WOMEN AND THE
EUROPEAN LABOUR MARKETS

WOMEN AND THE EUROPEAN LABOUR MARKETS

Edited by

ANNEKE VAN DOORNE-HUISKES
Erasmus University of Rotterdam

JACQUES VAN HOOF
Dutch Open University in Heerlen
University of Leiden

ELLIE ROELOFS
Dutch Open University

P·C·P
Paul Chapman
Publishing Ltd

Paul Chapman Publishing Ltd
144 Liverpool Road
London
N1 1LA

British Library Cataloguing in Publication Data

Women and the European Labour Markets
    I. Doorne-Huiskes, A. Van
    331.4094

ISBN 1-85396-298-8

Typeset by Whitelaw & Palmer Ltd, Glasgow
Printed and bound by Athenaeum Press Ltd, Gateshead, Tyne & Wear

A B C D E F G H   9 8 7 6 5

POPULAR LOAN

This book is likely to be in heavy
demand. Please RETURN or RENEW it no
later than the last date stamped below

Contents

64 culture
_236 - 249_

139 hours
_84-85_

Contributors

BETTINA BOCK works for an organization consultancy and does research on career developments of men and women and women in non-traditional professions.

ANNEKE VAN DOORNE-HUISKES is a Professor of Women's Studies at the Faculty of Social Sciences of the Erasmus University of Rotterdam. She also works as a consultant for organizational change and equal opportunities policy. She has published books and articles on women's careers, pay differences between men and women and the effects of equal opportunities policies.

NOOR GOEDHARD is currently head of the Wetenschapswinkel (the science shop) of the Erasmus University of Rotterdam, a research institution that works for non-profit organizations which have no funding for research purposes. She engages in research on industrial relations.

ANNE-WIL HARZING is a lecturer at the Faculty of Economics of the University of Maastricht. She has published on expatriate management and international human resources management.

JACQUES VAN HOOF is professor of sociology at the Dutch Open University in Heerlen and the University of Leiden. He is mainly interested in the present transformations of work organization, industrial relations and the labour market, and their consequences for social inequality. He has also written on the relations between education/training and work.

ATTIE DE JONG is a partner in an organization consultancy and is an expert on positive action.

TANJA VAN DER LIPPE is a research fellow at the Department of Social Sciences of the University of Utrecht. She specializes in the field of domestic work and time budgeting.

JANNEKE PLANTENGA is a lecturer at the Economic Institute of the University of Utrecht. Her main fields of interest are the history of women's work, changing working time patterns and (European) social policy. She is the Dutch member of the European Commission network of experts on the situation of women in the labour market.

LIESBETH POT is a member of the European Commission network on child care and other measures to reconcile employment and family responsibilities. Until 1989 she was a research fellow at the Dutch Child Care Association. At present she works for the Dutch Care and Welfare Institute (NIZW) where she is responsible for the child-care programme.

ELLIE ROELOFS works for the Dutch Open University. She is a lecturer at the Department of Social Sciences. Her research topics are (European) social policy and technology and innovation policy.

JOOP SCHIPPERS works as an associate professor at the Economic Institute of the University of Utrecht. He specializes in research on women's labour-market position and male/female inequality. He is also a member of the Dutch National Council on Equal Opportunity for Women (Emancipatieraad, The Hague).

KEA TIJDENS is a senior lecturer at the Faculty of Economics of the University of Amsterdam. She has published articles and books on the impact of information technology and clerical works, occupational segregation and the gender gap in the banking sector.

TINEKE VAN VLEUTEN is an expert on policy and legislation and was a member of the Equal Opportunities Commission in the Netherlands from 1988 to 1994.

Acknowledgements

This book is based in part on the course `Women and Labour-Market Positions within the European Community', written for the Dutch Open University (Ou). Besides most of the authors of the present book, Marga Bruyn-Hundt and Marijke van Vonderen-van Staveren also contributed to the coursebook. We wish to thank first the Faculty of Social Sciences of the Ou and its Dean, Professor Jos Claessen, for encouraging the project and for providing the much needed financial support for the translation and editing.

Others assisted in one way or another: Judith Tersteeg and Josine van Zijl provided secretarial assistance, Jan Hendriks and Jan Hornstra (Taalvorm e.s.) helped with preparing the manuscript, Albert Kampermann and John Schobre provided logistical support.

In particular we would like to thank Cecilia Willems, who translated most of the chapters from Dutch. We truly admire her professionalism and are grateful for her commitment.

ANNEKE VAN DOORNE-HUISKES
JACQUES VAN HOOF
ELLIE ROELOFS

Introduction

For some time now the European Union has been concerned with the position of women in the labour markets of its member states, as its many directives, recommendations, action programmes and research projects demonstrate. On 1 January 1995, 3 new member states – Finland, Austria and Sweden – joined the Union. Two of these countries have a long tradition of encouraging equal opportunities for men and women and it is expected that they will continue this tradition within the European Union. The facts show that even now, in the mid-1990s, their support is sorely needed. Although the share of women in paid employment has increased in each country over the past few decades, nowhere has sexual inequality in the labour market been eliminated.

The present book assesses whether any progress has been made in the field of sexual equality in the 12 member states of the European Union. The assessment rests on 3 themes. The first of these concentrates on the facts. How can we describe the situation of women in the labour markets of the member states when compared with that of men? Are there significant differences between the member states? What changes have become apparent in recent decades with respect to women's jobs? What can we expect to see in the years ahead?

The second theme has to do with explanations. Are there economic and sociological theories that explain why sexual inequality in the labour market is so doggedly persistent? How can we integrate the insights gleaned from these two disciplines into a single theoretical framework? Can a similar theoretical framework provide indicators for a policy promoting equality between the sexes?

The third theme explores the policy measures introduced by the European Union to promote equal opportunities between men and women. Which policy instruments have been developed? How are they applied within the member states? How effective are they? In addition to the European Union as an institutional frame of reference for an equal opportunities policy, we will also look at the role of the European trade unions in this respect.

In Chapter 1 Janneke Plantenga reviews changes in women's participation in the European labour market. There has been an across-the-board rise in participation, although there are significant differences from one country to the next in the pattern of change. Atypical employment and part-time work are still largely women's affairs, even though the number of men who work part time is gradually rising in most of the member states. Here, too, we find striking differences between the various countries. Chapter 2 makes clear that the rising number of women in the labour market has had little or no effect on occupational segregation by sex. Janneke Plantenga and Kea Tijdens also demonstrate that the occupational segregation of men and women within professions is an equally stubborn phenomenon.

The fact that women and men consistently perform different types of work goes some way towards explaining the differences in pay between the sexes in every country of the European Union. In addition, as Joop Schippers explains in Chapter 3, work-related skills are also important. There are, nevertheless, still grounds for suspecting employers of discrimination, either because, as Chapter 3 indicates, some employers display 'a taste for discrimination', or because they apply the principle of statistical discrimination.

Other examples of discrimination (statistical or otherwise) can be found not only in relation to sex but also in relation to ethnic background. In Chapter 4 Anne-Wil Harzing demonstrates that in Belgium, the Netherlands, Germany and the United Kingdom women from ethnic minorities generally have a poor position in the labour market. This is undoubtedly also the case in the other member states. To explain this phenomenon we need to go beyond the qualities of the women themselves. Here, too, it is difficult to ignore the evidence of discrimination.

In Chapter 5 Bettina Bock and Anneke van Doorne-Huiskes look at women's careers from a life-course perspective. This perspective makes clear how consecutive decisions with respect to educational programme, career and career interruptions have a cumulative effect on women and their position in the workplace. Such decisions are guided largely by the way in which men and women divide the unpaid work in the home. Comparative research such as that presented by Tanja van der Lippe and Ellie Roelofs in Chapter 6 shows how, in every country, women shoulder the larger share of the burden of domestic work. This pattern is proving particularly difficult to change, partly because both national governments and the European Union consider this as chiefly a private affair, with policy intervention being unwelcome.

Following these descriptive chapters, which also include various theoretical comments on sexual inequality in the labour market, Chapter 7 looks more explicitly at a number of economic and sociological explanations for this phenomenon. Anneke van Doorne-Huiskes and Jacques van Hoof outline these explanations and try to integrate them into a framework of rational choices under institutional constraints. A similar perspective can be useful in a comparison between countries. The institutional features of various countries are analysed as a structure of incentives, which in some cases encourages equality between men and women and in other cases discourages it.

The chapters following Chapter 7 focus on policy issues. In Chapter 8 Ellie Roelofs outlines the most important institutions within the European Union and describes in detail its policy instruments and measures in the field of equal opportunities. The most important contributions which the European Union has made to promote equal opportunities for men and women are the directives adopted in the 1970s and 1980s and the decisions of the European Court of Justice. Beyond this, the scope of the equal opportunities policy is limited because any proposals on this subject must be adopted unanimously within the Council of Ministers. In Chapter 9 Tineke van Vleuten looks more specifically at the legal instruments of the European Union. She concludes that legal developments at the European level have made a significant contribution to improving the labour-market position of women. This contribution is particularly clear in the direct effect of the principle of equal pay in all the member states and in the broad interpretation of the term 'pay'. In addition, all the member states are obliged to apply the principles of equal treatment by integrating it into their national law.

Child-care facilities are yet another important instrument for promoting equal opportunities for men and women in the labour market. In Chapter 10 Liesbeth Pot surveys the present state of affairs within the European Union with respect to this issue, concentrating on 4 countries: the UK, Denmark, Belgium and the Netherlands. She argues for the further reconciliation of work and family responsibilities because such a policy contributes in the end to a higher social and economic standard for all. Child-care facilities are often part of a broader approach to positive action. In Chapter 11 Attie de Jong and Bettina Bock survey the various positive action programmes on behalf of women which have been introduced in a number of European organizations. It is in the public sector in particular that positive action has achieved a certain level of success. In the private sector, on the other hand, the resistance to such measures as preferential treatment and targets has remained fierce. The business community is more receptive to individual approaches within the context of human resources management (HRM). But if women are actually to benefit from such an approach, work–family policies will have to be integrated into HRM, a move which is also in the interest of men with care responsibilities.

Chapter 12 describes another strategy to improve the position of women in the labour market: comparable worth. In this strategy it is not the individual but the job which is the object of policy intervention, as Anneke van Doorne-Huiskes explains. The principle of equal pay for work of equal value, regardless whether this work is performed primarily by men, women, white people or people of colour, is the starting point of the comparable worth strategy. This principle is a very recent one. Job evaluation systems are firmly entrenched sociological institutions. They often reflect traditional ideas about the value placed on women's work when compared with that of men.

Chapter 13 describes the role of the European labour movement in the area of equal opportunities. Noor Goedhard and Jacques van Hoof show that the participation of women in the labour movement is much greater in some European member states than in others. Trade unions do not differ much from other organizations, where structural and cultural constraints make it more difficult for women to further their careers and restrict the amount of influence they have on decision-making. This chapter also looks at the role of women in the European Trade Union Confederation (ETUC) and explores whether women can influence European social policy through this channel. The example of the directive on maternity leave is discussed to show that a gap exists between the demands of women (as voiced by the ETUC's Women's Committee) and the end results of European policy-making.

In Chapter 14, finally, the changes which have affected the position of women are viewed from the broader perspective of general overall changes in the labour market. The result is a somewhat mixed picture. Jacques van Hoof and Anneke van Doorne-Huiskes indicate that important results have been achieved in the field of equal opportunities in the workplace. But in view of the tumult in the European labour markets, unqualified optimism is difficult to maintain. The next few years will probably see a wave of new job losses, including in those sectors in which women work. Job growth will be largely in the low-skilled sectors. The generally accepted optimistic scenario of a few years ago, which projected an overall upgrading of employment, has lost much of its persuasiveness. On top of that it is expected that competition and pressure to perform will increase within organizations. Industrial relations will furthermore be increasingly dominated by the trend towards flexible working practices, decentralization and deregulation.

Naturally it is not only women who will have to deal with these changes. Men's jobs and careers will feel their impact as well. Neither will the effect of such changes be the same in each country, as demonstrated by the discussion (in the final chapter) of Esping-Andersen's recent study on the rise of a post-industrial service proletariat. The European Union has recognized this specific concern. It will be interesting to see how its social policy in this field evolves further.

CHAPTER 1

Labour-Market Participation of Women in the European Union

JANNEKE PLANTENGA

INTRODUCTION

Throughout Europe, women's labour-market behaviour is changing rapidly. Today, the arrival of a first child no longer means the automatic end of a woman's working life. Some opt to continue working or to stop after a second birth, others stay at home temporarily, while a number attempt to combine their paid work outside the home with their caring tasks by reducing their working week. However, these developments have not led to greater equality in the labour market. Job segregation between men and women is still considerable and wage differences hard to eradicate. Furthermore, there are also considerable differences in the nature of labour participation: women appear to be largely over-represented in atypical employment. Partly as a result, women's labour-market position still appears to be relatively vulnerable; in many European Union countries their unemployment rate is considerably higher than that of men.

This chapter aims to provide an overview of women's labour-market participation. The central focus is on the changing patterns of work and working time, giving facts and figures about activity rates, part-time work and unemployment. The analysis is highly descriptive; later in this volume more attention will be paid to possible explanations. The chapter ends with some discussion about future developments.

LABOUR-MARKET PARTICIPATION

In recent decades the significance of women's labour has increased strongly throughout the European Union. Women have taken up most of the new jobs created in the Union, and have demonstrated an increasing commitment to the labour market, particularly over the core child-rearing years. An important indicator in this respect is the share of women in the total work-force; Table 1.1 provides some post-war data. These data show a clear rising trend in all member states. For example, in 1950 women's share of the UK labour force was 30.7%; by 1991 this percentage had risen to 43.2. In so far as data are available, it would appear that the strongest increase has taken place

Table 1.1   **Women's share in the total labour force, by member state, 1950–91**

	1950	1975	1985	1991
Belgium		32.5	37.8	40.0
Denmark		39.2	45.7	46.6
FR Germany	35.1	36.5	39.7	40.9
Greece				35.8
Spain				35.3
France	35.9	37.8	42.7	44.3
Ireland		26.3	31.4	34.1
Italy	25.4	27.0	34.4	37.1
Luxembourg		28.2	34.9	35.8
Netherlands		24.2	34.9	39.5
Portugal				43.8
United Kingdom	30.7	38.3	41.4	43.2
Europe 9		34.8		
Europe 10			39.3	41.1
Europe 12				40.6

SOURCE: Eurostat, Labour Force Survey (1975, 1980, 1985, 1991)

in the Netherlands: in 1975 less than a quarter of the labour force was female; in 1991 this share had risen to 39.5%.

The rising number of women in the labour force is due to a number of diverse developments. First, men's labour-market participation is falling. In the first post-war decades this drop was due primarily to increasing participation in education. People remained at school for longer and therefore entered the labour market later. In recent years the participation level has also been influenced by early retirement options. Older employees stop working at an earlier age due to all kinds of early retirement schemes. When the labour-market participation of women is examined, it appears that the activity rates of young women have fallen for the same reasons as their male counterparts. However, this drop has been more than compensated by the changing labour-market behaviour of married women. Influenced by changes in education, number of children and relative wage rate, the labour-market participation has increased rapidly and the 'working married woman' phenomenon has become widely accepted.

Women's increased labour-market participation can be illustrated using the participation profiles in Figure 1.1. These profiles show participation in relation to age, with participation defined as the number of women within a specific age group who are active on the labour market divided by the total female population in the same age group. Where possible, Figure 1.1 shows participation rates in both 1975 and 1991 to allow a comparison over time. In addition, for 1991 the participation profile of men is included to give some insight into the still remaining inequality between men and women.

Based on Figure 1.1, it can be concluded that women's participation levels have increased in all member states, especially in the 25–50 age group, but considerable differences remain, both between men and women and between individual member states. In Denmark, for example, participation hardly declines with age, while in Belgium and Luxembourg falling participation in higher age groups can be observed. The UK shows a different profile. There are two clear 'peaks'; after an initial decline, participation rises again in higher age groups. These differences can be traced back to four different participation patterns which are more or less dominant in a specific country, and whose combined effect ultimately results in the actual participation pattern (Plantenga, Schippers and Siegers, 1990).

FOUR PATTERNS

The first participation pattern to be discerned is the two-phase pattern. The point of departure here is the familiar division of labour between men and women: the man as breadwinner while the woman cares for the home and family. This means the woman is active in the labour market until her marriage, or at the latest until the birth of her first child. In this participation pattern, high levels in young age groups go hand in hand with low levels in higher age groups. According to Figure 1.1 this type of pattern plays an important role in Ireland and – to a lesser extent – in Luxembourg; the participation level after the 25–29 age group falls very rapidly in both countries. The rigid division of labour which forms the basis of the two-phase pattern is no longer endorsed by everyone so women's labour-market behaviour can be described increasingly in terms of the three-phase pattern. This pattern is characterized by an initial period of paid work which is temporarily interrupted for a number of years for the birth and care of children, and then followed by paid work. The UK's actual participation pattern appears most clearly influenced by this three-phase pattern, but its influence is also apparent in the German Federal Republic (data shown are pre-reunification figures) and in France. In these countries, after a low participation level in the 25–29 and 30–34 age groups – the so-called 'child-trough' – the level increases once again in the higher age groups.

The third participation pattern is of particular importance in agricultural areas. In this agricultural/traditional pattern, civil status as a determinant for labour-market participation plays a subordinate role. After a period at school, paid work outside the home sometimes follows, but many girls also work in their family's business, e.g. farm. A marriage brings about change only in the sense that the wife now works in her husband's business. As the boundaries between this type of labour and household work tend to be vague, the labour is not always recognized as such, and official statistics often show a relatively low participation level, especially in younger age groups. According to Figure 1.1 this agricultural participation pattern particularly plays a major role in Greece.

Finally, a new pattern has emerged during the past decade. In this pattern ties with the labour market remain – also during the family phase. Paid and unpaid work are combined through leave options, child-care facilities and part-time positions, resulting in a labour-market participation which barely falls with age: in other words, the 'child trough' disappears. This so-called 'parallel' pattern requires a specific social infrastructure which is by no means

Figure 1.1   Activity rates by age in the European member states, 1975–91

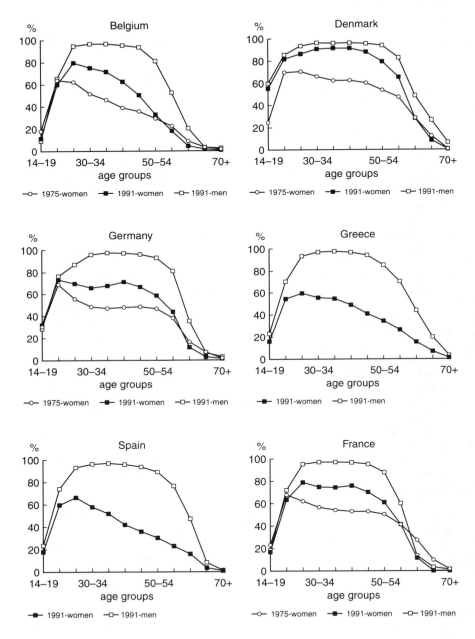

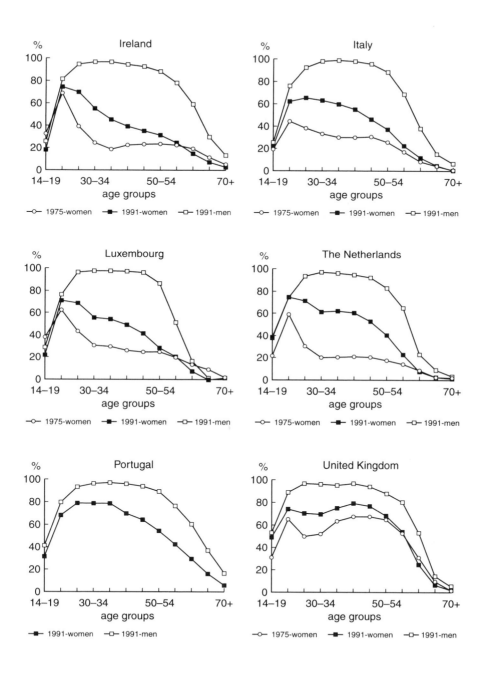

present in all member states. It would appear from Figure 1.1 that this pattern is particularly prevalent in Denmark. The participation level here averages around 20 percentage points higher than elsewhere, and participation levels hardly decline in the higher age groups.

Whereas four different patterns of labour-market behaviour can be discerned for women, it appears that men's behaviour is rather less varied. Children and/or civil status hardly play a role, resulting in male participation that can be characterized primarily as 'carefree'. The age profile is a reversed 'U'. As men tend to leave care of home and children to their wives or partners, labour-market participation does not decline in the 25–30 and 30–35 age groups, nor are weekly working hours subject to adjustment.

Of course, child care is an important cause in the difference in men and women's labour-market behaviour. Children cost both time and money. As women's hourly wage is usually lower than that of men, and because socio-economic circumstances stimulate a division of tasks, a certain level of specialization occurs in the sense that the time costs are borne by the woman and the monetary responsibilities by the man. Thus, the presence of children in a household has a negative effect on female labour supply and a positive influence on male labour supply. In effect, this sketches the rationale behind the two-phase participation pattern of women and men's carefree pattern; given the circumstances, specialization in the household would seem a logical choice for married mothers, and breadwinning for married men. This specialization will be permanent under certain circumstances. However, it is also possible that the woman considers re-entering the labour market once the children are older. It can be assumed that time costs decline as children grow older and that the monetary costs increase. If the woman does re-enter the market, the three-phase pattern is achieved. Finally, the parallel pattern should be seen primarily from a long-term perspective. The short-term advantages of specialization prove to be disadvantageous in the long term, given the fact that an absence of some years usually always has a negative effect on careers. It is this consideration which leads to the continuation of ties with the labour market, even during the phase when there are young children in the home, and in spite of the fact that this actually involves a double burden. In some cases time pressure is limited somewhat by a reduction in the number of paid working hours.

Besides the child factor, women's participation is also influenced to a great extent by education and training. Educational attainment tends to increase earnings potential and employment aspirations as well as access to the more intrinsically rewarding jobs (Rubery, Fagan and Smith, 1994, p. 44). As a result, highly qualified women more often pursue an uninterrupted career and, should an interruption occur, they more frequently take up the reins again. This educational effect proves to be very strong in the southern member states where, in general, women's participation tends to be relatively low. This might indicate that throughout Europe the participation behaviour of women with higher education shows fewer differences than that of women with lower levels of education (Meulders, Plasman and van der Strickt, 1992, p. 26).

ATYPICAL EMPLOYMENT

The main focus so far has been the changing level of labour-market participation. However, this is only part of the story. The restructuring of the European labour market from the mid-1970s has meant the rise of all manner of flexible labour relations, varying from part-time work to subcontracting, which are often known collectively as 'atypical employment' (see Meulders, Plasman and van der Strickt, 1994). The most striking thing about this development is not the actual introduction of these kinds of labour, as fixed-term employment, part-time work, home work and temporary employment already existed in most countries. What is new is the unprecedented spread through all member states during the 1980s.

Women appear to be largely over-represented in atypical employment. While the standard full-time labour contract is usually based on the male breadwinner, flexible labour relations seem to mesh with the needs of women in the sense that they are able to combine paid work outside the home with care obligations. Thus, the proposition could be defended that the development of atypical forms of employment has facilitated the insertion of women into the world of paid employment. However, the price that has to be paid for this insertion seems high. Atypical employment is generally characterized by relatively low wages, limited work security and the lack of any career prospects. Based on this cluster of factors, many authors have concluded that these new labour relations are not actual advances for women; instead of giving them real opportunities, they make use of their weak labour-market position and thus do no more than perpetuate it. In most countries this discussion on the pros and cons of flexible labour relations has concentrated on the part-time work phenomenon. This can probably be explained by the fact that the availability of this type of work has grown spectacularly and many women indicate they would like to work part time. Moreover, the (dis)advantages of a part-time position are not so obvious that all discussions becomes superfluous; whereas the disadvantages of home work or min–max contracts quickly tip the balance into the negative, a final judgement on part-time work is less self-evident. For these same reasons, the rest of this section will be devoted especially to the part-time work phenomenon.

PART-TIME WORK

Table 1.2 provides some data on part-time employment in the countries of the European Union for the second half of the 1980s. When interpreting this table, it should be noted that the full-time/part-time distinction is usually made on the basis of a spontaneous answer given by the person interviewed. In a number of countries there is a rather more specific classification which is based wholly or partly on the number of hours worked. Employees in the Netherlands, for example, are considered part-timers if the hours worked according to their labour contract amount to less than 31 per week, or if they work between 31 and 34 hours in a specific sector where these hours would be considered less than normal (Eurostat, 1988, p. 57).

Table 1.2   **Part-time employment, 1983 and 1991**

	1983				1991		
	SHARE OF PART-TIMERS IN TOTAL NUMBER EMPLOYED		SHARE OF WOMEN IN PART-TIME EMPLOYMENT		SHARE OF PART-TIMERS IN TOTAL NUMBER EMPLOYED		SHARE OF WOMEN IN PART-TIME EMPLOYMENT
	MEN	WOMEN			MEN	WOMEN	
Belgium	2.0	19.7	84.0		2.1	27.4	89.3
Denmark	6.5	43.7	84.7		10.5	37.8	75.5
FR Germany	1.7	30.0	91.9		2.7	34.3	89.6
Greece	3.7	12.1	61.2		2.2	7.2	62.9
Spain					1.6	11.2	77.5
France	2.5	20.0	84.6		3.4	23.5	83.9
Ireland	2.7	15.4	70.7		3.6	17.8	71.6
Italy	2.4	9.4	64.8		2.9	10.4	65.4
Luxembourg	1.0	16.7	80.0		1.9	17.5	83.3
Netherlands	6.8	49.7	78.3		15.7	59.8	70.4
Portugal					4.0	11.0	67.6
United Kingdom	3.3	41.3	89.6		5.4	43.1	86.0
Europe 10	2.8	27.4	85.7		4.3	30.8	82.8
Europe 12					4.0	28.5	82.4

SOURCE: Eurostat, *Labour Force Survey* (1983, 1991)

The data in Table 1.2 show that the share of part-time employment increased in almost all the member states between 1983 and 1991. Exceptions are Greece, where the share of both male and female part-timers has fallen, and Denmark, where the importance of part-time work in female employment has declined. In 1991, in total 28.5% of the female labour force in the European Union worked part time, against 4% of men. However, it should be noted that there are considerable differences between countries. For example, in the Netherlands no less than 59.8% of the female labour force works part time; a percentage that is clearly much higher than that for every other member state. Only the UK comes relatively close, with 43.1% in 1991. Denmark is a good third with 37.8%. If we look at the part-time share of men, the Netherlands again tops the table, with Denmark a fairly close second, recording 15.7% and 10.5% respectively.

Based on Table 1.2 we can also see the unequal division of part-time work between men and women. Of the total number of people working part time, over 80% are women. West Germany appears to have the most oblique division; almost 90% of part-time jobs are occupied by women. In this respect the differences between men and women are all the greater when age is taken into account. Male part-time work is (still) a primarily incidental and temporary phenomenon, concentrated at the start and the end of men's working lives, whereas for women it is a structural given.

The different role played by part-time work in the working lives of men and women can be illustrated using Figure 1.2, which shows the composition of male and female labour participation within the European Union. It distinguishes between full-timers, part-timers and the unemployed, according to age. The figure shows clearly that male part-time work plays a role primarily in the 14–24 age group; 7.6% of the male labour force in this group is employed part time. This concerns, for example, schoolchildren and/or students who are trying to pick up extra money through a small part time job. In the 25–49 age group the importance of part-time work declines to around 2%, and increases once again in the over-50 category. A very different pattern emerges when the figures for women are examined. In the younger age groups the importance of part-time work is relatively limited. Thus, in the 14–24 age group, 14.5% of the female labour force is employed part time; this percentage increases to 26.4 in the 25–49 category. Part-time work is not, therefore, a temporary phenomenon at the start of a working life, but a way to combine paid work with unpaid care responsibilities in the home.

The fact that women especially work part time and the fact that the quality of these jobs leaves a lot to be desired has raised doubts in a variety of quarters on the desirability of this development. Part-time work is seen to do no more than improve quantitatively the position of women in the labour market, whereas in qualitative terms little has changed. Thus, part-time work does not actually affect the prevalent social division of labour; in contrast to their full-time male counterparts, part-time working women have little prospect of building a career and thus continue to combine their household and caring tasks with a paid job. As a result, there can be no question of a breakdown of traditional role patterns.

Whereas this 'pessimistic' reading of part-time work focuses on the frustrating constants in society, the 'optimists' hold a different view. They point out the role of part-time work in the rise of the parallel participation pattern, because it creates the opportunity to combine paid and unpaid work in an acceptable fashion. Applied in this way, part-time work offers the option of uninterrupted labour-market participation; no mean feat if one considers that this type of option was until recently hardly open to (many) women. Moreover, a more fundamental question is raised on whether an equality strategy based on women's full-time labour-market participation is not one-sided. In this full-time strategy the same 'carefree' participation pattern enjoyed by men is advocated for women, without any clear answer on how to tackle the responsibilities normally associated with women's lives. Rather, the perspective should be turned around. The stress should no longer be on women participating in the labour market in a 'male' way, but, rather, that men should participate like women in the caring tasks. Seen in this light, it is no longer necessary to interpret part-time work as an exclusively negative choice. Instead, the positive aspects of part-time employment (for both men and women) are pointed out, because in this way involvement in work and care can be shaped humanely.

The problem – as is usually the case – is that both camps are partly right. Part-time work is usually no more than a confirmation and a continuation of the marginal position of women. Small part-time jobs especially – roughly, jobs of 15 hours or less per week – do not guarantee economic independence, they appear to have emerged purely in the interests of employers, and they do little more than create a force of marginal workers. In contrast, part-time work can also imply the promise of change. Based on the conviction that full-time

Figure 1.2   Participation rate by age and position in labour force, Europe 12, 1991

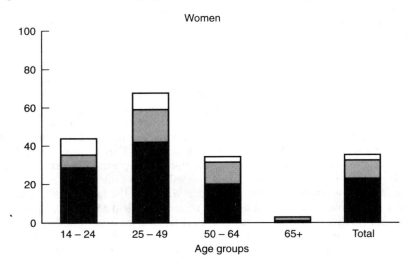

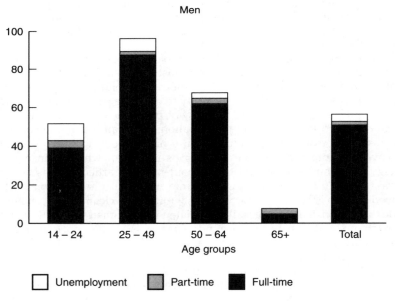

SOURCE: Eurostat, *Labour Force Survey*, 1991

work is not the only key to (socio-economic) equality, part-time work offers women and men the possibility of escaping the all-or-nothing option in the labour market, and thus of shaping a life in which work and caring tasks occupy a balanced place (Plantenga, 1994).

UNEMPLOYMENT

The fact that men and women still participate in the labour market under different conditions and circumstances is also apparent from unemployment figures. Table 1.3 shows unemployment percentages for the various European member states for 1983, 1987 and 1991, classified according to gender. These data show that, within the European Union, the female work-force has to contend more with unemployment than has its male counterpart. If the situation is examined country by country, it appears there are major differences, especially in Spain, Greece and Italy. The differences are considerable in Belgium and the Netherlands, while the UK is the only member state with a lower female unemployment rate.

When interpreting the data in Table 1.3, it should be noted that these are not always reliable or complete. Differences in definition can influence their comparability, while agreements on who is or is not considered unemployed can also effect differences between men and women. In the Eurostat definition, in principle everyone older than 14 who is without a job but is actively looking for work is registered as 'unemployed'; whether or not someone is registered as such at a labour exchange is not taken into account. This approach avoids an important source of distortion. However, the Eurostat definition does not fully exclude the possibility of underestimating the number of unemployed. The condition 'actively looking for work' means that someone has undertaken concrete steps to find a job within the past four weeks. If this condition has not been met, the person is registered as 'inactive' or as 'not available for work'. However, it is far from certain that a number of these inactives wouldn't welcome a paid job, but have given up trying to find one, for example because they live in a region of high unemployment or because their position in the labour market is weak through lack of education, or age, sex or ethnicity. Such 'discouraged workers' would accept a job if they were encouraged to do so and/or if the possibility of obtaining one improved. But at this point in time they are not registered as unemployed. Research on the numbers in this 'discouraged workers' category shows that in 1989 it included around 1 million EU citizens who were ranked as inactive and that women are strongly over-represented in this group. Incorporating these inactive people into a 'potential labour force' would cause the EU unemployment rate to be revised upwards by about 1% overall, and by nearly 2% for women. In Italy and Ireland especially, but also in Belgium and the Netherlands, there appear to be considerable numbers of discouraged workers (Commission of the European Communities, 1991, pp. 54–5). In short, the real differences between men and women are probably (far) greater than those contained in Table 1.3.

More generally it can be assumed that behind these abstract unemployment figures is hidden a world in which women more than men are confronted with social circumstances related to poverty and unemployment. Greater restrictions on mobility, the restraints placed on them by family responsibilities, the difficulties involved in acquiring retraining and learning new skills, and the very difficulties involved in registering for work and searching for work on a regular basis, make it harder for women to overcome the problems of unemployment (Eurostat, 1993, p. 61).

Table 1.3 **Unemployment percentages, by gender, 1983–91**

	1983		1987		1991	
	WOMEN	MEN	WOMEN	MEN	WOMEN	MEN
Belgium	17.8	8.1	17.6	7.3	10.6	4.6
Denmark	10.4	9.2	7.1	5.2	10.0	8.3
FR Germany	7.5	5.8	7.9	6.1	4.8	3.6
Greece	11.7	5.8	11.4	5.1	12.9	4.8
Spain			27.9	17.0	23.2	12.0
France	10.5	6.1	13.5	8.7	11.7	7.2
Ireland	16.0	14.3	19.1	17.6	16.6	15.4
Italy	14.4	5.7	16.5	7.5	15.8	6.8
Luxembourg	5.0	2.3	3.8	1.8	2.1	1.1
Netherlands	13.8	10.9	14.1	7.5	10.0	5.6
Portugal			9.7	5.8	5.7	2.6
United Kingdom	9.8	12.0	10.4	11.5	7.4	9.4
Europe 10	10.7	7.7	11.9	8.2		
Europe 12			13.2	9.1	10.7	7.1

SOURCE: Eurostat, *Labour Force Survey* (1983, 1991)

DISCUSSION

The picture which emerges from the foregoing is not wholly positive. There is certainly a rise in women's labour-market participation, but the differences between men and women remain considerable, especially when the nature of labour contracts is examined. The picture is also strongly fragmented. Danish women face very different problems from those confronting Portuguese women, while there is also a world of difference between the French and British labour markets. Such differences make it difficult to speculate on future developments. Is a certain convergence probable in men's and women's participation patterns, or will considerable differences remain? What are the future ramifications of labour-market inequalities? Does the increased participation of women through part-time work indicate a real integration in the labour market, or is this a signifier of a new, undesirable segmentation, especially in terms of the quality of the jobs? These questions become all the more pressing now unemployment in the European Union is rising.

This disappointing economic development has already led to an intensified interest in the demand side of the labour market. Traditionally, when women's low participation level is at issue, great attention is given to labour-market supply factors. The lack of (affordable) child care is pointed out, and the discouraging effects of breadwinner facilities. Increasing unemployment does not make these factors less relevant, but the need to broaden supply has become considerably less pressing. The central question now is more how the demand for labour can be stimulated. In all the proposals put forward to solve the problems, two global scenarios can be distinguished. These can be described as the redistribution scenario and the restructuring scenario. In the latter, the growth of numbers of jobs is central, and it plays a prominent role in former EU commissioner Jacques Delors's White Paper which advocates an increase of 15 million jobs before the millenium based on a healthy, open, decentralized, more competitive and fair economy. Measures to be taken include wage moderation, lifelong training, flexibilization of the labour system and the implementation of trans-European infrastructural projects in the fields of information, transport and energy. The redistribution scenario is intended as a complement. It is not concerned primarily with the creation of more jobs, but with the redistribution of existing work among a larger number of people. The most important instruments are reduction of working time and the stimulation of part-time employment. What can be expected from these scenarios in terms of women's future labour-market participation?

At first sight both scenarios should be valued positively. A creation of jobs is absolutely necessary given the high levels of unemployment, whereas the redistribution scenario shows real similarities to an old women's movement point of contention. Still, some prudence seems in order. The tone of the discussion on working-time reduction, for example, is different from that of 20 years ago. It is more defensive, and also more interwoven with the discussion on flexibilization. It is therefore highly improbable that there will be a generic reduction in working time in the short term. Much more probable is a development in which a four-day working week results from a negotiating process in which reduction is agreed in exchange for, say, Saturday work, or more generally in exchange for a more flexible use of labour, without all kinds of additional payments for inconvenient hours. In this sense working-time reduction is oriented more towards a flexibilization of work and working times than towards a reconciliation of work and family life. If this flexibilization aspect is emphasized too strongly, even the difference between the redistribution and the restructuring scenarios disappears and the former will become part of a general move toward restructuring of the labour market.

This more or less settles the agenda for the 1990s and beyond. Restructuring of the European labour market and a redistribution of paid work is necessary to increase the labour-force participation of men and women. This will not be sufficient, however, when the unequal position of women is taken into account. To tackle this inequality, more attention should be paid to the compatibility between family responsibilities and labour-market participation and the shared roles between men and women. This means that apart from restructuring and redistribution, a reconciliation scenario is also needed. Only a policy that goes beyond the potential conflicts between the restructuring, redistribution and reconciliation scenarios will result in a fair, equal society.

REFERENCES

COMMISSION OF THE EUROPEAN COMMUNITIES (1991) *Employment in Europe 1991*, Directorate-General Employment, Industrial Relations and Social Affairs.
EUROSTAT (1988) *Labour Force Survey, Methods and Definition*, Office for Official Publications of the European Communities, Luxembourg.

EUROSTAT (1993) *Unemployed Women in the EC. Statistical Facts*, Office for Official Publications of the European Communities, Luxembourg.

MEULDERS, D., PLASMAN, R. and VAN DER STRICKT, V. (1992) Position of women on the labour market of the EC. Developments between 1983 and 1990. Network of experts on the situation of women in the labour market, in *Report of the Equal Opportunities Unit*, DGV, Commission of the European Communities.

MEULDERS, D., PLASMAN, O. and PLASMAN, R. (1994) *Atypical Employment in the EC*, Dartmouth, Aldershot.

PLANTENGA, J. (1994) Le phénomène du travail à temps partiel: faits, toile de fond et consequences, in R. Plasman, (ed.) *Les femmes d'Europe sur le marché du travail*, L'Harmattan, Paris.

PLANTENGA, J., SCHIPPERS, J. J. and SIEGERS, J. J. (1990) Een afwijkend patroon? Een vergelijkend onderzoek naar participatie en segregatie op de arbeidsmarkt in Nederland en de Bondsrepubliek Duitsland, 1960–1985, *Mens en Maatschappij*, Vol. 65, pp. 337–54.

RUBERY, J., FAGAN, C. and SMITH, M. (1994) Changing patterns of work and working time in the European Union and the impact of gender divisions, Network of experts on the situation of women in the labour market, in *Report of the Equal Opportunities Unit*, DGV, Commission of the European Communities.

CHAPTER 2

Segregation in the European Union: Developments in the 1980s

JANNEKE PLANTENGA AND KEA TIJDENS

INTRODUCTION

As Chapter 1 has made clear, the labour-market participation of women in the European Union has increased quite dramatically. Whereas the activity rate of men, especially in the older age categories, is declining, that of women is growing, partly through changes in education and training, number of children and wage rate. The central question in this chapter is what happened to levels of occupational segregation during this period. Has the traditional unequal division of labour remained intact, or has increasing labour-market participation meant women have broken through the old boundaries?

Research on 2 levels was required to answer these questions. The first part of the chapter focuses on developments in the labour force and is primarily quantitative in orientation. The first section will chart (changing) levels of occupational segregation; an insight will be given into the share of women (and men) in the occupational sectors, the relative under- or over-representation of women (or men) in those sectors and the level of concentration. In the next section we try to 'measure' the level of occupational segregation, thereby using different segregation indices. The second part of the chapter focuses on developments at the workplace and is primarily qualitative in orientation; attention is drawn to the segregational dynamics among one, male-dominated, new occupation that has grown extremely in the 1980s, i.e. the computer professional. Finally, in the last section, some conclusions are drawn.

Before starting, a few notes will be useful on the statistical material. As a comparative approach demands harmonized data, the Eurostat data, the Eurostat Labour Force Survey is an obvious source of information. However, until 1992 Eurostat collected but did not publish occupational data based on the international classification scheme ISCO 68. Problems with this classification have resulted in Eurostat moving in 1992 to a new system of occupational classification: ISCO 1988. As this transition will take some time, no harmonized data set is yet available for international comparisons. Given this situation, the material used in the first section of this chapter is based largely on the report 'Occupational segregation of women and men in the European Community', published in 1993 (Social Europe, 1993). This report is based on the national reports produced by the EU network of experts on the situation of women in the labour market. Within this report, the structure and trends which emerge from the Eurostat data have where possible been checked against data provided from national sources.

THE EXTENT OF OCCUPATIONAL SEGREGATION

Women's work and men's work are highly segregated. The most striking form of segregation is no doubt the fact that women perform most of the unpaid domestic work, whereas men perform most of the paid work; a subject which is more fully discussed in Chapter 6. However, even within the area of paid work, segregation remains a major feature of the EU labour market. When revealing the unequal distribution of men and women throughout the occupational structure, at least 3 different dimensions should be distinguished. The first is the level of segregation within a specific occupation: the share of women (or men) in that occupation. The second is the extent of under- or over-representation. This is an important figure because the share of women in a specific occupation tells us little if it cannot be compared with the percentage of women in the total working population. The third dimension concerns levels of concentration, i.e. the extent to which the female (or male) working population is concentrated in a specific occupation. The differences between these 3 dimensions become clear when one realizes that segregation may remain the same in a specific occupation with a high share of women (the percentage of women remains the same), whereas at the same time the level of over-representation may decrease (because the share of women in the total working population increases) and the level of concentration may increase (because of higher than average rises in employment in the occupation).

Table 2.1 offers a first impression of the extent of occupational segregation in the European Union between 1983 and 1990, and the degree of under- or over-representation. This table shows the share of women by occupational sectors in the different European member states. Given the fact that the share of women in total employment in Belgium in 1990, for example, is 37.5%, it can be concluded that women in that year are strongly over-represented in occupational sector 5 (service workers). Women are also over-represented in sectors 0/1 (professional, technical and related workers), 3 (clerical and related workers) and 4 (sales workers). At the same time, there is a clear under-representation of women in sectors 2 (administrative and managerial workers), 6 (agricultural, animal husbandry and forestry workers, fishermen and hunters) and 7/8/9 (production and related workers, transport equipment operators and labourers). This pattern of over- and under-representation is – with minor differences – reflected in all member states of the European Union.

The data from Table 2.1 also enable us to compare the share of women employed in major occupational sectors for the years 1983 and 1990 for 11 of the 12 member states: data for Italy are not available. It appears that women have increased their share of total employment over the 1980s, but the rate of change varies by occupational sector. In sector 0/1 (professional, technical and related workers) women are increasing their shares in all countries –

Table 2.1 **Share of women's employment by occupational sector in 1983 and 1990**

	0/1 PROFESSIONAL		2 MANAGERIAL		3 CLERICAL		4 SALES		5 SERVICES		6 AGRICULTURE		7/8/9 PRODUCTION		9A ARMED FORCES		TOTAL	
	1983	1990	1983	1990	1983	1990	1983	1990	1983	1990	1983	1990	1983	1990	1983	1990	1983	1990
Belgium	46.8	49.6	13.4	16.6	44.6	52.8	48.7	48.5	63.1	63.4	27.4	24.7	14.2	13.2	4.2	8.0	34.4	37.5
Denmark		63.6		16.4		70.4		46.3		68.7		11.7		21.3		3.8		45.9
FR Germany		41.4		19.0		62.3		57.2		67.2		41.7		15.9		0.3		39.9
Greece	37.0	43.2	14.3	10.1	47.3	50.2	32.0	37.3	42.5	43.0	43.3	44.4	15.4	17.2	2.6	8.2	32.7	35.2
Spain		46.1		8.5		48.1		43.9		57.3		27.0		12.4		0.2		31.9
France	41.1	42.5	14.1	10.3	64.9	69.1	48.0	48.6	69.3	68.6	34.5	32.4	15.8	15.0	5.0	7.2	40.7	42.7
Ireland	43.5	46.6	10.7	16.5	60.3	65.1	37.2	36.8	52.1	52.9	13.0	9.8	12.7	14.4	0.2	1.0	30.6	33.2
Luxembourg	36.0	37.7	1.1	8.6	44.7	46.9	57.8	53.0	74.1	72.1	29.3	26.8	6.1	5.4	3.4	6.8	32.7	34.5
Netherlands		42.6		11.6		57.6		41.7		71.0		23.0		8.3		0.0		37.5
Portugal		54.7		19.8		50.0		42.1		65.2		49.7		26.5		0.0		42.0
United Kingdom	42.9	47.7	6.9	33.0	68.7	72.0	48.2	49.7	71.8	70.1	14.2	16.9	15.2	16.4	5.3	7.7	40.5	45.3

SOURCE: Social Europe (1993) appendix table 1 (Eurostat, Labour Force Survey)

although the range of female share varies from 38% in Luxembourg to 64% in Denmark. Also in clerical work (ISCO 3) the share of women is growing in most countries, with the result that such work tends to become a predominantly female occupation, with very high shares in Denmark, France, Ireland and the UK. On the other hand, the production, transport and related workers (ISCO 7/8/9) remain predominantly male; the female share has remained constant or even declined.

Differences in the level of concentration between men and women refer to the extent to which women are confined to a narrower range of occupations, compared with men. This requires data on a more desegregated level, dividing major occupational sectors into occupational classes. National data reveal that the level of concentration is indeed higher for women than it is for men. In 1990 in the Netherlands, for example, 52% of the female employment is concentrated in only 5 occupations, of which 06/07 (medical, dental, veterinary and related workers) is the largest. No less than 12.5% of the female labour force is employed in this class. Instead 51.4% of the male employment is concentrated in 11 classes, the largest of which (02/03, architects, engineers and related technicians) accounts for only 6.2% of male employees (Plantenga, Van der Burg and Van Velzen, 1992, p. 15).

Various studies have already pointed out this difference in concentration and attempted to find explanations for it. Tijdens (1990) draws attention to the effect of the occupational classification used. In general, occupations in which many women work are not as precisely defined as occupations where a lot of men are employed. One well-known example is the broad, barely specified occupational class 32 (stenographers, typists and card- and tape-punching machine operators). In total, this class has only 2 occupational groups (3-digit level) and 8 occupations (4-digit level). Whichever way you look at it, this is exceptionally low when compared to, for example, the fairly well-specified occupational class 95 (bricklayers, carpenters and other construction workers), which is subdivided into 8 occupational groups and 62 occupations. A variety of explanations can be given for this less differentiated structure in 'women's' occupations. According to Tijdens:

> First, the basic occupational description . . . dates from 1968. It can be assumed that in comparison with today, at that time the traditional male skilled occupations were more dominant in the occupational structure than the 'new' service occupations. In other words: the occupational classification is 'lagging behind'. De Kiewit and Teulings (1990) add that Taylorism in industry has led to a much finer definition of tasks than in the clerical and administrative sector. Secondly, based on the smaller spread of women in the job levels, it can be assumed that women's occupations have a less hierarchical character than men's occupations. This would mean that less occupations can be distinguished. Thirdly, it can also be assumed that professional identity in a number of women's occupations is less developed – cleaning someone else's home is not a profession.
>
> Tijdens, 1990, p. 16

In fact, the biases in the classification system used are one of the reasons for Eurostat moving to the new occupational classification system mentioned in the introduction.

Besides the fact that the statistics offer a distorted image, the strong concentration of the female labour force in only a few occupational classes must also be explained by the problematic integration of women in men's occupations. A number of studies have shown that the progression of integration of women is considerably more complex than that of men into women's occupations (Ott, 1985; Pringle, 1989; Williams, 1989). The last section of this chapter examines the background to this phenomenon.

MEASURING LEVELS OF OCCUPATIONAL SEGREGATION

Table 2.1 gives only a rather rough picture of the dynamics of occupational segregation. In order to answer the question whether occupational segregation has increased or not in the 1980s, it is necessary to 'measure' occupational segregation more precisely.

In the literature several indices for measuring this type of segregation are used. A number of problems attach to these indices, which do not necessarily demonstrate an identical trend. In order to describe developments as thoroughly as possible, the various trends indicated by the segregation indices will be compared. In addition, an attempt will be made to gain an insight into the methodological demands which should be met by a measurement tool, by an in-depth examination of the pros and cons of generally accepted segregation indices.

Segregation indices

A much-used index for measuring occupational segregation is the 's index', also called the index of dissimilarity, which is defined as:

$$s = 0.5 \ S \ M_i \ / \ M - F_i \ / \ F$$

where M_i = number of men in occupational category i, M = number of men in labour force, F_i = number of women in occupational category i, and F = number of women in labour force.

The index of dissimilarity can be interpreted as the sum of the percentage of the male labour force and the percentage of the female labour force which would have to change its job in order to eliminate all occupational segregation. The value of the index is equal to zero if the percentage distribution of the male and female labour force over the distinguished occupations is the same. The maximum value of s is 100, in which case the segregation in men's and women's occupations would be complete.

The index provides an indication of the differences in the structure of female and male employment, but the interpretation is not without problems. Index s is expressed as the sum of the percentage of the male and the percentage of the female labour force, but adding percentages does not tell us very much. As the percentages are generally based on different numbers of men and women, and are thus not equivalent, index s does not give a clear answer about the number of people, male and female, who should change occupations to achieve a non-segregated occupational structure. There are hosts of conceivable movements, which would all result in a non-segregated occupational structure. In addition, there is the interconnected problem that index s does not take into account the structure of the labour force. The suggested movements could, for example, mean that the number of infant-school teachers was reduced by half, whereas the number of plumbers doubled – which would be a very unrealistic course.

Nor is the interpretation of changes in s entirely without problems. It appears that changes in the value of index s can be attributed to 3 factors: a changed numerical ratio between men and women within occupational categories; a changed distribution of the total labour force over the occupational categories; and changed numerical ratios between men and women within the total labour force (see among others Blau and Hendricks, 1979; Blackburn, Jarman and Siltanen, 1991). Thus, the value of index s varies not only as a result of changes in occupational segregation between men and women within a specific group. Changes in the occupational structure or the gender composition of the labour force can also lead to changes in the value of the s index.

Alternative measuring tools have been suggested to tackle these problems, such as the S index and the WE index, used by the Organization for Economic Co-operation and Development (OECD) in its publications. Upon analysis, however, it appears that both indices can be traced back to the s index and are thus confronted with the same methodological limitations and interpretational problems (Blackburn, Jarman and Siltanen, 1991). Blackburn, Jarman and Siltanen therefore conclude that the s, S and WE segregation indices are all unsuitable as tools to measure occupational segregation. They emphasize the need for a totally new approach. In their view, segregation should no longer be seen as a quantity to be measured from some fixed point but, rather, as a characteristic of the labour market and a relationship which can be described using suitable measures of association. They support this argument by formulating the so-called Basic Segregation Table (see Table 2.2).

By using the Basic Segregation Table (BST), the index of dissimilarity can be reformulated as the proportion of all women working in women's occupations reduced by the proportion of all men employed in women's occupations: $[F_f/F - M_f/M]$. When such a formulation is used it becomes clear that a change in the number of women's occupations, resulting from changes in the occupational structure, will lead to a change in the value of index s. Similarly, it appears that an increase or decrease in the number of women resulting from changes in the gender composition of the labour force will change the definition of women's occupation. This also has consequences for the value of index s. Changes in the marginals of the BST appear to result in a situation whereby changes in the index can no longer be interpreted in terms of changes in occupational segregation as such. In addition, it appears from the formula that index s can achieve its maximum value of 1 only if the number of women is equal to the number of people employed in women's occupations and the number of men is equal to the number of people in men's occupations. In that case $F = F_f = N_f$ and $M = M_m = N_m$. The M_f and F_m cells in the BST will not be filled, and the relationship between gender and men's and women's occupations is at a maximum. Blackburn, Jarman and Siltanen suggest monitoring for the undesirable effects by ensuring the marginals no longer differ from each other. By defining women's occupations as those

Table 2.2 **The Basic Segregation Table: women and men in women's and men's occupations**

	Women	Men	
Women's occupations	F_f	M_f	N_f
Men's occupations	F_m	M_m	N_m
Total	F	M	N

where

N = total labour force

N_f = total number of people working in women's occupations

F = number of women in labour force

F_f = number of women in women's occupations

etc.

occupations with the highest ratio of women to men which together contain the same number of workers as there are women in the labour force, they make the table symmetrical ('matching marginals'). Whatever happens to the numbers of women and men in the labour force, the classification of occupational categories is adjusted to preserve this symmetry. As a result, the measure of association can take on a maximum value of 1 in every conceivable situation, and comparison in time and for countries are possible.

According to Blackburn, Jarman and Siltanen, the most useful tool to measure the connection between gender and men's and women's occupations is the measure of association tau B, also called 'index of segregation'. They believe this index can be interpreted as a measure of the extent to which gender and gendered occupations vary together – how far women's occupations are staffed by women and men's by men. The maximum and minimum values of this segregation index have been defined for all situations as 1 and 0 respectively. The tool suggested by Blackburn, Jarman and Siltanen is, as they themselves admit, probably not the solution to all the problems related to measuring occupational segregation. But, in comparison with the frequently used *s, S,* and *WE* indices, the advantage of their measure is that it can at least be used to compare situations in various countries and at various times.

Measuring occupational segregation

Table 2.3 then provides the values of the index of dissimilarity and the index of segregation for the years 1983, 1987 and 1990, using the Eurostat ISCO data on a 2-digit level. The countries have been ranked using the index of dissimilarity to run from countries with high levels of segregation at the top to those with low levels of segregation at the bottom. It shows that Denmark had the highest segregation score in 1990 and Greece the lowest. Unfortunately, no data for Denmark are available for 1983 and 1987 so no trend can be inferred for it. The low level of segregation in Greece seems to be the result of a 'recording' in the agricultural occupations and should be treated with some suspicion (Social Europe, 1993, p. 32).

Table 2.3 **Indices measuring trends in occupational segregation in employment, 1983–90**

Countries ranked by level of segregation	1983	1987	1990
Denmark			
Index of dissimilarity			.59 (1)
Index of segregation			.59 (1)
Luxembourg			
Index of dissimilarity	.63 (1)	.61 (1)	.59 (1)
Index of segregation	.61 (1)	.56 (2)	.54 (3)
United Kingdom			
Index of dissimilarity	.62 (2)	.59 (2)	.57 (3)
Index of segregation	.59 (2)	.57 (1)	.56 (2)
Netherlands			
Index of dissimilarity		.54 (6)	.57 (3)
Index of segregation		.50 (6)	.51 (6)
Ireland			
Index of dissimilarity	.57 (3)	.56 (3)	.56 (5)
Index of segregation	.52 (4)	.52 (4)	.53 (4)
France			
Index of dissimilarity	.54 (5)	.54 (6)	.54 (6)
Index of segregation	.53 (3)	.53 (3)	.53 (4)
Germany			
Index of dissimilarity		.55 (5)	.54 (6)
Index of segregation		.52 (4)	.51 (6)
Spain			
Index of dissimilarity		.51 (9)	.53 (8)
Index of segregation		.46 (9)	.48 (8)
Belgium			
Index of dissimilarity	.55 (4)	.56 (3)	.47 (9)
Index of segregation	.49 (6)	.49 (8)	.48 (8)
Portugal			
Index of dissimilarity		.47 (10)	.46 (10)
Index of segregation		.43 (10)	.43 (10)
Greece			
Index of dissimilarity	.53 (6)	.53 (8)	.43 (11)
Index of segregation	.50 (5)	.50 (6)	.35 (11)
Number of countries ranked	6	10	11

SOURCE: *Social Europe* (1993), p.35 (Eurostat, *Labour Force Survey*, ISCO (68) 2-digit data)

When it comes to developments in time, index *s* records a quite substantial decrease in the level of segregation in Greece, the UK, Belgium (after an initial rise) and Luxembourg. In other countries the level of segregation has remained more or less the same or has risen (Netherlands and Spain). If we compare these results with those for the index of segregation, some discrepancies can be found, which is, of course, no surprise given the compositional change as a result of the rising female share of the labour force in all EU member states. On the whole the extent of the segregation measured with the index of segregation is slightly lower, but more important are the differences in the changes over time. Compared to the level of segregation measured by the index of dissimilarity, the index of segregation records a less substantial rise in segregation in the Netherlands, less substantial falls in segregation in the UK, and Belgium, and more substantial falls in Luxembourg and Greece. Using the information provided by this index, it can be concluded that in 5 countries the unequal distribution of men and women over occupational classes has declined in the period under examination, whereas in another 5 countries this distribution has remained the same or has risen.

Summarizing, it has become clear that measuring segregation is not an unequivocal matter. For this reason, we used 2 index measures which are premised upon different conceptual approaches, notably towards the changing female share of the work-force and the question of over- and under-representation. Although, for some countries, these indices indicate a slight drop in the level of segregation, they also indicate that occupational segregation remains an important feature of the European labour market. Table 2.3 also makes clear that there is no simple relationship between the extent of segregation and the extent of female participation. Whereas Ireland and Luxembourg score high on the segregation indices, both countries are characterized by a low level of participation; the UK and Denmark not only have a high level of segregation but also a high level of participation. This is a rather disturbing outcome from a policy point of view as it seems to indicate that occupational segregation is likely to remain a pervasive and persistent characteristic of all labour markets.

SEGREGATIONAL DYNAMICS AMONG COMPUTER PROFESSIONALS DURING THE 1980s

Whereas the previous section focused on segregation in the labour force, in this section attention is drawn to segregational dynamics at the workplace. To illustrate the dynamics in the 1980s for EU countries, one occupation (computer professionals) is taken as an example. This choice is based on the fact that it is a new and rapidly expanding occupational area, with high levels of external recruitment, giving opportunities for women to enter. At the same time, it is a highly competitive, mobile labour market with a typically male definition. This raises the question of how in fact women are doing within this occupational area.

Computer professionals in the 1980s

In the 1980s the use of information technology increased tremendously, due mainly to the huge increase in the use of microcomputers from the second half of the decade onwards. This growth meant a declining dominance of large, centralized computer systems in favour of many small, decentralized systems. Whereas in the 1970s firms usually carried out designing and programming in their Electronic Data Processing (EDP) departments, by the 1980s this had partly been contracted out, as can be seen from the growth of software houses as well as from the availability of off-the-shelf packages (for Germany see Trautwein-Kalms, 1991). Moreover, end-user computing also influenced the EDP departments and many organizations established information centres, providing support to users and establishing intermediate jobs (Bergeron, Rivard and De Serre, 1990).

These developments have led to a differentiation of job titles within the occupational field, as well as to a changing number of workers within each of these groups (Tijdens, 1991a). A major change was that the lines between professional and non-professional users became less clear; the tasks of the systems analysts and the users became increasingly matched. Secondly, the number of computer operators decreased in favour of help-desk employees, supporting the decentralized systems. Thirdly, due to advanced technologies such as optical character reading, key entry tasks diminished. Fourthly, new managerial jobs came into being because EDP managers entered the higher managerial levels, reflecting the increased importance of information technology for the firm's business. The changing concepts of information systems within firms and the changing role of EDP departments are reflected by the changing qualification demands for computer professionals. Whereas qualifications in the field of electronics or programming used to be the key qualifications, the job requirements gradually become more business-oriented. In fact, Kahn and Kusalis (1990) found that in the USA a quarter of the information system managers at a certain job level did not have a degree in computer-related fields.

Despite the diversified occupational field, the occupational group is not classified in great detail in the ISCO-68 occupational classification. On a 3-digit level 4 jobs can be defined as EDP occupations: systems analysts and programmers (categorized as scientific jobs), and computer operators and key entry operators (categorized as service jobs). Managerial and other information technology jobs are not included, although they might be considered as computer professionals, together with the systems analysts and programmers. More detailed classifications of this occupational area depend very much on private studies, conducted by computer consultants or manufacturers themselves, but these sources lack a uniform definition of the occupations (see, for an overview, Commission of the European Communities, 1990).

Women as computer professionals

The computer professionals have been male-dominated occupations from the beginning (see, for the early development of the occupational group, Game and Pringle, 1983). In the 1970s the terminal was the most used piece of computer equipment. In EU countries male workers in skilled jobs used terminals mainly for systems analysis or programming, and they designed and controlled the computerized information systems, whereas female workers used terminals for key entry processing, and were regarded as marginal users in unskilled jobs (Bird, 1980; Chalude, 1984). Therefore, gender relations within the field of information technology were hierarchical.

The percentage of female computer professionals differs from one country

Table 2.4 **Share of female EDP employees in the Netherlands, 1979–93**

	PERCENTAGE OF FEMALE EDP EMPLOYEES				
	1979	1983	1987	1991	1993
Systems analysts	5.4	5.2	5.6	10.0	8.9
Programmers	7.9	8.8	10.3	12.8	13.0
Computer operators	25.5	15.1	(?)	(?)	(?)
Key entry operators	98.0	94.3	(?)	87.5	87.5

	NUMBER OF FEMALE EDP EMPLOYEES			TOTAL EDP EMPLOYEES		
	1979	1993	Increase	1979	1993	Increase
Systems analysts	800	7,000	875%	14,700	79,000	537%
Programmers	900	6,000	667%	11,400	46,000	404%
Computer operators	2,800	(?)	(?)	11,000	<5,000	<55%
Key entry operators	10,000	7,000	−30%	10,200	8,000	−22%

SOURCE: Tijdens (1991a) and Enquête Beroepsbevolking

NOTE: (?) means no reliable figures are available. This concerns figures below 5,000 or %.

to another, but in no EU country is this percentage estimated to be above 30 and in most countries it is closer to 20 (Social Europe, 1993, p. 70). These percentages seem to have increased in the 1980s; however, there is a lack of detailed information here. Statistical data by Eurostat provide only employment figures in the wider occupational group of statisticians, mathematicians, systems analysts and related occupations (ISCO 08). Interestingly, data gathered from national reports show that in southern countries such as Spain and Portugal women are better represented in the field of information technology than in most northern countries. Particularly in the Netherlands, the shares of female computer professionals are low – 9% among systems analysts and 13% among programmers in 1993 (see Table 2.4).

Table 2.4 also indicates that in the Netherlands, from the end of the 1970s to the beginning of the 1990s, the number of the predominantly male computer professionals multiplied by 5, whereas the number of predominantly female key entry typists decreased by approximately one quarter and the number of predominantly male computer operators even more. The percentage of female workers in the 2 growing occupations nearly doubled, whereas the share of women in at least one of the 2 decreasing occupations diminished slightly. This indicates that women are indeed making inroads into the high-status and fast-expanding computer professions, whereas their share among the low-status, declining operator occupations has slightly diminished. This last development seems to contradict the argument sometimes made (see, for example, Sullerot, 1968) that men withdraw faster than women from diminishing occupations.

Despite the growing share of women in most EU countries, the image of the high-status EDP occupations remains typically male. This is a world of big money, fast cars and very long working days. In Germany, for example, about 75% of the EDP staff (men and women) work 40 hours or more and 17% work even 50 hours or more, leading the author to conclude that these jobs give opportunities to ambitious young men (Trautwein–Kalms, 1989). These figures are confirmed in surveys conducted in the UK, and in the Netherlands (Beech, 1990; De Olde and Van Doorne–Huiskes, 1991). De Olde's research showed that female computer professionals spend on average 44 hours per week on their work, i.e. they work 37.5 hours per week, add 3 hours' overtime and spend an extra 3.5 hours on training in their own time. These long working hours pose serious problems for women trying to combine paid and unpaid labour. They either have to withdraw from their jobs, and face difficulties when trying to re-enter, or they have to negotiate on an individual level more flexible or part-time working hours. Female computer professionals seem aware of these difficulties. In a questionnaire among 617 female computer professionals, De Olde and Van Doorne-Huiskes (1991) found that 55% of the women agreed with the statement that the limited possibilities of working part time made combining work and motherhood a difficult business (13% disagreed). And 80% agreed that it would be very difficult to take a few years off, e.g. to take care of young children, and then go back into a computer job (5% disagreed).

Surprisingly, however, female computer professionals do not find their profession to be male dominated in general. Only 30% agreed with the statement that labour conditions, work methods and atmosphere at work were geared to male requirements (40% disagreed). The results are probably influenced by the fact that most women are young – 80% under 35 – and do not yet feel the need to emphasize (potential) tensions between gender identity and professional identity. This would also tally with the fact that women in the 30 and older age category indicated more often that work in automation was geared to male working-time patterns; the percentages were 37 and 23 respectively. These outcomes indicate that female computer professionals, facing a male-dominated culture, have to adapt in order to stay in the occupational group.

Occupational segregation is also related to wage differentials. The field of computer professionals does not deviate from other occupations in this respect. The few available statistics show that in every area of the computer industry male employees earn more than their female colleagues (Commission of the European Communities, 1990). This is confirmed in the Dutch survey mentioned earlier. No uniform conclusions can be drawn about wage differentials between women in the profession. Whereas a British survey indicates that non-technically qualified women do better than their colleagues with a science qualification, in the Dutch survey it appears that women with a technical background at university level earn more than their female counterparts from other university disciplines (Beech, 1990; De Olde and Van Doorne-Huiskes, 1991).

Theorizing the causes of occupational segregation

As segregation by gender is explained by several theories, are some of them useful to explain segregation in the EDP occupations? Below we will explore 3 theories, each with its own particular view about the main actor in this respect, i.e. the employee, the employer or the occupational group.

When gender segregation is explained by the employee's occupational choices, anticipating behaviour is supposed. Women, as the argument goes, seek occupations in which the effects on their income will be low in case of a career break, whereas men do not seek these occupations (Polachek, 1979). Therefore, women will have jobs with flat age–wage profiles (Jusenius, 1976). A second theory states that, due to their primary socialization, women choose occupations that are in accordance with their sex roles (Ireson, 1978). Moreover, gender-role socialization theories address the fact that women are oriented primarily towards their families rather than their careers. Gender-role socialization is a process by which families, peers, schools and the media influence society's expectations towards girls and boys. In this sense gender-role socialization contributes to the explanation of occupational segregation by gender-related occupational choices in childhood. Gender-role socialization can explain that girls (in contrast to boys) do not choose occupations that might require mathematics or technical qualifications, whereas boys do not choose occupations in which 'caring' is an important element. This theory is in accordance with the low and hardly increasing share of women in computer science in many EU countries (Social Europe, 1993, pp. 70–6). However, this theory has difficulty explaining the stubbornness of the occupational segregation phenomenon as such and the changeability of definitions of women's and men's work according to time and place.

Employers' hiring practices are the main focus in theories of statistical discrimination. Women are supposed to be more costly to employers than men, due to higher turnover or absence rates because of motherhood. This theory – to be discussed more fully in Chapter 3 – states that employers treat individuals on the basis of their group's average behaviour, because employers have no more specific information about an applicant than the gender he or she belongs to. Bergmann (1989) also focuses on employers' hiring practices by arguing that employers do not prefer women for male-dominated occupations (and men for female-dominated ones) because this would undermine labour relations and the status quo. Employers' personnel policies might also be influenced by male employees' strategies, as Bergmann (1986) has made clear, looking at segregation codes in firms. The content of these informal codes is that women should not exercise authority over men. Moreover, the control over sex-typing of tasks is a means to maintain patriarchal structures in the division of labour within the occupational field. These strategies also include sexual harassment – women in male-dominated occupations report sexual harassment much more often than women in female-dominated occupations (Gutek and Cohen, 1987). In fact, the segregation-coding process includes not 1, but 2 elements. The first is that the supervision of relationships at work should accord with the hierarchical relationship between genders at home as well as in society: women should not exercise authority over men. The second element is that, in contrast to men, women as a group are perceived as non-hierarchical: women should not exercise authority over women. Therefore, the segregation code establishes that women do not have a hierarchical relationship and, if they do, they should not supervise men. Workers, male and female, are likely to enforce this code. For the computer professions this mechanism is revealed in the fact that women are able to enter the professional field, but remain very scarce in higher managerial levels. This probably coincides with the code that young people should not exercise power over middle-aged people.

Strategies of occupational groups are analysed in the social closure theory, offering an explanation of the process by which occupational groups define occupational boundaries, including the definition of working hours, recruitment and jobs. The Weberian theory of social closure has been elaborated by Parkin (1979). He distinguishes 2 groups in the process of social closure, both following their own strategies. The privileged group follows a strategy of exclusion to keep their position by subordinating the groups they want to exclude. The subordinated group follows a strategy to appropriate some privileges of the subordinating group. Witz (1986) integrated the theories of patriarchy and of social closure and distinguished several closure strategies of the organizational groups: for example, to establish the exclusively male character of the professional organization by excluding women; to control routes of access to such resources as skills and knowledge; and to control the occupational boundaries by attempts to subordinate related occupational fields. Thus, in his opinion, occupational segregation is caused by male professionals trying to protect their qualification structures. This theory seems to be confirmed by a study of the Dutch computer professionals' association as they obviously try to maintain the occupation's male image in 2 ways: they establish the full-time availability image of the occupation and remain silent about the entrance of women into the professional group (Tijdens, 1991b). The strategy to control occupational boundaries was also confirmed, as the association made clear that the key entry operators did not belong to the occupational field. However, another low-status EDP occupation, the computer operators, was not excluded in such an explicit way as the key entry operators were. Therefore, this cannot be interpreted as an attempt to remain a high-status occupational group, but as an attempt to maintain the occupation's male image.

CONCLUSIONS

The rising activity rates of European women might be expected to lead to integration and equality and away from gender segregation and inequality. Evidence suggests, however, that no such expectation is justified. Women may be making inroads into some jobs previously dominated by men, but this is counterbalanced by the increasing feminization of female-dominated occupations, such as clerical and service sector work.

Some of the problems of women entering men's job have emerged clearly from studying the segregational dynamics among computer professionals during the 1980s. This study seems to confirm an important conclusion of the work of Pringle (1989) and Williams (1989), namely that the integration of men into women's occupations and that of women into men's are not symmetrical as professionalism is still defined exclusively in male terms. Women who enter men's occupations are confronted by an opposition between gender identity and professional identity which can only be bridged by adapting gender identity. In other words, women can enter the profession but they have to adhere to 'male' codes. In contrast, men in women's occupations make use of the male connotation associated with professionalism by describing specific elements in their work as masculine. This could apply to tasks with technical aspects or to management activities. In short, if women go into men's work, it is the woman who changes and not the work, whereas the opposite is the case when men enter women's occupations. In conclusion, we can state that integration of women into men's occupations (or integration of men into women's) does not make the work 'gender neutral'. What is at stake here is the gender definition of occupations and more is needed than simply a numerical adjustment. And as long as a job is generally considered masculine, the female computer professional will remain in an ambivalent and contradictory position.

REFERENCES

BEECH, C. (1990) *Women and WIT*, British Computer Service, London.

BERGERON, F., RIVARD, S. and DE SERRE, L. (1990) Investigating the support role of the information centre, *MIS Quarterly*, Sept., pp. 247–60.

BERGMANN, B. (1986) *The Economic Emergence of Women*, Basic Books, New York.

BERGMANN, B. (1989) Does the market for women's labor need fixing? *Journal of Economic Perspectives*, Vol. 79, no. 2, pp. 294–313.

BIRD, E. (1980) *Information Technology in the Office: The Impact on Women's Jobs*, Equal Opportunities Commission, London.

BLACKBURN, R. M., JARMAN, J. and SILTANEN, J. (1991) *International Comparisons in Occupational Gender Segregation: Assessing Two Popular Measures*, Sociological Research Group, working paper 9, Cambridge.

BLAU, F. D. and HENDRICKS, W. E. (1979) Occupational segregation by sex trends and prospects, *Journal of Human Resources*, Vol. 14, no. 2, pp. 197–210.

CHALUDE, M. (1984) *Office Automation and Work for Women*, Commission of the European Communities, Brussels/Luxembourg.

COMMISSION OF THE EUROPEAN COMMUNITIES (1990) *The Labour Market for Information Technology Professionals in Europe*, Brussels/Luxembourg.

GAME, A. and PRINGLE R. (1983) *Gender at Work*, Pluto Press, London.

GUTEK, B. A. and COHEN, A. G. (1987) Sex ratios, sex role spillover and sex at work: A comparison of men's and women's experiences, *Human Relations*, Vol. 40, no. 2, pp. 97–115.

IRESON, C. (1978) Girls' socialization for work, in A. Stromberg and S. Harkess (eds.) *Women Working*, Mayfield, California/Palo Alto, pp. 176–200.

JUSENIUS, C. L. (1976) Economics, *Signs*, Autumn, pp. 177–89.

KAHN, M. B. and KUSALIS, S. (1990) MIS professionals: education and performance, *Information and Management*, Vol. 19, pp. 249–55.

KIEWIT, A. DE and TEULINGS, C. M. (1990) Afbakening beroepsdeelmarkten voor de technische en administratieve sector, SEO, Research memorandum 9001, Amsterdam.

OLDE, C. DE and VAN DOORNE-HUISKES, A. (1991) Position of women in information technology in the Netherlands; education, job characteristics and proposals for an equal opportunity policy, in I. V. Eriksson, B. A. Kitchenham and K. G. Tijdens (eds.), *Women Work and the Computerization of Education*, North-Holland, Amsterdam, pp. 347–62.

OTT, M. (1985) *Assepoesters en kroonprinsen. Een onderzoek naar de minderheidspositie van agentes en verplegers*, SUA, Amsterdam.

PARKIN, F. (1979) *Marxism and Class Theory: A Bourgeois Critique*, Tavistock Publications, London.

PLANTENGA, J., VAN DER BURG, B. and VAN VELZEN, S. (1992) *Occupational Segregation in the Netherlands, Developments in the 1980s*, external report commissioned by and presented to the European Commission, Institute of Economics CIAV, Utrecht.

POLACHEK, S. (1979) Occupational segregation among women: theory, evidence, and a prognosis, in C. Lloyd, E. Andrews and C. Gilroy (eds.), *Women in the Labour Market*, Columbia University Press, New York, pp. 137–57.

PRINGLE, R. (1989) *Secretaries Talk. Sexuality, Power and Work*, Verso, London.

SOCIAL EUROPE (1993) *Occupational Segregation of Women and Men in the European Community*, Supplement 3/93, Office for Official Publications of the European Communities, Luxembourg.

SULLEROT, E. (1968) *Histoire et sociologie de travail féminin 2*, Société nouvelle des Éditions Gonthier, Paris.

TIJDENS, K. (1990) Beroepssegregatie en werkgelegenheid, *Tijdschrift voor Arbeidsvraagstukken*, Vol. 6, no. 2, pp. 13–23.

TIJDENS, K. (1991a) Decentralized office technology and women's work, in P. van den besselaar, A. Clement and P. Järvinnen (eds.), *Information System, Work and Organization Design*, North-Holland, Amsterdam, pp. 215–24.

TIJDENS, K. (1991b) Berufssegregation in der EDV, in W. Littek, U. Heisig and H. Gondek (eds.), *Strukturveränderungen und Beschäftigungsbedingungen im Dienstleistungsbereich*, Edition Sigma Rainer Bohn Verlag, Berlin, pp. 199–212.

TRAUTWEIN-KALMS, G. (1989) Die neuen haben alte Probleme, *Der Gewerkschaftler*, 7/89, pp. 26–7.

TRAUTWEIN-KALMS, G. (1991) Arbeits-und berufssituation qualifizierter Angestellter im Software-Bereich, in W. Littek, U. Heisig and H. Gondek (eds.), *Strukturveränderungen und Beschäftigungsbedingungen im Dienstleistungsbereich*, Edition Sigma Rainer Bohn Verlag, Berlin, pp. 213–29

WILLIAMS, C. C. (1989) *Gender Differences at Work. Women and Men in Non-Traditional Occupations*, University of California Press, Berkeley/London.

WITZ, A. (1986) Patriarchy and the labour market: occupational control strategies and the medical division of labour, in D. Knights and H. Willmott, (eds.), *Gender and the Labour Process*, Gower, Aldershot/Brookfield, pp. 14–35.

CHAPTER 3

Pay Differences between Men and Women in the European Labour Market

JOOP SCHIPPERS

INTRODUCTION

An individual's labour-market position does not depend only on the job he or she holds, but also on the payment received. This payment is the more important as it not only reflects the value the employer or society as a whole attaches to the individual's labour performance, but also constitutes the income an individual receives to pay for his or her (daily) needs in terms of goods and services. From the previous chapters we have learned that women's labour-market participation has been rising all over Europe during the past few decades, but that it is still lower than men's participation, especially if measured in hours, and over the life-cycle. Besides, we have learned that there is a considerable degree of segregation between men's and women's jobs. Women are more frequently found in occupations like nursing, teaching and caring, whereas men are more often found in technical and industrial jobs. Moreover, women are concentrated in a relatively small number of jobs, which makes them vulnerable to economic recession.

In this chapter we will discuss women's earnings and compare them with men's, in the context of women's lower labour-market participation and job segregation between men and women. Once again, we discuss and compare the situation in several European countries. As a rule, we will discuss the situation in the UK and introduce other countries wherever it is necessary to show that there are differences between those countries and the UK. In some cases we will also refer to countries outside the European Union. Recent facts and figures will be put forward for the community as a whole, while the history of pay differences will be sketched briefly. For the interpretation of the different figures we will introduce some theoretical notions concerning pay and pay differences. First, however, we need to clarify which facts and figures should be considered relevant if we want to get a complete and balanced view of pay differences between men and women, and deal with some methodological issues involved in establishing pay differences.

PAY DIFFERENCES BETWEEN WOMEN AND MEN: WHICH DIFFERENCES DO MAKE A DIFFERENCE?

Essentially, there are 2 ways to look at pay differences between women and men. One approach considers men's and women's hourly wages or – as economists like to put it – wage rates. Questions regarding the number of hours a worker is employed to work are ignored in this comparison. The second approach to pay differences also takes into account the time dimension and usually concentrates on annual incomes. Annual incomes depend on both the wage rate as well as the number of hours a worker has earned that wage rate over the year.

Both statistics can be considered relevant to judge women's labour market position. The wage rate informs us of the value an employer attaches to the worker's productive performance (and may be relevant when questions of discrimination and equal treatment arise). What matters most to the worker as an individual (whether male or female) is the total amount he or she receives for being active in the labour market. This annual income determines whether a holiday abroad or a new car can be afforded or whether there have to be economies on food and clothes. In general, the size of a woman's income decides whether or not she can be economically independent.

Looking at differences between women and men, it may also be of interest to consider lifetime incomes: the sum of all annual incomes over the life-cycle. With regard to this lifetime income we may make a distinction between labour income that is earned during the worker's career and a broader concept of lifetime income that also takes into account, e.g. pension income. If we look at lifetime income differences between women and men we can also take account of the fact that during the life-course many women interrupt their labour-market careers for shorter or longer spells to give birth to and take care of one or more children. As we have seen earlier (Chapter 1) these interruptions constitute one of the major differences in labour-market behaviour between women and men. Still, we should not forget that non-continuous careers have become a phenomenon with which many workers have to deal at some point in their life; people become unemployed, disabled or decide to go back to school for some time. So, nowadays we should not be surprised to find differences in lifetime incomes not only between women and men, but also among women and men respectively, depending on a number of causes for career interruptions.

No matter which variable one looks at (wage rate, annual income or lifetime income) it is always possible to distinguish between gross and net figures. Gross wage rates are most relevant from the employer's point of view. Apart from additional labour costs gross wage rates determine the costs of employing a worker, so will play a major role in the employer's calculations. Workers may be more interested in net wage rates. If a man considers working part time instead of full time his concern will be the drop in net earnings. The same holds for a woman who wants to change her part-time job into a full-time one. Their concern is not what happens to the employer's wage bill, but the effect on their own bank balance.

The higher the tax rates levied upon gross incomes the larger the difference between gross and net incomes. Differences in net incomes between women and men may follow from differential treatment of women and men in the tax system. If a tax system treats breadwinners differently from others or if taxes are charged on the household income instead of on individual incomes this may give rise to differences between women and men. If one wants to explain differences between women and men concerning net incomes it is wise not to forget the effects of the tax system. This warning is particularly relevant if one wants to make an international comparison; despite the unifying tendencies following from the establishment of the European Union after Maastricht we are still facing pervasive differences in tax systems within the Union.

METHODOLOGICAL AND MEASUREMENT PROBLEMS

Figures concerning wages and incomes can be acquired from different sources. If one wants a complete picture of incomes a potential source might be the figures from the tax authorities. From this source one may gain an insight into both gross and net figures. Apart from privacy problems and limitations on the access to such figures, one major objection to using incomes as registered by the tax authorities is that some of our fellow humans are less eager than others to pay taxes and therefore try to 'disguise' some of their income. As a consequence, incomes reported to the tax authority may systematically underestimate the nation's real income figures. Besides, this source does not usually contain data on working hours, which prevents a researcher from calculating hourly wage rates. Records containing gross (and sometimes net) incomes and working hours can be found at company level. Once again privacy problems may constitute a barrier to access to the information, while everyday life shows that small firms in particular do not always keep detailed records of all workers. In many countries the task of collecting these – and many other – data from companies is performed by a specialized government agency, such as HMSO in the UK or Eurostat at the level of the European Union.

Given the problems concerning the accessibility, completeness or reliability of the 'official' data many researchers investigating wage rates and differentials between women and men take refuge in collecting their own data. Usually these data are collected from a survey among, e.g., a few thousand households or individuals. The great advantage of such a survey designed specifically for the research question to be answered is that a whole series of relevant (and sometimes detailed) questions can be asked of the people being interviewed. Of course, it is not certain that the interviews will always produce correct and reliable information. People may not be willing to tell the truth, they make mistakes, and – with retrospective questions – their memory may fail them. As another disadvantage one should mention the limited size of many samples. As collecting data by way of both oral and written interviews takes a lot of time and money most researchers have to limit the number of interviews. The smaller the sample the larger the probability that the outcomes of the research cannot be considered representative of the population as a whole. Finally, it should be noted that high costs are pushing official statistical agencies towards relying on (large-scale) samples too.

Things grow even more complicated when one wants to make an international comparison. As yet, all European countries still have their own currency, while the prices of commodities and services differ between countries (and sometimes even within countries, as we can clearly see from the UK). To answer questions concerning differences in wealth or purchasing power between nationals of different countries we need a common denominator. The Organization for Economic Co-operation and Development (OECD) in Paris uses the US dollar as such a measure, while Eurostat prefers the European currency unit (ecu). Still, this is only the first step. Suppose an Italian and an English teacher both earn the monthly equivalent of 1,000 ecus, after taxes. From these earnings the Italian teacher may have to pay for medical services, while her English colleague can make use of the facilities from the National Health Service (NHS). On the other hand, public transport in the UK may be more costly, which – in its turn – favours the Italian teacher. So, the differential possibilities for consumption by women and men in different countries do also depend on the availability of public goods and services paid for by national or local taxes (like the NHS), public transport, educational facilities). In this chapter we will ignore such differences, as they would over-complicate our present analysis.

The conclusion from this section can be that it is not always easy to get the information required for an investigation of male–female wage rate or income differentials. When one has a dataset at hand one should carefully consider its source and keep an eye open for the problems inherent in the way the information was collected.

WAGE DIFFERENCES BETWEEN WOMEN AND MEN IN THE EUROPEAN LABOUR MARKET: FACTS AND FIGURES.

When we look at the statistics of gross wage rates of women and men in the European labour market the following picture results. In all countries of the European Union women's wage rates fall substantially behind men's. Table 3.1 contains information on women's relative wage, i.e. women's wages as a percentage of men's wages, for 1980, 1985 and 1991, the most recent year for which standardized figures are available for the European Union as a whole. This relative wage is calculated using average gross hourly earnings of manual (full-time) workers in industry for different years. Of course, these figures relate to part only of the working population: non-manual workers are omitted (see below), (in most cases) part-timers are left out and so are public sector workers. Still, these figures by Eurostat provide the only source of harmonized wage data allowing for inter-country comparisons to be made.

During the 1980s men's and women's wages measured in national currencies both show a steady increase, due partly to a rise in real wealth as well as to nominal (inflatory) increases. Women's wages as a percentage of men's vary strongly across Europe. Women holding manual jobs in Luxembourg earn about two-thirds of what their male colleagues in Luxembourg earn, while Danish women are far better off: they earn 'only' 15% less than their male colleagues. Women's relative wages have been rather stable during the 1980s. Only Greece shows an enormous increase, from 67.46% in 1980 to 79.18% in 1991. A more detailed picture for the UK shows a strong rise of women's wages as a percentage of men's during the mid-1970s,

Table 3.1 **Women's average gross hourly earnings as a percentage of men's, manual workers, 1980–91**

Country	1980	1985	1991
Belgium	70.25	74.29	75.59
Denmark	86.05	85.83	84.47
Federal Republic Germany	72.37	72.84	73.39
Greece	67.46	78.79	79.18
Spain	n.a.	n.a.	72.22
France	78.28	80.76	80.25
Ireland	68.70	67.30	69.51
Italy	83.22	82.74	79.30 (1989)
Luxembourg	64.71	65.29	67.95 (1990)
Netherlands	73.05	73.56	76.17 (1990)
Portugal	n.a.	n.a.	70.78
United Kingdom	69.77	67.09	67.15

SOURCE: European Communities (1992)

a rather stable development during the 1980s and a slight increase during the early 1990s (see Figure 3.1). In the next section we will discuss a possible explanation for an increase in women's relative wage rate.

A similar picture to that presented in Table 3.1 can be drawn for non-manual workers. The figures in Table 3.2, however, do not concern hourly wages, but monthly earnings. Remembering what was said in an earlier section, this implies that we may expect to find larger male–female differences, as men and women differ with respect not only to remuneration but also to working hours.

Table 3.2 reveals that the gap between male and female non-manual workers' monthly earnings varies from 45% in the UK to 27% in Portugal. So, variation is as strong as for hourly wage rates, but at a different level. Only Portugal shows non-manual women's relative earnings to be higher than manual women's relative hourly wage. In all other countries we find that relative monthly earnings for women fall behind the relative hourly wages.

Even though the figures presented in these tables are not always complete and relate only to selected – though large – segments of the labour market the general picture is clear: equal pay for women and men is still far off, despite the increasing participation of women in the European labour markets that was discussed in Chapter 1.

Before we discuss wage differences between men and women in more detail and try to put forward some explanations we want to conclude this section by presenting a comparison (for 1988) of wages for the countries of the European Union. For this comparison hourly wages of manual industrial employees (men and women together) were translated into ecus. Figure 3.2 shows that Danish workers earn the highest wages, while their Portuguese colleagues earn less than 20% of the Danish wage. Measured in ecus Figure 3.2 also shows that, e.g. a Danish woman who earns 75% of the wage of her male colleague is still better off than a British woman earning the same as her male

Figure 3.1   Women's hourly pay as a percentage of men's, employees aged 18 and over, excluding overtime

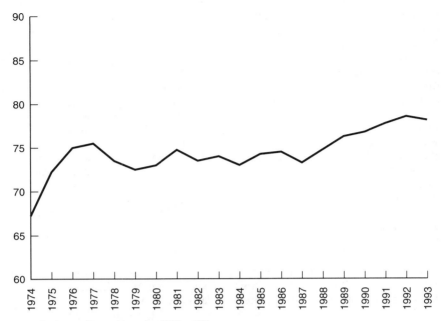

SOURCE: *Employment Gazette*, November 1993, p. 517

Table 3.2   **Women's gross monthly earnings as a percentage of men's, non-manual workers in industry, 1980–9**

Country	1980	1985	1989
Belgium	61.90	62.94	64.50
Denmark			
Federal Republic Germany	65.97	66.21	66.50
Greece	60.04 (1983)	64.31	66.20
Spain			
France	61.13	62.92	64.90
Ireland			
Italy *	72.34	68.52	
Luxembourg	49.74	55.18	55.60
Netherlands	59.11	64.12	64.50
Portugal			73.40
United Kingdom	54.48	54.75	55.20

* No separate figures available for men and women.

SOURCE: European Communities (1990)

Figure 3.2 Gross hourly wages of manual workers in industry in ecus, 1988

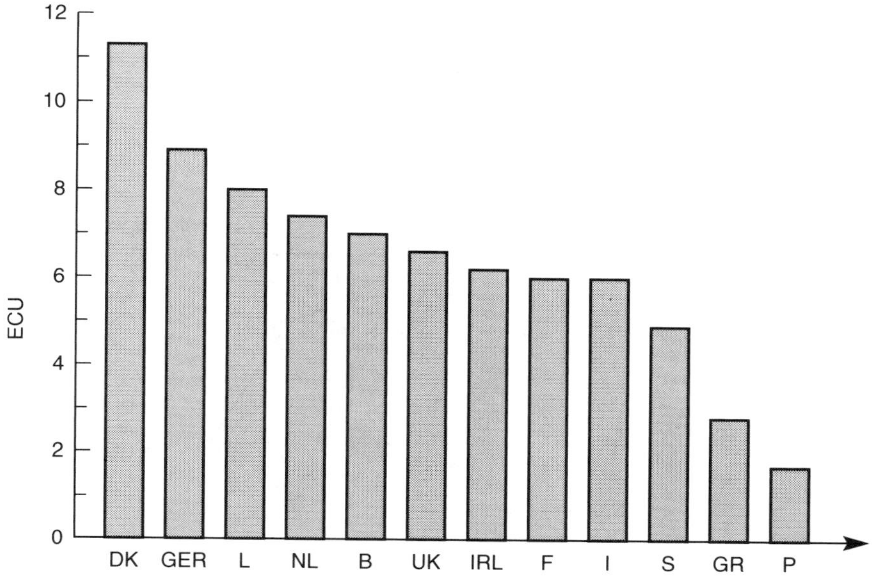

SOURCE: Commission of the European Communities, *Employment in Europe*, 1990, p. 60, Fig. 52.

colleague. So, when making comparisons it is always worth looking at different dimensions; in this case both the national and the European dimension.

WAGE DIFFERENCES: A MORE DETAILED LOOK

Beyond the mean

As said earlier, the figures presented in the previous section concern only industrial hourly wages and monthly earnings, and also reflect only mean values. Beyond this mean we may again find a world of differences. When discussing these differences it is impossible to go into the details of all EU countries. In most cases the UK, for which many detailed data are available, will be discussed as an example and the situation in the UK will be compared to one or more countries on the continent.

All countries of the European Union show an earnings distribution that can be drawn as a pyramid (see Figure 3.3): many people earning low incomes constitute the bottom of the pyramid and there are fewer people at the higher levels, while – in principle – the top of the pyramid reflects the income of the highest earner.

Having a job usually prevents an individual from falling to the bottom of the pyramid. This holds especially in countries that have some kind of legislation with respect to minimum wages to be paid to workers. While, for

Figure 3.3   The personal income distribution shown as a pyramid

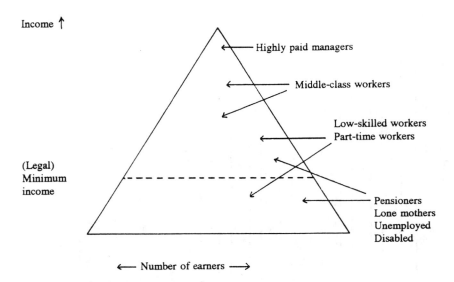

instance, in the Netherlands the minimum wage law was recently extended to part-time workers (among whom many women are found), Dickens, Gregg and Machin (1993) report that in Britain the 1993 Trade Union Reform and Employment Rights Act removed the remaining minimum wage protection for some 2.5 million low-paid workers by abolishing the last 26 UK wages councils. The government's case for abolition rested on 3 key arguments:

1 minimum wages do little to alleviate poverty, since most protected workers do not live in poor *households*;
2 when in operation, minimum wages reduced employment in the affected industries;
3 the problem of poverty that the wages councils were set up in 1909 to deal with are not relevant in today's labour market. However, Dickens, Gregg and Machin (1993) argue that:
    (a) 50% of families with at least one earner being paid wages council rates come from the poorest 20% of families;
    (b) the existing evidence suggests that abolishing the wages councils is unlikely to create jobs;
    (c) the widening earnings distribution in the UK implies that low pay is an increasingly important determinant of poverty. If anything – in their view – there appears to be an increasing need for minimum wage legislation in the UK.

After abolishing minimum wage protection the UK has drifted further away from European standards. While in 3 countries (Italy, Denmark and Germany) the regulation of minimum wages is left to employers and unions, who settle minimum wages in collective bargaining agreements, 7 countries set a national minimum wage. Ireland is also an exceptional case with only a partial system of minimum wage protection. Minimum wage rules or legislation are especially important to women. The EU reports that, e.g. in France, 14% of all women employed receive the minimum wage compared to only 5% of men.

Despite minimum wage protection many women run the risk of falling into the category of 'low-pay' workers, which is usually defined as that of individuals earning less than 66% of the national median level of earnings. EU statistics show that women are clearly over-represented among low-paid full-time workers in the Union. The share of the low paid who are female varies from 49% in Portugal to 82% in Germany in 1990 (see Figure 3.4). As part-time workers are excluded from these figures and women constitute the majority of part-timers these figures even underestimate the probability of women being found in the low-paid category.

Joshi (1990) points to the fact that because of their low participation 'lone mothers share with lone female pensioners the highest risk of poverty. Estimates for 1983 put 61% of both these categories below a poverty line defined as 140% of ordinary Supplementary Benefit assistance levels; a line which marked off 28% of all households and 43% of lone fathers' (p. 127). The lone mother 'appears to be trapped into poverty by the interaction of institutions and attitudes which are poorly adapted to people combining the roles of the carer and the provider' (p. 147).

So, at the bottom of the pyramid we find:

Figure 3.4   The percentage of low-paid full-time workers who are female in the European Union

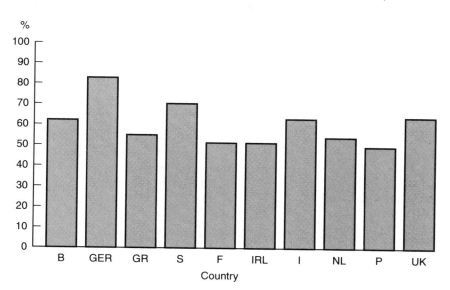

NOTE: Low pay is defined as less than 66% of the full-time median wage, except for Spain where the definition used is less than 40%, and data for Greece includes part-timers. No data for Denmark or Luxembourg.

SOURCE: CERC (1991), Table IV.9, as quoted in: EC, *Bulletin on Women and Employment in the EU*, Brussels, October 1994, p. 2.

1 lone mothers and pensioners, without a job or with just a small part-time job;
2 workers (many of them female) who hold jobs where pay falls short of (former) minimum wages.

Among men and women who *do* have jobs and even among workers holding full-time jobs we also find substantial wage differences. First, one can distinguish regional differences. In almost all European countries such differences can be found. Very often high-wage regions are located around the nation's capital (as in France, Belgium, Portugal, Greece and Spain). However, countries like Germany (Bavaria), Italy (the Po region around Milan), Spain (the Barcelona region) and – again – Belgium (the provinces of West and East Flanders) show that high-pay regions can also be found far from the capital. High-pay regions can usually be characterized by the presence of a concentration of service industries and a large number of high-tech jobs. As can be seen from Table 3.3, average earnings for both men and women (for manual workers and for all industries) in the UK also differ substantially by region.

It is not surprising to see that gross hourly earnings are highest in the South East. Lowest earnings for both men and women are recorded for Northern Ireland. When we look at the third column of Table 3.3 (women's wages as a percentage of men's in the same region) we find that women's position is most favourable in Scotland and Northern Ireland and least favourable in the East Midlands. Some 'wage watchers' are inclined to attribute these differences to religious, political and social differences in the background of the local population. However, such factors often remain vague and difficult to be measured. That is why, in the next subsection, we turn to a type of difference that is much more easily measured: wage differences related to the kind of industry.

Table 3.3 **Average gross hourly earnings (£) of manual workers in industry by UK region and women's relative wages, 1989**

REGION	MEN	WOMEN	WOMEN'S WAGES AS A % OF MEN'S
North	5.42	3.61	66.6
Yorkshire and Humberside	5.17	3.61	66.9
East Midlands	5.04	3.39	65.5
East Anglia	5.26	3.72	70.7
South East	5.52	3.79	68.7
South West	5.08	3.59	70.7
West Midlands	5.13	3.47	67.6
North West	5.23	3.62	69.2
Wales	5.27	3.61	68.5
Scotland	4.99	3.60	72.1
Northern Ireland	4.57	3.25	71.1

SOURCE: European Communities (1990)

Equal pay for equal work?

As we shall see later in this book legislation concerning equal pay both at the level of the European Union and at the level of separate countries concentrates on equal pay for equal work. Earlier we saw that the division of male and female workers over jobs and industries was quite different. Indeed, it was concluded that we can even speak of 'male' and 'female' jobs. The question we have to answer in this chapter is to what degree overall wage differences between women and men are related to the unequal distribution of women and men over jobs and industries. Table 3.4 shows the differences and similarities in pay for men and women for a selected number of industrial groups in the UK. Once again, we present both absolute figures and women's wages as a percentage of men's.

Table 3.4 shows clearly that in terms of pay there are very 'good' as well as very 'bad' industries. In some cases both men and women earn high wages, as in the tobacco industry, (there is in fact no industrial group in Britain where a woman can earn more). In other cases both men and women earn low wages, as in clothes manufacturing or the textile industry. Other cases show a 'mixed pattern': the industry is very rewarding for male workers, but far less so for female workers (as in the production of rubber and plastic), while the opposite can be said about foundries. Due to these differences women's wages as a percentage of men's vary strongly from 64.9 in the production of rubber and plastic to 83.7 in the industrial group for motor vehicles, parts and accessories. When we combine these figures with the earlier information concerning 'male' and 'female' occupations, there seems to be a slightly positive relationship between the percentage of women among the workers in an industry and women's wages as a

Table 3.4 **Average gross hourly earnings (£) of manual workers in selected industrial groups in the UK and women's relative wages, 1989**

INDUSTRIAL GROUP	MEN	WOMEN	WOMEN'S WAGES AS A % OF MEN'S
Production of electricity, gas, steam	6.47	4.41	68.2
Manufacture of ceramic goods	4.58	3.61	78.6
Motor vehicles, parts, accessories	5.84	4.89	83.7
Food industry	4.92	3.70	75.2
Tobacco industry	7.20	5.78	80.3
Textile industry	4.24	3.15	74.3
Manufacture of clothing	3.75	2.99	79.7
Paper, printing, publishing	6.64	4.51	67.9
Production of rubber and plastic	7.23	4.69	64.9
Manufacture of glass	5.17	3.61	69.8
Foundries	4.94	4.06	82.2
All	5.26	3.62	68.8

SOURCE: European Communities (1990)

percentage of men's. Typical female industries like textiles and manufacturing clothing show significantly above-average relative wages for women, while women's wages as a percentage of men's equal the mean value for typical male industries (the production of electricity, gas and steam, and paper, printing, publishing).

Figure 3.5   Country differences in inter-industry pay differentials

(a) The textiles industry

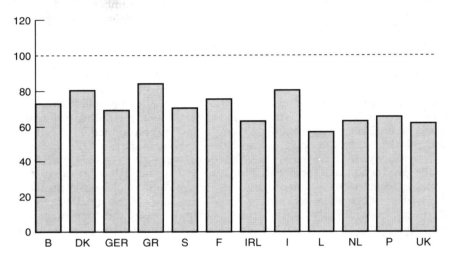

(b) The banking sector

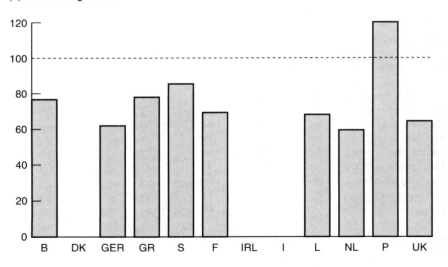

SOURCE: *Bulletin on Women and Employment in the EU*, Brussels, October 1994, p. 5.

Table 3.5 **Additional pay elements (£) in workers' average weekly earnings in the UK, April 1993**

	MEN			WOMEN		
	MANUAL	NON-MANUAL	ALL	MANUAL	NON-MANUAL	ALL
Average weekly earnings	274	418	354	177	269	253
of which:						
– overtime payments	38	12	23	11	5	6
– incentive payments, etc.	14	15	15	11	4	6
– shift, etc. premiums	10	3	6	5	3	3
All additions	62	30	44	27	12	15
As a percentage of total						
weekly earnings	22.5	7.1	12.5	15.0	4.5	5.8
Proportion of employees						
who receive:						
– overtime payments	51.9	19.4	34.0	28.1	16.3	18.3
– incentive payments, etc.	30.9	15.6	22.4	24.1	11.9	14.1
– shift, etc. premiums	22.9	6.1	13.6	16.4	8.9	10.2

NOTE: The figures refer to full-time employees on adult rates, whose pay for the survey pay-period was not affected by absence.

SOURCE: *Employment Gazette*, November 1993, p. 517

At the EU level the situation in some industries has been analysed in more detail. Figure 3.5(a) contains information on women's relative earnings for the textiles industry and 3.5(b) for the banking sector. Women's pay in textiles has been compared to the average pay of men in energy, manufacturing and construction, while women's earnings in banking are compared to average male non-manual pay in the same sectors.

For the textiles industry Figure 3.5 shows a rather stable picture. With the exception of Luxembourg women's relative wage rates vary between 60% and 80% of men's wages. In the banking sector there is more variation. Here Portugal is the exceptional case: women in banking earn 118% of the male earnings that are used for comparison.

Thus far the figures presented concern gross wage rates paid on a regular basis according to the labour contract between employer and employee. In addition, many workers also receive some additional benefits, like overtime payments, premium payments, etc. Table 3.5 summarizes some figures with respect to these additional benefits for the UK.

What becomes overwhelmingly clear from this table is that the gap between women and men in respect of additional payments is even wider than for regular pay. Not only do men earn about 3 times as much in additional payments as women, but also the percentage of women eligible for some kind of additional payments is much smaller than the percentage for men. For both men and women we can see that manual workers receive more than twice as much in additional payments as non-manual workers.

So, looking beyond the mean of male and female wages, we find all kinds of differences: differences according to region, differences according to industry, and within each region and within each industrial group there are again smaller or larger differences between men and women. The conclusion drawn earlier that there are large differences between men's and women's labour-market positions and employment situations can be extended to pay. Much of the overall difference between male and female earnings relates to the distribution of men and women over jobs and industries. However, if men and women work in the same industry equal pay is still an illusion. This conclusion can not only be drawn for the UK, but is valid for the other countries of the European Union as well, as can be seen from different studies based on national statistics (see, e.g. Schuld, Schipper and Siegers, 1994,) as well as from statistics collected by international organizations like the EU, OECD and the ILO (International Labour Organization). Even though countries, and regions within countries differ in this respect (as our regional excursion clearly illustrated), the differences between men and women appear to be substantial as well as very persistent (as our comparison for different years shows). In the following sections we will discuss some explanations put forward to account for the substantial and persistent earnings differences between men and women.

PAY DIFFERENCES AND PERSONAL CHARACTERISTICS: THE HUMAN CAPITAL APPROACH

Over the years different explanations have been put forward to explain wage differentials like those we established in the previous section. Many explanations relate the gross wage rate differential to differentials in 'work-related skills'. The basic framework regarding the relationship between earnings and skills has become known as the theory of human capital. Human capital can be defined as the body of knowledge and skills of a worker which enables him or her to perform a job. The concept of human capital concerns the qualitative dimension of labour as a factor of production (Mincer, 1974; Becker, 1975). A worker's stock of human capital determines to a large extent his or her position in the labour market. Neither the jobs workers perform nor the wages they earn in these jobs can be explained other than by reference to their stock of human capital (Schippers, 1987). Human capital is acquired through formal education at school and through working experience and on-the-job training.

The total stock of human capital an individual possesses depends on 2 factors:

1 the formation of new human capital, and
2 the depreciation of the existing stock of human capital (Mincer and Polachek, 1978; Mincer and Ofek, 1982).

During the first part of the life-cycle both men and women invest heavily in the formation of new human capital by way of schooling. This period is dedicated exclusively to investments in human capital which generate hardly any revenues for the time being. After schooling has been completed individuals join the labour force and enter the labour market. In general, from then on most of the additional investments in human capital take the form of on-the-job training, industrial courses or through experience. Most workers spend only a limited part of their working hours on investment activities, and even this decreases as they grow older (Ben-Porath, 1967; Mincer, 1974; Becker, 1975). Moreover, the existing stock of human capital wears out, and is subject to depreciation.

The investment profile of workers as described above is referred to as the 2-period model. Elementary human capital theory, which is used in the vast majority of studies trying to explain wage rates and wage rate differentials, presumes that after leaving school workers are continually present in the labour market. However, it is a well-known and well-established fact that this presumption does not hold for women. Women often take direct responsibility for household duties and the care of children. Therefore, their career profile is characterized by one or more interruptions. Besides, if they participate in the labour market, they often work only part time. Related to these differences are differences in investments in 'on-the-job-training' between men and women. As human capital theory is originally an equilibrium theory it usually ignores another well-known phenomenon, i.e. the existence of spells of unemployment, from which both men and women may suffer. These spells of unemployment may also be responsible for non-continuous careers patterns. During the 1970s unemployment rates reached figures unknown since the end of the Second World War. So, a model which explicitly considers career interruptions might be a valuable alternative to the traditional human capital model.

A deviating career profile (due to either unemployment or voluntary withdrawal from the labour market to care for a child) has a twofold effect on workers' wage rates. First, as a worker does not work during certain periods, less working experience is gained. Second, during periods of non-participation, the human capital stock suffers from additional depreciation due to a lack of maintenance. This effect is known as atrophy. Atrophy (literally: languishing) means the loss of market-oriented knowledge as a consequence of 'non-use'. For reasons of convenience, the loss caused of changing circumstances, for instance technological development, is also labelled atrophy. This additional depreciation cumulates with the depreciation of the human capital stock due to ageing and wastage. Due to forgone experience the wage rate will be lower the more interruptions occur and the longer the interruption lasts.

So, the basic message of human capital theory is that workers' earnings are closely related to their skills (acquired both by way of schooling and on the job) and that there are strong reasons to believe that women cannot acquire as much human capital as men, due to career interruptions or working in part-time jobs following the (unequal) division of caring tasks within the household. Even though – as we saw earlier – women's education no longer falls short of men's, the experience differential may explain why – on average – women earn less than men.

Many empirical studies for different countries – both in Europe and, e.g., in the United States, Canada and Australia – confirm the importance of human capital factors as a major determinant of workers' earnings and earning differentials between women and men (Polachek and Siebert, 1993). Still, most researchers also report that even though a large part (varying from 50% to 75%) of the earnings differential between women and men can be attributed to skill differences, women still earn less than one would expect given the human capital they *do* dispose of. For that reason the search for explanations for the wage gap between women and men has moved in another direction, which will be discussed in the next section.

PAY DIFFERENCES AND DISCRIMINATION IN THE LABOUR MARKET

Introduction

During the late 1960s and 1970s discrimination became a popular phenomenon in women's studies, as pay differences remained even though women's education and labour-market participation (and as a consequence their labour-market experience) increased. Many researchers think there must be 'more' to the male–female wage gap than just differences in abilities or human capital.

Economists – and many sociologists as well – try to explain human behaviour by using an analytical framework based on the confrontation of goals and restrictions, both of which limit the choices open to an economic actor. The distinction between goals and restrictions is fruitful when classifying economic theories on discrimination. The first category of theories considers discrimination one of the goals an economic actor pursues, which implies that, e.g. an employer aims not only to maximize profit but also to minimize association with a certain group of workers. It should be noted that when we talk about discrimination as a goal, we do not mean that discriminatory behaviour as such is one of the aims individuals try to realize; discriminatory behaviour follows from the desire not to associate with a certain group. So, the real argument is that desire.

The second branch of economic theories of discrimination does not consider discrimination a goal pursued by an actor with particular feelings against a certain group of workers, but only an instrument that is used to realize other goals, e.g. profit maximization. A major topic in this branch of theory is identifying the conditions under which groups of workers must be treated differently by an employer in order to maximize profit. When it is solely a means to realize a commonly accepted goal like profit maximization, discrimination does not in any way represent a moral value.

In the following subsections we will present the major lines of thought of both branches of economic theory on discrimination. One should first appreciate, however, that the economists' analysis of discrimination is always preceded by another step: establishing that there *is* discrimination. From economists' point of view discrimination is involved as soon as pay ratios or employment ratios between groups of workers deviate from productivity ratios between the same group of workers. So, if one group of workers is twice as productive as another, economists expect the first group to earn twice as much as the second. If this is the case, there is no reason to consider discrimination. If the first group earns either more or less than twice as much as the second group, economists label the deviation 'discrimination' and start seeking the nature of this discrimination.

'A taste for discrimination'

Pioneer work in the field of economic theory concerned with discrimination as an economic actor's end was carried out by the 1992 Nobel Prize-winner Gary S. Becker, who published his famous *The Economics of Discrimination* in 1957. He was the first to incorporate discrimination in the well-known neo-classical framework of utility and profit maximization. Models developed in this tradition concern 3 possible discriminating parties:

1 employers who dislike associating with certain groups of workers;
2 fellow workers who dislike working with or being supervised by certain groups of colleagues; and
3 consumers who dislike goods and services from firms owned by or managed by members of a particular group.

From the point of view of labour-market analysis (1) and (2) appear most relevant.

If an employer discriminates against a group of workers, employing members of that group renders 'disutility'. This implies that the employer who has both profit maximization and discrimination as goals prefers a certain level of profits reached without employing members of the disliked group over that same level of profits realized in combination with their employment. Indeed, he would even be prepared to settle for lower profits if it means that he could do with a smaller number of the group of workers he does not like to associate with. So, he acts as if the costs of these 'minority' workers equal the sum of both wage costs and an amount of money representing his 'suffering' from associating with them.

In a similar way, fellow workers who have a taste for discriminating against certain 'minority' workers act as if working with such disliked colleagues diminishes their wage rate. They calculate their *real* wage as the wage paid by the employer, reduced by an amount representing their dislike of the colleagues with whom or the boss under whom they have to work. This implies that they will be willing to accept this unwanted situation only if their employer pays them a compensating premium to the monetary value of the utility lost by accepting colleagues they do not like.

In both cases the discriminatory behaviour may result in wage discrimination or job discrimination or a mixture of the two, depending on the market situation and the behaviour of other employers and/or workers.

Suppose that only one employer in the whole labour market displays discriminatory behaviour. In that event 'minority' group workers will avoid that employer and seek employment at a non-discriminating firm, where they will receive the same pay as 'majority' group workers. The discriminating employer will employ only 'majority' group workers. So, his work-force will be strictly segregated, while no wage discrimination takes place.

If, on the contrary, all employers have a similar taste for discrimination, 'minority' workers will be faced with the same low wage offers everywhere. In that case they can either accept the reduced wage rate or choose to remain unemployed. As a result most companies will have a mixed work-force, while the same rate of wage discrimination pervades the entire labour market.

In case of discrimination by fellow workers similar results can be obtained. An employer who is faced with demands for discriminatory wage premiums by 'majority' workers may try to avoid these costs by employing either 'minority' workers or 'majority' workers only. So, the result will be complete segregation of the work-force. However, the employer may be forced to employ a mixed work-force and pay 'majority' workers additional wages if, e.g., for particular jobs workers cannot be recruited from one group. In that case partial segregation will be found together with wage differentials. It can be concluded that Becker's theory of discrimination based on individuals' tastes can (under certain assumptions) explain both wage and job discrimination. The next subsection will show, however, that competing theories also claim to be able to generate an explanation.

Discrimination as a means of maximizing profit

The second branch of theories concerned with labour-market discrimination regards the explanation of discriminatory behaviour advanced by Becker and others as 'too simple'. The main objection of the critics is that by including a certain aspect of economic behaviour in the individuals' goals 'everything can be explained'. They wonder whether it is possible to explain discriminatory behaviour without the additional assumption that people have a taste for discrimination. By seeking alternative explanations that can do without that assumption, researchers have looked in 2 directions.

One line of reasoning stresses the similarity between the market for goods and the labour market. Paying different wages to different groups of workers has some resemblance to the behaviour of a producer who holds a monopoly in the product market. Under certain conditions a monopolist will charge different prices to different buyers, not because he prefers one buyer to another, but simply because he wants to take every opportunity to make a profit. As he is the only supplier of the good he can charge prices that are higher than those charged where there is full competition.

In some cases an employer may face a similar situation in the labour market. In such a case we talk about a monopsony (i.e. a situation of a single buyer and many suppliers in a market for factors of production). A monopsony may occur in small company villages, for example, where the village has grown around a single industry (e.g. a mining plant or an air base). The main breadwinner of the household may have moved to such a place because of the high wages or the promising career opportunities. Their partners may find themselves confronted with rather restricted job opportunities, and – if they are keen to be employed – will have to settle for lower wages than they might have earned elsewhere. If such a situation occurs an employer who pays the partners (usually women) more than their reservation wage (i.e. the minimum wage necessary to make workers enter the labour market) will put himself at a disadvantage compared to an employer who pays just the reservation wage. Given the local circumstances the achievement of the goal of profit maximization prescribes wage discrimination or exploitation.

A second line of reasoning is in with the so-called search literature, which stresses that economic actors usually act under conditions of uncertainty. This hold for product markets as well as for the labour market. The problem an employer faces when attracting new workers is that of having to make them a wage offer based on future productivity. In order to make the 'right' wage offer the employer will estimate a worker's potential productivity. Such an estimate can be made in several ways, each having different costs and different revenues in terms of reduced uncertainty about the worker's productivity. Extensive testing of applicants for a job using specialized agencies can provide a lot of information about a worker's productivity; this way of acquiring information is, however, rather expensive. If one wants to hire, e.g., a manager or another worker of whom high productivity is demanded it may be worthwhile to choose an expensive method of selection. The costs of selecting the 'wrong' candidate may be quite high. If the vacancy is a low-productivity job the gains from selecting the best candidate instead of any other may be relatively small. The use of expensive selection methods in such a case may be inefficient. So, especially for low-productivity jobs the employer will prefer easy and cheap selection rules. A selection based on 'face values' like race, sex and age provides such a cheap rule. All of these characteristics are easy to identify, contrary to, e.g., ability, experience and attitude towards the job.

It is necessary, however, for such a rule to be actually used, that applying this selection rule will result in selecting the 'right', i.e. most productive workers. Phelps (1972) and Arrow (1973) have pointed out that 'previous statistical experiences' (Phelps, 1972, p. 659) might constitute an argument for using a certain selection rule. An employer will continue using a certain rule as long as he has the idea that it 'works'. He does not need to know why it works or whether it works for the right or wrong reasons. Essential to him is that the 'face values' just mentioned provide correct information on an individual's productivity.

Also statistical discrimination may result in either wage or employment discrimination. When an employer thinks that workers belonging to a certain group are less productive than other workers he might be willing to hire the less productive workers, but only if they are prepared to settle for correspondingly lower wages. Depending on the labour-market situation the workers involved will accept or refuse the wage offer. If the employer sets some minimum productivity standard he wants workers to meet, statistical discrimination will result in the decision not to hire workers from the group that is considered less productive.

Once again we are dealing with a situation where employers make a distinction between groups of workers, not because they have feelings against or in favour of either group, but just because it would be inefficient to pay workers more than what they (are expected to) contribute to the production.

The conclusion from this – brief and necessarily incomplete – survey of discrimination theories can be that even though the notion of discrimination is used in both branches of theories the content of the concept is quite different. The first branch comprises theories of discrimination where discriminatory behaviour follows from feelings against a certain group. The second comprises theories where economic agents are as such indifferent to workers from different groups. Circumstances in the market, however, force them to treat workers from different groups in a different way. These different origins of discriminatory behaviour call for a careful analysis of labour-market phenomena before judging this behaviour and developing labour-market policies against discrimination. In case of statistical discrimination compulsory hiring of 'minority' workers may be successful. During the 'experiment' employers may find that on average 'minority' workers are just as productive as the 'majority' workers who have been the only group employed so far. After some time the obligation to hire 'minority' workers could be withdrawn as employers would no longer use their traditional selection rule. Had discrimination been based on a taste for discrimination the 'experiment' could not have been successful, as the employer's behaviour does not originate from any belief (either right or wrong) concerning 'minority' workers' productivity. If compelled to hire 'minority' workers the employer will try to pay them less than 'majority' workers and, as soon as the hiring of 'minority' workers loses its compulsory character, will fall back into his or her old discriminatory routine.

Even though it is difficult to establish discriminatory wage differentials, there is evidence that discrimination is one of the determinants of the male–female wage gap. At the beginning of this section discriminatory wage differentials were introduced as the complement of those related to human capital. So, the more accurately we can measure workers' human capital the more likely it is that additional wage differentials should be labelled 'discriminatory'. Most empirical research in this field concerns the USA (see for an interesting overview Oaxaca and Ransom, 1994, as well as Polachek and Kim, 1994, and Slottje et al., 1994, all in a special edition of the Journal of Econometrics). However, recent studies by Schippers and Siegers (1989) and Schuld, Schippers and Siegers (1994) also offer some insight into the Netherlands, while earlier research by Chiplin and Sloane (1976) is available in respect of discrimination in the UK. More recently, wage discrimination in the UK was studied by Dolton and Makepeace (1985). Wright and Ermisch (1991) and Jenkins (1994). The empirical studies concerning male–female wage discrimination in the labour market show a wide variety with respect to the part of the wage gap that should be labelled 'discriminatory': some authors report percentages of no more than about 10, while others find percentages that amount to 30 or 40. As stated before, to a large degree these outcomes depend on the measurement of human capital and other factors.

Looking at the nature of discrimination against women many authors find it difficult to apply Becker's taste-based discrimination to the case of women. Contrary to what applies for, e.g., ethnic minority groups women live in the same houses and go to the same schools as men. Most men like to share their houses and their lives with a woman. So, discrimination against women is more likely to fall into the category of statistical discrimination: employers expect women to drop out of the labour market more often than men, to report ill more often, e.g. when their children are ill, and to show less commitment to the job. However, more sociologically oriented research shows that both types of discrimination easily intermingle (see also Chapter 5 of this book).

EVALUATION AND FUTURE DEVELOPMENTS

In this chapter concerning pay differences between women and men we presented figures for the European Union as a whole and more detailed figures for the UK with respect to wage and earnings differentials. Even though our figures show only part of the picture (the statistics available at the European level are limited to gross wages and earnings of workers in selected branches of the economy) at least this part of the picture shows convincingly the pay gap between women and men. Although this gap varies between countries – and within countries between regions and sectors of the economy – women everywhere appear to be in a disadvantaged position compared to men. In many cases this disadvantaged position leads women to fall below the 'poverty line' or – put differently – to find themselves at the bottom of the pyramid of earnings. Of course this picture is not a static one. We have learned that workers completing some sort of education may expect their income to increase, while getting more experience may also improve a worker's earning capacity. On the other hand, losing one's job or becoming disabled may have severe consequences for workers' earnings. Earlier in the book we saw that everywhere in Europe women suffer excessively from unemployment. As legislation with respect to unemployment benefits strongly differs between European countries, it is not possible to analyse the consequences for women's earnings in a straightforward way. Once again, there is a great need to look 'beyond the mean' as we also know – and Chapter 4 will deal with this item more thoroughly – that black and immigrant women, for example, are hit more severely by unemployment than other women. So, if there are lessons to be learned from this chapter, the first is, of course, that a substantial wage gap still exists between women and men. The second lesson, immediately following the first, should be that there is a wide variety in earnings and causes for earnings differentials both between women and men as well as among women and among men.

This trend of increasing variety is likely to continue during the next few years. As flexibility and removing rigidities seem to be the key words with respect to labour-market policy these days differences between workers are likely to increase. Even without such labour-market policies technical as well as commercial developments point in the direction of more specialization and less uniformity in production. As a consequence the labour market will become more and more heterogeneous. In such a heterogeneous market there is little room for standard labour contracts and more diversity in terms of both employment and fringe benefits will occur. Yet, there is also a countervailing power at work. The last few years have shown an increasing flow of verdicts by the European Court in Luxembourg widening the scope of application of the 'equal pay' principle. These verdicts, pressure from the emancipation movement, and the results from scientific research have favoured the case for job classification systems, which have been introduced in different firms in many European countries, to improve proper and balanced pay for different jobs. In some cases firms or local authorities even have followed examples from Canada and the USA and have introduced the so-called 'comparable worth' approach, which is explicitly aimed at improving women's wages. Chapter 12 will discuss job classification systems and comparable worth in more detail. Our concern in this chapter is that there seem to be 2 forces at work. One advances more liberty and results in more inequality and the other stresses the importance of fair and equal treatment, resulting in more equality. During the next few years women's wages will be determined by these two forces. Only time will tell whether one of them will get the upper hand.

REFERENCES

ARROW, K. J. (1973) The theory of discrimination, in O. Ashenfelter and A. Rees (eds.), *Discrimination in Labour Markets*, Princeton University Press, Princeton (NJ), pp. 3–33.

BECKER, G. S. (1957) *The Economics of Discrimination*, Chicago University Press, Chicago.

BECKER, G. S. (1975) *Human Capital* (2nd edn), National Bureau of Economic Research, New York.

BEN-PORATH, Y. (1967) The production of human capital and the life-cycle of earnings, *Journal of Political Economy*, Vol. 75, pp. 352–65.

CHIPLIN, B. and SLOANE, P. J. (1976) *Sex Discrimination in the Labour Market*, Macmillan, London.

DICKENS, R., GREGG, P. and MACHIN, S. (1993) Wages Councils: was there a case for abolition?, *British Journal of Industrial Relations*, Vol. 31, no. 4, pp. 515–29.

DOLTON, P. J. and MAKEPEACE, G. H. (1985) The statistical measurement of discrimination, *Economic Letters*, Vol. 18, pp. 391–5.

Employment Gazette, various editions.

EUROPEAN COMMUNITIES, Statistical Office (1990) *Earnings: Industry and Services*, Luxembourg, Vol. 1.

EUROPEAN COMMUNITIES, Statistical Office (1992) *Earnings: Industry and Services*, Luxembourg, Vol. 1.

JENKINS, S. P. (1994) Earnings discrimination measurement. A distributional approach, *Journal of Econometrics*, Vol. 61, pp. 81–102.

JOSHI, H. (1990) Obstacles and opportunities for lone parents as breadwinners in Great Britain, OECD, *Lone-Parent Families*, Paris.

MINCER, J. (1974) *Schooling, Experience and Earnings*, National Bureau of Economic Research, New York.

MINCER, J. and POLACHEK, S. (1978) Women's earnings reexamined, *Journal of Human Resources*, Vol. 13, pp. 118–34.

MINCER, J. and OFEK, H. (1982) *Interrupted Work Careers*, National Bureau for Economic Research, Working Paper no. 479, Cambridge.

OAXACA, R. L. and RANSOM, M. R. (1994), On discrimination and the decomposition of wage differentials, *Journal of Econometrics*, Vol. 61, pp. 5–21.

PHELPS, E. S. (1972) The statistical theory of racism and sexism, *American Economic Review*, Vol. 62, pp. 659–61.

POLACHEK, S. W. and SIEBERT, W. S. (1993) *The Economics of Earnings*, Cambridge University Press, Cambridge, UK.

POLACHEK, S. W. and KIM, K. M. (1994) Panel estimates of the gender earnings gap, *Journal of Econometrics*, Vol. 61, pp. 23–42.

SCHIPPERS, J. J. (1987) *Beloningsverschillen tussen mannen en vrouwen - een economische analyse*, Ph.D. dissertation, Utrecht University, Wolters-Noordhoff, Groningen.

SCHIPPERS, J. J. and SIEGERS, J. J. (1989) *Beloning, loopbanen en segregatie*, Ministerie van sociale zaken en werkgelegenheid, The Hague.

SCHILD, T. C. A., SCHIPPERS, J. J. and SIEGERS, J. J. (1994) Allocation and wage structure: differences between men and women, *Applied Economics*, Vol. 26, pp. 137–52.

SLOTTJE, D. J., HIRSCHBERG, J. G., HAYES, K. J. and SCULLY, G. W. (1994) A new method for detecting individual and group labor market discrimination, *Journal of Econometrics*, Vol. 61, pp. 43–64.

WRIGHT, R. E. and ERMISCH, J. F. (1991) Gender discrimination in the British labour market: a reassessment, *Economic Journal*, Vol. 101, pp. 508–22.

CHAPTER 4

The Labour-Market Position of Women from Ethnic Minorities: A Comparison of Four European Countries

ANNE-WIL K. HARZING

INTRODUCTION

In this chapter we will compare the position of women from ethnic minorities in the labour markets of a number of European countries. We have selected the Netherlands, Belgium, Germany and the UK. This choice is based, on the one hand, on the relative or absolute sizes of the female ethnic work-force and, on the other, on the availability of statistical data for each country. The ethnic groups treated will be those which are most strongly represented in the total ethnic work-force or population.

In this chapter we will concentrate on:

1 a comparison of the participation rates;
2 the unemployment rates;
3 the sort of work undertaken by women from ethnic minorities;
4 the wages of women from ethnic minorities.

A general conclusion that can be drawn from these case studies is that the labour-market position of women from ethnic minorities is unfavourable compared to that of women of the majority cultures. The possible reasons for this are outlined in the third section. In addition to factors such as education, culture and the economic sectors in which women from ethnic minorities are employed, discrimination appears to provide an additional explanation for the poor labour-market position of women from ethnic minorities. It is striking that in each of the four countries it is possible to divide the women from ethnic minorities roughly into two groups, one of which is noticeably worse off than the other. Given the similarities between countries, it might be worth considering whether a co-ordinated European policy might not work better than purely national policies, which in any case are not really effective in most countries. Therefore in the fourth section we will go into the current EU policy on women from ethnic minorities. The chapter will close with a short conclusion.

COMPARING LABOUR-MARKET POSITIONS

In this section we will attempt to compare the labour-market position of women from ethnic minorities in four EU countries: Belgium, the Netherlands, Germany and the UK. In general, numerical comparisons between the various countries are considered very difficult. Comparative statistical data are available regarding the rates of participation and unemployment for the various European countries (e.g. data from Eurostat, OECD, ILO), but such data do not differentiate between the positions of the various ethnic groups or countries of origin. Since ethnic minorities comprise a relatively small proportion of the population and work-force, the data can be treated as a good approximation of the data for the majority cultures. However, data regarding ethnic minorities can be obtained only from the diverse sources of national statistics. These national statistics cannot always be properly compared with one another, because they employ different definitions – for instance with regard to whether or not nationalized immigrants are counted as ethnic minorities – and are collected in diverse ways. In this chapter we have in fact chosen to use only the national statistics for each country, since the comparisons between various ethnic groups within a country appeared to be more important than comparisons of ethnic minorities across various countries.

The figures in the various tables should be treated conservatively, as indicators. Thus we cannot draw sweeping conclusions from small percentage differences. This is particularly so for ethnic minorities, since these figures are based on small, sometimes very small, populations. Because of the very long delays in processing statistical material, the data in this section relate mainly to the situation in the late 1980s and early 1990s. At the time of writing (1994) the rates of participation and of unemployment of the various groups of women might be expected to be somewhat higher. We have no reason to suppose that substantial improvements have taken place for women from ethnic minorities. In view of the growing nationalism in most European countries, our conclusions regarding unemployment are more likely to be on the positive side than on the negative side.

Size of the work-force (participation rate)

Table 4.1 shows the participation rates of men and women from the various ethnic groups in the Netherlands, Belgium, Germany and the UK. The participation rate is calculated as the percentage of the population between 15 and 64 (the potential work-force) who are in the 'actual work-force'. The actual work-force includes both those already working and unemployed people who are available for the labour market. The data for the Netherlands are derived from the Statistisch Vademecum 1992 *Minderheden in Nederland* (Roelandt, Roijen and Veenman, 1992). The average over the years 1988–91 has been used as far as possible because little significance can be attributed to year-to-year fluctuations for ethnic minorities. The data for Belgium are derived from *De vreemdelingen in België volgens de tellingen*, Statistical Studies series no. 92 (Grimmeau, 1991). The data for Germany relate only to the former West Germany, and are drawn from the report *Aspekte der*

Ausländerbeschäftigung in der Bundersrepublik Deutschland from the Institut für Arbeitsmarkt- und Berufsforschung der Bundesanstalt für Arbeit (Hönekopp, 1987). Since no specific statistics are maintained in Germany in relation to the rates of participation and unemployment of women from ethnic minorities, we had to rely on the somewhat older data from the report of the Bundesanstalt für Arbeit. The data for the UK are derived from the *Employment Gazette* of February 1991.

Table 4.1 shows that Moroccan women (in Belgium and the Netherlands), Turkish women (in the Netherlands and Germany), and Pakistani/Bengali women (in the UK) in particular have low participation rates. On the other hand, Surinamese and Antillean/Aruban women in the Netherlands, Italian women in Belgium and Germany, Yugoslav women in Germany and West Indian women in the UK have participation rates which are as high or even higher than the rates for women of the majority culture. Indian women in the UK have an intermediate position.

In all countries the participation rate is higher for men than for women, for both the majority culture and ethnic minorities. However, there are clear differences between countries and between groups within these countries. The participation rates of Dutch, Belgian and German women (expressed as

Table 4.1   **Rate of participation (%) by country, gender and ethnic origin**

The Netherlands					
	Dutch	Moroccan	Turkish	Antil./Arub	Surinamese
Women	54	22	32	58	52
Men	82	67	78	78	75

Belgium *			
	Belgian	Italian	Moroccan
Women	43	43	21
Men	79	70	67

Germany †			
	German	Italian	Turkish	Yugoslav
Women	34.5	39.5	26.7	51.0
Men	59.1	69.8	56.0	71.0

United Kingdom			
	British	West Indian	Indian	Pakistani/Bengali
Women	70	76	58	21
Men	89	85	84	77

* (Martens, 1991). The original participation figures for Belgium related to the work-force divided by the total population. With the aid of the age distribution of Italians and Moroccans, which is given in the same report (André, 1991), these figures are translated in terms of the work-force divided by the population between the ages of 15 and 64. The age distribution for Belgians of the majority culture is derived from Eurostat (1989).

† (Thon, 1987). These figures, like those for Belgium, relate to the work-force divided by the total population. Unfortunately, the lack of data as to the age distribution of Italians, Turks and Yugoslavs meant that it was not possible to recalculate these figures. This percentage is thus not comparable to the percentages given for the other countries, for which the participation rates are calculated as the work-force divided by the population between the ages of 15 and 64. For native Germans, 70% of the population is between the ages of 15 and 64 (Eurostat, 1989), so that the recalculated figures for German woman and men would be 49% and 84%, respectively.

percentages of the population between 15 and 64) are all at roughly the same level, although it must be noted that, in comparison with other countries, a very large portion (about two-thirds) of Dutch women work part time. The participation rate of British women is clearly higher, both in absolute terms and relative to the rate of British men. This might be due to the relatively low wages in the UK, a less comprehensive system of social security and the high rate of home ownership (and thus of high mortgages). However, there is no clear connection between the participation rates of women from the majority culture and from ethnic minorities within one country. In the UK, for example, we see some women from ethnic minorities with very high participation rates (the West Indian women), while Pakistani/Bengali women have a very low participation rate. Finally, it is striking that Moroccan and Pakistani/Bengali men have fairly low participation rates.

If we consider the various ethnic groups within a country, it can be seen that women of the majority culture do not have the highest rate of participation, in either absolute or relative terms, in Germany, the Netherlands and the UK. Yugoslav women in Germany have a clearly higher participation rate than German women, and the same is true to a lesser extent for Italian women in Germany. In absolute terms the participation rates of Antillean women in the Netherlands and West Indian women in the UK are also higher than the rates for women of the majority cultures. In relative terms this difference is even more marked, since the participation rates of Antillean and West Indian men are in fact lower than the rate for men of the majority cultures.

It must, however, be noted that the data for women from ethnic minorities contain large margins of error, so that we cannot draw really firm conclusions on the basis of these small differences. We should also be cautious in dealing with the participation figures for ethnic minorities in general. The population of ethnic minorities often has a different overall age distribution from the population of the majority culture, especially where immigration has been relatively recent. Often there will be more young people and fewer people of over 50 in the population of ethnic minorities. Since young people in general have a higher participation rate than older people, the participation figures of ethnic minorities may be overestimated. On the other hand, Antillean and Surinamese women who are more than 30 years old have a higher participation rate than Dutch women, while those younger than 30 have a lower rate (Roelandt, Roijen and Veenman, 1992). If the age structure of the two groups were the same, the participation rate of Antillean and Surinamese women would thus be significantly higher than for Dutch women. In brief, we can say that we certainly do not have to assume, prima facie, that the participation rates of all groups of women from ethnic minorities are lower than those of women of the majority cultures.

Unemployment

Table 4.2 shows the unemployment rates of men and women of the various ethnic groups in the Netherlands, Germany and the UK. The unemployment rate is calculated as the number of unemployed people divided by the actual work-force, and is derived from the same sources as were used to calculate the participation rate. However, the definition of unemployment and the

Table 4.2 **Unemployment rate (%) by country, gender and ethnic origin**

The Netherlands					
	Dutch	Moroccan	Turkish	Antil./Arub	Surinamese
Women	9	52	39	35	27
Men	6	33	29	28	25
Germany					
	German	Italian	Turkish	Yugoslav	
Women and Men	8.7	14.8	16.3	11.0	
United Kingdom					
	British	West Indian	Indian	Pakistani/Bengali	
Women	8	14	13	–	
Men	9	18	10	25	

recentness of the data differ from country to country, so that we must be very cautious in making comparisons between countries. For example, for the Netherlands we have used the number of job-seekers who are registered at the Employment Office and do not have a job, taken from the 1991 survey 'Sociale Positie en Voorzieningengebruik van Allochtonen en Autochtonen' (SPVA). The true number of job-seekers may be either lower or higher than the registered number, since some people who are registered are not really job-seekers, and some job-seekers do not register as such. One common reason for not registering with the Employment Office is that registration is not expected to help in getting a job. This reasoning is stronger for those belonging to groups with poorer prospects. The unemployment figures for women and ethnic minorities (and certainly for women from ethnic minorities) may thus be underestimated.

We can see that in the Netherlands the unemployment rate for ethnic minorities is very much higher than for the majority culture. Moreover, for all ethnic groups the unemployment rate for women is higher than that for men. It is striking that the differences in unemployment between men of various ethnic minorities are smaller than between women of various ethnic minorities. Moroccan women in particular, and Turkish women to a lesser extent, show up very badly. It is also interesting to note that women from ethnic minorities more often have temporary work contracts. Turkish and Moroccan women are almost three times as likely to have a temporary employment contract as Dutch women, and Surinamese and Antillean women are, respectively, almost twice and almost one and a half times as likely to have temporary work (Roelandt, Roijen and Veenman, 1992).

The data for Belgium are not in any sense comparable with the data for the Netherlands, Germany and the UK, because of differences in the way they are recorded. Therefore they have not been included in Table 4.2. In Belgium the percentages are generally calculated over the total population over 15 years old, rather than being calculated as proportions of the female and male work-forces, as applicable. Thus we have to multiply the percentages by a certain factor, according to the share of men, women and people of over 65 in the total population and the participation rates of men and women. The fact that only a small percentage of the Moroccan population consists of unemployed women certainly does not mean that we can conclude that unemployment among Moroccan women is low. Since there are fewer Moroccan women than men in Belgium, and their participation rate is very low, a fairly large proportion of the Moroccan women in Belgium who want to work, and are able to work, are in fact unemployed. We have made no attempt to recalculate the available unemployment figures because the calculation might result in an excessively large accumulation of errors. However, we can say that, in broad terms, Italian men and especially Moroccan men are more likely to be unemployed than are Belgian men. Italian and Moroccan women have even higher unemployment rates.

In Germany the unemployment rate for ethnic minorities since 1974 has been higher than that of native Germans (Bach, 1987). Between 1960 and 1974 the labour market was quite tight, with unemployment rates of 0.5% to 2%. Workers from ethnic minorities, the so-called guest workers, were recruited to relieve this scarcity in the labour market. In 1974 and 1975 the unemployment rate of native Germans increased markedly. However, unemployment among Germans from ethnic minorities increased even more strongly, a development which was repeated in the early 1980s. In 1984 (unfortunately, no more recent data could be obtained) the unemployment rate for native Germans was 8.7%, and the rate for Germans from ethnic minorities was 14%. Table 4.2 gives a breakdown by ethnicity. We can see that the unemployment of Italians and especially of Turks is clearly higher than that of Yugoslavs. Unfortunately, it was not possible to make any differentiation by sex. It is known, however, that women of ethnic minorities, like German women, are more often unemployed than men (Bach, 1987).

Finally, in the UK the situation is entirely different. With the exception of Indians, the unemployment rate for men in each ethnic group is actually higher than that for women, and for ethnic minorities the difference is even stronger than for the majority culture. The differences in unemployment rates for the various ethnic groups are also greater for men than for women. Here again we see that unemployment among women from ethnic minorities is higher than for women of the majority culture. The unemployment rate of Pakistani and Bengali women is not known, but given the total unemployment figure for this part of the population, it must certainly be more than 20%. That means that unemployment is highest for West Indian men and Pakistani/Bengali men and women. Indians are in a relatively good position.

Thus, unemployment among women of ethnic minorities in all countries is generally higher, often significantly higher, than unemployment among women of the majority culture. Turkish, Moroccan and Pakistani/Bengali women are in a particularly bad position, with unemployment rates which are even higher than for other women from ethnic minorities. With the exception of the UK, unemployment among women from ethnic minorities is higher than for men from ethnic minorities. Thus they appear to suffer double discrimination. However, the negative effect of belonging to an ethnic minority seems in fact to be stronger than the effect (usually negative) of being a woman.

Table 4.3   **Percentage of women doing unskilled work in Germany**

Nordrhein-Westfalen				
	German	Italian	Turkish	Yugoslav
Women	30	61	79	59
Germany				
	German	Ethnic minorities		
Women and Men	8	62		

Kinds of work

To begin with, we will examine the sectors in which women from ethnic minorities are strongly represented. Moroccan women are very much over-represented in cleaning work, both in the Netherlands and in Belgium. Italian women in Belgium are also slightly over-represented in this sector. Turkish women in both the Netherlands and Germany work mainly in the processing industry (assembly-line work) (Ankersmit, Roelandt and Veenman, 1990; Denolf and Martens, 1990). For Yugoslav and Italian women in Germany this is somewhat less marked, but they are also over-represented in this sector as compared to German women (Bundesanstalt für Arbeit, 1992). Antillean and Surinamese women in the Netherlands generally work in the same sectors as Dutch women (Most van Spijk, 1991). In the UK Indian and Pakistani/Bengali women are over-represented in industrial production, and especially in textiles and clothing (i.e. clothing ateliers). Relatively, many West Indian women work as nurses (Brown, 1984).

Next we examined which functions or jobs women from ethnic minorities have within these sectors. According to one study carried out in the Netherlands (Bouw and Nelissen, 1986), half of the work done by Turkish and Moroccan women is not done at all by Dutch women. Moreover, within a single sector (laundries), Turkish women do heavier work than Dutch women (Ankoné and Kaufman, 1984).

In Germany, as shown in Table 4.3, the larger part of the women from ethnic minorities perform unskilled work, while only about 30% of German women work as unskilled labourers. The situation for younger women (15–24) from ethnic minorities in Germany appears to be somewhat more favourable, but even so some 59% of them do unskilled work (Schultze, 1987). These figures are based on a study in Nordrhein-Westfalen. The figures for Germany as a whole do not differ that much, however, as can be seen in Table 4.3. In the UK West Indian and Indian women are more likely than British women to have a 'blue collar' job.

Wages

In the Netherlands Turkish and Moroccan women are the worst paid, partly because they do mainly unskilled work. However, Dutch women who do unskilled work earn more than women from ethnic minorities (Bouw and Nelissen, 1986). Moreover, under-payment is frequent for young Turkish and

Moroccan women, in particular (Brassé et al., 1983), and it is generally more common for girls than for boys.

In Belgium the greatest differences are again those between men and women, although women from ethnic minorities (and men) are paid less than people of the majority culture who work in the same sector. Moroccan women are on the lowest rung of the wage hierarchy. Within each sector they are paid the lowest wages, and they are also over-represented in the low-wage sectors. In wage terms, Italian women fall between Moroccan and Belgian women (Denolf and Martens, 1990).

In Germany women from ethnic minorities earn less than men from ethnic minorities working at the same function level. Turkish and Italian women earn less than Yugoslav women (König, Schultze and Wesse, 1986; Schultze, 1987), although this might be explained by their lower function levels and the larger number of part-time workers among Italian and Turkish women. The larger numbers of Yugoslav women doing shift work, and thus earning more because of shift allowances, may also be a factor. Unfortunately there are no comparable data for German women.

The data in relation to the UK are ambiguous. It is clear that the largest differences in wages are once more those between men and women. Men from the majority culture earn distinctly more than either men from ethnic minorities or women of British ancestry. The differences between women from ethnic minorities and women of the majority culture are smaller. According to some researchers, this is because women are often in a marginal position, and the differences between them and men are so great that there is little room for differences between women. Indian, and especially Pakistani/Bengali, women earn less than British women, while West Indian women on average earn somewhat more. This can be explained partly by the differences in function levels described above. If differences in age distribution are controlled for, British women on the whole seem to earn more than women from ethnic minorities (Brown, 1984).

Conclusion

To draw any general conclusions, we will necessarily have to generalize and leave some groups out of consideration. However, it is clear that women from ethnic minorities in general have a worse labour-market position than women of the majority cultures. It is also possible to distinguish roughly between two groups. Turkish, Moroccan, Pakistani, Bengali and to some extent Indian women have lower participation rates, face higher unemployment, and have poorer quality work and lower wages than women of either the majority culture or other ethnic minorities. For Italian, Yugoslav, Antillean/Aruban, Surinamese and West Indian women the participation rates in particular, but often also the kind of work they do and their wages, are more similar to those of women of the majority culture. However, unemployment in this group is clearly higher than among women of the majority culture. In the following section we will attempt to find an explanation for the poor labour-market position of women from ethnic minorities.

EXPLANATORY FACTORS

Economic sector

One of the causes which is often suggested for the high unemployment, low wages and dead-end work of women from ethnic minorities is the economic sectors they work in and the sort of work (i.e. unskilled labour) which they do. According to this reasoning, they find themselves in a disadvantageous position because they choose the wrong jobs.

In Belgium Moroccan women would appear to be over-represented in the sectors in which low wages are combined with job insecurity, little or no chance of promotion and unfavourable working conditions. This is also true for Italian women, although to a somewhat lesser extent. In the UK, too, women from ethnic minorities (especially Asians) are over-represented in the textile sector and industrial production. Both of these sectors are characterized by relatively low wages, high unemployment and unfavourable working conditions. In the Netherlands Turkish and Moroccan women are over-represented in the industrial sector and in cleaning work, and in these sectors they have mainly unskilled jobs. These sectors are also characterized by falling job numbers, especially for unskilled workers. In Germany we also see an over-representation of women from ethnic minorities in these sectors, and they do mainly unskilled work.

However, this factor hardly constitutes an explanation. We saw in the last section that women from ethnic minorities were over-represented in these sectors, begging the question of why women from ethnic minorities work there. A partial explanation can be found in their lower educational levels and their culture.

Education

Education can be an important explanatory factor for all the aspects of the poor labour-market position listed earlier. A lower educational level generally leads to unsatisfactory jobs, higher unemployment and lower wages. Moreover, the participation rate of women with lower-level training is in general lower than that of women with higher-level training. Thus, if women from ethnic minorities have a lower educational level than women of the majority culture, this factor could explain their poorer labour-market position. Let us consider this country by country.

In the Netherlands Moroccan and Turkish women are clearly less well educated than Dutch women. Almost two-thirds of the Moroccan women and a quarter of the Turkish women have not had any schooling at all. Another half of the Turkish women and 17% of the Moroccan women have only primary education. All Dutch women have completed some form of education, although 23% have had only primary education. For the Surinamese and Antillean women, 6% and 5% respectively have had no schooling whatsoever. Apart from this, their situation is comparable to that of Dutch women (Most van Spijk, 1991). Lack of education could thus offer an explanation of the low participation rates and poor labour-market position of Moroccan and Turkish women. Nevertheless, Turkish and Moroccan women are more likely to be unemployed than Dutch women with the same educational level (e.g. no more than primary education or lower vocational education/lower general secondary education) (Roelandt, Roijen and Veenman, 1992). The educational level of Antillean and Surinamese women would lead us to expect a participation rate comparable with that for Dutch women, and this is indeed the case. However, the higher educational level of Antillean and Surinamese women does not result in a comparable unemployment rate: they are roughly three times as likely to be unemployed as are Dutch women. This is indeed a worrying situation, since, if investing in education does not bring returns in the form of a better chance of getting a job, the motivation to undertake a course of higher education may be reduced.

In Belgium Moroccan immigrant women of the first generation have a very low educational level. Two-thirds of the adult population in Morocco are illiterate, and for women from rural areas the proportion is as high as three-quarters (Peytier, 1991). Most Moroccan women are thus illiterate when they arrive in Belgium. If we consider the statistics on the educational level of the total group of Moroccan women (thus including the second and third generations), we see that almost half have no diploma of any kind and more than a third have only primary education (Deboosere, 1991). Because education is compulsory in Italy, Italian women generally have at least a diploma from lower secondary education. They are thus, on average, much more highly educated than Moroccan women. In the second generation, a large proportion of the youngsters from ethnic minorities fall one or more years behind while at primary school. After primary school the overwhelming majority of these youngsters go on to technical or vocational education, which in general offers poorer prospects of getting a good job than does a broad general education, which is much more likely to be taken by young Belgians. This situation also applies, to an even greater degree, for young Moroccans (Deville and Dequeeker, 1988). The data on the labour-market position of Italian women show that they have a higher participation rate than Moroccan women, along with relatively better jobs and higher wages. This could be due partly to their better education. Unemployment is also high among Italian women, however.

In Germany Yugoslav women are better trained than Italian and Turkish women. They are more likely to have a school diploma, stay at school longer, and more of them have completed a vocational education than of the Turkish and Italian women (Schultze, 1987). We also find that the second generation of immigrant women are better educated, because they have studied in Germany. It does seem that non-German youngsters have more difficulty in findings a post-secondary school trainee post in a business during their vocational training (König, Schultze and Wesse, 1986), and in Germany participation in this form of education is very important if one hopes to obtain anything better than unskilled work. Yugoslav women have a higher participation rate and a better labour-market position than Turkish and Italian women. Their higher educational level could thus, in part, explain this better labour-market position. We have also noted that the second generation of immigrant women are somewhat better placed as regards the kinds of work they do. Nevertheless, some 59% of these women still work in unskilled jobs. A better education does not lead directly to a much better labour-market position.

Table 4.4 **Female educational level (%) in the UK by ethnic origin**

	British	West Indian	Indian	Pakistani/Bengali
Above GCE A-level	12	16	12	–
GCE A-level or lower	49	49	45	24
No qualifications (16–59)	38	35	44	72
No qualifications (16–24)	21	19	23	60

In the UK the picture is quite clear (see Table 4.4). The educational level of Indian women is almost equal to that of women of the majority culture. Many of them have no qualifications (i.e. no education at all, primary education alone, or only some secondary school education), but that is also true for British women. West Indian women are in fact slightly better trained than British women, since only 35% of them have no education and 16% have higher education, as compared to 12% of British women (*Employment Gazette*, 1991). However, it must be noted that some of these qualifications were not gained in the UK. The extent to which courses in the lands from which they have come meet the standards of the British education system is not clear. The educational position of Pakistani/Bengalese women is clearly worse, with 72% having no schooling whatsoever and almost none of them having higher education. In the UK, as in almost every other country, young people are better trained than older people. The percentage of girls having no qualifications is broadly comparable for the British, West Indian and Indian groups. The number of Pakistani/Bengali girls without schooling is falling more slowly, however, with some 60% between 16 and 24 years old have no qualifications. Despite the fact that, with the exception of Pakistani/Bengali women, women from ethnic minorities are as well or better trained than British women, they are under-represented in higher functions and more likely to be unemployed. Other research shows that in 1981, 25% of the unemployed West Indian men had completed their 0-level exams, as compared to 9% of men from the majority culture, and that there were twice as many unemployed Asian academics as white academics (Ohri and Farugi, 1988). Thus, in the UK, lack of education explains the poorer labour-market position even less than in other countries. There is, however, a clear relationship between education and the rate of participation. The less-educated Pakistani and Bengalese women have a clearly lower participation rate.

Culture

Culture is often suggested as an explanatory factor for the poor labour-market position of women from ethnic minorities. This suggestion is often accompanied by a reference to Islam, which is said to be the reason that Islamic women and girls participate less in the labour market. Conceptions of honour and shame, in particular, are involved. Work outside the home means a loss of honour for the man because, on the one hand, he appears not to be able to support his family and, on the other hand, the women come in contact with men without the husband or other males of the family being present. It is true that the participation rates of Islamic women are much lower than those of women of the majority culture and of other ethnic minorities. Nevertheless it is clear that, when it is financially necessary (for example, if the husband is unemployed or does not earn enough), Islamic women are often also permitted to work outside the home.

An Islamic background would thus to some extent explain the low participation rate, but it does not account for other factors such as high unemployment, dead-end work and low wages. It is, however, true that Islamic women, in part because of traditional conceptions of gender roles, have little schooling in general. This is also applicable, though to a lesser degree, for the second (and third) generations. In the Netherlands the rates of participation in education of Turkish and Moroccan girls are lower than for Dutch girls. In the 12–14 age group the rates for Turkish, Moroccan, and Dutch girls are 92%, 98% and 100%, and in the 15–17 age group they are 77%, 82% and 95% respectively (Most van Spijk, 1991). This could also indirectly explain the higher unemployment and the lower-level work. But we have also seen that, even when they have the same schooling, Turkish and Moroccan women are more likely to be unemployed.

Culture and religion can, however, certainly play a role in the choice between different kinds of work. Working at home encounters fewer objections than working outside the house, and jobs in settings such as clothing ateliers where the employees are almost all women are less objectionable than other kinds of work. And these are precisely the sectors in which wages and working conditions are poorest.

It is clear that for other groups of women from ethnic minorities, culture cannot play any significant part in explaining their poor labour-market positions. Among Italian women (and even more, among Italian men) conceptions of gender roles are still rather traditional. However, Yugoslav, Antillean, Surinamese and West Indian women are generally more progressive than Dutch, Belgian, British or German women as regards women's participation in the labour market, economic independence and the equality of men and women. What they all have in common, however, is that they come from cultures which differ from the majority cultures. And it begins to appear that this could in fact be an important additional explanatory factor for their poor labour-market position.

Discrimination

Economic sectors, education and culture provide at best partial explanations for the poor labour-market position of women from ethnic minorities, and then often for specific groups only. There must be another factor which explains the poor labour-market position of men and women from ethnic minorities. It would appear that the difference in nationality, race or culture can explain a great deal. This is in fact a residual category explanation, i.e. if other factors do not provide sufficient explanation there must be a degree of discrimination on the basis of nationality, race or culture. However, we can also give a number of examples of more or less active and directly demonstrable discrimination.

In the Netherlands many employers state quite plainly that they prefer employees of the majority culture, and justify this with various arguments:

1 they assume that ethnic minorities entail extra cost and effort because they need more supervision and attention;
2 they are thought to be a higher business risk because they are less motivated, more often sick, and take longer holidays;
3 it is often said that people of ethnic minorities do not fit into the team or that there is customer resistance (Reubsaet and Kropman, 1986; Bouw and Nelissen, 1986).

In a recent study by Bovenkerk, Gras and Ramsoedh (1994), in which a Dutch and a Moroccan applicant with identical qualifications and the same command of Dutch applied for work, it was found that there was abundantly clear evidence of discrimination in at least 38% of the cases. In many cases the Moroccan was told during the first telephone conversation that the vacancy had already been filled, while it was still open for the Dutch applicant.

A study of the labour-market position of ex-miners in Belgian Limburg showed that one year after losing their jobs 92% of the Belgian workers, 78.5% of the Italians and 24% of the Turks had found new work. Even if Turks speak better Dutch and/or have a higher educational level and/or have completed extra training, their chances of getting a job are lower than for Italians (Denolf and Martens, 1991).

In Germany ethnic minorities often miss out in the allocation of trainee posts for vocational training. On the employers' part, more or less objective drawbacks, such as lack of school education, difficulty with the German language and plans to return to their parents' country, play a role (Mehrlander, 1989). But we should question to what extent these factors really are present among ethnic minorities. Moreover, such arguments could be rationalizations for other reasons which are not considered socially acceptable. Employers also state quite plainly that the different cultural and social background of Turkish youths, in particular, could give rise to conflicts with German employees. In small and medium-sized businesses, moreover, it is thought that customers will not accept employees belonging to an ethnic minority (Beer and Collingro, 1988).

In the UK a group of ethnic minorities was asked whether they had ever been refused a job because of their race or skin colour. Of the West Indians, 26% of the men and 23% of the women answered in the affirmative, while the percentages for the Asians were rather lower, at 10% and 8% respectively. This difference can be explained largely by the higher number of 'don't know' answers from the Asian respondents. The percentage who said 'no' is roughly the same for the two groups. When asked whether some employers discriminate on the basis of race or skin colour, 77% of the West Indians said yes. Only 5% of the West Indian women and 7% of the West Indian men said no (Brown, 1984). Foreign youngsters also have less chance of getting a place in YTS (Youth Training Scheme) projects, which offer better prospects. Many personnel managers are distinctly unenthusiastic about taking on employees from ethnic minorities (Lee and Wrench, 1982).

All in all, it would appear that men and women from ethnic minorities are, or were, a useful solution for employers who have had difficulty findings employees from the majority culture to perform a particular type of work. As soon as substitutes are available who differ less from men of the majority culture – e.g., if more women of the majority culture participate, or, as in the example of Germany, when East German workers became available – the ethnic minorities find themselves relegated to second-best choice. The reasons given for this vary from more or less objective ones, such as lack of education and knowledge of the national language, to indubitably discriminatory ones, such as being a different culture. Even the objective reasons are sometimes more a matter of presupposition (of course they will want to go home, they won't speak German/Dutch well enough, etc.) than of fact.

Conclusion

This section has shown that the economic sector in which many women from ethnic minorities work is in fact not an explanation for their poor labour-market position. The question is why they end up in those sectors or jobs. Lack of education could be one reason, but we have seen that this argument holds for only part of this group (especially for Turkish, Moroccan and Pakistani/Bengali women) and, even then, they are more likely to be unemployed than women of the majority culture with the same education, or they are paid less. A third explanation, culture, may to some extent explain this group's low participation rate, but offers only very indirect reasons for their high rate of unemployment, dead-end jobs and low wages. Indeed, a large group of ethnic minority women (e.g. Antillean, Surinamese and West Indian women) come from relatively emancipated cultures which should in fact constitute a positive factor.

We have, therefore, found that the labour-market position of women from ethnic minorities is clearly worse than that of other women, without discovering any satisfactory explanation for that difference in the characteristics of the women themselves. There is one factor which may provide an important supplementary explanation, however: simple discrimination on the basis of race, nationality or culture. The title of a book edited by F. Bovenkerk (1978) puts it succinctly: *Because They Are Different: Patterns of Race Discrimination in the Netherlands (Omdat zij anders zijn: patronen van rassendiscriminatie in Nederland)*. And whether this discrimination is open and conscious or is the result of an unconscious negative estimate of ethnic minorities, the result is in any case the same: a drastically poorer labour-market position for ethnic minorities in general and for women from ethnic minorities in particular.

POLICY AT EUROPEAN LEVEL

In this section we will examine the extent to which something is being done about the poor labour-market position of women from ethnic minorities at the EU level, looking at measures in three areas. Naturally we will begin by looking at measures focused particularly on women from ethnic minorities, but we will also consider what policy initiatives are in place for women, and for ethnic minorities, in general.

Women from ethnic minorities

To begin, we will discuss EU policy specifically targeting women from ethnic minorities. This section will be very short, since there is almost no policy. On 17 and 18 September 1987 the Commission organized a seminar on 'Immigrant women and employment'. The participants, representing member states, unions and immigrant organizations, emphasized the need to put an end to specific discrimination against women who do not have a suitable educational background and who are often squeezed aside, into the less well-paid sectors. The European institutes were asked to undertake concrete experiments for the improvement of the situation of those women, either under the provisions of the Social Fund, or via the programme for equal opportunities for men and women. One of the recommendations of the seminar was an appeal to the Commission to encourage all member states to fight against discrimination.

The problem discussed during the seminar were seen by some people at the Commission as matters to be handled under the equal opportunities programme, and by others as questions related to racism and xenophobia. In this chapter we have seen that the poor labour-market position of women from ethnic minorities has more to do with their belonging to an ethnic minority (discrimination being a significant factor here) than with their being women. The latter point of view was quickly dropped, however, and an approach based on the equal opportunities programme resulted, in 1988, in a communication from the Commission to the Council on both the social and the employment situations with the goal of achieving better social and occupational integration of women from ethnic minorities. The final report of the seminar fed into a number of smaller studies, scantily subsidized by the Commission. But to date not a single concrete measure for women from ethnic minorities has been put into action (European Parliament, 1991).

Women

According to the Commission, then, the problems of women from ethnic minorities must be considered under the umbrella of the equal opportunities programme. We will now examine what measures have been taken in this field. On 21 May 1991 the Council published a resolution regarding the third EU action programme for equal opportunities for men and women, covering the period from 1991 to 1995. The goal of this action programme is to encourage women's full participation in the labour market in every respect, and to increase the value of their contribution to the labour market. Attention was drawn to three specific areas:

1 *The implementation and development of the law.* The implementation and development of existing legal procedures should be ensured, and women must be fully alive to their legal rights and obligations. Furthermore, understanding of specific issues relating to equal pay for work of equal value and the concept of indirect discrimination against women should be deepened.

2 *The integration of women into the labour market.* Both the quantity and the

quality of the participation of women must be increased. Special attention should be given to barriers to women's access and participation in employment, such as the combination of work and family.

3 *The improvement in the status of women in society.* The participation of women in the media and in the social and economic decision-making process must be encouraged (Commission of the European Communities, 1991).

Of course we have to ask precisely what women from ethnic minorities can hope to gain from this. The answer is: not much, apparently. A general policy focused on equalizing the positions of men and women will not be sufficient to remove the disadvantages under which women from ethnic minorities labour. Some effect can be expected only in areas in which differences between men and women are more important than those between the majority culture and ethnic minorities. Thus, women from ethnic minorities might well share in the benefits of measures focusing on equal wages for equal work for men and women, but this action programme will presumably not persuade employers to hire more women from ethnic minorities. It is also probable that the women from ethnic minorities who are now relatively better off will benefit most from this action programme, because they differ less from women of the majority culture.

Ethnic minorities

Has anything been done for ethnic minorities in general, then? There is at least a report; the Evrigenis Report (1985), which sets forth 40 recommendations for combating racism and xenophobia. Thus far, only 2 of the report's recommendations have been realized in full at EU level: the 1986 Joint Declaration against racism and xenophobia and the Eurobarometer for racism and xenophobia in the EU. The events surrounding the declaration against racism and xenophobia and their sequel illustrate the state of EU policy in this area, and will therefore be described briefly.

The 'Declaration against racism, racial discrimination and xenophobia and in favour of harmonious relationships between all the communities in Europe' was signed on 11 June 1986 by the chairpersons of the Parliament, the Commission and the Council, as well as by representatives of the member states in the Council. But this was no more than a declaration, and not a series of recommendations to member states. A 1988 proposal from the Commission to fight racism and xenophobia ultimately received the approval of the Council after a 2-year tug-of-war. However, the resolution which was adopted no longer resembled the original Commission proposal. Every mention of citizens from outside the EU had been dropped, even the passage which called urgently for a policy of preventive education and information to be put in place to promote good relations between the various cultures and to make a clear and objective evaluation of the position of employees from ethnic minorities. The statement that racism and xenophobia were obstacles to the free movement of people within the Community had already been killed, along with the Commission's promise to encourage the establishment of immigrant organizations at Community level in order to achieve a better dialogue between the immigrant communities and the institutes of the

Community. The member states are not required to report on the implementation of the resolution, and the Commission will also not compile a report. Moreover, a declaration was attached to the resolution, in which it was specified that the implementation of the resolution should not entail any extension to the powers of the European institutes as defined in the Treaties.

The result was that the Commission distanced itself from the proposal. The Council described the text, as it was ultimately approved, as an important step forward towards the eradication of racism and xenophobia between citizens of the various member states. But the judgement of the European Parliament was that the resolution was a backward step, because residents coming from outside the Community were deliberately not mentioned, so that the text clearly ran counter to the spirit and content of the joint declaration against racism and xenophobia of June 1986 (European Parliament, 1991).

In short, we can say that there has not been any concrete policy decided on in any of these three areas which might lead to an improvement in the poor labour-market position of women from ethnic minorities.

CONCLUSION

We have seen that in each country considered, the labour-market position of women from ethnic minorities is worse than that of women of the majority culture. Sometimes their position is also to some extent worse than the position of men from ethnic minorities, but there are also countries in which the reverse applies for some groups. The position of women from ethnic minorities also appears – with the exception of under-payment – to be determined more by their belonging to an ethnic minority than by their being women. We can roughly distinguish two sub-groups within the population of women from ethnic minorities in the various countries. On the one hand, the Turkish, Moroccan, Pakistani/Bengali and to some extent Indian women form a group with a lower participation rate, higher unemployment, poorer quality of work and lower wages than women of both the majority culture and other ethnic minorities. As for the group comprising Italian, Yugoslav, Antillean/Aruban, Surinamese and West Indian women, their participation rates, in particular, but often also the kind of work they do and their wages are closer to those of women of the majority culture. However, the unemployment levels in this group are also clearly higher than among women of the majority culture.

The economic sector in which many women from ethnic minorities work is not an explanation for their poor labour-market position. The question is, why do they end up in those sectors or jobs? Lack of education might be an explanation, but we have seen that this applies only to a limited group of women from ethnic minorities. And even then it appears that they are more likely to be unemployed than women of the majority culture who have the same education, or that they are paid less. A third possible explanation, culture, was found partly to explain the low participation rate for the same group, but it is only a very indirect explanation of their high unemployment, dead-end jobs and low wages. There is a large group of women from ethnic minorities (e.g. Antillean, Surinamese and West Indian women) whose relatively emancipated cultures would be expected to have positive effects. Direct or indirect discrimination therefore seems to provide an important supplementary explanation for the poor labour-market position of ethnic minorities in general and women from ethnic minorities in particular.

At EU level little is being done to improve the position of women from ethnic minorities. The decision-making process is very slow and, if proposals are accepted by the Council, these are no more than very watered-down versions of the originals. Even then, it is a matter of waiting to see whether the measures which are taken have any effect in practice.

In short, we could say that emancipation and training for the group comprising Moroccan, Turkish and Pakistani/Bengali women might bring an improvement, though perhaps only a small one, in their labour-market position. However, this would require policy measures which specifically target these groups. But in general it would be better to try anti-discrimination programmes, which should not be entirely voluntary in character. A recent study by the NIA (Dutch institute for employment conditions), for example, showed that affirmative action plans for women are implemented only if the government provides direct subsidies (Breedeveld, 1992). Thus we would certainly not expect employers to apply policy plans for men or women from ethnic minorities without some compulsion or financial stimulus. Since concrete policy at EU level will probably remain an illusion for the present, national authorities will have to accept this responsibility.

REFERENCES

ANDRÉ, R. (1991) Evolutie van de buitenlandse bevolking tussen de tellingen van 1890 en 1981, in Grimmeau (1991).

ANKERSMIT, T., ROELANDT, TH. and VEENMAN, J. (1990) *Minderheden in Nederland*, Statistisch Vademecum 1990, SDU, Uitgave van het Centraal Bureau voor Statistiek en het Instituut voor Sociologisch-Economisch Onderzoek (ISEO) van de Erasmus Universiteit Rotterdam, Den Haag.

ANKONÉ, E. C. M. and KAUFMAN, W. J. (1984) *Turkse en Marokkaanse vrouwen in Utrecht: een verkennend onderzoek naar hun positie en ervaringen*, Gemeente Utrecht, ROVU, Afdeling Onderzoek, Utrecht.

BACH, H.-U. (1987) Entwicklung und Struktur der Ausländerarbeitslosigkeit in der Bundesrepublik Deutschland seit 1960, in Hönekopp (1987).

BEER, D. and COLLINGRO, P. (1988) *Zur Situation der beruflichen Bildung von ausländischen Jugendlichen in der Bundesrepublik Deutschland*, Paper voor de conferentie Berufliche Aus- und Weiterbildung und Arbeitsmigration, Freie Universität, Berlin.

BOUW, C. and NELISSEN, D. (1986) *Werken en zorgen: een vergelijkend onderzoek naar de arbeidservaringen van Turkse, Marokkaanse en Nederlandse vrouwen*, Ministerie van Sociale Zaken en Werkgelegenheid, Den Haag.

BOVENKERK, F. (ed.) (1978) *Omdat zij anders zijn: patronen van rasdiscriminatie in Nederland*, Boom, Meppel.

BOVENKERK, F., GRAS, M. and RAMSOEDH, D. (1994) Werkloosheid bij allochtonen gevolg van bewuste uitsluiting, *NRC Handelsblad*, 18 March 1994.

BRASSÉ, P. *et al.* (1983) *Jonge Turken en Marokkanen op de Nederlandse arbeidsmarkt*, Universiteit van Amsterdam, Instituut voor Sociale Geografie, Amsterdam.

BREEDEVELD, M. (1992) Voorkeur of willekeur, *Intermediair*, Vol. 28, no. 13, p. 45.

BROWN, C. (1984) *Black and White in Britain: the Third PSI Survey*, Heinemann, London.

BREUGEL, I. (1989) Sex and race in the labour market, *Feminist Review*, Vol. 32, pp. 49–68.

BUNDESANSTALT FÜR ARBEIT (1991) *Ausländerbeschäftigung 1980 bis 1990,* Sonderdruck aus Amtliche Nachrichten der Bundesanstalt für Arbeit, no. 10/1991, Bundesanstalt für Arbeit, Nürnberg.

BUNDESANSTALT FÜR ARBEIT (1992) *Arbeitsmarkt in Zahlen. Sozialversicherungspflichtige Beschäftigte am 30. Juni 1991 im Bundesgebiet,* Bundesanstalt für Arbeit, Nürnberg.

COMMISSION OF THE EUROPEAN COMMUNITIES (1991) Equal Opportunities for Women and Men. The third medium-term community action programme – 1991–1995, *Women of Europe,* supplements, no. 34.

DEBOOSERE, P. (1991) *Onderwijsniveau bij Islammigranten en regionale spreiding,* VUB, Centrum voor Sociologie, Steunpunt voor demografie, Brussel.

DENOLF, L. and MARTENS, A. (1990) *Aspecten van de werkgelegenheid van migranten. Loonstructuur, loopbaanontwikkeling na de mijnsluiting en kansen bij het interprofessioneel overleg,* Sociologisch Onderzoeksinstituut, Leuven.

DENOLF, L. and MARTENS, A. (1991) *Van mijnwerk naar ander werk. Onderzoeksrapport over de arbeidsmarktpositie van ex-mijnwerkers,* Sociologisch Onderzoeksinstituut, Leuven.

DEVILLE, R. and DEQUEEKER, G. (1988) *De leefwereld van veertiejarigen. Een vergelijkend onderzoek bij jongeren uit een sociaal begunstigd en een sociaal achtergesteld milieu: Vlamingen en immigranten uit Italië en Marokko,* Sociologisch Onderzoeksinstituut, Leuven.

EUROPEAN PARLIAMENT (1991), Committee of Inquiry on Racism and Xenophobia, *Report on the Findings of the Inquiry,* Office for Official Publications of the European Communities, Luxembourg.

EUROSTAT (1989) *Employment and Unemployment,* Luxembourg.

GRIMMEAU, J. P. (1991) *De vreemdelingen in België volgens de tellingen,* statistische studiën, no. 92, Nationaal Instituut voor de Statistiek, Ministerie van Economische Zaken.

HÖNEKOPP, E. (ed.) (1987) *Aspekte der Ausländerbeschäftigung in der Bundesrepublik Deutschland,* Institut für Arbeitsmarkt- und Berufsforschung der Bundesanstalt für Arbeit, Nürnberg, BeitrAB 114.

KÖNIG, P., SCHULTZE, G. and WESSE, R. (1986) *Situation der ausländischen Arbeitnehmer und ihrer Familienangehörigen in der Bundesrepublik Deutschland. Repräsentativentersuchung '85.* Forschungsbericht no. 133, Bundesminister für Arbeit und Sozialordnung, Bonn.

LEE, G. and WRENCH, J. (1982) *In Search of a Skill: Ethnic Minority Youth and Apprenticeship,* A Summary, CRE, London.

MARTENS, A. (1991) Vreemdelingen in onderwijs en tewerkstelling, in Grimmeau (1991).

MEHRLÄNDER, U. (1989) The current situation of young Italians in the transition from education to employment: Federal Republic of Germany, *International Review of Comparative Public Policy,* Vol. 1, pp. 209–22.

MOST VAN SPIJK, M. VAN DER (1991) *Allochtone vrouwen in Nederland,* Adviescommissie Onderzoek Minderheden, Leiden.

OHRI, S. and FARUGI, S. (1988) Racism, employment and unemployment in A. Bhat (ed.) *Britain's Black Population: A New Perspective,* Gower, Aldershot.

PEYTIER, E. (1991) *Het internationaal jaar van de strijd tegen het analfabetisme in Marokko: een reisverslag,* Vlaams Centrum voor Integratie van Migranten.

REUBSAET, T. J. M. and KROPMAN, J. A. (1986) *Beter opgeleide Antillianen op de Nederlandse arbeidsmarkt,* Instituut voor Toegepaste Sociologie, Nijmegen.

ROELANDT, TH., ROIJEN, J. H. M. and VEENMAN, J. (1991) *Minderheden in Nederland,* Statistisch Vademecum 1991, SDU, Uitgave van het Centraal Bureau voor Statistiek en het Instituut voor Sociologisch-Economisch Onderzoek (ISEO van de Erasmus Universiteit Rotterdam, Den Haag.

ROELANDT, TH., ROIJEN, J. H. M. and VEENMAN, J. (1992) *Minderheden in Nederland,* Statistisch Vademecum 1992, SDU, Uitgave van het Centraal Bureau voor Statistiek en het Instituut voor Sociologisch-Economisch Onderzoek (ISEO) van de Erasmus Universiteit Rotterdam, Den Haag.

SCHULTZE, G. (1987) *Soziale Situation ausländische Mädchen und Frauen in Nordrhein-Westfalen,* Staatssekretärin für die Gleichstellung von Frau and Mann beim Ministerpräsidenten des Landes Nordrhein-Westfalen, Düsseldorf.

THON, M. (1987) Ausländer in der Bundesrepublik Deutschland – Bevölkerung und Erwerbsbeteiligung, in Hönekopp (1987).

CHAPTER 5

The Careers of Men and Women: A Life-Course Perspective

BETTINA BOCK AND ANNEKE VAN DOORNE-HUISKES

INTRODUCTION

In this chapter we look at the careers of men and women from a life-course perspective by exploring how careers develop in relation to other areas of life. It is particularly important when attempting to explain the course of women's careers that we do not view the various spheres of life in isolation. We will not deal with all the aspects of a career or life-course, but instead focus on certain periods which in our opinion are of the utmost importance where differences between men and women are concerned: type of vocational education, entry into the work-force, career breaks and re-entry and resumption of a career. We also show that differences which arise at the start of a career are cumulative and eventually lead to a less favourable career for women.

The differences between men and women which influence the latter's opportunities from the start are related to the traditional roles that men and women expect to play. Girls assume that they will combine a job with child care at a later stage. Boys make the assumption that they will have a full-time job and a wife who cares for the children. Even today, many women take these expectations into account when making career decisions, while employers adjust their career policy on women accordingly. Both therefore contribute in their own fashion to maintaining the status quo, i.e. women's inferior position on the labour market and the lack of equal opportunities for women.

During the past few decades, important shifts have occurred in the working patterns of women in practically all the countries within the European Union. More and more women are participating in the labour market. This increase is particularly sharp among married women and women with young children. In addition, an increasing number of women re-enter the work-force after a period of domestic labour.

In spite of these changes, the basic pattern does not seem to have altered: the arrival of children still signifies an important encroachment on the professional careers of women but not on those of men. This difference is obvious long before a woman has children. Men and women display different behaviours at a much earlier stage, anticipating as it were the division of roles when their children are born. The differences already assert themselves in the choice of vocational education.

VOCATIONAL EDUCATION

The careers of men and women differ from the outset because girls and boys choose different vocational education programmes. This initial distinction perseveres during the rest of their careers, so that they are likely to make different choices and decisions which ultimately cause their careers to diverge even more.

The difference in educational level between men and women has become much smaller during the past few decades, but a clear gender-specific distinction can still be seen in the type of vocational training which men and women select: men tend to choose programmes in the 'hard' sector – technology, economics, physical sciences – while women choose programmes in the 'soft' sector: languages, welfare, administration (Blossfeld, 1987; Sørensen, 1990; Ten Dam, Urling and Volman, 1991). In the Netherlands more women than men have not had or completed vocational training (Bock and Hövels, 1991).

A broad complex of factors comes into play when attempting to explain the educational choices of men and women. Formally, there are no programmes where admission is based on gender. In principle, all educational programmes are accessible to women. The obstacles presented by 'masculine' programmes become evident at a different level. On the one hand, there is the necessary preliminary training and experience. Women usually do not satisfy these requirements to the same extent that men do, for example because they have chosen certain subjects rather than others during secondary school. More direct obstacles are also of importance: prejudices upheld in the social environment, minority status in the classroom, discrimination by teachers and fellow students, and women's own prejudices and anxieties. Naturally, the fact that women are pre-ordained to enrol in a 'feminine' educational programme through socialization and social role-playing plays an important part, in the same way that men are steered towards 'masculine' programmes: their interest in 'soft' versus 'hard' subjects is in large part acquired.

We can explain why women choose certain educational programmes and professions by looking at their expectations for the future and for life in general. Many women expect to interrupt their career at some time in the future due to the birth of children. In anticipation, according to this theory, these women choose professions which demand less time, effort and commitment, as such investments do not pay off (Sanders, 1992) or because these professions offer better opportunities to combine work and child care (Desai and Waite, 1991). Desai and Waite argue that:

> If some occupations have characteristics like flexible work schedules, short hours, or absence of extensive travel that make them relatively easy to combine with childrearing, as long as women give primary responsibility to childrearing these occupations may be more attractive to women than to men, at least on average. Women may be willing to trade off earnings, chances for advancement, or interesting work for this convenience.
>
> (Desai and Waite, 1991, p. 564)

A recent article in which a comparison was made between a Dutch and a British study concludes that, even today, many young Dutch and British girls still anticipate interrupting their careers as a consequence of having children (Chisholm and Du Bois-Reymond, 1993). A large number of girls further expect to work part time in the future and to combine domestic duties and work in this way. Only a minority foresee the possibility of working full time and combining this with child-rearing. So even at this early stage most of the girls have taken into account that their future role as mother will limit how ambitious they can permit themselves to be in their careers. The level of aspirations, however, depends on the level of education attained.

Ultimately, in the background, social role patterns and the career expectations of men and women play an important part in every explanation of the educational choices that women make. As a result of these differences, women and men prepare themselves for their careers differently and start their careers under different conditions and with different chances. This often means that women's career opportunities are slighter than men's from the moment that they choose their educational programme. Blossfeld (1987 and 1991) concludes that the choice of vocational training largely determines career opportunities.

Entering the work-force

After completing vocational training, the next crucial step is the entry into the work-force. A person's first job has been shown to have a major influence on the future development of a career (Blossfeld, 1985, 1987, 1990 and 1991).

Having studied the entry into the work-force and the careers of 3 different cohorts of men and women in Germany, Blossfeld (1985) established that the level of initial entry is crucial for any further career progress. The level of entry determines which opportunities for promotion and transfer to other professional sectors there are. He interprets this using the segmentation theory: according to him, occupations can be divided into more or less separate, self-contained segments. The most self-contained are those segments which incorporate the higher-level professions, known as the primary segment. Hardly anyone ever transfers into or out of these professions. The segments become less self-contained as the required qualifications drop: the largest number of transfers occurs between occupations with no required qualifications, the so-called secondary segment. Within the segments, careers are reasonably stable. The segments are separated from one another by qualification barriers, but also by processes of statistical discrimination. On the basis of both the educational prerequisites and the general expectations with respect to their labour-market behaviour, employees in the secondary segment are usually not eligible for occupations in the primary segment (Blossfeld, 1990).

According to Blossfeld, the limits of any subsequent career are determined by the initial entry into the work-force. Those who can only obtain a position in the secondary segment due to a generally weak situation on the labour market will be permanently disadvantaged by the self-contained nature of the primary segment. Even if the situation on the labour market changes at a later stage, the low level of entry into the work-force cannot be compensated completely (Blossfeld, 1985). Blossfeld believes that women in particular are affected by this because they have fewer opportunities than men to compensate for a low level of entry through career and promotion processes. The disadvantage they experience in comparison to men in a similar age group will be reinforced during their subsequent career (Blossfeld, 1990).

From the beginning, women have fewer opportunities than men to obtain a position in one of the 'better' segments. Apart from bias and discrimination, differences in vocational training and career choice play an important role. Women's occupations are found mostly within the secondary segment of the labour market, as appears from several studies (Barron and Norris, 1976; Blossfeld, 1987; Di Prete and Soule, 1988; Rubery and Tarling, 1988; Crompton, Hantrais and Walters, 1990). Women who work in these occupations are at a disadvantage from the start compared with men and women who work in the primary segment. This initial disadvantage will have a permanent influence on their subsequent career.

The fact that men and women have different occupations or careers can to a large extent be attributed to their own expectations and decisions. it appears that women base their occupational or career choices on different motives and expectations from men. Dutch research involving the career choices of graduates of technical training programmes showed that women give less consideration than men do to the salary they can earn in a profession and the opportunities for promotion, and more to the scope which the position offers to work part time in the future (Sanders, Lindenberg and Van Doorne-Huiskes, 1991; Sanders, 1992). Women, more than men, give preference to positions at a lower job level and which require less commitment – findings confirmed in American research (Desai and Waite, 1991).

It is more important to distinguish between different categories of women. The Dutch research shows that the positions described above are preferred by those women who expect to have children at a future stage. Women who do not have these expectations choose careers which resemble those of men. This is confirmed by American research: women who want to keep working are less likely to choose so-called 'women's' jobs, which are less difficult to combine with a family. Desai and Waite (1991, p. 564) have found: 'This process of recruitment of women into "convenient" occupations operates only for women who plan not to work over the long run. Women who prefer to be employed show little effect of occupational characteristics reflecting the ease of combining work and motherhood.' Prior research showed that women who planned to work over the long run invested more in their vocational training than those who intended to stop working at some stage (Shaw and Shapiro, 1987, cited in Desai and Waite, 1991).

We see, then, that there are both structural and individual factors which contribute to the fact that men and women occupy different positions at the start of their career, positions which ultimately lead to different opportunities in the future. In general, women find themselves at a disadvantage not only at the beginning of their careers, but also, and perhaps more importantly, with respect to any future career chances. The double set of expectations, or, rather, the double set of tasks which women take on, seems to be the most important cause: both employers and women themselves make allowances by anticipating their future 'second job' in the household. This expectation also influences the structure of the labour market and the way that jobs are arranged.

INTERRUPTION AND RESUMPTION OF CAREERS

Patterns

Evidence for the importance of women's double set of expectations can also be found in the fact that many women still interrupt their careers upon the arrival of their first child. In the Netherlands, according to recent research, half of women (53%) still suspend their occupational activities upon the birth of their first child (De Jong and De Olde, 1994). Of the remainder, an overwhelming majority (91%) switch to part-time work; only a small minority continue with full-time employment. Many women who continue working after the birth of their first child stop after the birth of a second or third. According to another Dutch study, 80% of women who continue working after having their first child stop upon the arrival of their second (Beets and Moors, 1991, cited in Hooghiemstra and Niphuis-Nell, 1993).

British research has led to comparable results, but clear differences exist between the 2 countries. According to Joshi and Hinde (1993), p. 203), 'In Britain, the key question is not whether a woman resumes employment, but when'. These authors have conducted research on 2 generations of women: those who had a child in 1946, and daughters of these same women who had children in the 1970s. The study shows that the younger generation of women returned to work sooner and more often than did their mothers. Among the older women, 10% returned to work within a year after the birth of their child; on average, the women interrupted their careers for 9 years. Among the younger generation, 20% resumed working within a year, the average absence being 5 years.

Joshi and Hinde conclude on the basis of their research that not only the opportunity to return to the labour force has increased, but that the factors which influence the behaviour of women have also changed. Among the older generation of women, the rate of re-entry varied according to the occupation of the husband and the region in which the women lived. Women whose husbands worked in white-collar occupations were much less likely to return to the labour force than women whose husbands were self-employed or who worked in a blue-collar occupation, whether skilled or unskilled. During the 1970s these factors no longer seemed to play a role. Joshi and Hinde (1993, p. 220) argue that: 'The increase in female employment is partly due to the weakening of negative influences, and a "catching up" by "lagging" classes and regions . . . and accommodated by a shift in industrial structure towards less regionally specialized service industries.' Alongside this, the fact that the combination of work and motherhood has been accepted by more and broader sections of the community and that women's wages have increased plays an important part. In addition, the increase in part-time positions has made the combination of work and motherhood easier.

McRae (1993) has also conducted research on the labour-market behaviour of mothers in Britain. Her research involved a sample of nearly 5,000 first-time mothers whose children were born in 1987–8. McRae shows that during the preceding 10 years in Britain, the number of women returning to work within 8 to 9 months after the birth of their child doubled: in 1979 that figure was approximately 20%: by 1988 it had increased to 45%.

Where full-time work is concerned, the return to work tripled: in 1979 around 6% of women resumed work on a full-time basis; by 1988 nearly 20% did so. The figure varied widely between social classes; the return percentages are the highest in the professional and management positions. In her study McRae tries to discover which factors play an important role in determining whether mothers resume their careers. Her conclusion is that the advantages associated with have a better labour-market position and a higher social class make it possible for women who have these advantages and who want to resume work actually to do so. These women have a better salary and can therefore afford good child care; they often occupy a position in the public service, which offers better facilities for the combination of work and parenthood; they often have jobs in the service sector and can thus come to agreements on flexible working hours more easily. All the above factors facilitate a rapid return to the labour market. Women from lower social classes and with an inferior position on the labour market have less money to arrange child care; access to workplace facilities and to jobs with flexible working hours is restricted.

According to McRae, these results indicate increasing polarization between women: the women in a stronger social position can resume their careers sooner after giving birth and improve their position on the labour market. The relative lag that the women in a weaker social position experience seems to increase accordingly. This theory demands further empirical proof. An interesting question would be to see if a rise in educational level would reduce this polarization.

German researchers speak of an increasing polarization in the lifestyles of women (Berger, Steinmüller and Sopp, 1993). They do not refer to class differences in this case, but to a growing contrast between various types of career which women pursue. Based on their research, it appears that younger women in particular often pursue 'masculine' careers and continue to work full time without interrupting their career for family matters. In a sense these women distance themselves from the traditional female career model, in which the main issues have revolved around the adjustments and compromises required to combine work and family. Berger, Steinmüller and Sopp conclude:

> In sum, since the 1950s and 1960s . . . a 'break' in the typical female life-course patterns seems to have occurred. 'Typical' housewife life courses have decreased, while life courses leading into or continuing within the active labour force have become more widespread. For younger women, shifts from 'normal' housewife courses towards 'normal labour-force courses' can be observed. For women, it therefore seems appropriate to speak of a tendency of 'polarization' or 'dualization' between the two life-course models.
>
> (Berger, Steinmüller and Sopp, 1993, p. 56)

All in all, from the research described above the trend appears to be towards fewer career interruptions. A shift is evident from the dominant bimodal model to different and more complex models. Fewer women break off their careers entirely after the birth of their first child until all their children have been born (bimodal model), but instead continue their careers in various ways between births. Only seldom do they do this by continuing to work full time, however. More often and in increasing measure, women keep working on a part-time basis. Apart from this, a number of women interrupt their careers and resume working after a certain period of time. There are important differences between countries so far as the different types of models are concerned.

As we pointed out earlier, British women are less likely to interrupt their careers than are women in various other countries. A growing number of women resume their position in the shortest time possible after giving birth, and increasingly on a full-time basis. In the Netherlands, more than is the case in other European countries, the trend towards fewer career interruptions has been made possible by an enormous increase in part-time positions: more work is done on a part-time basis in the Netherlands than anywhere else in Europe (Plantenga, 1993). The vast majority of the women who continue working after the birth of their child cut back on the number of working hours. Most women choose so-called 'small' part-time positions. Pott-Buter (1993, p. 206) argues that 'Of all women participating part-time in the Netherlands in 1988, one third had a job of less than 10 hours a week, while 40% worked more than 10 but less than 20 hours a week.'

Unique in the Netherlands is that part-time work is found not only in the lesser-paying jobs and sectors, but more often than not among the 'better' positions: this is because there are considerable opportunities for part-time work in government departments. In most of the other European countries part-time work has been restricted to lower-paying positions requiring few qualifications (Crompton, Hantrais and Walters, 1990; Joshi and Hinde, 1993; McRae, 1993). At any rate, the fact that career opportunities are severely hampered by part-time work applies to nearly all countries (see below).

The trend towards shorter and ever-fewer interruptions and more part-time work can be observed in Germany as well. Schupp (1991) is under the impression that part-time work makes it easier for women to resume work at some stage, in spite of their obligations at home and their wish to care for their children in the best way possible. Even women who had no previous intention of returning to work resume their careers at an earlier stage than expected thanks to part-time work.

A part-time job can thus be considered a transitional 'phase' in a woman's career on the way to complete resumption of her career. The comparison with one of the Scandinavian countries, where women have long continued to work after having children, raises the possibility that an increase in the number of part-time positions could also be a 'phase; which a country passes through as it develops an employment structure within which women and men have equal opportunities to choose similar life-course models.

Since the 1980s the number of women working on a full-time basis in Sweden has increased (Sundström, 1993). Until them, the growing number of women in the work-force was mainly attributable to their taking up part-time positions. From 1970 to 1982 the percentage of women working part time rose from 38 to 47%. Since 1983 more women have switched from part-time to full-time jobs than vice versa. This development was made possible by an increase in the number of child-care centres and by liberal maternity leave schemes. In addition, according to Sundström, the 1983 tax reform stimulated this trend by lowering the tax rate for full-time employment and increasing taxes for part-time work. A part-time position, and with it the decision to choose a 'female' life-course model, were made much less inviting from a financial point of view.

Whether and for how long women interrupt their career to raise children is related in all countries to their occupational and educational level. Women who have gone through higher education are more likely to continue working without an interruption or to interrupt their career for a shorter period of time than women with a lower level of education (Martin and Roberts, 1984; Steward and Greenlagh, 1984; Crompton, Hantrais and Walters, 1990; Dessens, Van Doorne-Huiskes and Mertens, 1990; Desai and Waite, 1991; McRae, 1993). Other characteristics of the job also play an important role: women will keep working when the position offers better opportunities to combine work and motherhood (Glass, 1988; see below).

Re-entry: motives and obstacles

To predict why women choose to re-enter the work-force, it is on the one hand important to consider their motives for doing so, but on the other we should also look at the obstacles which stand in their way. Both factors can help clarify the process of interrupting and resuming a career.

MOTIVES   British and German research has shown that women initially mention material motives when considering a return to work; the need to contribute to the household income (Martin and Roberts, 1984; Brannen, 1989; Steenbuck, 1989). It is striking that they often referred to it as 'extra' money, intended for the odd extra expense or those non-essential luxuries. This applies even if they had contributed to the household income for years and if their contribution was actually needed to cover basic needs (Brannen, 1989). American research showed that, according to the men and women involved, women's earnings are generally not used to cover 'basic needs' but to cover 'consumption needs' instead: according to this study, it is not economic necessity but the wish to acquire a certain 'standard of living' which motivates women to resume working (Eggebeen and Hawkins, 1990). Women's jobs are often seen as 'extra' and 'voluntary'. By defining women's contribution to the household income in this way, couples can avoid calling the role of the husband as breadwinner into question. Such a definition implies that the expenses incurred by both partners working away from the home come out of the woman's pocket. Brannen (1989, p. 42) has found that 'Despite the fact that *both* parents were in full-time employment, child care was seen as mainly the women's financial responsibility, in the same way that the children were seen as the responsibility of mothers' (original emphasis).

The relative value of a woman's position decreases in this way, and with it her contribution to the household income.

It should be clear that the studies described above apply only to situations which typically occur in relatively rich, Western countries. In countries where the average income is lower than in the West, a wife who works is often readily accepted since that is the only way to acquire a more or less adequate family income. Braun, Scott and Alwin (1994, p. 39) have found that 'Specifically, the East Germans display a nearly universal acceptance of the importance of both husband and wife contributing to the household income, which is not the case in West Germany.' In 1989, for example, 86% of the female professional population in former East Germany was employed. According to Roloff (1992 and 1993), this can be accounted for by the financial situation of most families. During that period, women earned an average of 40% of the household income. In this case one can no longer speak of a 'voluntary' or 'extra' contribution. (Even after the 'Wende', it still goes without saying that women (want to) continue working. The financial situation for most has not so much as improved; besides, work, even for women, was considered a common part of life under the former political structures (Roloff, 1992 and 1993). In spite of this, it appears that women are the first to be dismissed when redundancies are announced.).

According to a Dutch research project on women who resume working (Heiligers, 1990), a majority of women mentioned social motives for re-entering, namely the need for more social contacts (88%). A second motive was the wish for further personal development (69%) and in third place we find financial necessity (38%) and the wish to earn their own money (44%).

Women in Britain and Germany also indicate the desire for more social contacts as a motive to re-enter the work-force (Brannen, 1989; Steenbuck, 1989). These women do not regard being at home alone as something positive. One of the reasons they return to work is to break out of their isolation. The desire for more social contacts applies not only to the sociability, but also to the inspiration and reaffirmation found in professional contacts with other adults (Steenbuck, 1989).

A reason given by mainly highly educated women for resuming their work is career satisfaction (Brannen, 1989). Strikingly enough, in Brannen's study hardly any women identify long-term career goals as a motive for resuming work, and none at all mentions the risks associated with an unnecessarily long absence from the labour market – risks that apply to both the future career and to the chance of resuming work at all. Dutch research indicates that women who interrupt their career do not consider the long-term consequences. Women who do keep working indicate a firm commitment to their profession and career as the most important motive (De Jong and De Olde, 1994). According to American research, ambition and career opportunities are mentioned as long-term motives (Gerson, 1985). Women are pulled in two directions. They are under immense social and emotional pressure to have children and to care for them personally at home, but they also feel the 'pull' of their own ambitions and plans for a career.

OBSTACLES   There are various obstacles to re-entering the work-force. One is the lack of adequate child-care facilities; another is a shortage of part-time positions or jobs with flexible working hours (Engelbrech, 1989; Heiligers, 1990; Hooghiemstra and Niphuis-Nell, 1993). For many women these factors represent the minimum conditions which must be met before re-entry is in any way possible: child care has to be arranged and the circumstances of the job must be such that domestic duties and career can be combined.

In addition, a woman's subjective experience of her duties and responsibilities as a mother seems to be a very important factor in the decision either to continue or interrupt her career or to resume working. Women often find it difficult to entrust the care of their child to another person (Gerson, 1985; Glass, 1988; Engelbrech, 1989; Morée, 1992). They want to spend as much time as they can with their children and reduce the amount of time that they entrust them to someone else's care. They do this by interrupting their career, or by working a limited number of hours per week (Boek and De Jong, 1994). Many women in the Netherlands are convinced that it is detrimental to the development of their children if they are cared for by others. They are particularly distrustful of institutionalized forms of child care (De Jong and De Olde, 1994).

Attitudes towards child care are influenced in particular by the availability of child-care facilities and the national policy on combining employment and motherhood (Crompton, Hantrais and Walters, 1990; Sørensen, 1990; Lane, 1993; Plantenga, 1993; Braun, Scott and Alwin, 1994). In those areas where there is no shortage of child-care centres, it is also emotionally more gratifying for women to make use of them and to continue or resume working. It is not only the presence of these practical facilities which encourages them; the social climate in countries with a larger number of child-care facilities often offers more support as well. Braun, Scott and Alwin have found that:

> Not only was the working mother the norm, but also women's dual roles reflected a way of life promulgated by state ideology and fostered by the provision of alternative child-care arrangements . . . For these reasons, combining motherhood and employment is far more difficult for (former) West Germans than was the case in the (former) East. It is, therefore, not surprising that West Germans are more likely to perceive the negative consequences for families of working mothers than East Germans.
>
> (Braun, Scott and Alwin, 1994, p. 38)

The nature of the work that women have previously performed is also an obstacle to re-entry into the labour force. For example, the availability either of jobs within a certain radius of the place of residence or of part-time positions may be a consideration. But the quality of the work is also an important factor. This is clearly shown by the rapid return to work of highly educated women: their jobs clearly have more to offer because they are generally more interesting and offer more opportunities for development (Gerson, 1985; Sørensen, 1990). Research conducted in the Netherlands involving young women with a lower level of education (Jorna and Offers, 1991) shows that women base their decision to return to work partly on the employment conditions and the opportunities offered by the position to develop further their own qualifications through education and training. American research on why young women leave the work-force supports the Dutch findings (Glass, 1988). According to this study, besides the family situation the employment conditions have an important influence on the decision either to continue or to cease working in case of pregnancy. Glass (1988, p. 238) argues that 'Improved job conditions (in terms of pay, prestige, and job satisfaction) and presence of existing preschool children (implying prior experience with child care) also increased the likelihood of continuous employment for pregnant women.'

Consequences of career interruption

Women who interrupt their careers experience a lasting disadvantage with respect to their future career prospects. The manner in which they plan this interruption can limit the damage, but in general a career interruption means fewer career opportunities. They earn less, they are promoted less often and they work in lower-status occupations more frequently than women who do keep working. A career interruption also brings with it more immediate disadvantages or costs, i.e. lower wages compared to women who continue to work. British research has shown that women over the age of 25 who plan to have children can reckon on earning only half the income they would have earned otherwise. The years lost through career interruptions, the decrease in the number of working hours and the loss of income due to having to work in lower-level occupations all contribute to this effect (Davies and Joshi, 1990, cited in McRae, 1993).

British research conducted during the early 1980s (Steward and Greenlagh, 1984) shows that women's income decreases as the number and the duration of their career interruptions increase. According to this research, not only a career interruption but even part-time work has its costs. Part-time work results in a 7% wage rise over a 10-year period; full-time work, on the other hand, shows an increase of another 16% over the same period (Steward and Greenlagh, 1984).

German research shows comparable results: women who resume working after an interruption often work in temporary jobs, do part-time work or work in occupations below their educational level (Brinkmann and Engelbrech, 1989; Engelbrech, 1989, in Schupp, 1991). On the other hand, part-time work rather than a career interruption can reduce the drop in income by half (Galler, 1988, cited in Schupp, 1991).

Such results are confirmed by Dutch research: an interrupted career has negative effects on income growth (Groot, Schippers and Siegers, 1988; Schippers and Siegers, 1988). These effects are usually explained by the human capital theory: less capital is being accumulated and existing capital is not being bolstered and maintained and thus decreases in value. During a career interruption no work experience or relevant know-how can be acquired; the knowledge and experience gained up to that stage may diminish in value due to new developments on, for example, the technological front; and part of the acquired knowledge and experience is lost because it cannot be applied. Groot, Schippers and Siegers (1988) have calculated that the value of human capital is reduced by 2% each year in this fashion. If part-time work replaces a career interruption, the reduction is less, although even part-time work clearly results in a lower income. The Emancipation Council in the Netherlands has calculated that a career interruption results in a loss of income amounting to 0.6 to 1.1% annually (Emancipatieraad, cited in Dessens, van Doorne-Huiskes and Mertens, 1990).

Apart from a loss of income, another consequence is a reduction in professional status. According to a study mentioned previously by Joshi and Hinde (1993) 36% of the women from both generations returned to a lower-level position after the birth of their children than the one they had held previously. There are major differences on this point associated with the level of work performed prior to the birth. Of the women who had a professional job before having children, the vast majority (84%) succeeded in returning to a position at the same level. Only a small minority of women (16%) returned to a lower-level position. Of those who had previously performed office or factory work, roughly half (57% and 43% respectively) returned to a job at a lower level (Joshi and Hinde, 1993). A study conducted by McRae (1991 and 1993) shows that fewer women experience a drop in status than in the past. In particular, women with professional jobs are returning to similar positions with increasing success, often with their former employer. In addition, the decision to resume working full time or part time is important. Those who favour the part-time option have to accept a loss of career status in most cases, unlike those who resume working full time after the birth of a child. The loss of status in part-time jobs is most apparent among 'managers and administrators' and 'clerical and secretarial jobs' and least among 'professional and associate professional and technical jobs' (McRae, 1991).

According to Dex (1987), women themselves are partly to blame for the drop in status because they readjust their priorities when children are born. The hours of work now take priority over the type of work they want. Martin and Roberts (1984, p. 167) reached the same conclusion. 'Women wanting part-time work . . . tended to trade off such aspects of a job as good pay, security and the opportunity to use one's abilities in favour of convenient hours.'

The attention given to working hours is understandable, since women, in addition to their job outside the home, generally have complete responsibility for the children and domestic duties. Brannen (1989, p. 43) has found that 'Moreover, in combining their careers as mothers and workers, women simply assumed that the child's routine had to be fitted around their own working days and not those of the father.' This means, for example, that it is women who take children to and from the child-care centres and do the household duties in addition to their work, and also that they are the ones who have to take time off work whenever the children need the presence of a parent, for example in case of illness (Van Dijke, Terpstra and Hermanns, 1994).

The fact that both the man and the woman work outside the home has little effect on the ease with which women give greater priority to family responsibility than to their career (Gerson, 1985; Kruger, 1991; Sørensen, 1990). They do most of the 'family work' and make sure they can continue doing so when they resume work, for example by working part time. Women often have difficulty entrusting the care of their children to others because as 'mothers' they feel obliged to take the responsibility of care upon themselves (Gerson, 1985; Glass, 1988; Morée, 1992). A different interpretation is that they want to retain the authority of the emotional 'domain' (Backett, 1987; Lewis and O'Brien, 1987). On the other hand, men are usually not very forthcoming when it comes to taking over their share of the care tasks (Larossa, 1988; Hochschild, 1989).

It is clear that women who interrupt their careers for family reasons make a decision which has far-reaching consequences for their working futures. It is very likely that their career will suffer permanent damage when it comes to attainable job level, career status and level of income, not to mention any future career prospects. Many women have to be content with a lower-level job when they re-enter the work-force. This often implies that the position is less demanding and less interesting than the one they had before their career interruption. It is important to note that women can curtail slightly the damage done by, for instance, interrupting their career for a short time only, or by continuing to work on a part-time basis instead of stopping altogether. If they choose to work a relatively large number of hours instead of a few, they can limit the long-term damage. This will not be possible for all women to the same degree, and depends on the situation of each individual family and the level of social security in a particular country. As present developments with respect to the labour-force participation of women show, women have the biggest chance of achieving similar career goals to men in countries which have proper maternity leave and child-care arrangements. The Scandinavian countries still play a leading role in this respect. In addition, it is important that women themselves undergo a change in mentality by distancing themselves from their dominant role in child care, and that men shoulder their share of the practical burden of caring for their children.

CONCLUSION: CAREER AND THE DOUBLE LIFE OF WOMEN

It is not easy to interpret trends in the work-force participation of women when viewed within the context of the issues discussed in this chapter. On the one hand, in most countries of the European Union there is a clear trend towards fewer interruptions in women's careers but, on the other, results from many studies point to the persistence of the traditional division of roles between men and women and to the consequences of such a division for the careers of the latter.

More and more women, and especially mothers, are joining or re-entering the labour force, more child-care facilities are available and the number of part-time jobs has increased. The moral threshold with respect to re-entry and the combination of work and motherhood has been lowered over the years. It seems clear, however, that women still have to pay a heavy price for their temporary withdrawal from the work-force, in the form of lower status, less income, fewer future career prospects and a double set of tasks to be performed after re-entry.

A recurring issue in the careers of women is precisely this double set of tasks which women take on: in addition to their occupational careers, they also have a 'domestic career' as a wife and mother. It is not only women who view themselves in this way, but, more importantly, society at large which expects women to play this dual role. Regardless of whether a woman works outside the home or not, in most European societies she is still seen as the person who bears the major share of responsibility for the welfare of her family. As a consequence, the division of labour between men and women in the household is hardly changing (as will be shown in Chapter 6). And this is at the same time one of the most important reasons for the permanent difference between the careers of men and women. The specific expectations that women have of themselves and that society has of women appear to influence every career move dealt with in this chapter. On the one hand, this is because women want their career decisions to hinge upon their family situation, although they do not wish to sacrifice their career ambitions entirely in order to full their role as mother. On the other hand, it is clear from the types of opportunities available to women on the labour market that the underlying assumption is that family duties will limit their availability and involvement. The persistence of traditional role expectations, on both sides of the labour market, may explain why women are in a subordinate position and therefore why their participation is 'irregular' and 'different' from that of men.

According to Bernhardt (1993), all this indicates that the status of female employees as 'supplementary worker' has essentially not changed. She argues (1993, p. 29) that 'Thus the rather dramatic increase in female labour-force participation which has occurred over the last two or three decades has hardly changed women's role as supplementary workers.' Women are more likely to have paid jobs now than in the past, but in general they do not earn enough to be financially independent (Sørensen and McLanahan, 1987; Bernhardt, 1993). Plantenga (1993) concludes that women who choose to combine work and family are not actually challenging the traditional gender stereotype of women as 'carers' because their connection and identification with their careers remain tenuous.

The time has come to reflect on how paid work and caretaking can be combined without individual careers being damaged. In the report *Shaping Structural Change: The Role of Women* (1991), the OECD argues for the development of an active society, where compatibility of employment and family commitments is assured. Shared family and employment roles will, according to the OECD, increase the potential labour force, promote a better utilization of human capital, enhance gender equality and improve the quality of life. This degree of compatibility first requires us to update the so-called social contract, the implicit system of norms and values that gives women the primary responsibility for care at home and confers on men the role of breadwinner in European countries. Precisely how we are to intervene in this system is not elaborated on in detail in this report, which tries to promote a particular point of view. Nevertheless, it does draw attention to several issues: more flexibility in working hours; new models of employment which allow men and women to combine a career with family commitments while maintaining their quality of life; opportunities for career breaks, which should be viewed as opportunities for skills development and personal enrichment rather than as periods of inactivity; the necessity of establishing a specific social infrastructure to help women and men meet certain family obligations, especially the care of children and elderly relatives. The European Commission's Green Paper (1993) indicates the need for a more balanced society, within which employment and family care are divided more evenly between men and women. Like the OECD report, the underlying considerations of the Green Paper are that the 'resources' of women should be utilized in a more versatile fashion in order to establish a more efficient and just economic and social lifestyle. In addition, the resources of men can be better utilized if they are involved in an increasing measure in care and domestic tasks.

Obviously, an important question is how these general propositions can be translated into concrete measures within places of employment. There are very few examples or models of tried and tested career programmes set up to accommodate women and men who want to combine their careers with domestic tasks. The number of working examples of family-friendly policies is on the increase, however. The recent *UK Employer Initiatives* report (Working Mothers Association, 1994), which includes a survey of British companies, draws attention to working patterns like flexitime, home working, job sharing, part-time work and to benefits like child-care facilities/information and referral services, out-of-school child-care provisions, parental leave, career breaks, cafeteria/flexible benefits, and so on.

Important questions for further research and study are how these working examples stand up in actual practice, who the main users are, what the consequences are for the careers of the men and women involved, and how the different arrangements are being used. Until now, a successful combination of paid employment and domestic tasks was considered the employee's responsibility. In Europe there are only a few employers who regard family-friendly policies as an integral part of human resource management, which plays an important role in retaining human capital within the organization. When family-friendly policies are viewed from the perspective of human resource management, then the way is open to a businesslike and 'tailor-made approach. Employers and employees can arrive at arrangements which indicate how the employee's family obligations will be included in the career planning.

In the case of part-time work, a plan can be drafted beforehand stating how the number of hours to be worked will be divided. Any necessary adjustments in employment terms with respect to tasks and responsibilities at work can be discussed at the same time, bearing future career opportunities in mind. If the employee has a spouse or partner, his or her contribution to domestic tasks can also be taken into consideration. In this way the employer and employee consciously work on solving the problems created by the employee's temporary reduction in working hours ahead of time, as would be the case if he or she were to attend a training course during working hours. Both sides are bound by the agreement: the employer is obligated to enable the employee to perform his or her duties on the domestic front in the best way possible; the employee is obliged to be as available and dedicated as possible.

Such a 'contract' is relatively binding for both parties, and may be viewed by some women as a limit on their freedom of choice. In return, however, they reduce the chance that their careers will suffer a permanent setback. Once the domestic and family duties of employees are approached in a similar businesslike fashion, it will also become easier for men to negotiate these matters with their employers. There will be fewer risks with respect to their long-term career prospects, and any risks that do exist will be more predictable when a 'care contract' is agreed on by both parties.

REFERENCES

BACKETT, K. (1987) The negotiation of fatherhood, in Lewis and O'Brien (1987).

BARRON, R. D. and NORRIS, G. M. (1976) Sexual divisions and the dual labourmarket, in D. L. Barker and S. Allen (eds.), *Sexual Divisions and Society*, Tavistock, London.

BEETS, G. and MOORS, H. (1991) Hoe goed zorgt de overheid voor ouders en kinderen?, *DEMOS*, Vol. 7, pp. 49–52.

BERGER, P. A., STEINMÜLLER, P. and SOPP, P. (1993) Differentiation of life-courses, changing patterns of labour-market sequences in West Germany, *European Sociological Review*, Vol. 9, no. 1, pp. 43–65

BERNHARDT, E. M. (1993) Fertility and employment, *European Sociological Review*, Vol. 9, no. 1, pp. 25–42.

BLOSSFELD, H. (1985) Berufseintritt und Berufsverlauf; Eine Kohortenanalyse über die Bedeutung des ersten Berufs in der Erwerbsbiographie, *Mitteilungen aus der Arbeitsmarkt- und Berufsforschung*, Vol. 18, no. 2, pp. 177–97.

BLOSSFELD, H. (1987) Labor market entry and the sexual segregation of career in the Federal Republic of Germany, *American Journal of Sociology*, Vol. 93, no. 1, pp. 89–118.

BLOSSFELD, H. (1990) Berufsverläufe und Arbeitsmarktprozesse, in Neidhart, Lepsins and Esser (1990), pp. 118–45.

BLOSSFELD, H. (1991) Der Wandel von Ausbildung und Berufseinstieg bei Frauen, in Mayer, Allemendinger and Huinink (1991), pp. 1–22.

BOCK, B. B. and HÖVELS, B. (1991) *Een kwantitatief beeld van de groep voortijdige schoolverlaters*, ITS, Nijmegen.

BOCK, B. B. and DE JONG, A. (1994) *Carrières van vrouwen en mannen*, Ministerie van binnenlandse zaken, The Hague.

BRANNEN, J. (1989) The resumption of employment after childbirth; a turning point within a life course perspective, in M. Pijl (ed.), *Changing Patterns of Work*, 15th European Symposium of the International Council on Social Welfare. Noordwijkerhout, July 1989, pp. 32–47.

BRAUN, M., SCOTT, J. and ALWIN, D. F. (1994) Economic necessity or self-actualization? Attitudes toward women's labour-force participation in East and West Germany, *European Sociological Review*, Vol. 10, no. 1, pp. 29–47.

BRINKMANN, C. and ENGELBRECH, G. (1989) Beschäftigungsprobleme der Frauen, in H. Scherf (ed.) *Jahrestagung des Vereins für Sozialpolitik*, Beschäftigungsprobleme Hocherwickelter Volkswirtschaften, Berlin, pp. 533–60.

CHISHOLM, L. and DU BOIS-REYMOND, M. (1993) Youth transitions, gender and social change, *Sociology*, Vol. 27, no. 2, pp. 259–79.

COMMISSION OF THE EUROPEAN COMMUNITIES (1993) *European Social Policy: Options for the Union*, Green Paper, Brussels.

CROMPTON, R., HANTRAIS, L. and WALTERS, P. (1990) Gender relations and employment, *British Journal of Sociology*, Vol. 41, no. 3, pp. 329–49.

DAM TEN, G., URLING, M. and VOLMAN, M. (1991) *Sekseverschillen in het onderwijs*, Wolters Noordhoff, Groningen.

DAVIES, H. and JOSHI, H. (1990) The foregone earnings of Europe's mothers, paper for EAPS symposium, Barcelona, October.

DESAI, S. and WAITE, L. J. (1991) Women's employment during pregnancy and after the first birth, *American Sociological Review*, Vol. 56, pp. 551–66.

DESSENS, J., VAN DOORNE-HUISKES, J. and MERTENS, E. (1990) *Arbeidsmarkt en gezin*, OSA Paper W 72, The Hague.

DEX, S. (1987) *Women's Occupational Mobility – A Lifetime Perspective*, Macmillan, London.

VAN DIJKE, A., TERPSTRA, L. and HERMANNS, J. (1994) *Ouders over kinderopvang*, SCO-Kohnstamm Instituut, Amsterdam.

DI PRETE, T. and SOULE, W. T. (1988) Gender and promotion in segmented job ladder systems *American Journal of Sociology*, Vol. 53, pp. 26–40.

VAN DOORNE-HUISKES, J. (1992) Betaalde en onbetaalde arbeid: over oude spanningen en nieuwe uitdagingen, inaugural lecture 29 October 1992, Erasmus universiteit, Rotterdam.

EGGEBEEN, D. J. and HAWKINS, A. J. (1990) Economic need and wives' employment, *Journal of Family Issues*, Vol. 11, no. 1, pp. 48–66.

EMANCIPATIERAAD (1989) *Emancipatiebeleid in macro-economisch perspectief*, The Hague.

ENGELBRECH, G. (1989) Erfahrungen von Frauen an der 'dritten Schwelle', *Mitteilungen aus der Arbeitsmarkt- und Berufsforschung*, Vol. 22, no. 1. pp. 100–13.

GALLER, H. P. (1988) Familiale Lebenslagen und Familienlastenausgleich, in B. Felderer (ed.), *Familienlastenausgleich und demographische Entwicklung*, Schriften des Vereins für Sozialpolitik, no. 175, Berlin, pp. 83–112.

GERSON, K. (1985) *Hard Choices; how Women Decide about Work, Career and Motherhood*, University of California Press, Berkeley.

GLASS, J. (1988) Job quits and job changes, *Gender and Society*, Vol. 2, no. 2, pp. 228–40.

GROOT, L. F. M., SCHIPPERS, J. J. and SIEGERS, J. J. (1988) The effect of interruptions and part-time work on women's wage rate: a test of the variable-intensity model, *Economist*, no. 2, pp. 220–38.

HEILIGERS, P. (1990) *Het afwegingsproces bij herintreden, verschillen in de balans*, Congres Vrouwen/Mannen, Amsterdam.

HOCHSCHILD, A. (1989) *The Second Shift*, Avon Books, New York.

HOOGHIEMSTRA, B. T. J. and NIPHUIS-NELL, M. (1993) *Sociale atlas van de vrouw*, part 2. *Sociaal en Review*, Vol. 9, no. 3, pp. 203–7.

JONG, DE, A. and OLDE, DE, C. (1994) *Hoe Ouders Het Werk Delen*, VUGA, Den Haag.

JORNA, A. and OFFERS, E. (1991) Jonge Vrouwen, Hun Werk, Hun Toekomst, Den Haag.

JOSHI, H. and HINDE, P. R. A. (1993) Employment after childbearing in post-war Britain: cohort study, evidence on contrasts within and across generations, *European Sociological Review*, Vol. 9, pp. 203–27.

KERSTEN, A., VAN RU, C., SARIS, W. and VISSER, J. (1990) *Herverdeling van betaalde arbeid, Ideaal en werkelijkheid*, FNV, Amsterdam.

KRÜGER, H. (1991) Unterbrochene Erwerbskarrieren und Berufsspezifik, in Mayer, Allmendinger and Huinink (1991) pp. 142–62.

LANE, C. (1993) Gender and the labour market in Europe: Britain, Germany and France compared, *The Sociological Review*, Vol. 41, pp. 274–301.

LAROSSA, R. (1988) Fatherhood and social change, *Family Relations*, no. 37, pp. 451–7.

LEWIS, C. and O'BRIEN, M. (1987) *Reassessing Fatherhood*, Sage, London.

MARTIN, J. and ROBERTS, C. (1984) *Women and Employment – a Lifetime Perspective*, Dept of Employment, Office of Population Censuses and Surveys, London.

MAYER, K. U., ALLMENDINGER, J. and HUININK, J. (eds.) (1991) *Vom Regen in die Traufe: Frauen zwischen Beruf und Familie*, Campus, Frankfurt.

MCRAE, S. (1991) Occupational changes over childbirth: evidence from a national survey, *Sociology*, Vol. 25, no. 4, pp. 589–605.

MCRAE, S. (1993) Returning to work after childbirth; opportunities and inequalities, *European Sociological Review*, Vol. 9, no. 2, pp. 125–37.

MORÉE, M. (1992) *Mijn kinderen hebben er niets van gemerkt* (diss.), Utrecht.

NEIDHART, F., LEPSINS, M. R. and ESSER, H., (eds.) (1990) *Lebensverläufe und sozialer Wandel*, Kölner Zeitschrift für Soziologie und Sozialpsychologie, Sonderheft 31, Opladen.

OECD (1991) *Shaping Structural Change: The Role of Women*, Geneva.

PLANTENGA, J., (1993) *Een afwijkend patroon* (diss.), Amsterdam.

POTT-BUTER, H. A. (1993) *Facts and Fairy Tales, about Female Labour, Family and Fertility* (diss.). Amsterdam.

ROLOFF, J. (1992) Zu Problemen der Erwerbsbeteiligung der Frauen in den neuen Bundesländern, *Zeitschrift für Bevölkerungswissenschaft*, no. 4., pp. 465–75.

ROLOFF, J. (1993) Erwerbsbeteiligung und Familienstand von Frauen – ein deutsch–deutscher Vergleich, *Zeitschrift für Bevölkerungswissenschaft*, no. 1, pp. 105–12.

RUBERY, J. and TARLING, R. (1988) Women's employment in declining Britain, in J. Rubery (ed.) *Women and Recession*, Routledge and Kegan Paul, London.

SANDERS, K. (1991) *Vrouwelijke pioniers* (diss.), ICS, Groningen.

SANDERS, K. (1992) Indirecte beloningsverschillen tussen vrouwen en mannen, *Tijdschrift voor Arbeidsvraagstukken*, Vol. 8, no. 4, pp. 324–37.

SANDERS, K., LINDENBERG, S. and VAN DOORNE-HUISKES, J. (1991) Beroepskeuzepatronen bij vrouwen met een 'mannelijke' beroepsopleiding, *Gedrag en organisatie*, no. 4, pp. 43–60.

SCHIPPERS, J. J. and SIEGERS, J. J. (1988) Beloningsverschillen tussen mannen en vrouwen in Nederland, *Tijdschrift voor Arbeidsvraagstukken*, Vol. 4, no. 2, pp. 34–46.

SCHUPP, J. (1991) Teilzeitarbeit als Möglichkeit der beruflichen (Re)Integration, in Mayer, Allmendinger and Huinink (1991), pp. 207–32.

SHAW, L. B. and SHAPIRO, D. (1987) Women's work plans, *Monthly Labor Review*, no. 110, pp. 7–13.

SØRENSEN, A. (1990) Unterschiede im Lebenslauf von Frauen und Männern, in Neidhardt, Lepsins and Esser (1990), pp. 304–21.

SØRENSEN, A., and MCLANAHAN, S. (1987) Women's economic dependency, 1940–1980, *American Journal of Sociology*, Vol. 93, pp. 659–87.

STEENBUCK, G. (1989) Die Rüchkehr von Familienfrauen in den Beruf, *Zeitschrift für Berufs- und Wirtschaftspädagogik*, Vol. 85, no. 6, pp. 521–57.

STEWARD, M. B. and GREENLAGH, C. A. (1984) Workhistory patterns and the occupational attainment of women, *The Economic Journal*, Vol. 94, pp. 493-519.

SUNDSTRÖM, M. (1993) The growth in full-time work among Swedish women in the 1980s, *Acta sociologica*, Vol. 36, pp. 139-50.

WORKING MOTHERS ASSOCIATION (1994) *UK Employer Initiatives, Working Examples of Family Friendly and Equal Opportunities Policies*, Parents at Work, London.

CHAPTER 6

Sharing Domestic Work

TANJA VAN DER LIPPE AND ELLIE ROELOFS

INTRODUCTION

Despite their increasing involvement in the labour market, it is still women who do most of the work of looking after children and the home. This is true throughout Europe, although in some countries the husband's contribution within the household is greater than in others. In Scandinavia, for example, as pointed out in Chapter 1, it is perfectly normal for women to go out to work, even when they have children, and the husband's contribution is greater than in the rest of Europe. This is not only because men spend more time on housework but also because women spend less time on it. The present chapter focuses on the distribution of household and family tasks between men and women in the various countries of the European Union. We saw in the previous chapter that the position of women on the labour market is closely related to the distribution of work at home and the amount of domestic work required within the family.

Using comparative studies of the way time is budgeted, we first look at the participation of men and women in household work in a number of EU countries. We consider the significance of domestic work, the amount of time men and women spend on it, the influence of women's participation in the labour market on the amount of housework they do, and the influence of the make-up of the family, including whether or not there are any children. Various characteristics of the household and of the different countries are then compared in order to explain the level of participation in household and family tasks. This makes it possible to determine whether, besides household characteristics and levels of participation, there are specific country characteristics which influence the way time is used for domestic work. The next section then deals with the question of why men do not do more at home, despite the fact that in recent years far more women have undertaken paid employment. The final section examines the extent to which the policies of governments and employers influence the distribution of household tasks between men and women.

TIME SPENT ON DOMESTIC WORK IN VARIOUS EU COUNTRIES

Data and method

In order to understand the distribution of household tasks between men and women, we make use of studies of the way time is budgeted in various member states of the EU. These data are taken from the International Time Budget Archive assembled by the European Foundation for the Improvement of Living and Working Conditions (see Gershuny, Jones and Baert, 1991). The analyses dealt with Belgium, Denmark, the UK, France, Italy, the Netherlands and the former West Germany. The data cover a total of 25 years, but the period involved and the type of data differ from country to country. For Italy, for example, only a single study is available, whereas for the UK there are 3. The data also have the disadvantage that they are not very recent: the latest study dates from 1987. Nevertheless, the lack of other comparative information means that we are forced to rely on these data for insight into the distribution of household tasks.

The data were collected by means of the diary method, with respondents being asked to keep track of how they spent their time by filling in a diary over a certain period. This method varies to some extent from country to country. In some countries, for example, the main activity is filled in for a fixed interval (for example, for every quarter of an hour); in others, the intervals are open (i.e. the starting and finishing times are indicated). The period of time during which the diary was kept also differs from country to country. In some cases respondents were required to keep the diary for a single day and in others for a whole week. Even so, the diary method is considered the most reliable method of measuring the way people spend their time (Andorka, 1987; Juster and Stafford, 1991) and it gives an acceptable approximation of the actual situation (Knulst and Van Beek, 1990). It prevents respondents from exaggerating their favourite activities while neglecting day-to-day concerns and all sorts of trivial activities. The actual subject being studied is therefore not exaggerated, as sometimes happens when specialized questionnaires are used.

Although a broadly based study therefore has advantages for specific problems, it also means that not all subjects can be dealt with in detail. In the first place, the time budget study used here to ask about household activities did not ask about secondary activities. One example of a secondary activity is looking after children during meals, while preparing meals or during other household activities. It is therefore possible that the time devoted to supervising children is underestimated. Dealing with 'emotional matters' was not measured in the studies either. This area would include dealing with tensions, expressing affection, creating a pleasant atmosphere and encouraging good relations within the family.

An important point is also that one cannot simply use the amount of time devoted to household tasks and to family matters as an indication of the amount of work necessary in the household (see Knulst and Schoonderwoerd, 1983). For example, the fact that married women with a job carry out their household tasks in a shorter time than housewives in a similar living and family situation does not answer the question of whether the housewives deal with the tasks more thoroughly or whether they allow themselves more time for each chore than the women with a job. The time budget method applied does not allow us to answer this question. Probably there are differences in the women's attitudes to having a clean and tidy house and to whether or not they find housework enjoyable. These attitudes are probably closely related to education and age, with the importance women attach to having a clean and tidy house and to housework generally decreasing drastically the higher their level of education and the younger they are. Another significant element is the number of alternative activities available to them, both in the area of paid employment and in their free time. The more housework competes with other activities, the less time is spent on it. For full-time housewives, housework may be a way of 'filling up their time'. When interpreting the results of the studies, it is important to bear in mind that what is involved is the amount of time spent on the various activities and not actual 'performance'.

The various family and household tasks

A number of attempts have been made to define what is meant by domestic work (see, for example, Hagenaars and Wunderink-Van Veen, 1990). Cooking and cleaning, clearly, are household tasks, but how does one classify do-it-yourself activities and playing with the children? It is in fact difficult to distinguish clearly between household tasks and hobbies and recreational activities. This may also be difficult in the case of cooking, for example when preparations for a large dinner party are involved. The problems involved in deciding just what household tasks actually consist of has led to several definitions. 'Do-it-yourself', for example, may or may not be classified as a household task. Generally, a distinction is made between strictly household tasks and caring for children.

This chapter deals with household tasks within the context of a comprehensive definition, although it does examine the various aspects of housekeeping. Activities at home are termed 'domestic and family tasks'. They can be subdivided into housework, caring for children and do-it-yourself activities. This takes account of the categories available within the archive of data. Because we use data from different countries, which categorize tasks in different ways, it is difficult to arrive at an effective uniform system of categories. The following activities are considered to be domestic and family tasks:

1 *housework:* food preparation, baking, freezing, putting up preserves, washing up, putting away the dishes, washing clothes, hanging them out to dry, ironing them, making beds, dusting and cleaning indoors and out, tidying, putting shopping away, other manual domestic work, all types of shopping, travel related to domestic chores, housework not otherwise specified;
2 *caring for children:* looking after and supervising children;
3 *do-it-yourself activities* (described as *odd jobs*): mending clothes, tasks concerned with hot water or heating, decorating, repairs to the house, vehicle maintenance, pet care, gardening, care of dependent adults, housework done for others (unpaid), home paperwork.

Figure 6.1 Time spent on domestic work by men and women between the ages of 20 and 60 (in hours per week)

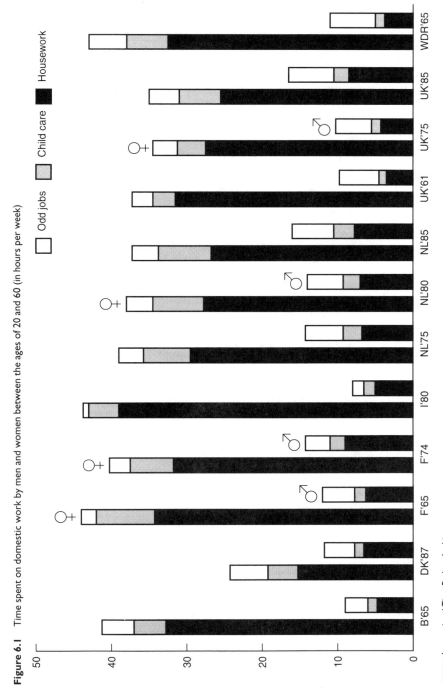

SOURCE: International Time Budget Archive.

Figure 6.1 shows how much time men and women devote to household work, caring for the children and odd jobs in 7 different countries. We can see that women devote the greater part of their household time to housework. In the course of time, women have come to devote less and men more time to housework in the 3 countries for which longitudinal data is available (France, the UK and the Netherlands). The same finding resulted from a comparison of time spent on housework in the UK and the USA (Gershuny and Robinson, 1988). This study also shows that the amount of housework has decreased. Gershuny and Robinson suggest that the reason is partly to do with the increased amount of time-saving equipment available, for example the washing machine and the microwave oven. This finding stands in contrast to those of studies of 2 decades ago (Robinson and Converse, 1972; Vanek, 1974; Walker, 1968), which concluded that the quantity of housework at that time was constant or even increasing.

There are major differences in the way time is budgeted in the different countries. This is due in part to the different survey methods used but, to some extent, the reason is also to be found in cultural and social factors. In Denmark, for example, there are far more women in paid employment than in the Netherlands and they are far more likely to work full time, meaning that they have less time available for the household. The fact that Danish men, despite their wives working full time, do not do more housework than Dutch men is probably due to the fact that in Denmark the state takes over some domestic and child-care tasks.

The first question to be dealt with is whether the distribution of domestic and family tasks between men and women in the various member states of the EU corresponds with the distribution of paid work in those countries. This is in fact the case. In Denmark, for example, figures for 1987 show that women carried out the most paid work (42% of the total amount) compared to women in other countries. As far as domestic and family tasks are concerned, Danish women do the least work, namely 66%. The wife's contribution to paid work can be determined by dividing the time she spends on it by the time the husband and wife spend on it jointly. (Their contributions thus add up to 100%.) In comparison to other countries, Italian women make the greatest contribution to household and family tasks, namely 84% (1980), whereas their proportion of paid work is relative small (27%). In the UK the percentages for 1985 were 67 and 34 respectively. In the EU countries examined, a larger contribution to household and family tasks is in general associated with less time spent on paid work. In the Netherlands the position is somewhat unusual. The figures for 1985 show that in relation to their contribution of 70% to the household (which can be considered average in comparison to all the countries investigated), Dutch women carried out a relatively small proportion of the paid work (25%). It is a well-known fact that in the Netherlands the number of women in paid employment has for a long time lagged behind in comparison to countries such as the UK and Denmark (see Chapter 1). Moreover, a relatively large number of working women work part time.

The amount of time women spend on paid employment

We now turn to the differences in the amount of time women spend on domestic and family tasks. An attempt will be made to explain these differences by taking into account some aspects of their environment along with personal characteristics.

The fact that women have done less household and family work over the past few decades is in part due to the greater extent to which they have undertaken paid employment. Chapter 1 dealt with the fact that although more women have gone out to work in all EU countries, the differences between the various countries have remained. Where paid employment for women is concerned, Denmark has always been the front runner. At the opposite end of the scale, there has been more variation: in 1973 the Netherlands brought up the rear, in 1983 Spain and in 1988 Ireland. We have also seen that in the Netherlands many working women only have part-time jobs, whereas in countries such as Italy and Portugal working women almost always work full time.

It therefore seems likely that there is a relationship between the amount of paid work women do and the time they devote to the home. We expect that the more time women work outside the home, the less time they spend on household tasks. People, obviously enough, have a restricted amount of time available, and if they spend more time on a given activity they will have less time to spend on other activities (Coverman, 1985). Besides paid work and household work, recreation may be one of those other types of activity.

Figure 6.2 Time spent on domestic work by women between the ages of 20 to 60 according to the number of hours spent on paid work (in hours per week)

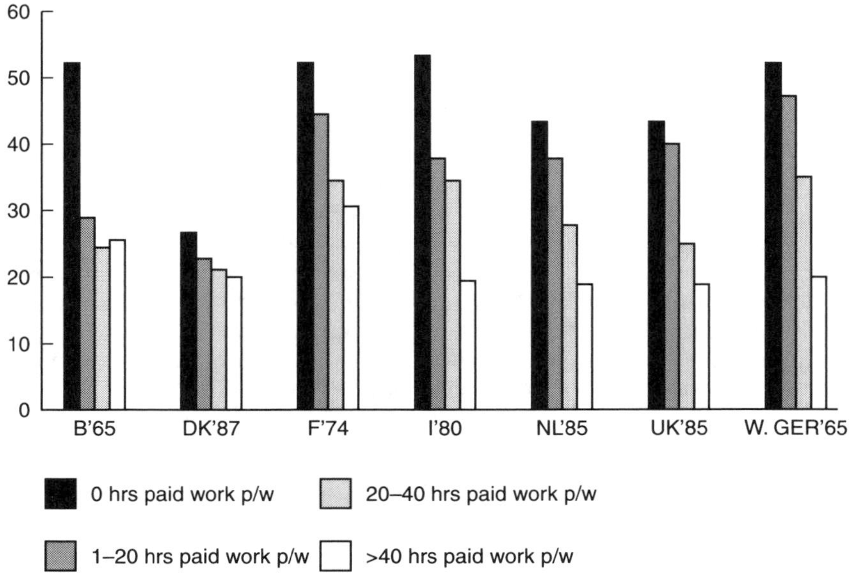

SOURCE: International Time Budget Archive.

Studies show that there is no perfect one-to-one relationship between household work and paid work. When less time is spent on paid work, a part of the time that becomes available is devoted to recreational activities rather than to household and family tasks (Grift, Siegers and Suy, 1989).

Figure 6.2 contrasts the number of hours women spend on household and family tasks with the time they spend on paid employment. (The most recent figures have been used for each country, although for Belgium and Germany the figures are from 1965.) Figure 6.2 shows that women carry out fewer household tasks the more they engage in paid employment. They do the least work at home if they are employed for more than 40 hours per week. This difference is probably due in part to the differing circumstances in which working women and housewives find themselves: women who go out to work have fewer children and are more often graduates of higher education than those who do not have a job. We will discuss these issues later.

Although there are differences between the various countries, the trend is always in the same direction. In almost all countries the wife's participation in housework drops below 20 hours per week if she works more than 40 hours per week. Denmark is an exception because full-time housewives in that country and women with a part-time job of only a few hours also do relatively little housework.

It is not possible here for us to go into the question of the extent to which men do more domestic work when their wife does more paid work, because we do not have data on both partners. Existing studies have come to differing conclusions. Some findings show that when women go out to work their husbands in fact do more in the household (Bird, Bird and Scruggs, 1984; Barnett and Baruch, 1987). Other studies indicate, however, that the proportion of housework done by the men increases, not because they do more but because their wife does less (Huber and Spitze, 1983; Hardesty and Bokemeier, 1989; Shelton, 1990). In the next section we will look more closely at the question of why men do not do more in the household when their wives go out to work.

Family situation

The arrival of children leads to a change in the way time is spent. More consumer goods (and thus a higher income) are necessary to look after children and more time is also necessary to take care of both the children and the household. In particular, the number of household and family tasks is greatly increased and it is primarily women who deal with these extra tasks. A comparative study covering 14 European countries shows that if one of the parents stops working because there are small children, it is always the wife (Ve, 1989). This has to do with the sex-specific socialization of men and women, structural differences in the position of men and women in society and considerations of efficiency (England and Farkas, 1986). Figure 6.3 compares the contribution of the wife to household and family tasks vis-à-vis the family situation. Once again, the wife's contribution has been calculated by dividing the time she devotes to the household by the total time that husband and wife devote to it together. (Although the husband's proportion is not shown in this figure, calculating it is perfectly simple. In the UK, for

Figure 6.3 Share in domestic work assumed by women between 20 and 60 years according to household situation (in percentages)

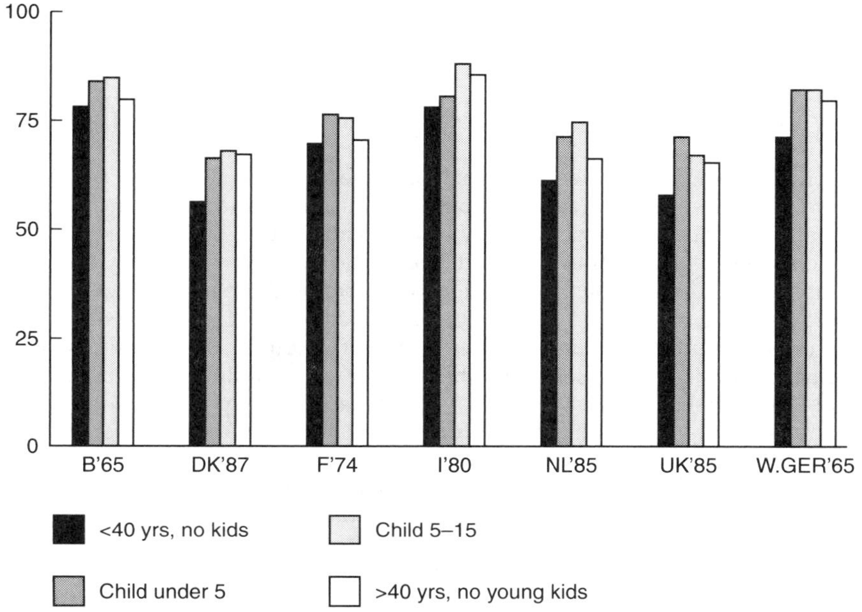

Legend:
- ■ <40 yrs, no kids
- ▨ Child under 5
- ▢ Child 5–15
- ▢ >40 yrs, no young kids

SOURCE: International Time Budget Archive.

example, a woman with children younger than 5 does 70% of the household work and her husband therefore does 30%.

Figure 6.3 shows that women deal with a greater proportion of the domestic and family tasks if there are children. Their proportion is clearly smallest when they themselves are younger than 40 years of age and they do not (yet) have children.

Other research shows that men and women with children are devoting an increasing amount of time to looking after them. Some researchers suggest that this is the result of a change in the significance of parenthood. A comparative study of 21 countries throughout the world, for example, covering the period from 1963 to 1978, shows that the value placed on children is related to the level of economic development of the country involved. The higher the level of development a country has achieved – and consequently the smaller the size of the average family – the more children start to take on a different significance for their parents in a number of ways. The psychological aspects of the significance of children for their parents gradually become more important. Above all, when economic development has reached a relatively high level, an increasingly heavy emphasis is placed on the psychological value of raising children and seeing them grow up, interacting with them, gaining pleasure from them and from doing things with them (Bulatao, 1979).

Developments in birth control mean that having children is increasingly a matter of conscious choice. In around 1960 that was still hardly the case at all: once people were married, children arrived as a matter of course. Choice came into it only if the parents decided that the family was becoming too large. Since the 1970s reliable methods of contraception have meant that having the first child (if a couple have children at all) and any further children has come to require a conscious decision.

Influence of various characteristics on domestic and family tasks

We have already identified a link between the home situation and the extent to which men and women participate in household and family tasks. Such situational features as whether they have a paid job and whether or not there are children have an important influence on the extent to which they carry out household and family tasks. In order to determine the real influence of such features, it is necessary to correct our calculations for other significant features. A multivariate analysis has been carried out to examine the relative influence of each circumstance on the number of hours devoted to household and family tasks. The results are set out in Table 6.1. Apart from household features and the differing periods during which the surveys were carried out, the 7 countries involved have also been taken into account in the comparison. By doing this we are able to establish whether the country of residence and the time period are also explanatory variables in their own right. The table can be interpreted as follows. If the household includes a child aged between 0 and 5 years, the wife has 19 hours per week of extra household and family tasks (including taking care of the child or children) in comparison with a childless woman whose situation is otherwise precisely the same with respect to the other features in the table. This difference is valid for all the member states. A man with a paid job of 40 or more hours per week does some 9 hours per week less housework than a man without a paid job whose circumstances are otherwise the same.

Table 6.1 shows that, regardless of the country in which they live, men and women spend less time on the household when they do more paid work. This result confirms the idea that people who do more paid work have less time available for the household. The age of the youngest child has even greater influence on the domestic work women do. The younger the child, the more time the wife spends on the household. In the case of men, children older than 5 years almost cease to have an effect on the time men spend on domestic and family tasks. This confirms that household and family tasks created by the presence of children are dealt with primarily by women. A study of 400 Dutch households carried out in 1990 also shows that the presence of young children is a very important factor in determining the amount of domestic work. The presence of children is a more important influence on the time spent than such features as level of education and social norms with respect to the division of roles (Van der Lippe and Siegers, 1994). Table 6.1 also shows that women who are graduates of higher education do less in the home than women with a lower level of education. For men, the level of education makes no difference. The older men and women are, the more they each do in the home than younger men and women.

The period of time is significant for both men and women. Regardless of the country in which they live, women did less in the home in the period between 1983 and 1990 and between 1971 and 1977 than in the period between 1961

Table 6.1 **Influence of various circumstances on time spent on domestic work.**

CIRCUMSTANCE	NON STANDARDIZED REGRESSION COEFFICIENTS* (T-VALUES)			
	WOMEN		MEN	
Paid work				
0 hours per week (reference group)				
1–19 hours per week	–6.50*	(–8.00)	–2.50	(–2.19)
20–39 hours per week	–14.47*	(–20.62)	–6.36*	(–10.04)
> = 40 hours per week	–21.51*	(–36.35)	–9.14*	(–18.91)
Presence of children				
No (small) children (reference group)				
Youngest child < 5 years	18.89*	(30.40)	4.13*	(10.09)
Youngest child 5–15 years	8.70*	(16.33)	0.48	(1.32)
Education				
Uncompleted secondary or less (reference)				
Completed secondary	–3.11*	(–6.78)	–0.82	(–2.53)
Above secondary education	–8.66*	(–10.42)	–0.93	(–1.87)
Age				
20–29 years (reference group)				
30–39 years	6.95*	(11.31)	2.63*	(6.13)
40–49 years	8.17*	(13.29)	3.19*	(7.47)
50–59 years	10.47*	(16.51)	2.74*	(6.57)
Period (survey time/period)				
1961–70 (reference category)				
1971–77	–3.02*	(–3.97)	0.75	(1.40)
1978–82	–2.47	(–1.86)	3.02*	(3.27)
1983–90	–2.45*	(–3.14)	5.79*	(10.43)
Country				
UK (reference group)				
Belgium	4.95*	(5.57)	–0.45	(–0.72)
Denmark	–5.71*	(–7.09)	–5.34*	(–9.45)
France	9.40*	(11.60)	3.39*	(6.93)
Italy	0.14	(0.10)	–12.21*	(–11.24)
Netherlands	0.95	(1.06)	0.05	(0.08)
West Germany	5.18*	(5.97)	0.57	(0.90)
Adjusted R-squares	.42		.12	

* Significant at 1% level

SOURCE: International Time Budget Archive (*n* = 7,079 women and 6,992 men)

and 1970. In the course of time, men have started to do more and more in the home. In the period between 1983 and 1990 they did almost 6 hours more than between 1961 and 1970. This time effect suggests that sex-specific norms with respect to carrying out household and family tasks have become considerably less rigid, shifting in the direction of a less unequal distribution of tasks.

When we compare the influence of the different countries, we must consider the fact that both the household characteristics and the different time periods included in the table are held constant. It would appear that women in Denmark devote significantly less time to the household than their counterparts in the UK. Danish men, also, do less in the home than men in the UK. It is quite possible that this is the result of the large number of child-care facilities available in Denmark, as mentioned above. It is much more usual for Danish children to be placed in day-care centres than for British children, for example (see also Chapter 10 on child care). It is also noticeable that men in Italy devote some 12 hours less to the household than men in the UK do, although there is no difference between Italian and British women. A possible explanation for this situation is that in Italy the norms with respect to the distribution of roles are different. It is not considered 'proper' for Italian men to involve themselves much in the housekeeping.

This analysis of the way in which women budget time for household and family tasks leads us to conclude that the presence of young children and the number of hours of paid work have a particularly significant influence. In the case of men, it is above all the number of hours of paid work per week which is relevant. Compared to these factors, the influence of the country concerned and the 'spirit of the times' are much less significant. For a man it is above all his availability, in relation to his hours of paid work, which determines how much time he invests in the household. In the case of women, it is not only availability which is important but also the need for household and family tasks, measured against the age of the youngest child. A similar analysis using housework and caring for children only (without do-it-yourself activities) does not produce a significant difference in the results.

THE CONTRIBUTION OF THE MALE PARTNER TO THE HOUSEHOLD

In the previous section we have seen that in most EU countries the contribution of the male partner to the household has remained restricted when compared to that of his wife. Why has the substantial increase in the number of women undertaking paid work led to only a modest increase in the male contribution to the household?

In this context, economics is an important factor. The results presented in Chapter 3 show that in every country men are able to earn more by means of paid work than women and that they – at least partly because of that fact – carry out more hours of paid work on average than women, even when we compare partners who each have a full-time job. It is therefore plausible to suppose that women devote more time to unpaid work. This is, however, not a satisfactory explanation, because the mechanism presented, namely 'men can simply earn more', is in itself a phenomenon requiring explanation. Studies have shown that even in households in which the male and female partners have basically the same earning capacity there is still an unequal distribution of tasks. This therefore leads to the assumption that more is involved than a simple weighing up of time and money (Hochschild, 1989).

A promising way of providing a better explanation of the unequal distribution of tasks is that of 'gender'. Gender can be seen as a social and normative construction in which the traditional distribution of tasks between men and women is considered to be so perfectly normal that breaking through it involves paying a high price socially and emotionally. This argument will be discussed in more detail in Chapter 7. Paid work and domestic work are culturally and historically determined tasks which are coupled to the concepts of maleness and femaleness (Berk, 1985). The categories 'women's work' and 'men's work' are not neutral ones. Domestic work is considered by many women to be something which is simply their own task, even if they are now playing an active role in working life. They cannot or do not wish to articulate clearly their wishes with respect to the redistribution of household tasks, and men are in general not helpful in this respect.

This is demonstrated effectively by Hochschild (1989) in a study of 50 double-income households from various levels of American society. She was a guest in the homes of a number of different families for a lengthy period of time and was thus able to follow closely the difficult negotiations on the distribution of household tasks. According to her, there are a number of dominant strategies during the negotiations between the partners. For example, some women negotiate directly and threaten divorce; some act as if they are helpless and incompetent where certain tasks are concerned; some do only the absolute minimum necessary in the household; some reduce the number of hours of paid work they do or take on the role of 'super mother'. Men often adopt a passive strategy by consistently forgetting to carry out their household tasks or by acting as if they are without the necessary skills for domestic work.

In some households, furthermore, it appears to be more acceptable for certain household tasks not to be carried out at all than for them to be undertaken by a member of the 'wrong' gender. Domestic work is still seen as a natural component of the female partner's role. In her study of the power of 'what is natural' in the relations between men and women, Komter (1989) shows how a number of power mechanisms are used to preserve existing distribution structures and prevent new ones being introduced. She speaks of hidden power mechanisms because these are used at a level which is hardly conscious, if it is conscious at all, and are often not recognized as such by those involved. Both men and women come up with arguments to legitimize the status quo: 'My husband simply doesn't have the time for housework' or 'He doesn't see what needs to be done, and I can do it just as quickly myself.' Men make use of similar arguments.

Summarizing, we can say that there are deeply rooted structures which are considered to be 'natural', which are characterized by normative considerations and which serve to slow down the introduction of an equal distribution of household tasks between men and women. These normative constructions are based on and supported by institutional and economic realities (van Doorne-Huiskes, 1992). Where such 'natural' situations are concerned, the future does not seem to be very reassuring. When considering their future, boys have a more traditional view of it in mind than girls. Girls more frequently expect that both partners will contribute to caring. As pointed out in the previous chapter, many girls do assume that in the future they will carry out fewer hours of paid work than their partner. This of course will influence their choice of occupation. In this respect they keep close to what they currently see women actually doing (Niphuis-Nell, 1992).

CHANGES IN THE DISTRIBUTION OF HOUSEHOLD TASKS?

This chapter has dealt with the distribution of household tasks and family tasks between men and women in various EU countries. In the course of the years the distribution of tasks has become less one-sided, but women still take upon themselves the lion's share of household work. This remains true even if they go out to work full time.

What do these findings mean for the future distribution of household tasks? Given the present rate of change, it can be expected that a more equal distribution will come about only slowly. That a more equal distribution can indeed be expected is justified on the one hand by the fact that changes are already taking place and on the other by the fact that women are increasingly aiming at a professional career. All the same, deeply rooted ideas of what is 'natural' in the distribution of tasks between men and women will slow down the process of change.

It is interesting to see what policies are being adopted by the various countries with respect to the distribution of household tasks between men and women. That government policy plays a role is made clear by the example of Denmark, where arrangements for child care are designed in such a way that the 2 partners need to spend less time, relatively speaking, on domestic work. Double-income households are the norm. Better child-care arrangements have undoubtedly made an important contribution to this situation. Chapter 10 will provide an overview of the state of affairs in the various EU countries with regard to child-care facilities, confinement leave and the possibility of maternity/paternity leave. Measures of this sort make it easier for women to combine their care and household tasks with paid work.

Similarly, by introducing legislation, governments can encourage or indeed force employers to apply various instruments. In this connection, the finding (Hogg and Harker, 1992) that in countries in which the government takes the initiative to encourage women to combine domestic and paid work – Belgium and Denmark are the examples given – employers also pursue a more active policy. Hogg and Harker have made an inventory of the various types of policy which companies apply in this respect. The inventory, incidentally, also covers policy instruments which are not intended primarily to make it possible for personnel to combine paid work and domestic work. The German department store chain Beck, for example, introduced a system of flexible working hours in order to be able to extend its opening hours. However, flexible working hours may also be attractive for people with a double role. Apart from flexitime, other policy instruments with which employers can encourage personnel to combine paid work and household work include part-time work, job sharing, flexiplace and teleworking, family leave, child-and/or adult-care support, information and referral services and financial assistance. Management changes are also seen by some companies as an important instrument which can indirectly create a more family-friendly environment. Policies on combining domestic and paid work are at present advocated by influential international organizations like the OECD. In its well-received report *Shaping Structural Change* a profound analysis is given of the closely interwoven connections between household work and paid work. The present division between the sexes means that the potential of women, in both the qualitative and quantitative sense, is in fact not being used to its full. A better distribution of domestic work and paid work is therefore necessary, and the report sets out a whole series of proposals for policies to encourage this. Besides encouraging the participation of women in public life, the report also argues in favour of a reassessment of the skills necessary for tasks which are usually carried out in the private sphere. This means, therefore, not only that girls should be encouraged to make different career choices but also that boys should learn to share responsibility for caring tasks.

The European Union also recognizes that the unequal distribution of domestic work is a bad thing for both women and men (Commission, 1993). In the Third Community Action Plan *Equal Opportunities for Men and Women*, which is dealt with in more detail in Chapter 8, one of the 3 main objectives is to integrate women into the labour market. Measures such as those taken within the framework of New Opportunities for Women (NOW) therefore aim to reconcile family and professional obligations (Commission, 1991). The Union also commits itself to this sort of action in its Social Charter. In practice, however, the Union follows a cautious course, as indeed their record on child care and parental leave shows. Where policy aimed at redistributing domestic work is concerned, the European Union must depend on the readiness of the governments of all the member states to take action.

Governments have always been cautious as far as the private lives of their citizens are concerned. Most governments have already shown reluctance to promote child-care facilities, and in dealing with the distribution of domestic and family tasks between men and women they are even more restrained. Denmark is an exception. We should also mention recent developments in the Netherlands, where the government has set up a working party to consider the 'redistribution of unpaid work and in that connection an increase in the responsibility of men for care tasks'. This commission's task is to make unpaid work better visible by, for example, studying the way in which time is used and by formulating scenarios for the future, partly on the basis of the OECD report. Activities are also being started which are keyed to the age of those concerned. These include, for example, developing educational materials and information packages for young people and for adults, organizing discussions, etc. Moreover, the Dutch government already decided some years ago to make domestic science a compulsory subject for all secondary school pupils because of its emancipatory function. It would therefore be wrong to conclude that the government has but little influence in the private sphere. The whole range of taxation measures and social security regulations, together with regulations covering working hours and school hours, are all means by which the government does indeed create the preconditions within which citizens organize their lives (Plan Redistribution of Unpaid Work

(*Werkplan Herverdeling Onbetaalde Arbeid*), 1994). How far the government goes in this respect is a political choice and differs from member state to member state. Moreover, whether or not the Dutch working party will succeed in getting many others to share its concerns is an open question. All too often, initiatives such as setting up such a working party are not followed up and are left in limbo (see also *Emancipatieraad*, 1994a and b).

In summary, there are hardly any signs that getting men to participate in unpaid work is actively encouraged by national governments, the European Union or employer initiatives (see also Hogg and Harker, 1992). Most of the initiatives which have been taken are directed mainly at women and at improving their opportunities for carrying out paid work.

REFERENCES

ANDORKA, R. (1987) Time budgets and their uses, *Annual Review of Sociology*, Vol. 13, pp. 149–64.
BARNETT, R. C. and BARUCH, G. K. (1987) Determinants of father's participation in family work, *Journal of Marriage and the Family*, Vol. 49, pp. 29–40.
BERK, S. F. (1985) *The Gender Factory: The Apportionment of Work in American Households*, Plenum, New York.
BIRD, G. W., BIRD, G. A. and SCRUGGS, M. (1984) Determinants of family task sharing: a study of husbands and wives, *Journal of Marriage and the Family*, Vol. 46, pp. 345-55.
BULUTAO, R. A. (1979) *Further Evidence of the Transition in the Value of Children*, East–West Population Institute, Honolulu, Hawaii (Paper no. 60-B).
COMMISSION OF THE EUROPEAN COMMUNITIES (1991) *Equal Opportunities for Women and Men: Third Action Programme 1991-95*, Brussels.
COMMISSION OF THE EUROPEAN COMMUNITIES (1993) *Growth, Competitiveness and Employment*, White Paper, Brussels.
COVERMAN, S. (1985) Explaining husband's participation in domestic labour, *The Sociological Quarterly*, Vol. 26, pp. 81-97.
DOORNE-HUISKES, VAN J. (1992) *Betaalde en onbetaalde arbeid: over oude spanningen en nieuwe uitdagingen*, Erasmus University, Rotterdam.
EMANCIPATIERAAD (1994a) *Met het oOG OP mer 1997*, Den Haag.
EMANCIPATIERAAD (1994b) *Plan Redistribution of Unpaid Work*, Den Haag.
ENGLAND, P. and FARKAS, G. (1986) *Households, Employment and Gender: A Social, Economic and Demographic View*, Aldine, New York.
GERSHUNY, J. and ROBINSON, J. P. (1988) Historical changes in the household division of labor, *Demography*, Vol. 25, pp. 537-52.
GERSHUNY, J., JONES, S. and BAERT, P. (1991) *The Time Economy or the Economy of Time: An Essay on the Interdependence of Living and Working Conditions*, Universities of Oxford and Bath, European Foundation for the Improvement of Living and Working Conditions, Dublin.
GRIFT, Y. K., SIEGERS, J. J. and SUY, G. M. C. (1989) *Tijdsbesteding in Nederland*, Swoka Onderzoeksrapporten, No. 65, Den Haag.
HAGENAARS, A. J. M. and WUNDERINK-VAN VEEN, S. R. (1990) *Soo gewonne soo verteert: economie van de huishoudelijke sector*, Stenfert Kroese, Leiden/Antwerpen.
HARDESTY, C. and BOKEMEIER, J. (1989) Finding time and making do: distribution of household labor in non-metropolitan marriages, *Journal of Marriage and the Family*, Vol. 51, pp. 253-67.
HOCHSCHILD, A. (1989) *The Second Shift: Working Parents and the Revolution at Home*, Viking, New York.
HOGG, C. and HARKER, L. (1992) *The Family-Friendly Employee: Examples from Europe*, Day Care Trust, New York.
HUBER, J. and SPITZE, G. (1983) *Sex Stratifications: Children, Housework and Jobs*, Academic Press, New York.
JUSTER, F. T. and STAFFORD, F. P. (1989) The allocation of time: empirical findings,

behavioural models, and problems of measurement, *Journal of Economic Literature*. Vol. 29, pp. 471-522.

KNIJN, T., VAN NUENEN, A. and VAN DER AVORT, A. (1994) Zorgend vaderschap, *Amsterdams Sociologisch Tijdschrift*, Vol. 20, pp. 70-97.

KNULST, W. and SCHOONDERWOERD, L. (1983) *Waar blijft de tijd: onderzoek naar de tijdsbesteding van Nederlanders*, Sociale en Culturele Studies 4, Staatsuitgeverij, Den Haag.

KNULST, W. P. and VAN BEEK, P. (1990) *Tijd komt met de jaren: onderzoek naar tegenstellingen en veranderingen in dagelijkse bezigheden van Nederlanders op basis van tijdbudgetonderzoek*, Sociale en Culturele Studies 14, Sociaal en Cultureel Planbureau/VUGA, Rijswijk/Den Haag.

KOMTER, A. (1989) Hidden power in marriage, *Gender and Society*, Vol. 3, pp. 187-216.

VAN DER LIPPE, T. and SIEGERS, J. J. (1984) Division of household and paid labour between partners: effects of relative wage rates and social norms, *Kyklos*, Vol. 47, pp. 109–36.

NIPHUIS-NELL, M. (1992) *De emancipatie van meizjes en jonge vrouwen: rapportage ten behoeve van een evaluatie van het meisjesbeld*, VUGA, Den Haag.

ROBINSON, J. P. and CONVERSE, P. (1972) Social change as reflected in the use of time, in A. Campbell and P. Converse (eds.), *The Human Being of Social Change*, Russell Sage Foundation, New York.

SHELTON, B. A. (1990) The distribution of household tasks, *Journal of Family Issues*, Vol. 11, pp. 115-35.

VANEK, J. (1974) Time spent in housework, *Scientific American*, p. 116.

VE, H. (1989) The male gender role and responsibility for childcare, in K. Boh *et al.*, *Changing Patterns of European Family Life: A Comparative Study of 14 European Countries*, Routledge, London/New York.

WALKER, K. (1968) Homemaking still takes time, *Journal of Home Economics*, Vol. 61, pp. 621-7.

CHAPTER 7

Gendered Patterns in Institutional Constraints: An Attempt at Theoretical Integration

ANNEKE VAN DOORNE-HUISKES AND JACQUES VAN HOOF

INTRODUCTION

The facts and figures presented in the previous chapters make clear that women account for an increasing share of the labour force within the European Union (see Chapter 1). This increase, however, does not mean that inequalities between male and female workers have disappeared. The large influx of women on to the labour market has not been accompanied by much diversification in the jobs they do. On the contrary, the pattern of concentration in a few sectors of activity has continued to prevail. This holds true for all the countries in the European Union (see Chapter 2). Such persistent occupational segregation can to some extent be attributed to the increasing number of women working in part-time jobs. Part-time work reinforces the concentration of women by confining them to a limited number of jobs and professions. This is especially true in the service sector, where women are employed part time predominantly as cooks, waitresses, cleaning staff, shop assistants and in lower-level clerical jobs.

Not only does segregation at the level of jobs and occupations appear to be persistent, but there is also a promotion gap between women and men. The number of women in top-level and decision-making positions remains low, although all of the countries of Europe have shown a slight increase in the number of women managers during the last decade (Davidson and Cooper, 1993).

Irrefutable evidence of pay differences between men and women was presented in Chapter 3. Much of the overall difference between male and female earnings appears to be related to the distribution of men and women over jobs and sectors. But that is not the whole story. Even if men and women work in the same sector or industry, they still do not earn the same wages. Because they often have low-paid jobs in a limited number of areas, work part time or do so-called atypical work, women are more likely than men to be unemployed. The UK is the only member state of the European Union where the female unemployment rate is lower than that of men; in all other member states, women's unemployment rates are higher (see Chapter 1).

One significant social fact which forms both the background to and main explanation for many of the labour-market inequalities between men and women is that unpaid labour in the home has remained to a large extent a woman's affair (Chapter 6). This domestic division of labour is deeply rooted in all European countries and seems to be beyond the reach of what is considered rational in an economic sense. Leaving aside the economic evidence, women's contribution to unpaid labour must be viewed as a firmly entrenched social construct, a system of norms and values about what is considered 'natural' in men's and women's work.

Of course, the various countries differ on these points. For example, in terms of their working life women in Denmark generally resemble men more than they do women in Spain or in Greece. The differences between countries require more clarification than this book has provided until now. These explanations will be given in the second part of this chapter. The first part deals with inequalities between men and women in the labour market in a more general sense, briefly discussing various economic and sociological explanations which are often referred to in the literature and in research. One important question is whether these two different points of view might be related to each other and, if so, to what extent and in what way. Moss Kanter's analysis of men and women in corporations (1993) could play a part in this attempt at integration.

ECONOMIC APPROACHES

The inequalities between men and women in the labour market have been studied from an economic as well as from a sociological point of view. One important economic explanation is the theory of human capital (Becker, 1965; Johnson and Stafford, 1974; Lloyd and Niemi, 1979; Polachek and Siebert, 1993). As mentioned in Chapter 3, this is an investment theory which views workers as a stock of human capital. The assumption is that the choices and decisions of the actors on both the supply and the demand sides of the labour market determine the position of workers in the labour force. Investments in human capital provide a certain degree of productive capacity. The general hypothesis of the human capital theory states that the more productive workers are, the higher up their positions in the labour force will be and the more money they will earn. If women are worse off than men, then it is because they are less productive workers. Women, the theory continues, generally make different decisions from men with regard to the length of their educational careers and field of study, on-the-job training, full-time and part-time work and continuation of careers once children are born (see Chapter 5). On average, such differences in investment profiles (Chapter 3) between men and women result in lower productivity for female workers, which is, according to the human capital approach, the main reason that their chance of achieving higher-level positions or higher earnings is smaller than that of men. Employers invest in the human capital of their employees and weigh the pros and cons of the long-term benefits of their investments. They expect that women are more likely than men to interrupt their careers and switch to part-time jobs when their children are born. These expectations mean that they are less willing to invest in the productivity of women.

When set alongside research data, however, the labour market seems more complex than the human capital theory suggests. Differences in rewards and in the quality of jobs can only partly be explained by differences in the stock of human capital. It was Gary Becker (1957) who introduced the concept of discrimination in the neo-classical framework of utility and profit maximization (see Chapter 3). It may be that employers, workers and customers have a 'taste' for discrimination, i.e. a preference for or against hiring, working with or buying from a group of – for example – black and female workers (England, 1992). This notion has been criticized, as Schippers makes clear in Chapter 3, for its rather psychological character. It is easy to see that the goals of individuals include some specific preferences, but a more significant question is how much these preferences explain. The idea of statistical discrimination allows for this objection. Without assuming that people have a taste for discrimination, it postulates that employers select their personnel and offer them wages by trying to estimate future productivity. In general employers wish to reduce the costs of selecting new personnel. If cheap selection rules are available and appear to offer the 'right' information, they will make use of these rules. A selection based on 'face values' like race, sex and age provides such cheap rules. In the opinion of the employer, previous statistical experiences legitimize the use of such selection criteria.

Statistical discrimination is also part of the so-called job-competition model, as worked out by Thurow (1975). A critique of the human capital approach, this model states that job characteristics are more important with regard to the level of pay than is the productivity on the supply side of the labour market. One significant job characteristic is whether the job is part of the internal or external labour market of a company. Internal positions in general have more growth potential than external jobs. They provide opportunities for on-the-job training, which external jobs do not. As far as the internal positions are concerned, people are hired for starting positions and through on-the-job training and career guidance are given a chance to rise in job level. Employers take decisions that give some people access to internal positions while excluding others. These decisions are made on the basis of estimated training costs. Relevant considerations are, for instance, whether or not the employees in whom the company has invested will recoup the costs incurred. The employees may quit the company within a few years, so that the cost of training them exceeds any possible gains. Women are generally considered less reliable employees than men. These 'previous experiences' are the basis of statistical discrimination. As there is a greater risk that women will interrupt their careers or work part time, such group characteristics are made applicable to individuals. Consequently, women have fewer opportunities than men to occupy positions on the internal job market and which are part of so-called promotion ladders. As a consequence, it is primarily the external jobs which are left for women.

Another, less elaborate theory is the segmented labour market theory (see, for example, Doeringer and Poire, 1971), which assumes the existence of primary and secondary segments on the labour market and within companies. Primary segments provide stable working relationships, good training opportunities and favourable promotion prospects. In the secondary segments these aspects are generally far less favourable. It is assumed that women rely more heavily on the secondary segments. This is because they have fewer opportunities to invest in their professional life, as they shoulder a larger share of the burden of unpaid labour.

SOCIOLOGICAL APPROACHES

Issues of inequality and social stratification are important in sociology as well. Traditionally, sociological theories stress mainly values and norms as significant behaviour-regulating mechanisms. Sociological explanations of gender inequality in the labour market have therefore focused on the significance of role expectations. Internalized role expectations are presumed to be the basis of human conduct. Variations in human conduct are generally attributed to varying degrees of completeness in the processes of internalization.

Role theories are based on functionalist notions of social systems and of the prerequisites which have to be met for these social systems to endure. These prerequisites are double-sided: external and internal. Families, as examples of important social systems, have to deal with the (external) necessity of making a living and with the (internal) need to preserve close caring relationships between the members of this specific social system. One significant aspect of the internal prerequisites is the process of socialization, whereby relevant norms, values and role expectations are passed down to the younger generation. From a functionalist point of view, such norms are in turn considered the most vital sources of cohesion in societies.

Not much imagination is required to identify which tasks functionalist theories considered mainly women's tasks and which men's. It is precisely this traditional view of the domestic division of labour which provoked such criticism during the 1960s and 1970s. Although these objections were relevant, the concepts of role expectation, socialization processes and the internalization of norms and values may go a long way toward explaining why inequality between men and women in the labour market is so persistent. As important elements of social culture, norms and values include ideas about what is natural, what is unproblematic, what is taken for granted with respect to the proper roles of men and women. The notion of 'gender' – as an institution, a social construction, a set of meanings and definitions of what is considered as 'normal' in men's and women's behaviour – is based entirely on classic sociological insights.

Traditional gender roles consign women to the home. Although many women in the European Union are engaged in paid labour, caring for husband and children is seen as their primary task in most countries. This cultural condition, which in many member states is still strongly embedded in structural and institutional arrangements, accounts for the fact that women have on average less time available for their jobs and careers than do men. The effect is that women lag behind in comparison to men, especially because the most demanding years on the domestic front often coincide with the important starting period of a career (Rossi, 1965; Coser and Rokoff, 1971).

Role expectations, however, have not only practical but also psychological consequences. During their socialization girls receive a double message about their future, causing them to develop ambivalent feelings about it (Bardwick and Douvan, 1971; Frieze *et al.*, 1978; Tavris and Offir, 1977). On the one hand the message is that paid work and an independent status are important aims worth achieving. On the other hand, they are told that being a wife and mother is a prospect both significant and worth striving for. Such ambivalence can severely impede the development of full commitment to a career, and it is reinforced by the fact that it is not only women who have contrasting role expectations. Employers are also influenced in their actions and decisions by similar considerations. As we have already mentioned in relation to economic theories, they expect less stable labour-market behaviour from women than from men. This means that women represent a greater risk factor for employers. Employers prefer to avoid risks, reducing the chance that women will end up working in an attractive position.

During the last decade, the theoretical model of the 'homo sociologicus', according to which behaviour is driven primarily by norms and values, has been the subject of considerable criticism. The main objection is that this normative approach does not take into account people's own considerations, choices and definitions of their situation, or their individual decisions. This criticism has been levelled by symbolic interactionists and sociologists who wish to integrate the economic model of profit maximization within a sociological perspective (see Opp and Hummell, 1973; Boudon, 1981; Lindenberg, 1985; Coleman, 1990). Our intention in this chapter is to present a similarly integrated approach and to demonstrate its usefulness as a frame of reference for discussing explanations of gender inequality and for indicating policy guidelines. Before expanding on this, we will first discuss the work of Rosabeth Moss Kanter (1993). Although her theoretical assumptions and empirical observations are not explicitly based on a theory of (rational) choice, her work can be linked to this.

Sociology of organizations: the view of Moss Kanter

Moss Kanter conducted research in the USA during the 1970s on the question of why women lag behind men in terms of job level. She carried out her research in a large international corporation. Kanter analysed the careers of men and women from the perspective of individual reactions to important structural characteristics of the corporation. One set of structural characteristics is related to the degree to which jobs offer opportunities for promotion and mobility. One of the central assumptions is that if people have jobs that offer little or no chance of further mobility, they will lose their aspirations and lower their level of ambition. 'Dead-end jobs', positions which offer no mobility opportunities, are uninspiring. When people know they cannot achieve a higher level in the organization, their commitment will decrease. Corporations often have various clusters of such dead-end jobs, positions that are not structurally connected to other positions. Because a relatively high percentage of women occupy these sorts of jobs, they in particular are faced with the psychological effects. As a result, women confirm an image that supports familiar stereotypes: women work primarily because they 'like' it; they find a pleasant working environment more important than achieving a career (see also De Jong, 1983). Women's reactions to a restricted environment are used as a basis and legitimation of existing practices. Most women are expected to have limited ambitions. Company attempts to offer women better jobs are consequently thought to be useful only to a limited extent.

Kanter's theory on the composition of groups of employees in terms of numbers, and the consequences of this composition on behaviour, is also interesting. She talks about tokens, people who differ from the rest of the group on the basis of a particular feature. Skin colour is one such feature, and so is gender. Tokens in a group stand a greater chance of being stereotyped than members of the majority group. A female manager in a group of male colleagues stands out. She is more likely to be viewed as a representative of her 'type' than as an individual with her own qualifications. Stereotyping frequently has a protective function for the majority: their culture can be maintained and does not come up for discussion. It is not easy for women in such a situation to escape from a restrictive role definition. In a manner of speaking, women can opt only for a particular feminine role or for behaving as inconspicuously as possible, neither of which is generally beneficial for a successful career.

Kanter's research has been criticized by feminist scholars because – as they argue – she neglects the aspects of gender and sexuality in her analysis of organizational structures and processes. Acker (1991) points out that Kanter's theory on numbers also applies to men as minorities in organizations which are dominated by women, but fails to account for gender differences in the situation of the token. Unlike women, she argues, men in women-dominated workplaces have far more chance of being positively evaluated and of being promoted to positions of greater authority. Empirical evidence to support this idea has already been presented by Ott (1985) in her research on male nurses and female police officers in the Netherlands. In her research on secretaries and on gender as an organizing principle of work relations, Pringle (1988) also criticizes the so-called gender-neutrality of Kanter's analysis of men and women in corporations. It remains to be seen if she is right in her arguments. It will be difficult to conduct more illuminating and innovative research into what secretaries are, how they behave and why they stay in the situations they are in.

We will now turn from the objections raised against Kanter to what is significant for our own theoretical point of view. One of the conclusions that Kanter reached is that women lag behind partly through their own actions. Such behaviour must not, however, be reduced to a set of attitudes acquired through socialization processes. Rather, it should be seen as a reaction to what is, to a greater or lesser extent, a constrained environment. Kanter does not explicitly state which principles or mechanisms people allow to guide them in their reactions to their environment. The concept of rational choice does, however, seem to be applicable to her work. Implicitly, Kanter states that people, through their behaviour, try to find a balance between their aspirations and the situation they are in. The avoidance of a too large a gap between their own behaviour and what is made possible by their environment, and the search for equilibrium or consonance between what they would like to achieve and what is actually possible, can be seen as a type of rational behaviour. The idea of a desire for balance, with unbalance being experienced as unpleasant, is based on Heider's (1946) cognitive consistency notion and Festinger's (1957) cognitive dissonance theory.

Towards an integration of theoretical insights: rational decisions in a constrained environment

It was Adam Smith, the 18th-century philosopher, who emphasized the assumption of self-interest as a basic principle of human behaviour. People, according to Smith, try to improve their condition of life or, in more formal terms, try to maximize their profit. The individual desire for profit will, through exchanges between people, lead to the development of social phenomena. These social phenomena, for instance the evolution of laws, norms and institutions to regulate the exchanges and interactions between people, constitute, as it were, the unintentional consequences of individual self-interest.

The maximization of profit, as a relevant basic principle of human behaviour and as a starting point for the analysis of collective phenomena, has expressed itself in the economy in particular. Under the influence of the 19th-century French sociologist and pedagogue Durkheim, the concept of values and norms as behaviour-regulating mechanisms has received much more attention in sociological theory and has been elaborated to a far greater extent than the individual desire for profit maximization. As stated before, however, the profit principle is being developed and applied to sociologically relevant phenomena in increasing measure. In this chapter we try to apply this approach to analyse the social phenomenon of gender inequality in the labour market. Important elements of this attempt are the extension of the principle of 'profit' by so-called sociological arguments, and the introduction of relevant institutional constraints. We hope in this way to avoid arriving at 2 highly one-sided views on the social phenomenon of inequality between women and men: the assumption that inequality between the sexes is caused exclusively by the individual choices of men and women or the opposite view that inequality is only a reflection of a constellation of norms, values and social arrangements, without any reference to individual considerations, definitions of the situation and behavioural choices.

Social phenomena, such as the inequality between men and women in the European labour markets, can be analysed from the point of view of the relevant actors who take decisions in a social context which is characterized by constraints. Before elaborating on these constraints, we will first say a few works about the objectives individuals strive to achieve when making their decisions. In principle, it can be assumed that people strive to reach the same goals or utilities. On this general level such goals and utilities are described in a vague and abstract manner. For example, physical well-being and social approval can be described as important and goals that all people strive to achieve. Focusing on the topic of this book – inequality between women and men in the European labour market – that could mean that both women and men endeavour to improve their positions during their careers. Such an improvement signifies a higher income (a rough approximation to the goal 'well-being') and higher status (likewise, a rough approximation to the goal 'social approval' or 'social standing'). This general proposition requires a far more subtle elaboration but, to simplify the argument, we will conclude that in their working life men and women aim to reach similar goals: a good job, a steady income, social approval and opportunities to move up to a better position. The reason that men and women do not achieve these goals in the same measure is because they must both work within constraints which – on average – turn out differently for the two sexes. Before we have a closer look at the 'gendered' nature of these constraints, we want to say a few words about the considerations and definitions of the situation which provide the basis for the decisions made by men and women.

A job or a career can be analysed as a continuing process of considerations and decision-making. Examples of such decisions are: should I continue in my current job, or should I try to find a better one; although I might not be able to manage financially, should I quit my full-time job and accept a part-time one; should I interrupt my career temporarily to look after my children, or am I taking too big a risk by doing so; should I attempt to re-enter the work-force, or would it be useless since I have done unpaid work for such a long time; should I accept the promotion or will it jeopardize my relationship with my partner? All these options have their pros and cons. These pros and cons can be expressed in a number of ways: economically, financially, socially, psychologically and emotionally. Economic prospects can be weighed against social rewards: 'If I keep my full-time job I will earn more and retain my chances for promotion, but concurrently I will be reproached for neglecting my children.' Sometimes practical advantages have to be compared to emotional cost: 'If I ask my husband to do more of the household chores it will make it easier for me, but at the same time I would find such a situation emotionally charged as he gives me the feeling that he does not really like doing housework.' Of course one can argue that in reality many women have no options at all; they simply have to earn a living, and that's that. Or they have no opportunity whatsoever to get a better job. This is true in many cases, but what this says from the theoretical perspective being presented here is that in these situations the constraints women face are so rigid that every other behavioural 'choice' comes at too high a price.

The relationship between benefits and costs is defined by each person individually. The theory predicts that one will make that choice which gives the greatest return of profit. This profit cannot be expressed in terms of money alone, as the above will have made clear. Profit can also be seen in terms of satisfaction, confirmation of role expectations and norms, and avoidance of conflict. This 'sociological' expansion of the definition of utilities or profits makes it possible to apply this theoretical point of view to social phenomena, for example the question as to why gender inequalities on the labour market are of such a persistent nature.

We would not be doing justice to the complexity of the phenomenon of sex inequality in the labour market, however, if we focused only on the behaviour and options available to the individual. People do not behave in a vacuum, but in an institutional context characterized by economic, social and cultural conditions. To obtain a clear understanding of why people behave in the labour market as they do, this institutional context must be mapped out precisely. If the differences in 'social outcomes' between men and women are at stake, then the way in which this institutional context differs in its characteristics for men and women needs to be clarified. It is precisely these differences in institutional constraints which account for how differences in the behavioural patterns of men and women are established. In turn, these differences in behaviour reproduce the social phenomenon of gender inequality in the labour market.

Institutional constraints at 2 levels

In this section we make a distinction between 2 institutional contexts, both of which are important if one is to understand the behaviour of men and women in the labour market. The first refers to the institutional constraints at the macro level of society. Which institutional arrangements have implications for what men and women are doing in the labour market and how do these implications work out? The second institutional context refers to organizations and companies. Which institutional constraints are present here and how will they influence the decisions men and women take about their jobs and careers? On both levels a 'gendered' institutional context can be assumed. This means that the relevant institutional conditions have – on average – a systematically different impact on the behaviour of men than they have on women. This differing impact results in a different set of pros and cons influencing men's and women's behavioural choices. By relating institutional constraints to individual choices in this way, a theoretical connection is made between the macro (or meso) level of institutions and the individual level of behaviour. This is an important connection, not only in a theoretical sense, but also for policy reasons. If the European Union wishes to diminish social inequality between men and women, it needs to understand the causes of these persistent patterns of inequality. An important element is that specific constraints lead the behaviour of men and women in different directions. If this behaviour is to change, the constraints must be altered. Before we discuss the various policies intended to effectuate this change in the following chapters, then, we first need an overview of what the relevant constraints are.

Institutional constraints can be described both in cultural and in structural terms. The most important cultural constraints within which men and women arrange their occupational lives are the values and norms, role expectations and 'taken-for-granted' assumptions which define men's and women's social tasks. There are interesting differences in emphasis between the welfare states of Europe on this point, which we will discuss later. Despite national differences in the degree to which traditional value patterns still apply, in general we can say that the role of breadwinner and the role of domestic and family caretaker are still divided largely along gender lines. This division has an important impact on the cost–benefit ratio which applies to the labour participation of men and women. It is generally 'more expensive' for women to focus on their careers than it is for men. The cost varies, not only from one country to the next, but also between various groups of women within each individual country. For example, it is generally more 'taken for granted' – and therefore less 'expensive' in a social sense – that highly educated women will continue to work throughout their entire lives than it is for women with a lower level of education. This assumption is related in turn to the benefits of performing highly skilled work. Such benefits are not simply financial, but also have to do with status, commitment and intrinsic satisfaction. At this level, benefits serve as a powerful incentive to ignore traditional value patterns, much more so than when work outside the home produces few rewards. Such mechanisms have a cumulative effect. For example, if a woman decides to continue working full time after having children, her chances of achieving a successful career will increase. Career interruptions related to family duties, on the other hand, reduce these chances (see Chapter 5). As a woman sees her chance at a successful career grow, she will be less prepared to make concessions on this point. The opposite is true when her career opportunities have been reduced due to interruptions earlier on in life.

Cultural constraints not only affect the behaviour of men and women in the labour market directly, they also do so indirectly. Cultural conditions do in fact constitute the basis of structural arrangements in Europe which affect the decisions men and women take in their occupational life. Examples of important structural arrangements are taxation and social security systems. These kinds of systems are implicitly or more explicitly based on norms and values related to the social tasks of men and women. If these tax and social security systems make clear distinctions between the role of breadwinner and the role of caretaker, then they will generally discourage women's occupational participation. If they are based largely on gender equality and on an individual approach to each citizen, then they will encourage women's paid labour. Such encouraging and discouraging effects can be interpreted in terms of benefits and costs. The more discouraging the effect of the tax and social security system on women's paid labour and careers, the higher the costs which have to be met by those women who wish to achieve an independent social status. The variation between European countries in the extent to which the effects of these institutional constraints are encouraged or discouraged demonstrates the importance of analysing patterns in men's and women's labour-force participation in terms of rational decisions in a constrained environment. We deal with this in greater detail in the next section of this chapter.

It is not only tax and social security systems which can be analysed in terms of institutional constraints. Another significant institutional fact is, for instance, the availability of child care and parental leave for working parents. If there are ample facilities, women have a better chance of engaging in paid labour than if those facilities are hardly available. Here also, there are significant differences between European countries (see Chapter 10). Legislation, case law and the degree to which positive action programmes are implemented in a country can also be considered institutional constraints, within which women have greater or fewer opportunities to develop a career and to reach an independent socioeconomic status. The countries within the European Union are all subject to the same legislative regime so far as equal pay and the equal treatment of men and women in the labour force are concerned. Yet the legal variation within the Union is reason enough to include legislation, case law and positive action as relevant institutional contexts in relation to men's and women's paid labour (see Chapters 9, 11 and 12).

The question of more or less implicit genderedness is not confined to the macro level of social institutions. It also applies to the way in which corporations are organized, both culturally and structurally. As stated earlier in this chapter, Moss Kanter (1993) has focused in her analysis of the careers of men and women on the connection between structural and cultural constraints within corporations and the 'decisions' people make about their jobs and careers. Their positions in the opportunity structure and their proportional representation within groups considerably influence the opportunities available to them to build up a career. The implicit genderedness of these structural conditions becomes clear when we consider that women are more often confronted with its disadvantageous consequences than are men.

Besides opportunity structures and proportional representations, there are other organizational constraints which affect the 'price' of a career for men and women. Recruitment and selection procedures, for example, determine whether or not a person will be employed by a company. If job advertisements are directed solely at men, or radiate a distinctly 'male' profile, women will have to overcome further obstacles and thus incur higher costs in order to be considered for a position. The same is true for selection procedures. If the requirements are not stated precisely, the chance exists that they will be broadened during the selection procedure because, for example, some applicants may be overqualified for the position. This has a disadvantageous effect on newcomers to the labour market, such as women and people of colour, because they often do not have extra qualifications at their disposal.

In analysing the gendered character of organizations, cultural characteristics must also be considered. An organization's culture can be defined by values and norms, by ideas about what is positive and worth striving for in the organizational context. Schein (1985) speaks of 'taken-for-granted assumptions', i.e. assumptions which have a high level of self-evidence within a corporation. In general, these taken-for-granted assumptions are not up for discussion, unless fundamental alterations are in process. The increasing number of women in significant positions and the growing ranks of employees, both women and men, with family commitments could well induce such a process of fundamental change.

Opinions about the place of women within an organization are hardly ever stated explicitly, but they are a part of organizational culture. Opinions may, for instance, be held about women not being able to perform certain duties, whereas other duties are regarded as typical women's tasks. These types of taken-for-granted assumptions are generally not neutral classifications, although they are often expressed and experienced this way. They usually imply relationships of authority or inequality, which are expressed by the structure of the organization and in the way jobs are evaluated (see Chapter 12). For example, the primary jobs in industry, which are those that contribute directly to the production process, are often filled by men. Positions derived from these, usually in the office, often form a women's domain. A similar classification occurs in the higher echelons. Managers are often men. Support staff functions, like those in the personnel department, are more often filled by women. Inequalities in the evaluation of the different jobs, and thus disparities in earnings, are legitimized by referring to the more or less central contribution that the job in question makes to the primary production process.

The influence which organizational culture has on the career opportunities of men and women also becomes manifest in the opportunities to work (temporarily) on a part-time basis in higher-level jobs. Research conducted in the information technology sector in the Netherlands (De Olde and Van Doorne-Huiskes, 1991) revealed that companies there had decisive ideas about the amount of dedication and commitment required from professionals. The culture 'radiated' by the companies was young, dynamic, enthusiastic and professional, backed by the independence, autonomy and capability of the information technologists. Within this enthusiastic working environment certain women-unfriendly attitudes became apparent at the same instant. Not because female fellow workers were excluded from the organization – on the contrary, women were regarded as competent colleagues – but because working part time at this level was found unsuitable. Part-time work, even if the job was for 30 hours per week, was thought to conflict with the necessity of being continuously available to the customers. Total commitment to the company was an important feature of the culture, as was the principle that customers should deal with one consultant only. There were few challenges to this culture, particularly by men. The result was that most women found themselves in a dilemma around the age of 30. In view of their professional experience they should have come into consideration for senior positions. However, promotion to this level was hard to combine with raising children. The companies lost well-qualified and experienced female employees in that way. If career patterns had been made more flexible, both the companies and the female professionals would have benefited. Similar flexibility for male professionals would have offered men a chance at a better 'work–family fit' as well. We will deal with this more extensively in Chapter 11.

We conclude that institutional constraints in societies and in corporations have a different impact on men than they have on women when it comes to the 'price' of trying for a better job on the labour market. These differences have consequences for the decisions men and women make about their work and family life. At the same time, the collective response of countless men and women to the gendered institutional environment has created a persistent social phenomenon: gender inequality in the labour market.

Differences between countries: the impact of welfare state regimes on the roles of men and women

Until now the focus in this chapter has been on inequalities between men and women. There has been little discussion so far of the difference in socio-economic position between women in the countries of the European Union. These differences are important, however, because they indicate that institutional constraints in the European countries are not all of one type and have different impacts on the lives of women (and of men). In the 1980s Chatab, Van Doorne-Huiskes and Ultee (1987) carried out an international comparative project focusing on the relationship between some specific institutional constraints and the extent and quality of female employment. They started from the assumption that as a country achieves a higher level of economic development, and as a country experiences a longer period of social democratic government, the inequality between men and women in the labour market will decrease. The economic hypothesis is based on the theory of industrial societies (Kerr, Dunlop and Myers, 1960), which states that an industrial society will not be able to function without a well-educated labour force. As the level of education rises the income differences will – most likely – diminish, not only within the male working population, but also between men and women. The political hypothesis is based on the conviction that social democratic parties will put greater emphasis on equality between citizens than will denominational or liberal parties. An empirical test, based on data collected in 22 countries, proved these theories right: as countries achieve a higher level of economic development, the differences between men and women – both in participation rate and level of remuneration – become smaller. The same holds for the span of social democratic government: the longer a country experiences social democratic government, the smaller the inequalities between men and women.

Research such as this, which is based on a large number of countries, is relatively abstract in nature. It does not reveal a great deal about the specific arrangements of each country and the influence which these arrangements have on the socio-economic positions of men and women there. For some time now feminist social scientists have debated the impact of welfare state regimes on the degree to which women can achieve full citizenship. This debate has focused far more on specific institutional constraints (Langan and Ostner, 1990; Borchorst, 1991; Lewis and Astrom, 1992; Plantenga and Van Doorne-Huiskes, 1992; Lewis, 1993) and has made extensive use of the typology devised by Esping-Andersen, although not without criticism. Esping-Andersen (1990) distinguishes 3 different types of welfare states based on issues of stratification, employment and decommodification. Decommodification is described as the degree to which people are independent of pure market forces. One important criticism levelled by feminists is that Esping-Andersen does not deal systematically with the position of women in the welfare states and that the notion of decommodification is focused entirely on the relationship between the market and the state. For women, however, the importance of the welfare state is not only that they become more or less independent of market forces but that they become more or less independent of family responsibilities. Welfare states therefore can be differentiated not only in the way they guarantee a livelihood without reliance on the market but also in the way they guarantee a livelihood outside or alongside the family (Plantenga and Van Doorne-Huiskes, 1992).

Esping-Andersen distinguishes the following 3 types of welfare state: the social-democratic welfare state regime, the conservative/corporative welfare state regime and the liberal welfare state regime. The social-democratic welfare state can be described as a regime which promotes equality among its citizens and which is committed to guaranteeing full employment for men as well as for women. The costs of raising a family are consequently largely socialized, to maximize the individual's capacity to achieve economic independence. An elaborate system of public services such as child care, sick care and elderly care ensures that everyone who is able to participate in the labour market in fact does so. One of the basic assumptions of the social-democratic welfare regime is that men and women are equivalent. The tax system is individualized and the government takes a neutral position *vis-à-vis* the choice of a particular lifestyle and/or division of roles. The emphasis on equal opportunities does not necessarily mean that the outcomes for women and men are equal. As we remarked earlier in this chapter, the labour market is still highly segregated along gender lines, because women work to a large extent in public services. In addition, the fact that women do the bulk of the remaining unpaid labour is not really challenged (Leira, 1993). Important for the argument in this chapter is, however, that the institutional constraints of the social-democratic welfare states encourage more than discourage women's employment. Cultural and structural constraints in this particular welfare state regime are still 'gendered', specifically in relation to unpaid work, but less so than in the other regimes. Within Europe, Denmark, Finland, Sweden and Norway come nearest to this particular welfare state regime.

Within the so-called conservative/corporatist welfare state regimes, the family plays an important role as the anchor of social stability and individual happiness. Unlike the social-democratic welfare state, this welfare regime is not so much an employer as a financial compensator. The state sees to financial compensation whenever the outcomes of the market are considered unaccept-able or whenever labour-force participation is thought of as undesirable. The role of compensator reveals itself in an elaborate system of breadwinner facili-ties within the social security and tax systems. Men and women are not treated as equal. Whereas men are seen as paid workers, women are seen primarily as wives and mothers. Because the emphasis is on the preservation of the tradi-tional family structure and not on labour-force participation, child-care and parental leave facilities are rather underdeveloped. Within Europe, Germany and Italy come nearest to this kind of welfare state.

In the liberal welfare state regimes, means-tested social assistance and modest social security plans predominate. There is a great belief in the blessings of the market and in its self-regulating capacity. Whereas one can say that the social-democratic welfare state regime treats men and women as equivalent, and the conservative/corporatist treats them as different, the liberal welfare state regime treats men and women as equals, disregarding differences in care responsibility. The necessity of state-provided child-care or parental leave facilities is more or less denied (Lewis, 1993). Because liberal welfare states have only a limited system of breadwinner facilities, the labour-force participation of women is rather high. This liberal welfare state regime applies to the USA. Within Europe, the UK comes nearest to this type, especially since the Thatcher government.

As interesting as the topic of welfare states and their impact on the roles of men and women may be, this chapter is not the proper place to continue this discussion. The important point for this chapter is that the theoretical perspective of individual choices within a context of institutional constraints provides a useful starting point to analyse socio-economic differences between women in the countries of Europe. Like the analysis of social inequality between women and men, the primary emphasis is not on what people hope to achieve by their actions. To put it in its simplest form, the assumption is that all Europeans have more or less the same goals or utilities. Instead, the emphasis is on the nature of the relevant institutional constraints, whose specific incentives steer the behavioural choices of people in a particular direction. These behavioural choices in turn constitute the basic fundaments of collective or social phenomena.

CONCLUSIONS

This chapter has presented a theoretical analysis of gender inequalities in the European labour market. One of the important questions raised was whether and how economic and sociological points of view might be related to each other. To attempt this type of integration, a simple model of behaviour has been used based on the assumption that people try to maximize their 'satisfaction' within a context of institutional constraints. Relevant constraints in the case of gender inequalities are social norms, values and taken-for-granted assumptions about what is 'natural' in the behaviour of women and men, and structural arrangements which reflect these cultural ideas. These are, for instance, tax and social security systems, legal systems and the degree to which care facilities are available. It is not only society as a whole which constitutes a relevant institutional context for analysing gender inequalities in the labour market; the institutional context of corporations or organizations in a more general sense also has to be taken into account. Institutional constraints appear to be 'gendered', in the sense that the conditions for maximizing satisfaction for men and women differ. It is precisely this genderedness which has to be reduced when equality between the sexes is a policy goal.

Societies differ in the degree to which they can be described as gendered. That is an important explanation for the socio-economic differences between women in Europe.

An analysis in terms of institutional constraints makes clear that the most important points of departure for improving the position of women in the European labour market lie in changing the institutional context. That is by no means a minor transformation process. The following chapters will explore this idea in more detail.

REFERENCES

ACKER, J. (1991) Hierarchies, jobs, bodies; a theory of gendered organizations, in J. Lorber and S. A. Farell (eds.), *The Social Construction of Gender*, Sage Publications, Newbury Park.
BARDWICK, J. M. and DOUVAN, E. (1971) Ambivalence: the socialization of women, in V. Gormick and B. K. Moran (eds.), *Women in Sexist Society*, Basic Books, New York.
BECKER, G. S. (1957) *The Economics of Discrimination*, University of Chicago Press, Chicago.
BECKER, G. S. (1965) A theory of the allocation of time, *Economic Journal*, Vol. 80, no. 200, pp. 493–517.
BORCHORST, A. (1991) The Scandinavian welfare states, patriarchal, gender-neutral or woman-friendly?, paper presented at the European Research Conference 'Women in the Changing Europe', University of Aalborg, Denmark, 18–22 August 1991.
BOUDON, R. (1981) *De logica van het sociale*, Samsom, Alphen aan den Rijn/Brussels.
CHATAB, J., VAN DOORNE-HUISKES, J. and ULTEE, W. C. (1987) Ongelijkheden tussen mannen en vrouwen; enige verklaringen van verschillen tussen geindustrialiseerde landen getoetst, *Sociale Wetenschappen*, Vol. 30, pp. 279–300.
COLEMAN, J. S. (1990) *Foundations of Social Theory*, Harvard University Press, Cambridge, Mass.
COSER, R. L. and ROKOFF, G. (1971) Women in the occupational world; social disruption, *Social Problems*, Vol. 18, pp. 535-54.
DAVIDSON, M. J. and COOPER C. L. (eds.) (1993) *European Women in Business and Management*, Paul Chapman, London.
DOERINGER, P. B. and PIORE, M. J. (1971) *Internal Labour Markets and Manpower Analysis*, Heath, New York.
ENGLAND, P. (1992) *Comparable Worth. Theories and Evidence*, Aldine de Gruyter, New York.
ESPING-ANDERSEN, G. (1990) *The Three Worlds of Welfare Capitalism*, Polity Press, Cambridge.
FESTINGER, L. (1957) *A Theory of Cognitive Dissonance*, Stanford University Press, Stanford.
FRIEZE, I. H. et al. (1978) *Women and Sexroles*, Norton and Company, New York.
HEIDER, F. (1946) Attitudes and cognitive organization, *Journal of Psychology*, Vol. 21, pp. 107–12.

JOHNSON, G. E. and STAFFORD, F. P. (1974) The earnings and promotion of women faculty, *American Economic Review*, Vol. 64, no. 6, pp. 888-903.
DE JONG, A. M. (1983) *Gelijke behandeling en het personeelsbeleid*, Kluwer, Deventer.
KERR, C., DUNLOP, J. T. and MYERS, C. A. (1960) *Industrialism and Industrial Man*, Harvard University Press, Cambridge, Mass.
LANGAN, M. and OSTNER, I. (1990) Gender and welfare, towards a comparative framework, paper presented at the Social Policy Association Conference, Bath (UK), 12–15 July 1990.
LEIRA, A. (1993) The 'woman-friendly' welfare state? The case of Norway and Sweden, in Lewis (1993).
LEWIS, J. (ed.) (1993) *Women and Social Policies in Europe*, Edward Elgar Publishing Ltd, Hants (UK).
LEWIS, J. and ASTRÖM, G. (1992) Equality, difference and state welfare: labour market and family policies in Sweden, *Feminist Studies*, Vol. 18, pp. 59–87.
LINDENBERG, S. (1985) An assessment of the new political economy, *Sociological Theory*, Vol. 3, no. 1, pp. 99-114.
LLOYD, C. B. and NIEMI, B. T. (1979) *The Economics of Sex Differentials*, Columbia University Press, New York.
MOSS KANTER, R. (1993) *Men and Women of the Corporation*, Basic Books, New York.
OLDE, C. DE and VAN DOORNE-HUISKES, J. (1991) Positions of women in information technology in the Netherlands: education, job characteristics and proposals for an equal opportunity policy, in I. V. Erikson, B. A. Kitschenkam and K. G. Tijdens (eds.) *Women, Work and the Computerization of Education*, North-Holland, Amsterdam, pp. 347-62
OPP, K. D. and HUMMELL, H. (1973) *Soziales Verhalten und soziale Systeme*, Athenäum, Frankfurt.
OTT, M. (1985) *Assepoesters en Kroonprinsessen. Een onderzoek naar de minderheidspositie van agentes en verplegers*, SUA, Amsterdam.
PLANTENGA, J. and VAN DOORNE-HUISKES, J. (1992) Gender, citizenship and welfare: a European Perspective, paper presented at the first Conference on Sociology, Vienna, 26–29 August 1992, p. 23.
POLACHEK, S. W. and SIEBERT, W. S. (1993) *The Economics of Earnings*, Cambridge University Press, Cambridge (UK).
PRINGLE, R. (1988) *Secretaries Talk*, Verso, London.
ROSSI, A. S. (1965) Women in science: why so few?, *Science*, 28 May, pp. 1196-202.
SCHEIN, E. H. (1985) *Organizational Culture and Leadership. A Dynamic View*, Jossey-Bass, San Francisco.
TAVRIS, C. and OFFIR, C. (1977) *The Longest War*, Harcourt Brace, New York.
THUROW, L. C. (1975) *Generating Inequality*, Basic Books, New York.

CHAPTER 8

The European Equal Opportunities Policy

ELLIE ROELOFS

INTRODUCTION

Does Europe have anything to offer women? The answer to this question may vary from country to country. The previous chapters indicated that there is considerable variation between the various member states in the labour-market position of women. If we compare the labour-market positions of men and women, however, we also find striking similarities between countries. This chapter will explore one of the factors behind such similarities and differences: the European Union's policy on women. We shall see that equal opportunities policy belongs to those areas of social policy in which the European Union is most active when it comes to policy that has a direct impact on its citizens. It is important to note that European social policy is subject to various restrictions. For a clear understanding of the way in which equal opportunities policy is given shape, we must understand the possibilities and impossibilities of social policy in general. This requires some knowledge about the way in which decision-making takes place and who are the most important agents in this process. We will also be looking at the policy instruments. Next we will turn to the various policy initiatives intended to improve the position of women, focusing on, in addition to the equal opportunities directives, the first 2 action programmes and the role of the structural funds. We will explore in detail the third action programme (1992–5), and, in the final section, discuss what the concrete contribution of the European Union has been with regard to improving the position of women in the labour market.

EUROPEAN UNION, ECONOMIC UNION OR COMMON MARKET?

Article 2 of the Treaty of Rome (1957), one of the founding treaties of the European Union (formerly the European Community) describes the most important aims of the Union as follows:

> The Community shall have as its task, by establishing a common market and progressively approximating the economic policies of member States, to promote throughout the Community, a harmonious development of economic

activities, a continuous and balanced expansion, an increase in stability, an accelerated raising of the standard of living and closer relations between the States belonging to it.

From the very beginning the European Union concentrated on setting up a common market; in other words, its intention was and is to break down existing trade barriers between the member states, including import tariffs, differences in technical specifications, and domestic regulations which prevent citizens of other member states from practising a certain profession. Its aim is to achieve the free movement of capital, services, goods and people between the member states. Most of its policy initiatives focus on achieving this aim – a good example is the '1992' project, in which the Union attempted to accelerate the process of creating one large internal market by setting out a series of strictly planned directives. The December 1992 deadline was viewed largely as an intermediate step and served mainly a symbolic function. The process of European integration, then, is largely one of economic integration. Its budget is evidence that the Union tends to emphasize aspects of policy other than those its member states do. It devotes a disproportionally large amount of its resources to agriculture and fisheries – in 1992, 50.7% of the EU's overall expenditure of 63.9 billion ecus (European currency units: a unit of account in which all the various EU currencies are represented, worth approximately £1.30) (Commission, 1993).

The principal framework in which the Union develops its policy is formed by the Treaties. Their importance, however, can be overestimated (Nugent, 1991; Cram, 1993). A reference in one of the Treaties is no guarantee that initiatives will in fact be taken in a certain field. Conversely, according to Nugent (1991), the Union sometimes acts in areas over which it actually has no legal jurisdiction. For example, those parts of the Treaties setting out a common policy on transport and on macro-economic co-operation have led to only very limited concrete policy measures; on the other hand, since the early 1970s the Union has been quite active in the field of environmental policy, a subject for which the Treaties make no provision.

The Treaties do provide a legal basis for social policy, although the articles which refer specifically to this subject bestow only very restricted powers on the Union and are, moreover, unclear in their intentions (Crijns, 1990). Compared with the Union's economic policy, which includes the setting up of a common market and the policy on agriculture, its social policy has always lagged behind. Social integration generally becomes an issue only when it is viewed as an element of economic integration, an attitude which becomes clear if we look at the Union's social policy framework. There are 3 social policy areas in which the Union is clearly active, and all 3 are relevant to its economic objectives. The following examples will serve to illustrate.

The first area of social policy in which the Union is active is the co-ordination of social insurance schemes. The member states consider it desirable to develop a policy on this issue because the free movement of people, and therefore the optimum functioning of the common market, is hampered by existing major differences in national social security schemes. Union policy is directed in particular at co-ordinating the various systems more effectively, leaving the individual systems intact. The EU's policy determines which rules apply, for example, to someone who lives in a country other than the one in which he or she works. The policy is concerned largely with employees, the self-employed and their families, and not with benefits recipients.

In no other field of social policy is the Union as active as on the issue of health and safety at work. The reason it has focused so much attention on this issue can, once again, be traced to the fact that major differences in working conditions can have a direct impact on international competitive relations. In the very worst case, that would mean that the member states with a progressive policy would see their position deteriorate. Health and safety in the workplace is the only aspect of social policy on which the most powerful decision-making body of the Union, the Council of Ministers, votes by qualified majority rather than unanimously.

The third area of social policy mentioned frequently is the equal treatment of men and women. Here too, considerations of competition played an important role in motivating the first policy steps. It was the French government which insisted on a set of regulations at European level, because France had already begun to introduce legislation on equal pay for men and women. The French were afraid that the major differences in pay between the sexes in the other member states might turn out to be economically disadvantageous for France. Another explanation frequently heard with regard to the interest that Europe has given to equal opportunities policy is the fact that, by doing so, the Union is reaching 50% of its electorate. In effect, the policy is being used to convince a large number of citizens of the importance of Europe.

It seems, then, that even the decision-making on a common social policy is motivated by economic considerations. Cram (1993), however, questions this economic motivation (to which the Union itself has consistently subscribed, incidentally). She argues that there are many other social factors – for example, legislation on employment terms and conditions – which have an impact on competition but which have not been made the subject of a common European policy. In Cram's view the development of a policy does not hinge on whether a social issue will have an effect on competition. More relevant is whether the policy will cost the Union any money. That is because it is easier to co-ordinate the various policies of the member states if it is the employers and not the national governments which must bear the financial consequences of doing so. Although this theory on the background of EU policy should be investigated in greater detail, it is obvious that the instruments which the Union chooses to set out its social policy generally require only limited investments, especially when compared with the investments made by the national governments.

The social policy framework is restricted not only to certain policy themes and instruments but also to specific target groups. These restrictions are reflected in the Social Charter signed by 11 of the member states in 1989. The Charter sets out the basic social rights of the 'citizen', but it is actually more concerned with the employee: its formal title is 'The Community Charter of Fundamental Social Rights for Workers'. The Charter is a frame of reference for future social policy. Women are mentioned as a separate category in an article on the necessity of equal opportunties. Indeed, the policy on this issue is restricted almost exclusively to the labour-market position of women, whereas other social categories, such as ethnic minorities or the disabled, are given far less attention.

Before discussing the nature of the policy initiatives which the Union has taken for the benefit of women, we will first look at the various institutions and instruments which play a role in developing this policy.

POLICY AGENTS AND POLICY INSTRUMENTS

In the previous section it became clear that the European Union is actively involved in a large number of issues, but that it gives certain issues far more attention than others. The set of tasks which the European Union has set for itself is unlike that of the national member states. The latter determine whether or not a decision is taken in Brussels, through their direct representatives in the Council of Ministers, the Union's most important decision-making body. Other agents which assist in decision-making are the European Commission, the European Parliament and the European Court of Justice. On the issue of policy as related to women, the following bodies are also important: the Equal Opportunities Unit, the Information Office of Women's Organizations and Press and lobbies such as the European Network of Women (ENOW).

Policy agents

THE COUNCIL OF MINISTERS   The ministers who sit in the Council change according to the issue being decided upon. Decisions on women's issues often require the presence of the Ministers of Social Affairs. The Council is the most important legislative body and votes on proposals submitted by the Commission after the European Parliament has been consulted. The process of decision-making is often quite slow because the Council is frequently required to decide by unanimous vote. This also applies to the policy on equal opportunities. The requirement of unanimity has delayed or blocked a large number of initiatives – specifically in the field of social policy – for many years. The European Council, composed of the government leaders of the member states and the president of France (the head of state), meets twice yearly. It is the European Council which takes the most important political decisions on the future of the Union.

THE EUROPEAN COMMISSION The European Commission, the administrative executive of the Union, plays the main role in the decision-making process. The Commission has the major task of preparing policy and implementing decisions. The top ranks consist of 17 commissioners who are each responsible for specific policy domains. In theory they act independently, but they are nominated by the member states, so that in practice the Commission is clearly political in nature. Indeed, the member states compete for the portfolios which they consider important. The commissioners are backed up by an administrative staff divided into 23 directorates-general and about a dozen services. The duties and responsibilities of the Commission are described in the Treaties as follows:

1 to introduce initiatives; in theory, the Commission alone has the power to propose legislation at the European level;
2 to draft and develop Community policy;
3 to implement Community legislation;
4 to ensure compliance by the member states with Community Treaties and decisions (de Gier, 1991).

With regard to social policy, the Commission has always been obliged to adjust its pace and scope to the wishes of the Council. The member states have been reluctant to relinquish authority on social issues to the Union. The Commission has therefore learned to manoeuvre carefully and to increase its level of influence incrementally, step by step.

There are 2 directorates-general covering women's policy issues: DG-V (Employment, Industrial Relations and Social Affairs) and DG-X (Information, Communication and Culture). The Equal Opportunities Unit falls under the first, and the Information Office of Women's Organizations and Press under the second.

The Equal Opportunities Unit drafts policy proposals targeting the improvement of the position of women. The unit is also responsible for implementing policy as formulated in the so-called Equal Opportunities Action Programmes. That means that it prepares decisions as to which of the many organizations submitting project applications within the framework of the action programme will in fact be awarded financial support. The Unit has an important task in co-ordinating research and the various networks which have been set up by the EU. It also collects data on the state of affairs in the various member states and monitors the level of compliance with EU regulations in the field of equal opportunities. The Information Office provides women with information on developments in the various members states and on the EU policy which concerns them.

THE EUROPEAN PARLIAMENT The European Parliament is elected directly by the citizens of the various member states and has only limited powers. It thus cannot be compared with a national parliament. The European Parliament supervises the policy-making process of the Commission. It has a right of co-decision in respect of the budget but for most other issues its role is only advisory and the Council is authorized to disregard its recommendations. Despite its limited formal powers, the Parliament does have some influence on the political agenda and the decision-making process in the Union: it exercises this influence by continually demanding attention for certain issues, by asking questions and by submitting reports to the Commission to convince it to take action. The European Parliament is an indisputable proponent of a European social policy. It plays an important role in drafting equal opportunities policy. For example, it asked for legislation on equal pay years before the first EU legal measure on this subject came into effect (Pillinger, 1992). The Parliament has also made its interest in equal opportunities policy clear by setting up a parliamentary committee on the rights of women. This committee analyses the impact that all different types of EU policy will have on women and advises other parliamentary committees on its findings (Ophuysen, 1994).

THE EUROPEAN COURT OF JUSTICE   The judicial power of the European Union is exercised by the European Court of Justice, which has its seat in Luxembourg. The Court is an independent body which monitors compliance with EU law by adjudicating in disputes between the member states or between the member states and the Commission. It also has an important task in interpreting EU law within the context of the so-called preliminary ruling procedure. Citizens may submit an appeal to their national court based on a specific EU law, and the national courts may request a ruling from European Court on that particular point of EU law. The role of the Court has grown increasingly important. One reason is that many EU laws are somewhat ambiguous, so that the Court is regularly asked to interpret them. The issue of equal opportunities is a good example of a policy domain in which the jurisprudence of the European Court has played a pioneering role. Chapter 9 will discuss this jurisprudence in detail.

LOBBIES AND ADVISORY ORGANIZATIONS   Lobbies play an important role in the European decision-making process. They are important channels of information for both Parliament and the Commission and attempt to influence the Union's policy. Women's organizations have made an important contribution to creating a European policy for women. In the early 1980s various organizations decided to join forces in the European Network of Women (ENOW), set up to give women and their representative organizations a sounding board allowing them to represent their interests more effectively at the EU level and helping them understand the various developments in the member states. ENOW has managed to stay alive thanks to the grassroots efforts of many women (Pillinger, 1992). In recent years the organization has focused in particular on the issue of poverty.

In 1987, at the initiative of the European Commission, the European Women's Lobby was set up as a co-operative effort between women's organizations in the 12 member states. 'Its aim is to ensure that there is continual progress in policy development and that a constant dialogue is maintained between women's organisations and the Community institutions' (Pillinger, 1992, p. 73). The European Trade Union Confederation (ETUC) has also founded a women's committee focusing on women's issues in the European labour movement. This committee, which will be further discussed in Chapter 13, is represented in the Women's Lobby and, through ETUC representatives, on the Commission's Advisory Committee on Equal Opportunities (Pillinger, 1992). The agricultural organization COPA, furthermore, has a committee which is concerned with women's affairs and which is also represented on the Advisory Committee. The latter committee, which was founded in 1980, is the successor to an *ad hoc* advisory group which met regularly from 1974 onwards to advise the Commission on policy measures. The present Advisory Committee is an official advisory body to the Commission. In addition to representatives from COPA and ETUC, the Committee has representatives from the national governments (Ophuysen, 1994). In 1993 the 'Black women in Europe' network was founded to deal with the special problems encountered by women from ethnic minorities. As Chapter 4 made clear, these women often face additional challenges.

Figure 8.1   Stages in the EU policy-making process in the field of Equal Opportunities

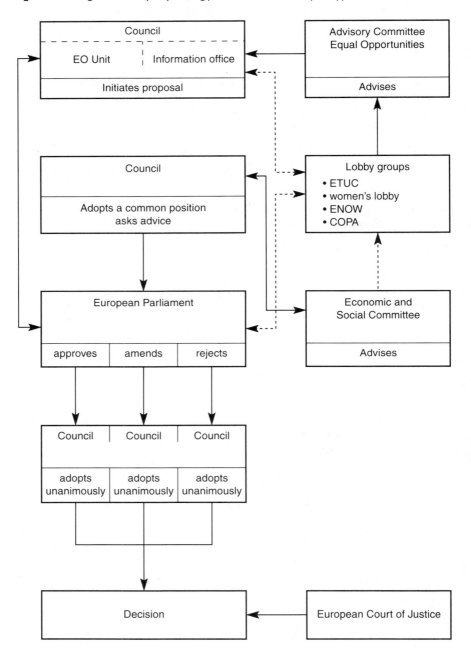

Figure 8.1 puts the policy agents described above in diagrammatic form.

Policy instruments

Policy can be formulated in a number of different ways. In this chapter we will adopt the classification used by Cram (1993), who distinguishes between 4 types of policy instruments: regulatory policy, 'soft' law, EU action policy, and process and organization.

Regulatory policy consists of regulations, directives and decisions laid down by the Commission. Table 8.1 indicates the important differences between these instruments.

When a legal measure is directly applicable, individual citizens are able to initiate judicial proceedings in their national courts based on the measure. It need not have been integrated into national law.

The instruments discussed above are binding on states and/or on individuals. In the field of equal opportunities policy, the European Union has made particular use of the directive, the most appropriate policy instrument for bringing norms in the various member states in line with one another. The advantage of the directive is that it gives the member states a certain period of time in which they are required to amend their legislation in accordance with the EU's norm. Regulations, on the other hand, are immediately binding, and decisions are unsuitable because they are not generally applicable. So far the EU has adopted five important directives in the field of equal opportunities. We will discuss these in the following section.

Soft laws are the recommendations and opinions set out by the Council and the Commission. Compliance with the 2 instruments is much more voluntary than in the case of a directive, for example. There are no sanctions attached to these instruments, and it is therefore up to the member states (and/or individuals) to determine whether, and how, they intend to comply with them. An example of a 'soft law' is the Recommendation on Childcare, which came into effect in 1992 and which is intended to encourage more effective child care and leave of absence arrangements, and a better distribution of responsibility between men and women with regard to child-rearing and child care. This aspect of EU policy will be discussed in detail in Chapter 10. Other examples of soft laws are the 1984 recommendation on positive action and the 1987 recommendation on vocational training for women.

Table 8.1   **Instruments in EU regulatory policy**

REGULATION	DIRECTIVE	DECISION
Always directly applicable	May be directly applicable	May be directly applicable
Binding in its entirety	Binding only in respect of the intended result	Binding in its entirety
Addressed to all the member states, not to individuals	Addressed to a number of member states, not to individuals	Addressed to individual member states and individual citizens

In addition to the instrument of law, the European Union uses its financial resources to steer developments by subsidizing a whole range of different projects. This is the EU's action policy. For example, the European Social Fund (ESF) makes resources available for employment and training projects for women. Besides projects set up within the framework of the Equal Opportunities Action Programme, attention is also given to women within the Action Programmes on Poverty, while young women are one of the target groups of the education and training projects aimed at reducing unemployment among young people. The scope of this type of policy initiative is limited; in the final assessment, they reach only a small number of women. We will discuss action policy in the next section, when we turn to the Equal Opportunities Action Programmes.

We call the fourth type of policy instrument process and organization. The name refers to the process of decision-making by means of committees and organizations and the process of laying down rules and procedures in order to create a framework within which substantive policy (soft laws, regulatory policies) can be developed. Cram (1993) demonstrates that this is the most common type of policy with regard to social issues in general at the European level. That is probably true of equal opportunities policy as well. In recent years the Union has actively encouraged women's organizations and set up various relevant networks. A number of expert networks were founded focusing on the following themes: child care, the position of women in the labour market, positive action in companies, the implementation of the directives governing equal treatment, diversification of occupational choices, equal opportunities in education, equal opportunities in radio and television, positive action among senior civil servants and women and decision-making. Two other networks which might be mentioned here are IRIS and LEI (Local Employment Initiatives). IRIS (founded in 1988) is a network of educational and training projects for women (around 335 projects in 1992) and LEI (established in 1984) is a network of people who provide advice and assistance to women who want to start up their own company. In the long run, these types of initiatives help to broaden political support for equal opportunities policy.

It is specifically the Council and the individual member states themselves which consistently put the brakes on the development of social policy and, consequently, on the development of equal opportunities policy. Decision-making is hence often a question of being very patient. Over the years, the Commission has built up the necessary experience in establishing policy in increments.

With regard to women as a specific group, until now the most tangible results have been achieved by means of regulatory policies and EU action policy. These are after all the instruments that affect citizens directly. The former European Commissioner of Social Affairs, Mr Vredeling, even claimed that equal opportunities was one of the few policy domains in which EU policy surpasses the policy of the member states (Warner, 1984). In the following section we will explore in detail the policy initiatives taken to promote equal opportunities between men and women.

EQUAL OPPORTUNITIES POLICIES: A SURVEY

1957–1980

It has often been the case in the Union that the Court of Justice has interpreted the intention of a treaty in such a way as to create an opening for concrete policy measures focusing on women. These measures were directed exclusively on the labour-market position of women. In this sense equal opportunities policy does not deviate substantially from other social policy governing employees. Initially the only action undertaken to promote equal opportunities for women was the inclusion of article 119 in the Treaty of Rome (1957). As mentioned previously, the article was adopted to alleviate the French government's fears that wage differences between men and women would prove to be a competitive advantage for the other member states. It states:

> Each member state shall during the first stage ensure and subsequently maintain the principle that men and women should receive equal pay for equal work. For purposes of this article, 'pay' means the ordinary basic or minimum wage or salary and any other consideration whether in cash or in kind which the worker receives, directly or indirectly, in respect of his employment from his employer. Equal pay without discrimination based on sex means:
> a) that pay for the same work at piece rates shall be calculated on the basis of the same unit of measurement;
> b) that pay for the same work at time rates shall be the same for the same job.

The jurisprudence relating to this article will be discussed in the following chapter. It will suffice here to remark that until the early 1970s very little action was taken based on this article. Many member states failed to comply with the agreements governing its implementation. Large pay differentials between men and women persisted (Warner, 1984). However, when EU citizens began to initiate proceedings based on article 119 before their domestic courts, it became inevitable that the provisions set out in the article would be made more concrete. At the same time, the women's movement in the various member states had drawn attention to the fact that women were being put at a disadvantage. Warner (1984) concludes that more scope was created in the early 1970s for joint social policy. This was related, on the one hand, to the fact that more money was available for social expenditure, and, on the other, to the fact that political support for such measures had grown. It also meant that the political climate was more receptive to criticism of the social order by the rapidly growing women's movement. One consequence was the founding of the Equal Opportunities Unit; another was the establishment of an *ad hoc* advisory group for the Commission.

The 1974 Social Action Programme also drew attention to the disadvantaged position of women; the programme argued for an active policy in this area. In 1975 the first steps were taken and the first equal opportunities directive was adopted: the Equal Pay Directive 75/117/EEC. This directive expanded the concept of equal pay to cover 'work to which equal value is attributed' (Warner, 1984). The directive allows employees the possibility of starting proceedings against their employer without putting themselves in danger of dismissal. Implementing the directive was more difficult, and member states did not seem in any hurry to do so. In 1979 the Commission started a series of infringement actions (proceedings initiated when a member state is accused of violating EU law) against all the current member states, with the exception of Italy and Ireland, the only countries which had implemented the directive satisfactorily (Pillinger, 1992).

Aware that unequal pay was only one of the many aspects contributing to the disadvantageous position of women, the Commission quickly introduced a second directive, which came into force in 1976: the Equal Treatment Directive 76/207/EEC. This directive covers employment, vocational training and working conditions (Nielsen and Szyszczak, 1991). Once again the Commission found itself initiating a number of infringement actions – this time against Italy, Belgium, and Ireland (Warner, 1984) and the UK – to force them to implement the Equal Treatment Directive. Warner states that it was specifically the rulings of the European Court of Justice on this directive which allowed the Commission to introduce a wider interpretation of the concept of equality.

The third directive focusing on achieving greater equality between men and women, the Directive on Equality in Social Security (79/7/EEU), came into effect in 1978. The goal of this directive was to promote the equal treatment of men and women in social security. The member states once again resisted implementation of the directive. The Netherlands and Belgium even introduced legal measures which increased rather than diminished sex discrimination in social security. According to Warner (1984), one of the reasons that this directive met such fierce resistance was the growing economic problems in the late 1970s and early 1980s, and the accompanying sharp rise in unemployment. Despite its limited scope – the directive does not cover non-statutory social insurance, excludes certain insurance types and allows for exceptions – the directive has nevertheless had an impact. For example, in 1986 the Court decided that Great Britain should also allow married women to claim an invalid care allowance. The Netherlands lowered its unemployment benefit in an attempt to meet the requirements of the Union and to circumvent a rise in social security expenditure at the same time. It was not the only country to do so.

In addition to regulatory and process policy – under which the 3 directives, the founding of the Equal Opportunities Unit and the *ad hoc* advisory group can be classified – the Union also took steps during this period within the framework of the ESF (European Social Fund) directed at women. The ESF is one of the EU's 3 Structural Funds (the other 2 are the European Regional Development Fund, ERDF, and the European Agricultural Guidance and Guarantee Fund, EAGGF), whose aim is to assist underdeveloped regions, combat long-term unemployment and help integrate young people into the labour market. The ESF is a source of funding for many educational and employment projects, and a considerable part of its work is directed at women. Since 1977 one of the ESF's specific target groups has been women over 25 years of age. The funding earmarked for projects focusing on this group shows that such projects are not equally distributed among the member states. Warner (1984) describes how in the early 1980s, about 60% of the funding went to Germany. The reason she gives is that Germany is more attuned to the idea of long-range planning and that it was therefore one of the first to understand that women constituted an important potential market. In addition, German applications for funding surpassed those submitted by other countries both in quantity and quality, the level of government support playing an important role in this respect. Project proposals submitted by countries such as Italy, the UK and France were often innovative but also small-scale. In addition to projects for women over 25, there are also training projects directed at young women which are subsidized through funding tagged for young people in general. At the end of the day, however, only a small group of women benefit directly from such projects. This type of action policy is an essential component of policy governing the various equal opportunities action programmes.

Owing to various pronouncements by the European Court of Justice concerning article 119 of the Treaty of Rome and the 3 equal opportunities directives, women became aware that real opportunities were opening up at the European level to compel the member states to improve the position of women, despite the laborious process of implementation. Women's organizations began to concentrate on the Union more and more, and attempted to influence policy-making. Thanks to this external support, EU policy-makers who campaigned vigorously to promote equal opportunities policy were able to bolster their position further. This increased level of activity resulted in 1979 in the establishment of a parliamentary committee on women's policy to investigate the way in which the member states had interpreted/implemented the 3 equal opportunities directives.

The first 2 action programmes: policy in the 1980s

After the energetic initiatives of the 1970s focusing on equal opportunities policy – for which the directive served as the most important legal instrument – the 1980s saw the evolution of a different approach. The emphasis shifted from regulatory policy to process and action policy. An important cause was undoubtedly the deteriorating economic climate. But the member states were also less willing to back up European legal measures, after they began to realize what the first 3 directives actually implied for domestic law.

The first 4-year action programme for equal opportunities began in 1982. The Commission, pressured by the French Minister of Emancipation, finally adopted a proposal setting out a framework for equal opportunities policy, although only after raising a string of objections. The Equal Opportunities Action Programme 1982–1985 focused on the one hand on implementing and endorsing existing equal opportunities legislation, and on the other hand on achieving greater equality in actual practice through positive action programmes and other instruments. To gain a greater understanding of how the various member states interpreted the intentions of the EU directives, the Commission established a network in 1984 whose purpose was to monitor their implementation (Pillinger, 1992). In 1987 the network made its dissatisfaction known concerning the impact of the directives. According to network members, there was no evidence that the directives had had any effect whatsoever on labour-market structures. Their only impact had been at the individual level.

The first action programme not only concentrated on the implementation of the 3 existing directives but also announced the addition of 2 new directives. The Directive on Equal Treatment in Occupational Social Security (86/378/EEC) and the fifth directive (86/613/EEC), which provides for equal treatment in self-employment, were introduced in 1986. The first was intended to complement the Directive on Social Security, which governs statutory social security schemes only. It extends this coverage to occupational schemes which are not governed by the third directive and whose purpose is to provide specific groups with benefits intended to supplement or even replace those provided by statutory schemes (Nielsen and Szyszczak, 1993). The directive therefore governs non-statutory arrangements such as those set out in collective bargaining agreements or in private company schemes. As of 1993 all non-statutory pension schemes were to have been revised in accordance with the principle of equal treatment.

The point of departure of the fifth directive was the protection of women – particularly during pregnancy and motherhood – whose occupational status is not entirely clear. It covers women who work in family businesses, in particular in the agrarian sector but elsewhere as well. This directive is broader than the previous equal treatment directive because it attempts to define the legal status of self-employed workers based on their comparability with other working persons. It also rules out any discrimination on the basis of sex.

A sixth directive governing parental leave met with fierce resistance in the UK and was voted down (Nielsen and Szyszczak, 1993). The draft directive on part-time work suffered the same fate. Had it been adopted, it would have been one of the most far-reaching equal opportunities directives to date, intended to guarantee part-time workers the same rights (for example, in respect of health and safety at work, dismissal procedures, promotion, training and social facilities) as employees with a full-time appointment. Since many women work part time, a provision such as this one is extremely important to them. Once again, it was the UK which was the most pessimistic about the proposal. The British government believed that it would lead to ossification in the labour market (Pillinger, 1992).

In addition to the 2 new directives, the first action programme also resulted in a number of positive action strategies. These included the organization of symposia, the stimulation of research (for example, into the impact of the fiscal system on working women, opportunities for legal redress in the member states, and the protection of women during pregnancy and motherhood) and the sharing of information. To keep these initiatives going in the right direction, 3 new expert networks were set up whose task was to encourage/monitor positive action: the 'positive action in the private sector' network, the 'senior civil servants' working party and the 'equal opportunities in radio and television' network. Initiatives were also taken to set up networks focusing on linking projects in the various member states: IRIS (1988) and LEI. The purpose of IRIS is to foster improvements in vocational training for women; it is a network of vocational training programmes for women. LEI (Local Employment Initiatives) was identified by the Commission as an effective instrument. In 1987 a programme promoted through the LEI network was set up to assist women who wanted to start up their own company.

As was often the case, the Equal Opportunities Action Programme 1982–1985 was clearly a compromise measure: it certainly did not distinguish itself as being unambiguous and progressive. Pillinger (1992) remarks that the points of action formulated in the document fail to give the implementers sufficient authority actually to achieve the objectives. The lack of both financial support and support by the Commission meant that the implementation of major portions of the action programme depended largely on the efforts and willingness of the member states (Pillinger, 1992). It was up to the individual member states, then, to take the initiative to introduce changes. However, the action programme did assist in expanding the range of activities focusing on improving the position of women.

The policy instruments employed in the 1980s, then, were quite diverse. Because they were small-scale initiatives of limited duration, many of the activities commenced within the framework of the third action programme did not lead to real structural improvement. The Commission itself held a positive opinion of the first action programme, however, and a second programme was initiated (1986–90). Similar to the first programme, the second made use of such policy instruments as the provision of information, discussions, research and seminars. Legislation was mentioned only in passing. An important new area of attention in the second programme was technological change.

Third action programme: the new policy framework

The third action programme, which runs from 1991 to 1995, differs from the first 2 in that it is an attempt to create an interface with the Union's general structural and socio-economic policy. The key concepts in this regard are the co-ordination, complementarity and integration of policy, at the European, national and regional levels. Another important area of concern in the third action programme is the attempt to counteract the detrimental effects on women of the single European market.

The programme has 3 main objectives:

1 Implementation and development of legislation: this includes activities targeting the implementation and development of existing legal measures, and activities intended to heighten awareness of rights and obligations among European citizens.
2 The integration of women into the labour market: this covers activities intended to generate employment, encourage female entrepreneurship, improve the quality of working life for women by means of education and vocational training, and introduce positive action measures in companies, and activities whose purpose is to make it possible for women to reconcile their domestic and professional obligations.
3 Improvement of the social position of women: this includes consciousness-raising activities and information; encouraging the participation of women in the media and in economic and social decision-making.

There are various steps the Commission intends to take that fall under the first objective. For example, it intends to draft a document further defining the concept of 'equal pay for equal work'; draft a guidebook on occupational evaluation and classification; and provide a closer description of the concept of 'indirect discrimination'. The Commission has, furthermore, undertaken to evaluate the implementation of the fifth directive.

There are also several concrete measures which are intended to assist in the integration of women in the labour market (second objective). Principal among these are various proposals for new directives, some of which had actually been developed in the 1980s. The first, a directive governing the protection of pregnant women at work, was published in 1990 and came into force a year later. Once again, the British government raised serious objections to this directive, with the result that it now offers women scarcely any additional protection. In the UK some 60% of women do not have a right to pregnancy leave (Pillinger, 1992). The directive has done little to change that because it prescribes only the minimum norms which the member states are obliged to satisfy, forbidding them to lower the standards which are prescribed in their domestic laws. The Union does not intend to take other initiatives in this area: in theory it is up to the individual member states to implement policy on this issue.

The second measure was a recommendation governing child care, introduced in April 1992. The Commission had predicted that a directive such as the one proposed by the child-care network could not rely on sufficient political backing. The issue of child care was and is a controversial one at the European level. According to Pillinger (1992), the reason is that child care is generally regarded as an educational issue, and the Union has no legal authority in matters of education, an issue which has always remained the responsibility of the individual member states. For women, however, the availability of child care is frequently a basic requirement for entering the labour market. (In Chapter 10 more will be said on child care in different member states and EU policy).

The third action programme also announced 3 draft directives (Com (90)/228) concerned with non-standard working practices. The flexibilization of the labour market is a highly relevant theme for women because many of them work on call, or on temporary contracts which offer very little social protection. The draft directives are intended to give employees on non-standard employment contracts the same piece-rate benefits and rights as employees who work full time on a permanent contract. In the 1980s the Council blocked a forerunner of this draft directive, which was intended to govern part-time and temporary work. So far Germany and the UK have refused to support the new draft directive. Because these 3 draft directives are subject to majority voting rather than unanimity, there is more chance of their being adopted than the previous directive on part-time and temporary work.

The final draft directive proposed by the Commission (C176) transfers the burden of proof to the employer in the event of a dispute between employer and employee on the principle of equal treatment. This directive was blocked by the UK in the 1980s and has been on the European decision-making agenda for several years now.

The most important pillar of the third action programme is NOW (New Opportunities for Women). This initiative targets training and employment projects for women and is an attempt to bridge the gap between the EU's equal opportunities policy and its structural and employment policies. The Union has allocated 120 million ecus to NOW for a period of 3 years. Funding is provided through the ESF and the European Regional Fund. Projects are, furthermore, always co-financed by the member states. Projects which qualify for NOW funding are those intended to encourage women who wish to start up their own company, those which stimulate vocational training, career planning and advice, and start-up subsidies covering infrastructural services that facilitate the founding of companies by women. NOW also provides supplementary assistance for child care and technical help in setting up networks. The various expert networks can also offer support in these matters.

In addition to NOW, there are a number of other measures intended to achieve the second objective, i.e. the integration of women in the labour market. According to the Commission, these include measures to continue and expand the IRIS and LEI networks. The other networks also continue to play a role in the field of research, and encourage the various member states to share information and experience. In future, all of the various programmes funded through the Structural Funds will focus in some way on the issues of equal opportunities and, in particular, on the problems encountered by women in the labour market (Commission, 1991). The Commission also intends to take steps to help men and women combine family life and career more effectively. One such measure is a recommendation on the establishment of codes of behaviour governing protection during pregnancy and motherhood.

We will finish this review with a few comments on the steps which the Commission intends to take to improve the social position of women, i.e. the third objective of the action programme. In addition to continuing its information activities, and improving information channels and contacts between various sources of information, the Commission will also draw attention to the image of women in the media. Another theme is the position of women in decision-making, both in political life and in commercial organizations. Co-operation is being sought with the European Parliament and with organizations in the member states to influence public opinion and in this way to increase the participation of women in decision-making processes. A 'women in decision-making' network has already been set up to this effect, intended to identify barriers that prevent women from participating in decision-making. There are also plans to research this issue with the assistance of the employers and trade unions.

We have covered the most important developments in the field of equal opportunities policy in Europe with the help of our 7-league boots. Although the Treaty of Rome includes an article setting out the principle of equal pay for women and men, it was not until the mid-1970s that the Union undertook concrete measures in this direction. It introduced 3 directives on equal treatment whose main effect has been to improve the legal position of individual citizens. In addition, the European Court of Justice has made it easier for citizens to initiate proceedings based on the principle of equal opportunities for men and women.

Since the early 1980s the Commission has used its action programmes as a means through which it can state explicitly the goal of its equal opportunities policy and how it intends to formulate this policy. In addition to these action programmes, there have been other relevant policy initiatives affecting women, for example those developed within the framework of the European Social Fund or the anti-poverty programme. The Commission intends to focus in the future more specifically on equal opportunities objectives in developing and implementing other EU policy.

WOMEN AND EUROPE: A FERTILE ALLIANCE?

In Ireland, many woman are pleased with the initiatives taken by Brussels. The law in the Republic of Ireland is probably the least favourable to women of any in Europe. The Irish government has been forced repeatedly to amend its legislation under pressure of proceedings initiated by the Commission or by its own citizens. The entry into Union has accelerated the pace of progress on this island on the periphery of Europe. No wonder that many Irish women see the Union as a blessing.

Danish women, on the other hand, are considerably less pleased with what the Union has to offer them. A significant number of them voted against the Maastricht Treaty (Ophuysen, 1994). Denmark is in many respects a progressive country when it comes to socio-economic legislation affecting women. Nowhere else in the Union is child care so efficiently arranged, and nowhere else do so many women participate in working life. Many Danish women are afraid that what the Union has to offer them in terms of equal opportunities policy will not compensate for the disadvantages of the single market, i.e. the increasing liberalization of the European economy, fiercer competition and the loss of democratic control over decision-making.

For Spain, joining the Union has led to economic and political modernization. Thanks to the European equal opportunities policy, Spain has begun to set up the organizational framework for an emancipation policy focusing on women. The Spanish approach is relatively bureaucratic and top-heavy, with very few of the results trickling down to the bottom layers (Ophuysen, 1994). In other words, the Union's equal opportunities policy has had very little impact on the lives of Spanish women. Perhaps this will change in the near future.

We have described above 3 different member states. Each one has undergone an experience very different from the others. In fact, it is not surprising that they differ so sharply in this respect. After all, they each started from a very different point in respect of both socio-economic and cultural characteristics, and these differences resulted in distinct experiences with respect to Union policy. When it comes to an obvious structural improvement in the position of women at the macro-level, the results achieved in the majority of member states by the Union's equal opportunities policy are meagre (Warner, 1984; Mazey, 1988). The segregation of the sexes, for example, remains largely the same, as was documented in Chapter 2. Discrimination on the basis of sex has consistently been forbidden, but indirect discrimination in employment terms or job requirements continues to be a problem. Nor are the directives equally unambiguous. The directive on equal pay states, for example, that there should be equal pay for work of equal value. It fails to make clear, however, how work of 'equal value' can be determined (a subject that will be discussed further in Chapter 12). Hence the directives have failed to eliminate pay differences between women and men.

EU law has given women more legal instruments with which to insist on an improvement in their position. But the restricted scope of the equal opportunities policy is largely a result of the decisive role which the member states themselves play in the Union's decision-making process. Because issues concerning equal opportunities must be decided unanimously, it is highly unlikely that the European Union will be able to achieve more than the more progressive member states have. In addition, given the limited resources available to policy-makers (New Opportunities for Women (NOW) received 120 million ecu, i.e. less than 1 ecu per woman), it is not surprising that the policy measures seem to have had little effect. Mazey (1988) has correctly remarked that this does not imply that policy is not worth the effort; although there have not been any great leaps forward, progress is being made step by step. Let us assess the effects of the equal opportunities policy in some more detail.

The 4 policy types described earlier can serve as a useful instrument. There has, for example, been an undeniable movement toward the harmonization of European and domestic equal opportunities policies. Until recently, the southernmost countries of the Union had taken no steps whatsoever in this area, and the Union's programmes have provided them with a framework within which they can operate. Process policy is the most common policy instrument; the Commission has set up a series of networks to improve the exchange of information on needs, problems and policy-making. The networks play a pivotal role in equal opportunities policy, but they are not very effective. That is often the result of the very limited financial resources at their disposal.

In qualitative terms, regulatory policy is probably the most important category of policy instrument. Although the implementation of the relative directives has been quite laborious, European legislation produced results, thanks in particular to the pronouncements of the Court of Justice. These results do not, however, always mean an improvement in the position of women. For example, the Court's interpretation of article 119 in *Barber v Guardian Royal Exchange Assurance Group* prompted the Dutch and German governments to make efforts to amend this article in order to circumvent the financial consequences of the ruling. Various governments have had to amend domestic social security and other legislation (for example on anti-discrimination) to bring it into line with the equal opportunities directives. However, these changes did not automatically lead to an improvement in the labour-market position of women. In their research into the effects of the directive governing equal treatment in social security in the UK, Hoskyns and Luckhaus (1989) concluded that the directive has on the whole produced very few tangible results for women. It did not, in any event, lead to an individualized system of social security, and any changes were implemented at the expense of men. The directive led to a reduction or even cancellation of certain social security benefits in other member states as well; they were not prepared to take on the additional expenditures (Nielsen and Szyszczak, 1993).

There are a number of directives awaiting adoption, but in recent years they have been the subject of difficult negotiations. The member states are evidently shocked by the consequences of previous directives and are extremely cautious when it comes to new legislation in this area.

The third type of policy mentioned in this chapter was called 'soft' law. This includes recommendations, opinions and even resolutions. The member states are not formally bound by this type of legislation. It means that they themselves have more far-reaching discretionary powers, as the wide range of interpretations given to the 1984 recommendation on positive action made clear. In some countries (e.g. Belgium), the recommendation led to formal legislation, whereas in others (the Netherlands and the UK) organizations and individuals were expected to take the initiative. The former policy approach is not necessarily more effective than the latter. France, for example, has had legislation on positive action since 1983. French companies are in theory obliged to publish an annual report on the distribution of men and women over the various occupational levels. The actual results are disappointing, however. Very few companies satisfy the requirements set out by the law. In Chapter 11 we will look in greater detail at the various positive action initiatives undertaken by the different member states. It is difficult to say to what extent the positive action policy pursued by the various member states has been influenced by the Union's recommendation and to what extent the domestic trade union movement and women's movement have played a role.

Finally, we come to action policy, the fourth type of policy instrument mentioned previously. We will restrict our discussion here to an evaluation of the second Equal Opportunities Action Programme which was carried out at the Commission's request (see Lefebvre, 1993). It is of course too soon to pass judgement on the third programme. The Commission's study focused on the effects of equal opportunities measures financed by the ESF. It is clear that within overall structural policy (i.e. policy developed within the framework of the ESF, ERDF and EAGGF which is to some extent aimed at social objectives), women are only a very minor area of concern. There are very few projects aimed specifically at women: 89% of the participating women are involved in projects within a general programme. This varies from member state to member state, however. Denmark, Germany and the Netherlands have a relatively large number of projects focusing specifically on women. Another important point is that women tend to participate in training and education projects; only in Denmark do women participate relatively more than do men in employment assistance schemes. Because training and education are further removed from actually entering the labour market than employment assistance schemes are, they do not make as direct a contribution to finding a job.

Another problem uncovered by the researchers is the lack of co-ordination between equal opportunities policy and the structural employment policy stimulated by the Union in the various member states. Only Denmark and the Netherlands have integrated the activities intended to stimulate employment among women into their domestic employment and training plans. Greece, Portugal and Ireland, on the other hand, have not even set up a monitoring system to provide an accurate picture of the labour-market position of women. That means that it is difficult for these countries to determine what the specific problems of women are and to take these problems into account when taking policy decisions. Another example which demonstrates that there is too little co-ordination is the fact that the various equal opportunities networks have had very little impact on the way in which the employment and educational projects funded by the ESF are set up, managed and evaluated. Many of the project staff members have never even heard of the networks. Co-operation between the networks also leaves something to be desired. Denmark is the only country to stimulate co-operation.

Summarizing, very little attention is given to the issue of the labour-market position of women, either at the national or at the regional level. Nor is much information made available on this subject; indeed very little information has been collected to begin with. The principles enshrined in the equal opportunities policy have had only a very minor effect on other ESF-funded projects.

NOW is an attempt to formulate a response to the critique given above. Its purpose is to integrate the objectives of equal opportunities policy into more general economic and social policy. It remains to be seen, however, whether the third action programme will indeed achieve much more than the first 2 did. After all, the directive lost popularity as a policy instrument in the field of equal opportunities after a flying start in the 1970s with the first 3 directives on equal treatment. It seems as though the member states have been traumatized by the consequences of these directives and are reluctant to use such a powerful instrument again. Another reason to question the scope of the third action programme is the fact that, in formulating its objectives, it leaves the member states a wide margin of discretionary power: as a document it is all too ambiguous. The 1993 Green Paper on social policy also covers the issue of the labour-market position of women to some extent, but no distinct line of argument can be discerned. The Green Paper is intended to stimulate discussion, ultimately resulting in a plan setting out the future social policy of the European Union. The closing chapter will go into further detail and will explore whether the intentions formulated in the Green Paper with respect to equal opportunities policy are in fact realistic.

REFERENCES

COMMISSION OF THE EUROPEAN COMMUNITIES (1991) *Equal Opportunities for Men and Women 1991–1995, Women in Europe*, no. 34, Brussels.
COMMISSION OF THE EUROPEAN COMMUNITIES (1993) XXVIE *General Report on the Activities of the European Communities 1992*, Brussels.
CRAM, L. (1993) Calling the tune without paying the piper? Social policy regulation: the role of the Commission in European Community social policy, *Policy and Politics*, Vol. 21, no. 2, pp. 135–46.
CRIJNS, F. C. L. M. (1990) *Europees recht*, Open universiteit, Heerlen, p. 145.
GIER, H. G. DE (1991) *Instituties en besluitvorming op EG-niveau*, in J. von Grumbkow *et al.*, *Sociale zekerheid: Europese trends*, Open universiteit, Heerlen.
HOSKYNS, C. and LUCKHAUS, L. (1989) The European Community Directive on equal treatment in social security, *Policy and Politics*, Vol. 17, no. 4, pp. 321–35).
LEFEBVRE, M. (1993) *Evaluation of Women's Involvement in European Social Fund Cofinanced*

Measures in 1990, Office for Official Publications of the European Communities, Luxemboug in 1990.

MAZEY, S. (1988) European Community Action of behalf of Women: the limits of legislation, *Journal of Common Market Studies*, Vol. XXVII, July, pp. 63–84.

NEILSEN, R. and SZYSZCZAK, E. (1993) *The Social Dimension of the European Community*, Handelshøjskoelens Forlag, Copenhagen.

NUGENT, N. (1991) *The Government and Politics of the European Community*, Macmillan, Basingstoke.

OPHUYSEN, T. (1994) *Vrouwen en Europa, Over werk, beleid en invloed in de EG*, Stichting Burgerschapskunde, Leiden.

PILLINGER, J. (1992) *Feminising the Market Women's Pay and Employment in the European Community*, Macmillan, Basingstoke.

WARNER, H. (1984) EC social policy in practice: Community action on behalf of women and its impact in the member states, *Journal of Common Market Studies*, Vol. XXIII, December, pp. 141–67.

CHAPTER 9

Legal Instruments at the EU Level

TINEKE VAN VLEUTEN

INTRODUCTION

The European Union has traditionally played an important role in the development of legal instruments for improving the position of women in the European labour market. This chapter deals with the instruments that have been developed over time and discusses whether and how they have improved the position of women in the labour market. We first examine the role of the European Commission and the European Court of Justice and then present a brief survey of legislation in the member states. As the principle of equality is crucial in eliminating labour-market inequalities, its implementation is subsequently discussed. We describe the general characteristics of Community law in the area of equal treatment and offer a summary of the case law in this field. We conclude with some considerations on the effectiveness of Community law.

LEGAL INSTRUMENTS, STATUTORY INSTRUMENTS

From 1974 onwards the European Commission became actively involved in promoting equal treatment for male and female employees in its action programmes. The action programmes resulted in a number of directives on equal pay and equal treatment. During this same period the European Court of Justice in Luxembourg likewise issued some important judgements in proceedings initiated by individuals (the *Defrenne* cases – see below).

By the second half of the 1970s, then, a body of Community legal instruments based on the principle of equal treatment had come into existence. Those instruments are becoming more concrete and are still being implemented. It appears from this process that legislation is not always necessary for the development of new legal instruments; it is often on the basis of existing legislation that new instruments are developed. Crucial to this process is that the EU Treaty provides for an independent judicial institution, the Court of Justice, which is qualified to test national laws against Community law, and whose decisions make an independent contribution to legal developments.

The Treaty itself says little of a concrete nature about equal pay and equal treatment. It contains a title on Social Policy, Chapter 1 of which (articles 117 to 122) discusses 'Social Provisions'. These provisions are general in nature; they have the aim of improving the standard of living of workers and of harmonizing social systems (article 117), of promoting co-operation in the social field (article 118) and of imposing an obligation to maintain the principle of equal pay for men and women (article 119).

The EU Treaty, then, in fact lays down only the norm of equal pay. The European Court decided quite early on, however, that equal treatment should be a fundamental principle of Community law. In time, article 119 was extended by further directives and by the Court's own rulings to such an extent that it became the core of Community law on equal pay and equal treatment. (The judgements will be referred to in this chapter by their abbreviated designation. The interested reader is referred to the works listed in the References, including Ellis (1991) and Prechal and Burrows (1990), which contain summaries of the judgements mentioned.)

The Defrenne judgements

The Belgian stewardess Gabriel Defrenne became well known during the 1970s for the great tenacity of her litigation. In 1968 Defrenne was dismissed from her job as a stewardess for Sabena because she had reached the age of 40. The airline's pursers were not dismissed at that age and, moreover, had better overall employment conditions, for example with respect to pension rights. In the years following her dismissal Defrenne initiated various court proceedings against Sabena and the State of Belgium. She based her position on the principle of equal pay as set out in article 119, a legal instrument that had already been proved effective in proceedings initiated by a number of EU female civil servants (Sabatini).

Although the Court found for Defrenne on a number of points of principle – for example, the Court declared that she had the right as an individual to invoke the equal pay principle and that equal treatment was a basic tenet of Community law – she herself gained little by her tenacity. The Court, for instance, extended no retroactive effect to its judgement concerning equal treatment, and this meant that the compensation awarded to Defrenne on the grounds of unfair dismissal was limited to 12,000 Belgians francs. Neither were her pension rights honoured, since these were not part of her employment agreement but were based on Belgian legislation.

The European Commission and the EU directives

In addition to the Treaty, the EU's directives are a principal source of law on equal pay and equal treatment. Directives are rules based on Community law which derive their legal force from the Treaty itself. They must be adopted unanimously by the Council of Ministers and create an obligation on member states to take measures at the national level so that specific results are achieved within a certain period of time. A summary of the various directives currently in force is given in Chapter 8. In general, EU citizens are not entitled to invoke these directives as individuals since they must first be incorporated into national legislation and a certain amount of time is given to member states to do so. Sometimes directives have a direct effect, i.e. when concrete enough to be applied in individual cases. As we have already mentioned, that was certainly true of the equal pay norm and therefore of the first EU directive which further elaborates this norm.

The period of time permitted for incorporation of the first 4 EU directives on this subject (equal pay, equal treatment, social security and pensions) into national legislation has meanwhile come to an end. At the beginning of 1994 draft directives were being prepared on related topics, including the burden-of-proof issue in equal treatment cases, parental leave and family leave, pregnancy and maternity leave, and on completing the implementation of the principle of equal treatment. One issue being considered by the EU which has not yet led to a directive is that of sexual harassment.

An important instrument for the integration of legislation within the EU is the infringement procedure. This procedure can be instituted by the European Commission or by one or more member states in the event that another member state does not comply with the EU Treaty or directives, or does not do so within the allotted period of time. In practice it is the Commission which starts proceedings before the Court. The proceedings are preceded by reports and a formal warning. The Court can require the member state concerned to take the necessary measures. Infringement procedures may continue for a long time and are by no means always pursued to the bitter end. Often the member state concerned will submit to the views set out by the European Commission long before the case reaches its conclusion. For example, Dutch equal pay legislation was adapted in 1981 and 1988 on a number of points, and the equal value procedure was incorporated into equal pay legislation in the UK in 1984 after the intervention of the European Commission.

The European Court of Justice

The European Court of Justice derives its powers from the EU Treaty. Article 164 imposes a formal duty upon the Court to 'ensure that in the interpretation and application of this Treaty the law is observed'. The Court has a double function:

1 to ensure proper compliance with the economic and social purposes of the EU; and
2 to perform an integrating task with respect to the laws of the member states.

The Court implements these duties in several ways. In some of its earliest decisions (*Van Gend en Loos, Costa/ENELL*), the Court held that, due to the very nature of the EU, Community law was to be treated as supranational law and had supremacy over national law. Individuals seeking justice may, therefore, address the European Court of Justice after a final judgement has been rendered in their own country.

During the course of national proceedings, national courts may request the Court to give a ruling on the interpretation of Community law. The national court must then decide on the case pending before it with due observance of the Court's preliminary ruling. Furthermore, the European Commission may request the Court to give a ruling if a member state fails to adjust its national law to EU directives within the legally allotted period of time (infringement).

The Court has held that, if EU norms are unconditional and sufficiently precise, they automatically form part of the legal system of the relevant member state. Such norms are said to have direct effect and may be invoked by all individuals and institutions, not only against the government (vertical effect) but also against other individuals and institutions (horizontal effect). In the *Defrenne I* case the Court decided that the equal pay provision of article 119 had such direct effect.

On the other hand, the Court held that the principle of equal treatment was too complex to assume that it had direct effect. This principle requires further detailing by the national legislative authorities.

The Court's ruling is very important for matters which overlap the issues of equal pay and equal treatment. Direct effect of the equal pay principle was invoked, for instance, in the matter of equal treatment in the field of pensions. This stance was justified on the grounds that the pension contributions could be regarded as a wage component. The strategy failed in the *Defrenne I* case because the pension concerned was a statutory pension. In the more recent *Barber* case, however, pension rights were awarded because they formed part of the employment contract (they were contracted out) and thus fell within the scope of the equal pay principle.

On the basis of the requirement that national laws should conform to Community law (*Von Colson* and *Kamann*), the Court is empowered to give rulings on individual complaints and preliminary questions in the field of unequal treatment. The Court requires conformity not only with directives but also with the EU's resolutions and recommendations, which consequently obtain some sort of legal force.

Two strategies: legislation and case law

The legal position of women can be improved at a European level in 2 ways: via Community law in the broad sense of the word – the EU Treaty – and legislation based on Community law, and via case law developed by the European Court of Justice.

Both strategies have disadvantages. Individual parties and pressure groups may force court rulings by instigating trial proceedings. But trial proceedings may not always have the outcome desired by the individual. The *Defrenne* cases, for instance, show that issues of minor importance may play so prominent a role that they dominate the Court's decision. The conduct of trial proceedings is therefore a legal instrument that has its own restrictions. It is important to raise a vital legal question and the complainant must be able to carry the costs of the proceedings. Furthermore, the party concerned must be extremely patient (Defrenne litigated for 10 years).

A strategic disadvantage of a test case is the fact that rulings of the European Court have no generally binding effect: formally speaking, only the parties to the proceedings are bound by the decision. Nevertheless, the Court's decisions have a great impact, because the Court may be expected to give similar rulings in similar cases. However, due to the focus on the individual circumstances of the case, it will not always be easy to interpret the Court's decisions. This may lead to legal uncertainty.

Politicians and policy-makers will, therefore, prefer legislative instruments. At first sight, this offers the advantage of general force. But legislation, too, has its limitations. The legislative process can be very time-consuming and the final results may be affected by compromises. Moreover, there is no certainty that the new rules will be complied with in individual cases. There may also be uncertainty about the actual contents of the provisions or about the scope of the terms: what is the exact meaning, what is covered by a specific term? Such questions will not become relevant until the rules are applied. The more precise the norm, the more legal certainty exists in individual cases. Consequently, the substance of the rules is closely related to the effectiveness of legislation.

This effectiveness can be undermined by insufficient control on the implementation or by the lack of appropriate sanctions. The enforcement mechanism – i.e. the various ways in which the law or the legal system provides for enforcement – is, therefore, of great import.

In the course of time the European Commission has made great efforts to implement legislation in the field of equal pay and equal treatment. The directives include clear norms for national equal treatment laws. The Commission has been less outspoken about sanctions. It has not recommended special enforcement agencies such as an Equal Opportunity Commission. The European Court, however, has repeatedly held that effective sanctions must be guaranteed at a national level (*Decker* case) and that the state is liable if such sanctions are not available (*Francovich* case).

Interaction

In general, the main legal developments in the labour-market position of women have been brought about by European Court decisions and Community law. The rulings in the *Defrenne* cases were given almost simultaneously with the adoption of the first 3 EU directives on the principles of equal pay and equal treatment: the Commission and the European Court of Justice worked hand in hand at that time.

In the past decade, however, interaction between the 2 EU institutions has become more problematic. The recent discord within the European Commission and the Council has slowed progress considerably in adopting new directives or implementing existing directives. The Court of Justice, on the other hand, has acted as a pioneer by giving significant rulings in the field of equal pay and equal treatment. These rulings caused considerable unrest among the Council members. In an effort to restrict the Court's decisions on the equal pay principle, the member states even went so far as to annex a protocol to the Maastricht Treaty pursuant to which any decisions of the Court on article 199 are deprived of retroactive effect.

However, there still are major opportunities for developing new law, as may be inferred from a recent decision of the European Court of Justice in which pension rights were allocated retrospectively to women, albeit subject to specific conditions.

NATIONAL EQUAL OPPORTUNITIES LEGISLATION

Creating national legislation

EU directives do not explicitly require member states to introduce a specific equal treatment Act. They do, however, oblige them to introduce 'legal and administrative provisions' to implement the principles of equal pay and equal treatment. This may involve changes or additions to existing labour law or social security legislation, but it may also mean a new Act incorporating all the provisions relating to the equal treatment of men and women. Most member states opt for the latter course, although most of them have also simultaneously amended their labour legislation to meet EU requirements.

When the first EU directive on equal pay was introduced (1975), the countries of Europe had already introduced legislation on equal pay because of their ILO obligations. The ILO – the International Labour Organization – is an international body composed of employers and employees which currently resides under the banner of the United Nations. Since it was founded, in 1919, the ILO has supported the principle of equal pay and in 1956 this principle was laid down in an ILO convention. In about 1975 most Western countries had adopted their own equal pay legislation in anticipation of the ILO obligation. Most of the laws on equal treatment were passed in the following years, not only to comply with EU obligations but also as a result of social and political initiatives at national level. The first European country to introduce equal treatment legislation, in the form of the 1975 Sex Discrimination Act, was the UK. This Act applies to all areas of society, work and education, and it provides clear definitions of direct and indirect discrimination. The Act was inspired by its American predecessor, namely the Civil Rights Act of 1969, and is closely related to the Race Discrimination Act which was already in force in England at the time. The British legislation is therefore in its structure not entirely part of the EU legislative family because it covers more areas (see below: Features of Community law).

The only EU country with no specific equal treatment legislation is Germany. Germany has always taken the position that the constitutional principle of equality, on the basis of which any citizen may appeal to the courts, provides sufficient guarantees of equal treatment. In 1980, however, under EU pressure and as a result of an infringement procedure initiated by the European Commission, the Federal Republic did adopt a number of articles in the Civil Code dealing with equal treatment in employment. Other member states have formally complied with their EU obligations by passing separate legislation on equal treatment, often alongside or in addition to existing legislation on equal pay. France's 'Loi Roudy', for example, contains all the necessary elements of an adequate law on equal treatment, and lacks only an agency to enforce it. In 1981 the Netherlands, where political decision-making was for many years dominated by a discussion on whether to introduce broad anti-discrimination legislation similar to the US Civil Rights Act, introduced a 'narrow' law on equal treatment for men and women in employment at the insistence of the European Commission, which was brought into line with EU requirements in 1988, again at the insistence of the European Commission. Since the 1970s the Scandinavian countries have introduced extensive legislation to combat sex discrimination. The Scandinavian legislation gives an important role to labour and management. As enforcement agencies they have either the 'ombud' (the modern Scandinavian term for 'ombudsman'), or an equal treatment commission which fulls the 'ombud' function.

Role of the European Commission

The European Commission closely monitors the implementation of the directives which require the member states to incorporate provisions into national legislation. If necessary, it may start an infringement procedure against a country which deviates from certain provisions set out in the directives. Such procedures may concern issues such as forms of indirect discrimination in member state regulations covering marital status, family status, the position of the family breadwinner or family allowances. The European Commission has also started proceedings before the Court of Justice requesting a judgement concerning the legal exceptions to direct discrimination. The Commission, for example, supervises the 'list' of gender-specific occupational qualifications which are exempt from the equal treatment requirement.

Equal treatment commissions

The EU has never insisted on the member states setting up a special enforcement agency to ensure that equal treatment legislation is in fact enforced and complied with, but the EU is not opposed to this being done. When it joined the EU, the UK already had such a body, namely the Equal Opportunities Commission. The Scandinavian countries do have special enforcement bodies in the form of an ombud for equal treatment, with the exception of the EU member state Denmark.

Within the EU, the Netherlands is an exception in having an Equal Treatment Commission which, although it is empowered to deliver a judgement on questions of equal treatment, is not allowed to issue a binding one.

The EU model of legislation is therefore significantly different in its scope and manner of enforcement from that in other Western countries such as the USA, Canada, New Zealand and Australia. These countries have special enforcement agencies which also have powers in other areas involving discrimination: race, religious conviction, ethnic origin and disability. In that respect the equal treatment legislation in the UK and in the Netherlands (since the adoption of the 1994 Anti-Discrimination Act) is closer to the UK legislation than to the EU model.

EQUAL TREATMENT AS A LEGAL CONCEPT

The principle of equality

Equality is a crucial concept within the set of legal instruments developed to improve the position of women on the labour market. The principle of equality is a fundamental principle of Community law. An important question where actual implementation is concerned, however, is to what extent concrete form is given to that equality.

It is possible to take a formal position and to posit that it is the letter of the law which defines what precisely equal treatment is. This view of equality is referred to as 'formal equality before the law'. Formal equality does not yet mean that the position of men and women is equal. The right to equality must be seen in its social context. Rights may be all very well on paper, but if one is unable to exercise them they are not of much value in practice. Legal theory and international agreements consequently speak not only of 'rights' but of the exercise or enjoyment of rights.

This can be illustrated with the help of the following example. As long as a married woman requires her husband's permission to enter into an employment contract, one can speak of formal inequality between men and (married) women. When this legal requirement is removed, then the final formal impediment to women entering the labour market is removed. There is then formal legal equality with respect to access to the market. But this does not mean that married women are now actually able to enter the labour market. There is, after all, still a large number of other impediments which go unmentioned in the text of the law itself but which are present in the prevailing social conditions: lack of child-care facilities, lack of maternity or family leave, a low level of education among women or prejudice on the part of employers. Formal legal equality is by no means the same thing as actual legal equality.

Women still have unequal opportunities even after all legal obstacles have been removed. Not only do the practical barriers still exist, but there is still no substantive legal equality. Specific (government) policy is often necessary, a body of measures to create the preconditions for actual enjoyment of rights. And it is not usually possible to enforce compliance with government policy via the courts: political decisions are necessary together with financial resources, instruments for implementation and special facilities. Seen in this light, therefore, special rights for women, preferential treatment, positive action, are not in any way 'fringe benefits', but favourable measures which promote equality between the sexes.

When shall equality actually have been achieved? We must be honest: it remains difficult to say precisely what equality is. Feminist legal theory has made an important contribution to the debate on the principle of equality by pointing out that the substance of statutory norms are not as sex-neutral as they may seem at first glance. Such norms, after all, are a reflection of the dominant culture, in which a masculine lifestyle, masculine responsibilities and masculine time management determine the way public and private lives are arranged. The world of work, with its full-time working week and uninterrupted career path from school to work to retirement, which entrusts private concerns to the care of 'others' (i.e. women), is grafted on to that pattern. One thing is certain: as long as the masculine model continues to serve as the yardstick for equal treatment in the labour market, the principle of equality will not improve the position of women (see Hewlett, 1986). That is why, in the opinion of some, the principle of equality will do very little to improve the position of women within and outside the labour market, and women would do better to gain special rights for themselves (see Wolgast, 1980). Still others (MacKinnon, 1987; Scales, 1986; Minow, 1990) have pointed out the inherent imbalance of power between men and women, one which is difficult to tackle with the equality principle.

In our opinion, the principle of equality between the sexes will have a positive effect provided that equality is interpreted concretely. In other words, it must be related to its 'context', to the social situation. That requires an understanding of the workings of discrimination, in particular of the key concept of indirect discrimination.

The concept of discrimination

As a rule, the principle of equality is interpreted as a prohibition of discrimination. The prohibition of discrimination in EU provisions is merely a specific enunciation of the general principle of equality. The rule of thumb is: the more concretely we can define discrimination, the easier it is to demonstrate that certain individuals or groups are being discriminated against.

Direct and indirect discrimination

A distinction is traditionally made between 2 forms of discrimination: direct and indirect. Direct discrimination is understood to mean unequal treatment on the grounds of sex or on the grounds of a feature which is directly related to gender. In Community law direct discrimination is always forbidden. The argument of objective justification is inadmissible. There are a few legal exceptions: protective measures in favour of women are sometimes permitted, jobs where the fact of belonging to a particular sex constitutes a genuine requirement of the occupation to be carried out (e.g. model, singer) and preferential treatment to remove actual inequalities is permitted.

Indirect discrimination is unequal treatment on the grounds of features other than sex whereby persons of a certain sex are disadvantaged. In indirect discrimination the point is the adverse effect of measures or actions which in practice affect men and women differently. The intention to discriminate is unnecessary for there to be indirect discrimination; it is not a matter of intention but of the actual effect. If, for example, part-time workers have a weaker legal position than full-timers in a given company, then that may put women at a disadvantage, since women generally work part time. The regulations relevant to part-time work therefore discriminate indirectly.

It is only for indirect discrimination that legislation allows the argument that there are grounds for objective justification. It is not entirely certain just what constitutes an objective justification, and this can sometimes lead to problems. A broad view of 'objective justification' can, after all, undermine any ban on discrimination. If, for example, 'business reasons' or 'financial difficulties' are accepted by the courts as justification in and of themselves, there will be very little reason to comply with anti-discrimination legislation: discrimination will generally be cheaper than equal treatment. In general, it is assumed that indirect discrimination must serve a reasonable purpose and also that there must be a balance between the goal and the means; and, finally, that it must be shown that the aim could not be achieved in a different, less discriminatory manner.

Discrimination as a social phenomenon

The legal way to tackle discrimination is via the individual person who is disadvantaged and who is seeking redress. However, the individual victim of discrimination is by nature in a weaker position and may need special protection. The law does have experience in balancing the interests of parties whose powers are unequal. Protection of the weaker party – a reasonable distribution of the burden of proof, for example – is an element also found in labour law or tenancy law, and can be applied to discrimination cases by analogy. The social side of discrimination is legally more difficult to tackle: it is traditionally the domain of the social sciences. It cannot be denied, however, that most forms of discrimination are not by nature individual but in fact general. It is groups and not individuals whose interests are damaged by discrimination. This impingement is not merely incidental and has a certain level of continuity. In Anglo-Saxon countries there is the term 'patterns and practice', meaning general patterns and practices of discrimination. In the USA one speaks of 'systemic' or systematic' discrimination, in other words discrimination which is an intrinsic part of the system itself. This does not mean that the discrimination is intentional but that groups of individuals are systematically – and structurally – placed or kept in a weaker position as a result of discriminatory patterns or practices.

To combat this form of discrimination, new legal methods are necessary, and these are in fact being developed. The term 'indirect discrimination' is a good reference point. It is often possible, after all, to demonstrate statistically the negative impact of a given measure or treatment. The legal question is then: to what extent is statistical proof, as in the social sciences, also legally admissible, and what objective justification is admissible if the negative effect is demonstrated statistically? We will return to this point when we look at the judgements rendered by the European Court.

It is now already clear, however, that if one wishes to combat the systematic, structural nature of discrimination effectively, one must be able to act jointly as a group (class action) and that interest groups (unions, women's movement) must have the right to act on behalf of a group which is being discriminated against.

Equal pay for equal work

The principle of equal pay for equal work has a special place when considering the issue of equality. Although the equal pay norm can be seen as a form of equal treatment which focuses on pay, historically speaking the principle of equal pay for equal work preceded the principle of equal treatment.

The original equal pay norm has been given more substance by the fact that there is no longer strict adherence to the requirement that 'the same work' or the 'same job' must be paid equally. Instead, what is considered is the matter of equal pay for work of equal value. The concept of work of equal value makes it possible to compare men's work and women's work even if we are not dealing with the same job or workplace. Research has shown that it is precisely this sort of pay discrimination which is widespread, and that the position of women is significantly improved if it can be tackled by legal means.

Summary

The disadvantaged position of women on the European labour market can be tackled by legal means if this position is defined in terms of inequality, discrimination and unequal treatment. In the background is a view of substantive, concrete equality before the law, which posits that one should not be satisfied with the removal of formal legal obstacles but that one should also take account of the actual unequal positions of women and men when determining equality.

In the legal approach to this issue, the provision of concrete norms is important. The more concrete the actual form given to the principle of equality, the simpler it is to demonstrate that persons or groups find themselves in a disadvantaged position and therefore have the right to equal treatment. The concepts of direct and indirect discrimination play a decisive role in this context. Direct discrimination, with a few legal exceptions, is always prohibited. In the case of indirect discrimination, the argument of objective justification is admissible. Discrimination against individuals is easier to tackle by legal means than are the more structural forms of discrimination (systematic discrimination). New legal measures are currently being developed to deal with the latter.

COMMUNITY LAW IN PRACTICE

Features of Community law

In order to determine the manner in which the EU enhances the legal position of women on the European labour market, it seems useful to emphasize some specific features of Community law in the field of equal treatment. These features are closely connected with the genesis and purpose of the EU and the way in which the EU has interpreted the principle of equality over the years. The features concerned can be summarized as follows: individualization, non-sexism, social policy and restriction to employment and vocational training. Furthermore, EU policies focus mainly on combating sex discrimination, and not on other forms of discrimination (such as racial discrimination).

The EU was established as an economic union and its purposes are related to the free movement of goods and services. As regards the issue of labour, the EU follows a policy of preventing unfair competition. There is a clear connection between the EU rules and the ILO conventions in the field of equal pay and equal treatment. EU policies are aimed at the individual workers, regardless of their sex. This means that there is no place for family concepts within EU policy. Breadwinners are not accepted as a separate category, since this would lead to a type of indirect discrimination: more men than women can be categorized as breadwinners. Consequently, provisions concerning the position of breadwinners will be accepted only in very special circumstances.

For the same reasons, EU policy can be described as gender neutral. As regards the position of women on the European labour market, this implies that efforts are made to make the relevant rules and regulations symmetrical. However, this is not always to the advantage of women. For instance, the European Court of Justice rejected the unequal treatment of men and women with respect to pensionable age. If women are allowed to retire on their 60th birthday, so should men (the *Barber* case). Community law affords little leeway for special rights for women, except for protective measures related to pregnancy and onerous working conditions. In other words, the EU fights sex discrimination rather than discrimination against women.

Apart from economic policies, the EU also endeavours to attain specific social objectives. This may be inferred from the place allocated to article 119 in the chapter on 'Social Provisions'. Due to the attention that the EU institutions have devoted since 1974 to the enhancement of women's legal position on the labour market, the social aspects have gone through a process of liberation. At present, the emancipation objectives now occupy a more prominent place within EU policies. This denotes a concept which can be compared to that of 'substantive legal equality', discussed above in the section: Equal treatment as a legal concept. The new EU regulations concerning parental leave, for instance, must be seen against this background. The same applies to the promotion of positive action, meaning that women and men must be afforded an equal opportunity to participate in the labour market. Once again, these regulations are marked by gender neutrality: both parental leave and positive action are, in principle, applicable to both sexes.

EU policies with regard to women are limited to the fields of employment and vocational training. Unlike Anglo-American law on equal treatment, Community law does not interfere with life outside the labour market, such as the tertiary sector or ordinary education. EU policies specifically address equal access to the labour process, equal career opportunities, vocational training, employment conditions and, in certain circumstances, social security.

EU policies exclusively concern themselves with sex discrimination. This scope, too, differs from the Anglo-American systems, in which actions against sex discrimination are simply a an element of a more comprehensive set of policies aimed at fighting other types of discrimination, particularly that on the grounds of race. The main advantages of the EU approach are that its rules concentrate on the special position of women and that women within the EU have not as yet been forced to compete with other 'minority' groups to receive attention from the EU institutions. Community law distinguishes between several types of discrimination on the grounds of sex. The European Court of Justice has held that discrimination on the grounds of pregnancy should be treated as a form of sex discrimination and has recognized this form as direct discrimination. According to the second directive, a reference to marital and family status is considered contrary to the principle of equal treatment, although there may be circumstances which justify such a reference; the EU speaks of indirect discrimination in this respect

Legal developments to date

We have seen that the EU plays an important role in the development and actual application of the principle of equal treatment, not only through article 119 of the EU Treaty, but also through the decisions issued by the European Court of Justice. In view of the supremacy of Community law, the EU has a significant integrating impact on the national legal systems.

The EU's most significant contribution consists of the direct effect given to the principle of equal pay and the broad interpretation of the term 'pay'. This means that scope of the equal pay principle has expanded to the field of social security and pensions.

The standard of equal treatment is put into practice by means of the national laws on equal treatment, enacted as prescribed by the EU directives. The European Court of Justice contributes to this development by demanding conformity to Community law when interpreting the national standards. National courts often find it difficult to accept the direct effect of Union provisions and, more particularly, the concept of 'conformity'. British courts, for instance, are accustomed to the case law system, which means that they are unaccustomed to an approach which openly demands a degree of judicial policy-making.

But although the creation of law at a national level does not always proceed smoothly, it is possible to describe the current state of affairs on several significant issues.

The EU is very outspoken on various forms of discrimination on the grounds of sex. Direct discrimination is prohibited at all times, but there are a few statutory exceptions. In one of its *causes célèbres* (the *Dekker* case), the European Court of Justice held that discrimination on the grounds of pregnancy was a type of direct discrimination which could in no event be justified by any objective standard. Discrimination on the grounds of marital or family status is regarded as indirect discrimination for which objective justification might, in principle, be invoked. The EU is, however, very strict about the position of breadwinners.

The law provides for some specific exceptions to direct discrimination. A distinction on the grounds of sex may be made in the following events:

1 protective measures for the benefit of women;
2 in a very limited number of cases in which the sex of the worker constitutes a genuine requirement;
3 measures to remove existing inequalities which affect women's opportunities.

Due to the nature of the exceptions, the provisions involved should be given a strict interpretation. The European Commission demands that the exceptions permitted be expressly incorporated in the laws of the member states.

Protective measures are aimed at protecting specifically female interests in their working environment. Such measures concern primarily the protection of pregnant workers and any related issues (maternity leave) as well as the protection of women in working situations which may be considered onerous for them, for instance the prohibition against working night shifts. This latter form of protection is often criticized, since it makes it very difficult to draw the line between protection and paternalism. The current tendency, supported by the European Commission, is to abolish the protective measures because they appear to prevent women from accessing the labour market.

The performance of some occupations (e.g. that of model or singer) is traditionally linked to members of one of the sexes. It is, in principle, permitted to make an exception for cases where the sex of the worker constitutes a determining factor. On the other hand, gender-specific jobs from part of a cultural concept which is subject to changes in the course of time. The EU demands that national legislation maintain a list of gender-specific exceptions and that these lists be updated from time to time. There is a tendency to diminish the number of exceptions which are permitted.

Positive action can be defined as any action to give members of a group which is discriminated against such preferential treatment as will abolish any actual inequalities. In the past, preferential treatment was also referred to as positive discrimination, but this term has been abandoned because it has acquired negative implications.

Preferential treatment is a collective term, emerging in various forms ranging from the well-known sentence 'if male and female applicants have the same qualifications, female applicants will be given precedence' to positive action. Positive action can be defined as 'an integral set of comprehensive measures to grant underprivileged groups an advantaged position on a temporary basis for purposes of removing any existing inequalities'. Preferential treatment may form part of such positive action. Positive action is usually presented in the form of a position action plan with various measures, targets and timetables (see Chapter 11). Preferential treatment should be approached with great care because Community law is gender neutral. To achieve the effect intended by preferential treatment, that is, to enhance the position of female workers, it is of the utmost importance to ensure that the measures target women exclusively. Where preferential treatment for men is allowed, the measures concerned often result in a confirmation of traditional stereotypes. Moreover, there have been several occasions on which men successfully opposed preferential treatment by invoking the principle of equal treatment, since certain measures favoured female workers to an excessive degree.

The European Court of Justice has clarified the standards of indirect discrimination. Indirect discrimination can be described as unequal treatment on grounds other than sex, though having the effect of discriminating against members of one of the sexes. It is thus not allowed to apply a criterion which appears to be gender neutral but which has a detrimental effect on members of one of the sexes. At present, indirect discrimination may be demonstrated on the basis of statistical data (the *Bilka Kaufhaus* and *Nimz* cases).

In the same cases the European Court of Justice specified the objective grounds for justification in greater detail. If the adverse effect of a certain criterion or measure is shown (for instance, on the basis of statistical data), it will be up to the employer to prove that the end is justifiable in objective terms. The conditions in this respect are that the means applied by the employer:

1 are proportionate to the intended goal or, in other words, that means and end are in balance;
2 are suitable for attaining the objective set;
3 are necessary for the purpose or, in other words, that there are no other, non-discriminatory means to achieve the same goal (*Bilka Kaufhaus* case).

An important question in this respect might be whether any deviating treatment of part-time workers constitutes a form of indirect discrimination. The European Court of Justice was still reticent in the *Jenkins* case, but clearly stated in the *Bilka Kaufhaus* case that unequal treatment of part-time workers basically constituted discrimination against women and that it was up to the employer to present objective justifications for his actions (*Bilka Kaufhaus* and *Nimz* cases). Consequently, part-time employment has become a suspect criterion and requires strict scrutiny. Seniority has not yet reached that stage.

One of the significant elements of the *Bilka Kaufhaus* case was that the European Court of Justice rendered a decision on the burden of proof. Once the adverse effect for women is demonstrated, the employer will have to prove that women are not confronted with any disproportionate disadvantage from specific arrangements for part-time workers. Non-transparency may also constitute a reason for reversing the burden of proof. If a pay scheme has any adverse effects on women and is also completely non-transparent, the employer will have to prove that the differences in payment for men and women are justifiable (*Danfoss* and *Nimz* cases). This ruling by the European Court of Justice takes precedence over national procedural rules and applies in all member states.

The concept of pay has been discussed before, in the *Defrenne* cases. The European Court of Justice interprets 'pay' very broadly, namely as all present and future benefits paid in cash and in kind, provided that they are paid either directly or indirectly by the employer to the employee (*Defrenne I*). This interpretation covers the employee's gross salary including any pension and social security contributions paid by the employer as well as bonuses, expense allowances and entitlements upon termination of the employment relationship (e.g. supplements to sickness benefits, claims from severance pay schemes) (*Liefting* and *Kowalska* cases).

If an employee accrues pension entitlements in the context of his or her employment relationship, such entitlements are covered by the concept of 'pay' as defined in article 119 of the EU Treaty. Men and women should be treated equally in the field of pension entitlements. The European Court of Justice has set the condition that the pension scheme must arise from an agreement between the employer and the employee or from a unilateral decision taken by the employer. No governmental contributions may be paid and the pension scheme must by necessity arise from the employment relationship (*Barber* case). This ruling also relates to collective employee pension schemes and, furthermore, to collective occupational pension schemes (*Barber*). As stated in the *Defrenne I* case, only statutory pensions fall outside the scope of article 119. Statutorily guaranteed pension schemes and collective agreement arrangements are covered by the concept of pay as defined in article 119 of the EU Treaty. Note that the provisions concerned have direct effect and need not be incorporated in greater detail in national legislation. The Court's rulings are, therefore, positive law for all member states. The decisions of the European Court of Justice contradict part of the literal text of the fourth directive on pension schemes. It is not clear as to what extent the *Barber* judgement has retroactive effect. A protocol attached to the Maastricht Treaty with respect to article 119 provides that no retroactive effect may be given to Court decisions on wage issues, but recent judgements of the European Court of Justice provide evidence that this provision is subject to certain restrictions. For instance, a Dutch part-time female worker who had been excluded from pension schemes was granted pension rights because she had initiated legal proceedings in 1986. In order to obtain the pension entitlement, however, she still had to pay all pension contributions.

The rules on pensions apply equally to the employer's contribution to social security schemes: these contributions are also regarded as a wage element (*Liefting* case). The term set for implementation of the EU directive in matters of social security has meanwhile expired. All member states must have adjusted their national law. If not, the relevant member state can be held liable for damages (*Francovich* case) and the European Court of Justice may even grant direct effect to rules which were not subject to such direct effect before.

Article 119 provides that equal pay without discrimination based on sex means:

1 that pay for the same work at piece rates shall be calculated on the basis of the same unit of measurement;
2 that pay for work at time rates shall be the same for the same job.

Furthermore, it may be inferred from the first directive that the principle of equal pay not only applies to equal work but also to 'work to which equal value is attributed'.

Equal work or work of equal value can be proved by means of a 'comparator'. The European Court of Justice does not accept any 'hypothetical comparator', but allows comparison with a female worker's predecessor or a male worker who performs less (but earns more). Under Community law the 'comparator' need not work in the same company, a rule which is infringed regularly in national legislation.

Comparing work or jobs can be achieved on the basis of a job classification system. The system applied must have been implemented on the basis of objective criteria. It may contain elements which generally favour one of the sexes, but it must be in balance as a whole (*Rummler Dato Truck* case). If the employer applies a completely non-transparent system, it will be up to him to prove that the system is not discriminatory (*Danfoss* case). The European Commission is working hard to adopt further directives on job classifications. Particularly due to the work of the trade unions, the courts in the UK are now beginning to compare inequality of work which should have been treated as work of equal value under the job classification systems (*Wendy Smith* case). New legal instruments are, therefore, under development in this area. The role of the job classification systems in breaking down labour-market segregation will be discussed in Chapter 12.

EFFECTIVENESS OF COMMUNITY LAW

Role of the EU institutions

For reasons which were initially of a purely economic nature, the European Union has played a significant role in developing the legal instruments intended to combat unequal treatment of female workers on the European labour market. However, how effective are these instruments? This is not an easy question, since improvements in the labour-market position of female workers cannot be attributed simply to the effect of legal instruments introduced to combat discrimination on the grounds of sex. Such developments may also have been the result of autonomous cultural changes, such as altered views on the position of women or changed economic circumstances (like the growing lack of qualified workers, which has led to a greater demand for female staff).

Nevertheless, we may conclude that legal developments at the European level have made a significant contribution to improving the labour-market position of women. Various factors play a role in this respect:

1 the direct effect attributed to the principle of equal pay and related matters;
2 the effect of 'conformity' as required by the European Court of Justice for interpreting the rules of Community law;
3 the force derived from the European Commission's policies to adjust national legislation in the field of equal treatment;
4 the EU obligation to adopt national rules governing parental leave and other matters affecting the labour-market position of women.

Due to its supranational position, the Union can also break through deadlocks within the member states at both a political and legal level. This can be illustrated, for instance, by the political battle fought in Germany over the equal treatment legislation, which was settled by the European Court in an infringement procedure initiated by the Commission, or by the fact that the European Commission put pressure on the Netherlands to enact at the very least a 'narrow' law on equal treatment after political discussions on civil rights seemed to have bogged down. After EU intervention the UK broadened its equal pay legislation by introducing the concept of work 'of equal value'.

When joining the Union, the countries of Southern Europe (Greece, Spain, Portugal) adopted laws on equal treatment in conformity with the EU directives, even though the political basis in those countries was inadequate at the time.

EU contribution to the development of legislation

The EU has made a significant contribution to the development of an appropriate set of rules to combat discrimination on the grounds of sex. This contribution was particularly noticeable where it concerned the clarification of norms and the interpretation of concepts required for a proper approach to equal treatment problems. The Union is gradually expanding equal treatment norms to areas which go beyond the actual concerns of labour, such as pensions and social security. Furthermore, the Union is working to enhance the judicial position of those discriminated against and it also provides the basis on which the principle of equal pay can be worked out.

Enforcement of and compliance with the EU norms have thus far led to many problems. The European Court demands realistic sanctions to complete the rules of Community law in the field of equal treatment, but there is little supervision of compliance in practice.

Proper anti-discrimination legislation is inconceivable without clear norms. The greatest contribution which the EU has made thus far is to clarify the distinction between direct and indirect discrimination by declaring unequal treatment on the grounds of pregnancy a form of direct discrimination and on the grounds of marital and family status a type of indirect discrimination. The EU has provided reference points for a review of objective justifications and has also made it clear that exemptions from the norm of equal treatment should be interpreted restrictively (see the section: National equal opportunities legislation).

The decision to extend the term 'pay' to include pension and social security entitlement has deeply affected labour and management and the social insurance and pension sector. The reason for this impact is that the interpretation of the relevant provisions, which have direct effect, must be adhered to at the national level. In its judgement in the *Barber* case, the European Court broke through the deadlock in the decision-making process concerning the directives on pension and social security. However, this approach by the European Court also has a disadvantage. At present, legal developments are based exclusively on court decisions, and this leads to uncertainty and interpretation difficulties. The member states have made an attempt to limit the consequences of the *Barber* case by amending the EU Treaty, but the scope of this amendment is by no means certain given the more recent decisions issued by the European Court.

Community law has also resulted in judicial improvements. In recent decisions the European Court has provided a basis for achieving a more balanced distribution of the burden of proof. It is no longer the person discriminated against who must produce all the evidence. Part-time work is considered a suspicious criterion, which means that the burden of proof will be shifted from the employee who is discriminated against to the employer as soon as there is adequate proof that the part-timers concerned are mainly female. The decision by the European Court takes precedence over national procedural law and, therefore, has effect in all member states.

The developments in the field of equal pay have thus far mainly focused on the term 'pay', but due to the 'equal value' notion, the opportunities to battle against unequal pay practices outside the direct workplace have increased. The review of job classification systems against EU norms also contributes to efforts to eliminate segregation on the labour market. For instance, the EU is developing a legal basis for a 'comparable worth strategy' (see Chapter 12). The requirements for a proper job classification system have become stricter and the European Court has held with regard to a non-transparent remuneration system that it is the employer who must prove that the system is not discriminatory. The European Commission is, therefore, working on a policy to fight segregation in the labour market through job classifications. New developments can be expected in this field.

Effectiveness

The effect of anti-discrimination legislation depends on whether the enforcement mechanism is adequate. At present, the European institutions themselves are assuming a share of the responsibility for enforcing and complying with the equality norms by means of court decisions and directives. This may be the reason the Union has never made any attempt to support the establishment of national enforcement agencies in this field. However, compliance within the member states is not always perfect. On the other hand, special legal proceedings have been set up; class actions and actions by interest groups are allowed in various member states. Specific enforcement agencies are noticeably absent within the EU, except for the UK and the Netherlands. French legislation on equal treatment is a good example of an excellent form of legislation that is nevertheless poorly complied with. This indicates that it is impossible to do without an enforcement agency and that highly motivated interest groups (such as unions and pressure groups) are also an absolute necessity.

This view is supported by American research into the macro effects of anti-discrimination legalization in the 1970s, which showed an increase in labour-market opportunities for women and an improvement of their position on the labour market as a result of statutory obligations and administrative measures against discrimination. Both the supervisory measures of enforcement agencies and trial proceedings instigated by the civil rights movement proved to be important factors for actual compliance (Leonard, 1985).

Once again: the principle of equality

Reviewing the major decisions issued by the European Court in the field of equal treatment, what strikes us is that the proceedings are often initiated by a man who feels harmed by the principle of equality (*Lieftink*, *Barber*) or that the litigating woman does not benefit from the decision (*Defrenne*). Is this the irony of fate, or is there some more deeply rooted social phenomenon which sees to it that the principle of equality will ultimately benefit only men? As it is, Community law developments should be followed attentively: the economic objective of the struggle against unfair competition lingers on in the background, and the EU's rules are non-sexist and not aimed specifically at women.

On the other hand, emancipation aspects are clearly recognizable in the European Commission's policies and the European Court's decisions. The most striking decision in this regard concerns the protection of pregnant workers, in that the employment-related risks of pregnancy are now borne by the employer rather than the employee. The decision on part-time work have also indicated that the European Court rejects any treatment of women as second-class employees. Neither does the Court accept achieving equal treatment by depriving women of their privileges: equally poor is not equal. It is to be hoped that the European social policies in the field of equal treatment will continue to have their own independent force and that application of the principle of equality will continue to focus with due care on improving the position of women.

REFERENCES

ELLIS, E. (1991) *European Community Sex Equality*, Clarendon Press, Oxford.

HEWLETT, S. A. (1986) *A Lesser Life. The Myth of Woman's Liberation in America*, Warner Books, New York.

LEONARD, J. S. (1985) *The Impact of Affirmative Action*, a study submitted to the Dept of Labor, National Bureau of Economic Research, Inc., Harvard University Press, Cambridge, Mass., October 1985.

MACKINNON, C. A. (1987) *Feminism Unmodified. Discourses on Life and Law*, Harvard University Press, Cambridge, Mass.

MINOW, M. (1990) *Making All the Difference. Inclusion, Exclusion and American Law*, Cornell University Press, Ithaca/London.

PRECHAL, S. and BURROWS, N. (1990) *Gender Discrimination Law of the European Community*, Aldershot, Dartmouth.

SCALES, A. C. (1986) The emergency of a feminist jurisprudence, *Yale Law Journal*, Vol. 95.

WOLGAST, E. (1980) *Equality and the Rights of Women*, Cornell University Press, Ithaca.

CHAPTER 10

Policies for Children and Parents in Four European Countries

LIESBETH POT

INTRODUCTION

This chapter will focus on how governments in 4 European Union (EU) countries attempt to reduce the strains on women with young children who try to combine paid employment with caring for their children. Caring for young children is seen as one of the obstacles to women gaining an equal position in the labour market. Although comparative research has yet to be conducted into this issue, there are indications that a highly developed system of child-care and flexible-leave schemes reduce the strains and positively influence female employment. The situation on caring for children in 3 small EU countries – Denmark, Belgium and the Netherlands – is compared to that in the UK. What options were created, by whom, and what were the choices women with children were offered? What is the EU's policy on this matter and which instruments does it use? Which of these approaches seem attractive alternatives for the future?

The 3 small countries focused on have been chosen because of:

1 their physical proximity – comparing distant countries may seem less relevant;
2 their size – Belgium, Denmark and the Netherlands are similar in terms of surface area, although the Netherlands, where the population of more than 15 million almost equals that of Belgium and Denmark combined, is far more densely populated;
3 their social and cultural affinity.

Of the above reasons, the last one also holds for the UK. Another common aspect of all 4 countries is that they are bounded by the sea. Moreover, the Netherlands, Belgium and the UK all have former colonies and share a racially mixed population.

The information presented is based on material of the EU Network on Childcare (official publications, and not published internal country reports) and on other research. Wherever possible the most recent statistics and data are presented. Statistics for all 12 EU countries (prior to 1995, that is) may, however, be less up to date.

In this chapter EU policy on equal opportunities for women with young children is presented, followed by data on working parents with children in the 4 EU countries, and an overview of officially provided services for young children in the 12 EU countries. Also, unofficial arrangements and fiscal policy for parents with young children in the 4 countries are explored. Historical backgrounds of actual policies on women with children in the 4 countries are compared, and their policy objectives and instruments. Looking ahead, the chapter concludes by balancing the benefits and cost of these policies.

THE EUROPEAN UNION AND EQUAL OPPORTUNITIES: POLICY INSTRUMENTS

In a social action programme set up in 1974, the EU, the former European Community (EC), argued in support of women's equality in the labour force. Because the lack of adequate facilities for working mothers was viewed as one of the causes of inequality, the EU recommended giving 'immediate priority to the problems of providing facilities to enable women to reconcile family responsibilities with job aspiration'.

Although the European Commission (the executive body of the Community) did recognize the relationship between caring for children and equal opportunities in its First Action Programme on the Promotion of Equal Opportunities for Women (1982–5), the policy measures remained restricted. Opposition on the part of the UK government prevented the implementation of a 1984 Directive on Parental Leave and Leave for Family Reasons. Meanwhile, an international study was carried out on child-care facilities (Piachault, 1984). Participants at an EC seminar in Rome on parental leave and child care (1985) stressed the close connection between both policy instruments. In its second action programme (1986–90), the European Commission expressed its intention 'to propose recommendations for action in the field of day-care facilities' and set up a network of European experts to act as its advisers. This 'Childcare Network' (1986) was the sixth expert network, and was composed of an independent expert of each of the 12 EC countries plus a co-ordinator. In 1991, at the start of the third action programme of the European Commission, the network was renamed 'Network on Childcare and other Measures to reconcile Employment and Family Responsibilities', thereby indicating its broader scope.

Policy recommendations by the Network on Childcare

The first task of the network in 1987 was to conduct a survey into the types of care given to the approximately 40 million children under the age of 10 within the EC while their parents were away at work or in training. Previous research had lacked coherence or was incomplete. Furthermore, it did not cover those countries which had only recently become EC members, such as Spain and Portugal. The publication of the network's report, *Childcare and Equality of Opportunity* (Moss, 1988), compensated largely for the gaps in information.

The most important policy recommendations of this report to the Commission were that:

1 A global directive on child-care provisions should be drawn up, accompanied by recommendations concerning its implementation. The directive should ensure the accessibility, diversity, availability, quality, and quality control of child-care services; it should also guarantee that child-care personnel would receive adequate pay and terms and conditions of employment, be appropriately educated and trained, and that good relations should exist between the child-care service and parents.

2 Changes should be encouraged in organizations to make it easier to combine paid work and caring for children, to be achieved via a system of leave provisions, for example maternity leave, parental leave and special leave to care for sick children. Recommendations for implementation would also accompany these suggestions. The rejected directive on parental leave would be subject to a review.

In order to offer parents various choices based on their individual needs and circumstances, the connection between services for young children and leave provisions was emphasized. In 1992 the Council of Ministers adopted a Recommendation of Childcare; in 1995 the Commission will publish a *Guide to Good Practice*, advising countries how to achieve the various goals set by the recommendation. An official evaluation of the progress made under the recommendation will be held in 1995. Also forthcoming in 1995 is a network document on quality of services for young children to accompany the *Guide to Good Practice*. Although the Commission's competence is limited to promoting equal treatment between women and men, the Parental Leave Directive stresses (in an explanatory memo) that it is based on the principle of equal treatment for women and men and refers to the 1976 Directive on Equal Treatment. The network is of the opinion that all young children and all parents (mothers and fathers) in the EU should have equal opportunities and equal access to good quality services and leave arrangements.

ACTUAL POLICIES FOR PARENTS WITH CHILDREN: A COUNTRY COMPARISON

What policy measures have been taken by governments in the Netherlands, Denmark, Belgium and the UK with respect to the reconciliation of employment and family responsibilities? To get an idea of the scope of this problem, an overview of working parents (mothers and fathers) with children under the age of 10 in these 4 countries is given.

Working parents with young children

The most recent comparative data concerning working parents with young children are those gathered by the Labour Force Supply, published in *Mothers, Fathers and Employment 1985–1991*, by the European Commission.

Table 10.1 reveals significant national differences between the 4 countries with respect to the number of working parents with young children:

1 The Netherlands has the smallest percentage of working women with children under the age of 10 and, relatively speaking, the most significant

Table 10.1   **Working parents with one or more children under the age of 10, 1985–92**

| COUNTRY | PERCENTAGE EMPLOYED 1991 | | WOMEN 20–39 NO CHILD | CHANGE IN % OF EMPLOYED 1985–91 |
	WOMEN WITH CHILD 0–9	MEN WITH CHILD 0–9		WOMEN WITH CHILD 0–9
Belgium	60 [22]	94 [1]	81 [14]	+9.0 [+8.6]
Denmark	75 [28]	92 [2]	77 [15]	−0.8 [−5.6]
Netherlands	40 [35]	92 [8]	79 [29]	+16.7 [−15.7]
UK	51 [20]	88 [1]	87 [8]	+13.2 [+6.5]
E12	51 [20]	92 [2]	76 [9]	+8.7 [+7.3]*

The numbers given in square brackets indicate the percentage of part-time employment.
* Excluding Spain, Portugal and new German *Länder*.

SOURCE: *Mothers, Fathers and Employment 1985–91*, Equal Opportunities Unit, Commission of the European Communities (1993)

increase in this category between 1985 and 1991, followed by the UK.

2 The percentage of part-time employees is considerable in all categories.

3 In Denmark the percentage of working women with children almost equals the percentage of working women without children. Women with children do tend to work in part-time employment more often.

4 Men with children score extremely high in all 4 countries, but lower in the UK than elsewhere; the Netherlands has the largest percentage of fathers in part-time employment.

5 In the UK the percentage of employed mothers with children equals the average.

The countries differ further with respect to working hours, unemployment, and the number of single and married women with children in employment. The data do not offer any insight into 'hidden' unemployment.

Further points to be noted are:

1 In the Netherlands, of all women with children under 10 actually employed in 1991 (excluding those reporting to be unemployed), 87.5% had part-time jobs; in the UK part-time jobs counted for 67.5% of employed women with children. In both countries, these women worked 10–19 hours per week on average.

2 In Belgium the percentage of women working part time was only 36.5%; most of them worked 20–29 hours weekly, as was the case in Denmark, where 37% of the mothers with children under 10 years of age worked part time.

3 The highest rate of unemployment for women having young children was found in Denmark (12%); 9% in Belgium and 6% in both the Netherlands and the UK.

4 Single mothers with children worked less frequently in the Netherlands and the UK, but were more likely to be employed in Belgium and Denmark. They worked, however, for longer hours than married women. Unemployment in this category was considerably higher than for women with children who were either married or cohabiting.

These data reveal that the position of Dutch women with young children in the labour market compares unfavourably to the other 3 countries and also to the EU as a whole. Lower than average participation rates were found in Ireland (38%), Luxembourg (42%) and Spain (44%). The Netherlands and the UK share a sharp rise in the percentage of working women with children since 1985, as is the case – although to a lesser extent – for Ireland and Germany. Labour participation patterns in countries in the middle of the EU (the Netherlands, the UK, Ireland and Germany) seem to catch up with those in France, Belgium and Italy, but are still far below the Danish rate. Looking at the number of hours worked per week, the UK and the Netherlands share a high part-time employment and the shortest working week.

SERVICES FOR PARENTS WITH YOUNG CHILDREN

What arrangements have governments created for parents to take care of young children? These arrangements include leave systems to stay at home when children are still very young, and organized services for young children. 'Services for young children' also may include education schemes for young children where 'care' is an implicit function. By adopting this broader definition, the terminology used by the EC Network on Childcare is followed.

Leave provisions

Table 10.2 presents data on maternity, paternity and other official leave arrangements in all 12 EU countries in 1994, as published by the European Commission Network on Childcare (1994b). The discussion of this data will be restricted to Belgium, Denmark, the Netherlands and the UK.

In Belgium leave is intended above all as a measure against unemployment, as is the case in Denmark, which introduced a new type of leave in 1994. The schemes in both countries are not meant for child care only, but can be taken for other reasons as well, such as study leave or a sabbatical. The length of the leave may vary: see Table 10.2.

Belgian employers are allowed to take a total of 5 periods of leave during their working life. In the public sector this is a right; in the private sector it depends on the particular bargaining agreement or employment contract. A condition of the leave is that someone who is unemployed takes over. The leave may be taken for half of the working week. Public sector workers also may take up to 3 months of unpaid parental leave until the child has reached the age of 1. Fathers in the public sector receive 4 days of paid paternity leave; in the private sector they have 3 days off.

The new Danish 'child-care leave' is extended to unemployed people, as well as self-employed and family workers, who were excluded from former statutory parental leave. Payment is at 80% of the level of the unemployment benefit and the leave is an individual, non-transferable right for each parent. The minimum leave-period is set at 13 weeks, because Swedish studies show that the period should be long enough to allow

Table 10.2   **Statutory leave arrangements in 12 EU countries, 1994**

COUNTRY	MATERNITY LEAVE	PARENTAL LEAVE
Belgium	15 weeks: 1 week before birth, 8 weeks after, 6 weeks before or after. Paid at 82% of earnings for first month, then 75% up to a maximum level.	No statutory leave. Workers can take 6–12 months' 'career break', if employer agrees. Paid at flat rate BF10,928 a month.
Denmark	18 weeks: 4 weeks before birth, 14 after. Paid at flat rate (DKK 2,556 a week, approx. 65% of average earnings for industrial worker).	10 weeks, paid as for ML. In addition, each worker can take leave for child care, training or sabbatical of 13–56 weeks, of which 26 should be agreed by employer, at 80% of ML. This is an individual leave.
Germany	14 weeks: 6 weeks before birth, 8 after, plus 4 weeks extra for multiple or premature birth, paid at 100% of earnings.	36 months per family. DM 600 for the first 6 months, next 24 months income-related benefit. Leave may be shared between parents, under conditions.
Greece	14 weeks: 3 weeks before and 7 weeks after, 4 weeks before or after. Paid at 100% of earnings.	3 months per parent, not transferable, unpaid.
France	16–26 weeks: 4 weeks before birth, 10 after, 2 before or after, extra leave for third or higher order birth. Paid at 84% of earnings, but untaxed.	36 months per family. Unpaid for first and second child, then flat rate of FF 2,738 a month.
Ireland	14 weeks: 4 weeks before birth, 10 before or after. Mother can request extra 4 weeks. First 14 weeks paid at 70% of earnings (untaxed), extra weeks unpaid.	None.
Italy	5 months: 2 months before birth, 3 months after. Paid at 80% of earnings.	6 months, paid at 30% of earnings.
Luxembourg	16 weeks: 4 weeks before and 8 weeks after. Paid at 100% of earnings.	None.
Netherlands	16 weeks: 4 before birth, 10 weeks after, 2 weeks before or after. Paid at 100% of earnings.	6 months' reduced hours per parent, minimum of 20 hours' work per week and not transferable. Unpaid.
Portugal	90 days: 60 days after birth, 30 days before or after. Paid at 100% of earnings.	24 months, unpaid.
Spain	16 weeks: 6 weeks after and 10 weeks before or after birth. Paid at 75% of earnings.	12 months, unpaid.
UK	40 weeks: 11 weeks before birth, 29 after. Paid at 90% of earnings for 6 weeks, flat rate for 12 weeks and unpaid for remaining period	None.

SOURCE: European Commission Network on Childcare (1993, 1994a)

fathers to get used to their new domestic and caring tasks. It is expected that 75% of workers on leave will be replaced by unemployed workers and that the scheme will have no consequences for public spending. The leave will be evaluated after 3 years of operation, in order to study its effectiveness. After the birth of a child, fathers have 2 weeks of paid paternity leave.

In the Netherlands the statutory leave is to be viewed as a minimum: it does not, however, apply to women in a family business, or to the self-employed. Collective agreements may extend the period of parental leave. For example, public sector workers are offered more favourable arrangements: they may reduce their working hours by half for 6 months while still receiving about 75% of their salary. Because many women work part time and part of lost earnings is compensated for, this scheme for public sector workers turns out to be much more successful than statutory leave. Paternity leave depends on collective bargaining agreements.

The UK has not statutory parental leave; at individual company level arrangements do, however, exist, although coverage is limited.

Leave for family reasons and 'emergency' leave

In Belgium public sector workers are allowed to take 8 days of paid leave annually and a maximum of 2 months of unpaid leave for family reasons. In the private sector it depends on collective or individual agreements

Although in Denmark it is not considered as a right, almost all parents are allowed to stay at home on the first day of a child's illness.

The Netherlands does not recognize a general right to leave when a child is ill. In a few special cases provisions have been made in collective agreements.

In the UK parents have no legal right to take days off when a child or another member of the family is taken ill. Not unlike in the Netherlands, parents (mostly mothers) often report ill themselves.

Considering the opportunities offered to women with young children in these 4 countries to carry their 'double burden' through various leave measures, it becomes clear that the UK provides the least attractive scheme so far as legal rights are concerned. At individual company level arrangements may be better; company arrangements may cover men as well. Denmark has the most favourable system, especially since the introduction of its new 'child-care leave', and also in comparison to other countries of the EU.

Services for young children

Which government policies on providing services for young children exist in the EU, enabling parents to combine paid employment and caring for children? These policies comprise financial subsidies by central or local authorities, planning, (quality) control and other forms of public support (see Table 10.3). Because in none of the 12 EU countries public supply of provisions keeps up with demand, non-subsidized forms of child care are also referred to.

Provisions for pre-school children

The demand for services for young children is related, first and foremost, to the features of the official school system. Countries differ with respect to the age at which children are allowed to attend school (nursery, pre-school and primary school), the age of compulsory schooling, and the number of required classroom hours per day and/or week. These various factors influence the demand for supplementary services while parents are at work. The presence or lack of extensive provisions for pre-school children also has an impact on demand. Table 10.3 presents the latest available information (varying from 1986 to 1989) on the 12 EU countries. New comparable statistics are not yet available, but will appear during 1995. Therefore the latest data are discussed in relation to the 4 countries.

The child-care function of education

Table 10.3 reveals how widely the system of education in various countries differs. This would become even wider were the admission age to nursery or pre-school included. In some cases (France and Belgium) this is below 3 years of age.

In Belgium, for example, children may attend nursery school, free of charge, from the age of 2.5 years; 10–11% of all children under the age of 3 do attend.

Table 10.3 **Percentage of pre-school children attending subsidized/publicly funded provision, compulsory school age and length of school day**

COUNTRY	YEAR	USE BY CHILDREN UNDER 3 YEARS OF AGE (%) *	USE FROM AGE 3 TO COMPULSORY SCHOOLING (%) *	AGE OF COMPULSORY SCHOOLING (YEARS)	LENGTH OF SCHOOL DAY (HOURS) *
Germany	1987	3	65–70	6–7	4–5
France	1988	20	95+	6	8
Italy	1986	5	85+	6	4
Netherlands	1989	2	50–55†	5	6–7
Belgium	1988	20	95+	6	7
Luxembourg	1989	2	55–60†	5	4–8
United Kingdom	1988	2	35–40	5	6.5
Ireland	1988	2	55	6	4.5–6.5
Denmark	1989	48	85	7	3–5.5
Greece	1988	4	65–70	5.5	4–5
Portugal	1988	6	35	6	6.5
Spain	1988	n.a.	65–70	6	8

* Percentages refer to the number of full-time places relative to total number of children. The number of children actually attending may be higher, because some attend part time. In several countries the number of school hours increases as children get older. Playgroup attendance in the Netherlands, the UK and Ireland is not included in this table.

† Admission age to nursery or (pre)school is set at 4 years.

SOURCE: European Commission Network on Childcare (1990)

Children 18 months and older may be sent to playgroups, which are frequently connected with a nursery school.

In Denmark all 6- and some 5-year-olds attend nursery school 3 hours a day; in addition, most children also attend some other type of public service. As children get older the number of hours spent in school increases.

In the Netherlands most children attend primary school from the age of 4; per day they spend about 5 hours in the classroom, although this is frequently less for younger children. Playgroups for 2- and 3-year-olds are generally not open long enough to be an option for working parents: 6–7 hours a week for 2 days is the average attendance.

The Netherlands and Luxembourg are the only EU countries where children are admitted to nursery or (pre)primary schooling when they have reached the age of 4, while 3 years is the common age in other countries. Table 10.3 reveals this difference in the use of provisions from the age of 3 to compulsory schooling: although almost all children of 4 (95%+) in the Netherlands attend school on a voluntary basis, children of 3 are excluded, which is shown in their rather low percentage attendance. The Netherlands and the UK (and Ireland) are unique in the EU with respect to admitting children to primary school before compulsory age, for the UK at least indicating a failure to develop universal nursery education.

Privately run playgroups are also widely used in England, Wales, Scotland and Ireland by children aged 3 and 4 years. In this respect, the UK and the Netherlands are alike as far as the function of playgroups is concerned: they act as a substitute for nursery education, which is not yet (or is insufficiently) available for the age groups involved. Parents pay for this provision, while the nursery or pre-school in general is free of charge. Especially in the UK, various options for pre-school provision are used by parents to compensate for the lack of free, public education: private nursery schools, playgroups and (mostly part-time) nursery schooling. In the UK competition between services for children below compulsory school age is widely spread; this is not the case in the Netherlands, where – besides day nurseries – playgroups form the only centre-based option available for 2- and 3-year-olds.

Care outside school hours

Data concerning care outside school hours (meaning child care for school-age children before and after school, during lunchtime, on days off and during the holidays) are scarce and piecemeal. This is partly because of the many organizations and groups involved. In a number of EU countries this task traditionally falls to the school. Usually care outside school hours is organized locally; this makes it difficult to survey the situation at a national level.

For the 4 countries covered in this chapter, for example, national data on Belgium concerning the extent to which services are available outside school hours do not exist. This type of care is generally the province of nursery and primary schools and is set up locally. The services offered (meals, available space and supervision) differ widely from town to town, and are usually far from adequate. The average school day is relatively long, although there are no classes held on Wednesday. In Dutch-speaking Belgium a limited number of children between the ages of 3 and 6 are cared for by organized child-minders. In 1988 approximately 11% of the children between 3 and 14 years of age attended provisions during holiday periods. In Flanders these are organized by the Jeugdafdeling (Youth Department) and in French-speaking Belgium by the ONE, a service acting for the federal government as provider and supervisor of publicly funded child care. Care outside school hours not organized by schools, but offered as 'free time' for children, is a rather new phenomenon in Flanders, and is expanding rapidly.

In Denmark care outside school hours is organized both in child-care centres and in the schools themselves. Children who have reached compulsory school age attend these services in addition to regular school attendance. In 1989, 29% of all children between the ages of 7 and 10 attended such provisions; in 1992 their participation had gone up to 40%. Seventy per cent of care outside school hours was provided by services other than school-based ones; a recent trend is a shift to school-based centres.

The Netherlands has a limited number of services offering child care before and after school hours and during the holidays. In 1993, 0.8% of children between 4 and 13 years old (the age when they normally finish primary school) made use of centre-based provisions for care, mostly after school hours. Some day nurseries also accept schoolchildren and a number of centres have been set up exclusively to provide care outside school hours. Since the introduction in 1985 of a new primary school structure covering both nursery school and primary school, and a 1984 Act of Parliament requiring the provision of lunchtime care, schools have to provide space for children whose parents wish them to stay during the lunch break. The Act does not make provisions for lunch break supervision or the cost involved in providing supervision. About 90% of Dutch schools have made arrangements for child care during the lunch break. The introduction of continuous timetables in schools – particularly in the built-up area in the western part of the country – has aggravated rather than relieved the problem of child care after school hours. Activities during the holidays are usually arranged at the local level by various organizations.

In the UK nursery and primary schools usually provide supervision and meals during lunchtime. Lessons are from 9.00 to 15.30, but tend to be shortened in some schools. Most children go to nursery education on a part-time shift basis, so only full-time children can stay for lunch. It is estimated that care outside school hours reaches now over 0.5% of the children from 5 to 10 years. It is provided mostly in the schools themselves and free of charge for parents. For other services outside school, parents have to make a contribution. Services are concentrated in and around the larger cities: a third are situated in the London inner city area.

Other services for young children

It is almost impossible to form a clear picture of private, non-subsidized care for young children, precisely because such arrangements are generally unofficial and informal. Young children in every country of the EU – except Denmark – are cared for primarily by partners and relatives, usually by their grandmothers. A significant decrease is apparent, however, in countries such as Denmark and Sweden, where a large proportion of the labour force is made up of women and where public services are rather extensive. In both countries private arrangements are a minority. Another rather popular type of care is paid care at home, usually by someone who also does some light work around the home. Some households employ nannies or au pairs lodging with the family.

In Belgium the role played by private, non-subsidized services and/or workplace nurseries is growing. In 1992 licensed private day nurseries and child-minders in Flanders served 10,500 children under 6 years of age, or a quarter of all organized care (Vandemeulebroecke, 1993). Most centres are rather small.

Such provisions barely exist at all in Denmark, although 40% of day nurseries are independent and not run by local authorities (Jensen and Jensen 1991). There is, however, no difference between both forms of provision, either financially or with respect to objectives, standards and philosophy. The commitment to community-based services is strong; therefore, Denmark has little private unsubsidized provision or provisions by employers.

The number of such services in the Netherlands, on the other hand, has increased considerably in the 1980s, largely because the government has failed to take any steps toward meeting the rising demand for child care. A study conducted in 1990 by the Dutch Federation of Trade Unions FNV (Miedema and Pelzer, 1990) turned up approximately 5,000 places, either in non-subsidized workplace nurseries or in subsidized nursery centres where companies had reserved places for their employees. About one third of the total number of places available at that time were provided outside the subsidized (or public) sector. Although the percentage of children involved was small, there was a considerable increase in relative terms: from almost 0 to 0.75% of children up to the age of 4 (as opposed to 1.5% of children under 4 years in subsidized places). A new government scheme operating since 1990 ('Stimulative Measure on Childcare, 1990–1995') intends to enlarge the involvement of employers in providing services for children. In 1992, 25% of available places were bought by employers in the public and private sector, covering almost 10,000 places. Apart from services receiving some public funds, there are also a number of centres that are run privately, either by parents themselves or as small enterprises. In 1992 these centres covered 8,500 places, almost half financed by employers. Altogether, in 1992 services offered 47,100 places for children under the age of 13. In 1993 places were offered for almost 63,000 children, or almost 2.7% of children aged 0–12 (CBS, 1994). In 1992 places were available for 5.1% of the children under 4, while actual use covered 8.4% of children in this age group, because most of them are part-time users (CBS, 1993). In 1993 places for children under 4 (in all forms of centre-based services, excluding playgroups) had grown to 6.6% (CBS, 1994).

In the UK public services for young children hardly increased in the 1980s. Most local authority nurseries are accessible only to 'children in need'; working parents wanting group care have to turn to community and private nurseries or company-run provisions. As in the Netherlands, these private services have seen a large increase in the 1980s, while public services catered for only 1% of the children under 3. It is estimated that in 1988 private and voluntary day nurseries served somewhat over 1% of children under 3 years of age (Cohen, 1993).

Many parents opt for individual care provided by child-minders; this may vary from government-subsidized, organized or licensed services to unofficial or even illegal arrangements. For services subject to licensing, the number of children that can be cared for simultaneously is set at a maximum of 3 or 4 in addition to the child-minder's own children. In Denmark family daycare is part of the official public child-care system. Child-minders are well paid – although they cost less than daycare centres – and are considered government employees. In recent years the proportion of relatives and privately arranged child-minders has decreased: a greater number of parents prefer public services. Well over 71,000 children under 10 years of age are using family daycare schemes, covering about 21% of the supply of services.

Belgium has an official network of child-minders who receive a fee for their services, which is not subject to tax or social security deductions. The ONE negotiates places for about 4% of children under the age of 3. In Flanders in 1992, 63% of subsidized places for children under 3 years of age were realized through organized family daycare, covering about 19,000 places (Vandemeulebroecke, 1993). Child-minders must be licensed and are subject to supervision and monitoring. As with nurseries, parents pay a fee based on income. In addition to this official system there is also an extensive network of clandestine child-minding.

The Netherlands has had an organized system of family daycare since the late 1970s. At the end of 1993 there were about 230 family daycare agencies in operation, acting as intermediaries between parents and child-minders and at times also offering other services. About 6,400 children were offered care through these agencies (CBS, 1994). Companies also reserve places in family daycare for their employees, but to a much lesser extent than was expected at the start of the Stimulative Measure. Family daycare in the Netherlands is not subject to licensing or inspection as in Denmark and Belgium. In a few cases parents pay according to income, but payment is usually made directly to the child-minder and based on a fixed fee per hour per child. Tax and social security contributions should be paid only if the child-minders earn more than an annual tax-free amount. Therefore, most child-minders try to keep under this limit by having only 1 or sometimes 2 children in their care. The status of this type of work is still not clearly established or regulated and continues to be a topic of debate.

In the UK child-minders are the most common form of child care, after partners, relatives and friends. In 1988 over 5% of children under 5 were looked after by a child-minder. Most child-minders (80%) are registered; some receive support and training from local authorities or are assisted by the National Childminding Association. Child-minders are popular for two reasons: they are a cheap solution for local authorities and they correspond with the still strongly held belief that individual care suits young children better than group care (Moss, 1991). This also holds for playgroups, which are widely spread in the UK and in the Netherlands. There is not only an ideological explanation for the popularity of playgroups in both countries, which is unique in the European Union (outside the EU they are also popular in, e.g., the USA and New Zealand), but also a financial one. Playgroups were initiated in the 1960s by volunteers, mostly mothers of young children. In the UK they are still paid for primarily by parents; in the Netherlands local authorities offer some support. In both countries their existence not only points to an insufficient infrastructure for services for young children but also illustrates the rather low priority government policy gives to the needs of young children and mothers in a changing society. In both countries 'caring for children' is still seen as a primary responsibility of parents (mothers), in which the state should not interfere except when parents are not suited to their tasks or when the welfare of children is endangered. In this respect it is interesting to note that Dutch playgroups are under heavy pressure since in the 1990s the number of services for working parents has been enlarged, to care for children in need. In the UK playgroups offer a rather cheap alternative to a system – still lacking – of free nursery education. As a consequence, women in the UK and in the Netherlands have largely adapted their working hours to the caring needs of their children.

Fiscal provisions

Parents in Belgium are allowed a tax deduction for costs of child care to a certain maximum (up to 80% of the fee) per child under the age of 3. They must submit the necessary evidence and the service in question must be officially recognized. In addition, parents with children under 3 are entitled to a yearly deduction of BF 10,000 if one of the parents is not employed outside the home.

In Denmark no tax deduction or tax allowance is available for cost of child care.

Between 1984 and 1990 parents having two incomes in the Netherlands were entitled to a rather small additional allowance – on top of the existing family benefit – if they had children under the age of 12. This so-called 'child-care allowance' was, however, not linked to the actual use of child-care. In 1989, as part of a general reform of the Dutch fiscal system, the government decided to eliminate this allowance and to apply the consequential saving (estimated at an annual amount of NFL 130 million) toward expanding the number of places in services for children. Instead, a temporary government measure to encourage the provision of services for young children, the 'Stimulative Measure 1990–1995' was introduced. In 1993 the government spent NFL 260 million on child care. In 1991 the Supreme Court ruled that employees who did not receive compensation from their employers for child care were entitled to a tax deduction for any – proven – child-care expenditure exceeding the cost of attending a subsidized service. Employers buying a place for their employees in an official service receive an annual bonus of at least NFL 2,000. Private, profit-making companies organizing workplace nurseries are allowed to deduct some costs for tax purposes. Apart from a general child benefit introduced in 1975, the UK gives neither an allowance nor a tax deduction for the costs of child care.

Concluding this comparison of services for young children, the outstanding position of Denmark is apparent. Belgium offers a rather broad but incoherent system, in which – besides care by relatives and other private solutions – nursery schools and child-minders cover most of the demand. The Dutch system is still being set up, but offers some perspectives for growth, at least when compared to the UK, where private arrangements are predominant. In the UK the system is also growing, but it depends almost entirely on the operation of the private market.

POLICY BACKGROUNDS

This section reviews the history of government policy on organized services for young children. The history of such services is remarkably similar in most Western nations, with the possible exception of Denmark. The initial impetus for setting up nursery schools or day nurseries was the growing public concern aroused by the plight of young children during a period of increasing industrialization and impoverishment, as lower-class women were forced into employment, often in factories. Such initiatives usually came from charitable organizations or public and religious benefactors; government funding followed at a later date.

In Belgium privately funded daycare centres were set up in a few of the larger cities in around 1850. Important objectives were to alleviate poverty and reduce the mortality rate among children. Government support began in 1919 through a private organization for maternal care and child care. Initially the target group was restricted to lower-income groups and mothers forced into employment. This restriction was lifted in 1970, after which the number of services expanded rapidly.

In Denmark the first day nurseries were founded around the turn of the century. They were set up to help families living on a small income and were motivated by social conscience rather than by the goal of helping mothers enter the work-force. Their function was therefore primarily preventive. The government began to provide funding in 1933; to qualify, at least two-thirds of the children had to come from lower-income groups. Labour-market shortages in the 1960s led to a reorientation in policy and a sharp increase in government funding. A 1964 Act removed the two-thirds limit, which opened the way for general services.

The first day nurseries in the Netherlands were founded in 1872, set up as a result of growing concern about the health of young working-class children whose mothers – due to circumstances like lone motherhood or low family income – had been forced to work. Use of these nurseries was restricted to those in gainful employment. Local authorities began to subsidize such charitable organizations in the 1920s. In the 1960s the number of day nurseries was rather low: about 30. In an official report to the government on future policy (1974), a working group advised against increasing the number of day nurseries, as this was regarded as harmful to young children; mothers should be discouraged from working outside the home. In the mid-1970s the national government stepped in to fulfil a regulatory role, but expansion was not seen as a policy objective. Subsidies to day nurseries were meant primarily for children of parents with low incomes who worked or studied, and for children of disadvantaged groups. By then a total of about 150 day nurseries existed. During the 1980s the emphasis in policy slowly shifted to working women and women re-entering the work-force, but until 1990 the increase in the number of provisions was negligible (Pot, 1988, 1990).

The first day nursery in the UK was set up in 1816, followed by other initiatives after 1850. During the First World War public involvement in day nurseries started and during the Second World War a range of provisions for women employed in the war industries was set up with public assistance. In 1945, 1,300 day nurseries offered places for 62,000 children in England and Wales (Cohen, 1993). Twenty years later their number had been reduced by two-thirds; it was expected that women would – and should – withdraw from paid employment. Instead of services for young children a system of family and tax allowances was introduced in order to keep women at home. In 1975 these allowances were replaced by a child benefit, paid to mothers. Increasing demand for services for young children of employed women was hardly addressed, as the main role of women was still seen as being at home. During the 1980s services for children expanded primarily because employers, trade unions and others took the initiative. Public provision in the UK is for children in need. All else is a private responsibility, including employment of women, which is seen as a private decision.

This brief historical review shows clearly how the emphasis has gradually shifted from protecting working-class children to assisting working parents as part of an equal opportunities policy. The shift occurred most early in Denmark and much later in the Netherlands. In the UK, however, the government has not yet concluded that the changing position of women needs another policy.

SERVICES FOR YOUNG CHILDREN – POLICY OBJECTIVES

Services for young children can be viewed as instruments devised to achieve certain policy objectives. As has been noted, policies in Belgium and Denmark shifted emphasis in the 1960s and 1970s and policy objectives changed accordingly. The same process also took place in the Netherlands, although later and with more reserve. In the UK government policy has not shifted significantly, emphasizing a free market approach. In a way, the 'public/private partnership' which forms the underlying objective of the recent Dutch policy also aims at a free market approach for the near future.

A shortage of labour and a growing desire among women to engage in paid employment and improve their situation were almost constant factors behind the creation of additional child-care and leave alternatives – with the exception of the UK, where gainful employment and caring for children are seen exclusively as a private choice of parents. In the Netherlands the government took a stimulating role in enlarging the number of provisions as a stepping stone to further privatization. In addition, other policy objectives were set, although these were less explicit. Linking labour-market objectives and emancipation goals has frequently had positive effects on policy measures concerning the care given to young children.

In Belgium the expansion of day nurseries was related to women entering the work-force and was a response to this phenomenon. In the early 1980s the emphasis shifted towards expanding the family daycare system, partly for financial reasons, partly because parents preferred their children to be cared for in a home-like environment. The fiscal allowance for families with young children, introduced in 1989, must be seen as a concession to parents who do not or cannot use recognized or licensed services. Opponents are particularly critical of the fact that this measure could stimulate the growth of 'unofficial' child care, while the expansion of public services has stagnated. Therefore, licensing of private nurseries is now one of the objectives of child-care policies. 'Illegal' child-care practices should be brought under supervision, thereby at the same time recognizing the function of child care as a profession. The leave system was enlarged as a measure against unemployment. The funding created in 1992 by allocating 0.05% of wages in the private sector in order to contribute to the expansion of public services should also be regarded as a measure against unemployment.

Expansion in Denmark was also generated by a shortage of labour. In addition, the country's socialist tradition ensured that the welfare of children would be a priority on the political agenda as well. The result was a high-quality system of services combining objectives of 'care' and 'education'. A sharp drop in the birth rate in the 1960s undoubtedly also played a role. It should be noted that Denmark's birth rate has once again begun to climb, even though women form a larger proportion of the labour force than in any other country within the EU. The Danish government has taken a less 'neutral' position than the Belgian government: the emphasis is on providing publicly supported services for children and not on using fiscal measures to subsidize demand. The fact that Denmark has only one system for children under 7 years of age and not a mix of public and private arrangements, like most other Western countries, should be seen as a clear recognition that services for young children are a public responsibility. Although the conservative government tried to diminish the role of the state, this met with strong opposition from parents and workers. The expansion of services in the 1980s and 1990s has been remarkable: between 1988 and 1994 about 400,000 new places have been provided. In 1996 the Danish government will guarantee a place for each child aged 1–6 years.

Until now Denmark has been successful in preserving a rather coherent policy approach. Working with young children is recognized as a real profession, requiring good training and offering adequate pay and a proper trade union for support. Ideologically, services for young children are seen as a supplement to home and family care, and not as an extension of the formal education system. Child-care services have been expanded for economic reasons and to achieve economic policy goals concerning the family, population, welfare and young people.

By contrast, until the early 1980s child care in the Netherlands served to ensure that children from disadvantaged backgrounds received adequate care. It was not until the end of the 1980s that the government accepted some responsibility with respect to equal opportunities for women. Also, the concern that a shortage of labour would arise as a result of the dwindling proportion of young people in the Netherlands and the ageing of the population cleared the way for policy measures encouraging labour participation of women with young children. The 'Stimulative Measure' created about 50,000 new child-care places up to 1994; together with the existing number totalling about 70,000. In 1996 there should be about 80,000 places, to be financed mainly by employers and employees. Central government contribution is now one third of average costs; in 1996 this will further decrease, when local authorities take over. Although undoubtedly a huge task has been carried out, the future is quite uncertain, especially if the economy fails. Will individual employers see it as their task to pay for services for children? What will happen to child-care arrangements in collective agreements? Will there be a national regulation on quality or will this be left to individual centres and organized parents' groups?

In the UK the conservative government did not reach a comparable conclusion, although many groups and experts strongly argued in favour of children- and women-friendly policies. However, by passing the Children Act in 1989, the government for the first time clearly stated its responsibility for the promotion of the welfare of children. On the other hand, the Children Act accentuates parental responsibility for the care of young children, and does not recognize any support for working parents. 'It is for parents or those with parental responsibility to decide in the light of their own circumstances whether to take up paid employment outside the home while their children are young' (HMSO, 1991, p. 30). The 'Children Act' imposes a provision duty only for children in need and a regulation duty for all services and not a general child welfare duty. The promotion of equal opportunities is not regarded as an objective of the state.

In this respect the effects of the Dutch and the British policy measures for equal opportunities (for women) are comparable, although slightly different in outlook. The Dutch 'Stimulative Measure' should in the end lead to a self-supporting child-care system operating in the market, a shared responsibility of social partners and parents, who should have a large say in the quality of services; in the UK certain standards in services should be assured by local authorities, while private enterprise should guarantee a sufficient supply. Both countries are equally ambivalent in their policy objectives; their policy measures reveal an optimistic belief in the operation of the market.

It can be argued that it is an illusion to suppose that parents as consumers of welfare goods (in this case, of services for young children) are as well placed as private enterprise is to ensure and demand high quality services. Good quality care for young children is only a minor objective for employers, to be ensured only as long as it is consistent with economic goals and with a need for women in certain jobs. Women in lower-paid jobs, ethnic groups and children and parents in need are of no special interest to private enterprise and should be taken care of by separate services or at the expense of the taxpayer. In the Netherlands these groups are already excluded from 'public' services and so enlarge the already existing gap between rich and successful citizens and those who remain poor and invisible. In the UK a division between 3 groups is apparent: 'children in need', getting public services, a small group of parents getting employers' support and a large group relying on private services. In both countries services for young children are seen as necessary primarily for the economy – and not for the welfare of children and families.

A LOOK AHEAD

During the European Commission's second Equal Opportunities Action Programme, most of the participating countries saw increased activity in the area of child care, as has been shown earlier. The various results these countries have achieved through their policy measures illustrate that similar problems can be solved in many different ways. At the same time, it shows how closely legislation, social security systems and services for young children are related to social and political norms and values.

Denmark, furthest ahead of the 4 countries in quantity of services and leave provisions, seems to have made this development on its own initiative, as it could not compare its already existing system with other EU countries. Instead, much inspiration was gained from Scandinavian neighbours. The new membership of more Scandinavian countries in the EU may have a positive effect on leave arrangements and services for children in the older member states. The rather pragmatic approach of Belgian policies might easily divert attention from the real problems of working women with young children, although it offers a variety of choices. However, the role of fathers in caring for children is not positively supported by existing arrangements, which are inspired primarily by economic and financial considerations.

One can have reservations about the outcome of the public/private partnership approach of the Netherlands, at least in the form in which it is presented. In the 1980s experts, advisory groups and involved organizations strongly pressed the government to opt for a National Fund, made up of contributions from both government and employers, to be equally redistributed among parents demanding a place. France offers a rather good example of how such a fund can operate. Now, it is up to individual employers to decide if they wish to support services or not, as is the situation in the UK. Moreover, the existing form is too complicated and needs too much red tape to be carried out properly. Parents and workers in services are in no position to influence policies decided at higher levels. But maybe it is the only way in which at least some progress can be made. In the Netherlands and the UK the strong ideology of a mother at home, which was a public theme throughout the 1980s, has shifted to an underlying ideology that women are responsible.

Another possible way forward, at least for the time being, is the use of economic policies by which families and young children would gain, such as the conversion of measures tackling unemployment to expanding leave and child-care arrangements.

Most important is, however, a state policy recognizing that the welfare of women, children and men would gain by further reconciling care and employment, and that such a policy contributes in the end to higher social and economic standards for all.

REFERENCES

CBS (CENTRAAL BUREAU VOOR DE STATISTIEK) (1993) *Kindercentra 1992*, CBS, Voorburg/Heerlen.
CBS (CENTRAAL BUREAU VOOR DE STATISTIEK) (1994) *Kindercentra 1993*, CBS, Voorburg/Heerlen.
COHEN, B. (1993) The United Kingdom, in M. Cochran (ed.), *International Handbook of Child Care Policies and Programs*, Greenwood Press, London, pp. 515–35.
EUROPEAN COMMISSION NETWORK ON CHILDCARE (1990) Childcare in the European Communities 1985–1990, *Women of Europe Special*, no. 31, August, European Commission, Brussels.
EUROPEAN COMMISSION NETWORK ON CHILDCARE (1993) *Employment, Equality and Caring for Children. Annual Report, 1992*, European Commission, Brussels.
EUROPEAN COMMISSION NETWORK ON CHILDCARE (1994) *Annual Report 1993*, European Commission, Brussels.
EUROPEAN COMMISSION NETWORK ON CHILDCARE (1994) *Leave Arrangements for Workers with Children*, European Commission, Brussels.

HMSO (1991) *The Children Act 1989. Guidance and Regulations*, HMSO, London.
JENSEN, J. and JENSEN, C. (1991) I Servizi educativi e sociali per bambini e le lore familglie. Danimarca, speech at a conference in Bologna, April.
MIEDEMA, N. and PELZER, A. (1990) *Kinderopvang in Nederland. De FNV-enquête.* Stichting FNV-pers/Jan Mets, Amsterdam.
MOSS, P. (1988) *Childcare and Equality of Opportunity. Consolidated Report to the European Commission*, European Commission, Brussels.
MOSS, P. (1991) Day care for young children in the United Kingdom, in E. C. Melhuish and P. Moss (eds.), *Day Care for Young Children: International Perspectives*, Tavistock/Routledge, London, pp. 121–42.
PIACHAULT, C. (1984) *Day Care Facilities and Services for Children Under the Age of 3 in the European Community*, European Commission, Brussels.
POT, E. M. (1988) *Kinderopvang nu – Zorgen voor Morgen*, private publication, Amsterdam.
POT, E. M. (1990) Het overheidsbeleid voor jonge kinderen in de jaren tachtig, *Jeugd en Samenleving*, Vol. 4, April, pp. 283–92.
POT, E. M. (1992) Kinderopvang en Ouderschapsverlof, in *Vrouwen en Arbeidsmarktposities binnen de Europese Gemeenschap*, Open universiteit, Heerlen, pp. 59–81.
SGBO (1993) *Kinderopvang in Gemeenten. De stand van zaken per 31 december 1992.* Vereniging van Nederlandse Gemeenten, Den Haag.
VANDEMEULEBROECKE, L. (1993) Kinderopvang in Vlaanderen, *Pedagogisch Tijdschrift*, Vol. 5–6, September, pp. 309–25.

NOTE

The author wishes to thank Peter Moss for his comments on an earlier version of this chapter.

CHAPTER 11

Positive Action in Organizations within the European Union

ATTIE DE JONG AND BETTINA BOCK

INTRODUCTION

This chapter will provide an overview of what has taken place within the European Union in the field of positive action. The following topics will be discussed: the origins and development of the concept of positive action; the role of the European Commission in publicizing and promoting positive action; the degree to which positive action has been adopted in the various member states and the steps which the member states have taken to promote positive action. Several practical examples are given of positive action programmes in a number of European companies. Whenever possible we will explore the results which have been achieved by such measures. The chapter closes with a discussion of the relationship between positive action and modern organizational and management concepts.

THE ORIGINS AND DEVELOPMENT OF POSITIVE ACTION

The concept of positive action, i.e. a personnel targeting emancipation, was developed in the USA and is known there as 'affirmative action'. Affirmative action belongs to a larger body of law intended to eliminate discrimination and create equal opportunities for members of ethnic minorities, women and the elderly. The most important legislation setting out the principle of equal treatment in employment comprises the 1963 Equal Pay Act, Title VII of the 1964 Civil Rights Act and the 1967 Age Discrimination in Employment Act (Shaeffer, 1980). The underlying principle and main purpose of this legislation is to create equal opportunities for everyone regardless of colour, ethnic background, sex or age. The intention is to eliminate not only direct but also indirect discrimination.

Title VII of the American Civil Rights Act provides for the establishment of a commission entrusted with the task of supervising compliance with the Act: the Equal Employment Opportunity Commission (EEOC). The EEOC clearly has more authority than comparable bodies in Europe. It is not only authorized to conduct investigations itself but also has the option of bringing so-called 'pattern and practice' cases before the Federal Court and may establish guidelines on the implementation of personnel policy. In addition, the Civil Rights Act also makes it possible for private individuals who have been discriminated against to claim damages and demand that any further discrimination cease. With respect to the second, companies found guilty of discriminatory practices can be required to introduce a programme of measures in close consultation with and under the supervision of the EEOC (de Jong, 1984).

In addition to legislation, another instrument used in the USA to promote equal opportunities for minorities and women in employment is the Executive Order, i.e. a regulation issued by the president. The first president to make use of the Executive Order in the interests of equal opportunities was Roosevelt, who ordered a clause to be inserted in government contracts forbidding companies working in the war industry to discriminate against black employees. Presidents Kennedy and Johnson gradually extended the scope of the Executive Order to include other contracts and other minority groups, and in 1967 the clause was further extended to cover discrimination against women.

The Executive Orders not only forbade discrimination, but they also required companies to introduce specific measures which would ensure that minorities were proportionally represented in the work-force. In 1978 the Department of Labor established the Office of Federal Contract Compliance Programs (OFCCP) to supervise contract compliance (Shaeffer, 1980).

It is quite possible that Europe would never have heard of the concept of 'contract compliance' or 'affirmative action' if the EEOC and OFCCP had not joined forces and established joint compulsory guidelines to improve the position of minorities and/or women within companies which had been awarded government contracts. The guidelines were set out in Revised Order no. 4 and came into effect in 1970. Revised Order no. 4 offers a description of a positive action programme. The fundamental idea is to emphasize 'proportional representation' as the goal of an emancipatory policy. Proportional representation is contingent upon the percentage of women and minorities employed by the company compared with the number of workers qualified to fill positions within the company. It is not enough to achieve proportional representation throughout the company as a whole. Women and minority groups must be proportionally represented in each job category and in each department. If there is a discrepancy between actual participation and availability in specific categories, the company is obliged to establish targets for those positions in which the discrepancy has become apparent. It must also provide a schedule which indicates the expected rate of progress per year.

Other points set out in the Revised Order concern the responsibility of management for the implementation of the policy, the obligation to analyse any bottlenecks which impede the hiring or promotion of women and members of ethnic minorities, the obligation to undertake suitable measures to eliminate these bottlenecks and the obligation to publicize the policy within the organization and outside (Shaeffer, 1980).

Europe became acquainted with the model described in the Revised Order in early 1980. The European Commission played a significant role in popularizing this model.

THE ROLE OF THE EUROPEAN COMMISSION IN PROMOTING EQUAL OPPORTUNITIES FOR WOMEN

History of equal opportunities

As was already noted earlier in this book the Treaty of Rome, one of the founding treaties of the European Union (1957), includes an article (article 119) which states that 'Each member state shall ensure and subsequently maintain the application of the principle that men and women should receive equal pay for equal work.' When it became apparent that legislative measures were not enough to help women gain equality, the Union gradually set about establishing a series of directives whose object was to promote equal opportunities between men and women (for an overview of EU policy on equal opportunity, see Chapter 8).

Inherent in the principle of equal opportunities is the idea that women and men participate in the labour market under distinct conditions. The assumption that women and men were in theory each other's equal in employment gradually gave way to the realization that the two groups start out from very different points. On the one hand, these differences can be attributed to circumstances and structural conditions; on the other, they reflect differences between the characteristics of the individuals who make up the two groups. In relation to the first cause, creating equal opportunities meant changing the conditions under which men and women participated in employment; more child-care facilities would have to be established, for example, so that women and men were equally available for paid employment. With regard to the second, the goal of creating equal opportunities might make it necessary to treat individual cases differently, for example by giving extra support to women entering non-traditional occupations and by establishing preferential treatment practices and quotas for appointments and promotions. Preferential treatment practices and quotas no longer qualify as instruments to ensure equal opportunities between male and female employees; they are intended to emphasize a larger measure of equality between men and women as a group.

The Commission's arguments in favour of positive action

The Commission has put forward three specific arguments to explain why it encourages a policy of positive action: the pursuit of justice, efficiency, and an interest in what the citizens of the EU themselves feel is the most suitable division of labour between men and women.

The Commission views active policy as highly desirable within the context of social justice. The existing legal instruments have failed to eliminate real inequalities and the conclusion is that more action must be taken by governments, employers and employees and the other parties involved (Council Recommendation, 1984).

Besides justice, the Commission has also stressed the economic expediency of positive action. Indeed, the third action programme emphasizes this. One reason to support positive action is that demographic changes may put pressure on the labour market, so that the participation of women would consequently become indispensable for the future economic development of Europe. The third argument, which the Commission puts forward only sporadically, is that the citizens of the European Union are increasingly in favour of the notion that men and women should play an equal role within the family (Commission of the European Communities, 1987). Four out of 10 Europeans back the idea of a family in which both the man and the woman have careers that absorb equal amounts of time and energy. The number of people who still view the traditional family structure, in which the man goes out to work while the woman cares for the home, as the ideal has declined in one out of four respondents. Approximately 3 out of 10 saw the ideal family as one in which the woman's career took up less time and energy than her husband's and in which she assumed a greater share of the household responsibilities than he did. Those who advocated an equal division of household tasks constituted an absolute majority in the age category 15 to 39 (Commission of the European Communities, 1987).

Instruments: action programmes and positive action

The action programmes 'Equal Opportunities for Women and Men', set up by the Commission to cover the periods 1982–5, 1986–90 and 1991–5, and the Council's 1984 recommendation on the promotion of positive action all give a broad interpretation to the concept of equal opportunities. The recommendation on the promotion of positive action, issued by the Council on 13 December 1984, went beyond equal treatment, as did the action programmes. The recommendation calls upon the member states to use positive action to eliminate real inequalities which women experience in professional life and to promote mixed employment. The member states are encouraged to formulate a policy on positive action, set up positive action programmes in the government sector and encourage the private sector, employers and trade unions to take steps in the direction of positive action.

The Commission, acting within the broad context in which positive action has come to be seen, has introduced various directives whose goal it is to improve the opportunities available to women in the labour market. We discussed these directives in detail in Chapter 8.

The Commission's concept of positive action

Besides being an instrument for promoting equal opportunities by and within organizations, the Council has also viewed positive action as the process of providing information and increasing public awareness, diversifying the range of occupational options by means of adequate vocational training and stimulating measures aimed at a better distribution of tasks in occupations and in society at large.

The Council's definition of positive action was initially much broader than that applied in the USA. Gradually, the term positive action as used in the Commission's documents was reserved to refer to those measures related directly to the position of women in employment (Commission of the European Communities, 1986).

In 1988 the Commission published a *Positive Action Manual*, in which positive action was defined as follows:

> Positive action aims to complement legislation regarding equal treatment and comprises any measure contributing to the elimination of inequalities in practice. A positive action programme will allow an organization to track down and eliminate every form of discrimination in its employment policy and to neutralize the effects of past discrimination. A positive action programme is a comprehensive planning process which an employer chooses to undertake in order to try and achieve a more balanced representation of women and men throughout the work force and thus making possible a more efficient use of the available skills and talents in the work force.
>
> (Commission of the European Communities, 1988, p. 10)

This definition draws upon the American model, specifically with respect to:

1 management being made responsible for positive action policy;
2 the emphasis on research and on numerical analysis of the work-force;
3 the registration of results and regular assessment of the progress which has been achieved;
4 the possibility of taking steps within the context of the programme which are tailored to the concrete situation within the relevant organization.

The manual also includes a plan setting out various stages such as 'declaration of intent', 'analysis', 'recommendations', 'action' and 'evaluation'. The Commission's manual and the American model differ in one important respect: the European manual contains no reference whatsoever to proportional representation as the ultimate policy goal. The numerical 'targets' which are so characteristic of the American concept of affirmative action are nowhere to be found in the Commission's manual.

The Commission's activities

The Commission has itself undertaken activities within the framework of positive action and has encouraged the member states to do the same. For example, it has stimulated expertise within the EU by establishing expert networks such as the Network on Childcare. Another example from the first action programme is the Commission's support for research on the position of women in the banking industry and in broadcasting organizations, in particular television (Laufer, 1982; Gallagher, 1984).

The Commission was asked to encourage the exchange of experiences between the member states on this point and to report on the implementation of the recommendation by the member states. The 1988 *Positive Action Manual* was published in nine languages. The financial support provided by the Commission for positive action was restricted to small-scale pilot projects. In May 1991 the Council adopted the Commission's third action programme. This programme once again encourages the use of positive action programmes within organizations. The Commission has, for example, undertaken to provide financial support to model projects within the context of positive action programmes set up by employers and trade unions (Commission of the European Communities, 1991).

The Commission has also been entrusted with the task of reporting on the results of its positive action initiatives. In 1988, for example, it published a report on the recommendation on the promotion of positive action. In its report the Commission observes that some member states had taken steps to introduce positive action measures in the public sector, but that in most of the member states there had been scarcely any positive action initiatives in the private sector (Commission of the European Communities, 1988). In the third action programme the Commission has undertaken to publish an updated report on the activities implemented by the member states.

POSITIVE ACTION IN THE MEMBER STATES

In this section we will first provide a general summary of the policy that the member states have pursued in respect of positive action. There is a great variety in the ways the member states implement the Council's recommendation on the promotion of positive action. We will discuss, in the following order, the legal basis for positive action in the member states, the way in which positive action is publicized, the implementation of positive action in the public sector and the role which trade and industry play in introducing positive action initiatives in the private sector. By way of illustration, and as examples of 'good practice', we will discuss a number of positive action programmes developed by various European companies. Wherever possible we will also look at the results which have been achieved through these programmes.

Legal basis of positive action and publicity

Most countries of the European Union have inserted a clause in their Equal Opportunities Act which makes it possible to give preferential treatment to women or to men in order to eliminate existing inequalities.

In the UK the legal basis for positive action was initially restricted to training and education. Employers and training boards were allowed to organize special courses for women or men only if the target group was under-represented in the relevant occupation. This restricted legal basis was extended in 1985 when Parliament approved the Equal Opportunities Commission's Code of Practice, which sets out guidelines for establishing and implementing positive action programmes for women (Vogel-Polsky, 1989).

German law also provides for the preferential treatment of women. A recent debate concerns whether the quota schemes set up by the social democrats in a number of *Länder* to encourage the appointment of women to government jobs can be reconciled with the constitutional right to equal treatment. When a group of men challenged this practice as discriminatory, the lower German courts referred their claim to the Bundesverfassungsgericht (the Constitutional Court) for a ruling on the constitutionality of quota schemes. The case is still under review. In the meantime, the local courts have forbidden the *Länder* to appoint the women selected to fill these posts (Ministerium für die Gleichstellung, 1994).

In the Netherlands a 1989 amendment restricted the possibility of giving preferential treatment to women. In Denmark any form of preferential treatment must have the prior consent of the Minister of Labour, who is advised by the Equality Council in such matters. France has issued a general prohibition of unequal treatment in employment, but there are derogations applying to positive action and protective measures for women.

Most of the member states have organized large-scale publicity campaigns whose object was to make women more aware of their position in the labour market and of their right to equal treatment. In various countries, including the Netherlands, the campaigns also targeted employers. Some of the instruments used were: research and publication of research results on the position of women in employment; positive action pilot projects; manuals and guidelines for employers; study groups; brochures and films. One of many examples is the Positive Action pilot project in Germany, which was carried out at the request of the Bundesminister für Jugend, Familie und Gesundheit. Twenty-six companies took part in the project, including several large organizations such as Deutsche Lufthansa, Bayer and Hoechst. The project led to a research report and manual (Krebsbach-Gnath and Schmid-Jörg, 1985).

Positive action in the public sector

Positive action programmes are being carried out in government organizations in almost every country.

In the UK it is largely the local councils which have introduced policies on positive action. Some councils with a Labour majority have implemented positive action programmes for women and minorities which include sweeping measures on preferential treatment and priority in training. Other governmental bodies have also established plans to improve employment terms for women. One example is Customs and Excise, which received the Working Mothers Association (WMA) Award in 1992 for having the most progressive policy on women in the public sector. The WMA award is meant to 'highlight organizations for implementing family-friendly working practices to further the quality and quantity of women's participation in their workforce' (WMA, 1994). The Association was impressed by the wide variety of flexible working patterns at Customs and Excise, including job sharing, flexitime, term-time working and home-working (WMA, 1994). In addition, Customs and Excise has made great efforts to appoint women in a variety of different ways: by paying close attention to its job advertisements (and by subjecting them to an annual evaluation), by selecting at least one woman to sit on each selection committee, by developing a selection test based on life experiences and personal qualities which has no gender bias, and by increasing the number of candidates invited to interview to ensure a greater number of female candidates. These measures have been successful; the number of female executive officers has grown from 25% in 1984 to 36% in 1991 (WMA, 1994).

In Germany most of the *Länder* implemented so-called

Frauenförderungspläne in the early 1980s setting out measures and guidelines to promote the career paths of women in the public service. In general the goal is to have 50% of all positions occupied by women. Some *Länder* have also introduced quota schemes which give preferential treatment to women as a means of achieving this goal. A set of guidelines was agreed in 1986 at the national level to improve the position of women employed in government service. A deliberate decision was taken not to introduce a quota scheme in view of the controversial nature of this practice.

As of 21 April 1994 the *Gleichberechtigungsgesetz* (Equal Opportunities Act) came into effect setting out the following: all government services at the national level are obliged to draft positive action plans; to make it easier for women to combine working life and family responsibilities, all appointments must in principle be available as part-time positions; national-level committees and advisory councils are to work actively towards a female participation rate of 50% (Bunderministerium für Frauen und Jugend, 1994b).

In the Netherlands the national ministries are obliged to work with positive action plans. There is no similar obligation for the provinces and municipalities, but almost all provinces, larger municipalities and a relatively large percentage of medium-sized and smaller municipalities pursue a positive action policy. The plans generally set targets indicating what percentage of women should be employed in the various positions by a certain date. The percentages are generally based on the percentage of women enrolled in vocational training programmes associated with these positions. At the national level the targets are 30% women in the organization as a whole and 20% women in graduate-level positions by 1995 (Chalude, de Jong and Laufer, 1994). By the end of 1992, the overall participation of women was already approaching the target at 28.5%. With respect to graduate-level positions, however, women still have a long way to go: at the end of 1992, women occupied only 15.7% of such positions (Ministry of the Interior, *servicepuntinfo* no. 22, 1993).

In Belgium positive action is obligatory for all public sector organizations, from ministries to municipal bodies (Royal Decree, 27 February 1990). Government organizations are obliged to appoint an equal opportunity officer, publish a report concerning the employment situation of women and set up a scheme for positive action. Progress is monitored by 'internal working parties' in each government organization. At the national level there is a 'general working party' which monitors progress and drafts an annual report (Chalude, de Jong and Laufer, 1994).

The French government has introduced a large number of measures since 1982 aimed at achieving '*mixeté de l'emploi*' in its own organization. Besides measures targeting equal treatment, there are special courses for women and specific statistics which reveal the status of women in the organization. In addition, female job candidates cannot be rejected because the employer fears that family obligations may conflict with the requirements of the position. Women are in the majority in public sector positions (52%), but in the minority when it comes to top-level jobs (9%). Positive action plans have helped to improve the situation of women in the French government service; for example, the percentage of female heads of department rose from 11.8% in 1988 to 15.1% in 1991 (Chalude, de Jong and Laufer, 1994).

Positive action in trade and industry

In the majority of member states positive action in trade and industry is also viewed as the particular responsibility of employers and trade unions. In Italy and Denmark the trade unions play a major role in creating positive action programmes and in introducing employment conditions which make it easier to combine paid work and family responsibilities. The national governments do attempt to motivate companies to draw up positive action plans, often by making subsidies available for this purpose. However, none of the member states of the EU actually requires companies to pursue a policy of positive action.

The member state which has gone the furthest in this regard is France. Since 1983 companies are required to draft an annual company report on the position of women in the organization and to discuss this report with the works council (Roudy Act, July 1983). Compliance is monitored by the Ministry of Labour, but in practice the Ministry has delegated this task to the regional Labour Inspectorates (Emancipatieraad, 1987). The idea behind the Roudy Act was that by submitting an annual report on the position of women and by discussing this subject employers and employees would become more aware of the problem. Discussion in the works council could lead to proposals for improvement and to the drafting of an Equality Plan. Companies with an exemplary plan could apply for funding to finance implementation. The number of actual agreements has proved disappointing, however. There are now positive action programmes in a total of 30 French companies (Chalude, de Jong and Laufer, 1994). After 1986 a change in policy meant that it was no longer possible to co-finance such programmes. The obligation to submit an annual report on the position of women within the organization also seems to have faded quietly away.

Since 1987 small and medium-sized companies have been able to sign contracts with the government governing the training of individual women for positions in which females have been under-represented until now. More than 400 such contracts have been concluded so far (Chalude, de Jong and Laufer, 1994).

There is no explicit government policy in the UK to promote positive action in trade and industry, but the Equal Opportunities Commission plays an important role in this field. It can, for example, conduct its own investigation into the position of women in a specific organization or sector. It may furthermore establish guidelines and codes of behaviour which can be passed by Parliament. In addition, the Commission actively promotes positive action by organizing seminars and by encouraging networking between companies.

It is interesting to note that the business community itself has taken steps in the direction of positive action. In 1991 a group of entrepreneurs affiliated with the Business in the Community organization launched an 'Opportunity 2000' campaign to increase the quality and quantity of women's participation in the work-force. Companies are encouraged to set programmes and goals to improve the opportunities of women in all areas and at all levels. According to the second annual report, 188 companies joined the campaign in 1993, and most of these have adopted new and improved 'women-friendly' policies and practices (Opportunity 2000, 1993).

As in almost all other European countries, the business community in

Germany has never been required to draw up positive action plans. In 1985 the government ordered the compilation of a manual based on experiences drawn from a number of companies which had introduced positive action programmes and from companies abroad (Krebsbach-Gnath and Schmid-Jörg, 1985). Since 1989 there has also been a scheme in which companies can request funding to set up programmes targeting the reintegration of women who had interrupted their careers to have children. The Equal Opportunity Law adopted in 1994 also covers a number of measures aimed at trade and industry. There is now a right to claim damages in the event that discrimination on the basis of sex can be proved. Employers are also required to take steps to protect employees against sexual harassment at work (Bundesministerium für Frauen und Jugend, 1994b).

In the Netherlands the Ministry of Social Affairs and Employment introduced a so-called positive action 'stimulation scheme'. Organizations which appointed a positive action co-ordinator or which hired external consultants or organized positive-action activities could apply to be reimbursed the costs involved. The scheme was in effect from 1988 to 1992. Most of the applications for funding (88%) came from the municipalities. Applications submitted by commercial organizations generally requested reimbursement for external advice or to organize a specific activity (van Amstel, Berg and Verschuren, 1994).

The Dutch Loontechnische Dienst (Wages Service) and the Collective Employment Terms Service under the Ministry of Social Affairs and Employment conducted a study on the emancipatory provisions in collective bargaining agreements and the implementation of such provisions in organizations. The study showed that in approximately half of the collective bargaining agreements provisions had been made which were intended to improve the position of women. Most of these referred to child care (43%), sexual harassment (38%) and emergency leave (34%). Only 8% of the collective bargaining agreements contained provisions on positive action. The presence of certain provisions in collective bargaining agreements does not mean that companies actually pursue a policy on these issues. Actually, in only 4% of the companies investigated was there a systematic approach to positive action. Targets and preferential treatment are almost unheard of in companies, although 20% of companies had concluded agreements, signed declarations of intent and made arrangements to improve the position of women by taking more active steps during the recruitment process and by encouraging women to enrol in training and educational programmes.

In Italy a law came into effect in 1991 aimed at achieving equality between men and women in employment through positive action (legge no. 125 of 10 April 1991). Employers, vocational training centres and trade unions which intend to introduce positive action measures may apply to the Ministry of Social Affairs and Employment for full or partial reimbursement of the costs associated with these plans.

A national committee has been set up to advise the minister on granting these reimbursements. The committee consists of representatives from the trade unions, employers' associations and women's organizations. The committee is also authorized to establish codes of behaviour and to investigate the position of women within organizations. Equal opportunities advisers are appointed to monitor the regional employment committees and report to the national committee. Each company with more than 100 employees must draft a report every two years describing the position of men and women within the company, broken down according to occupation. For each occupation, the report must provide statistics on appointments, promotions, retirements and dismissals. The report is submitted to the trade union or unions associated with the company and to the regional equal opportunities adviser. After this law was announced, the Italian business community protested vigorously against the obligation to draft a report and announced that it did not wish to co-operate. The government did not respond to these protests by threatening sanctions and, given the present political situation, it is highly unlikely that it will still try to compel business to comply with this obligation.

In Belgium the government promotes positive action in the commercial sector by signing interprofessional agreements which contain agreements in principle to insert positive action provision in industry-wide agreements. The 1990 central agreement provides for the possibility of allocating financial resources from the Employment Fund for this purpose. There is a Positive Action Unit within the Ministry of Employment and Labour which assists employers, trade unions and companies in setting up positive action plans. In the first interprofessional agreement, 13 sectors signed up for positive action programmes and in the second (1991–2) 19 sectors. In the meantime, the Positive Action Unit has come to focus more on the companies themselves and not only on the sectors.

In addition, the State Secretariat for Social Emancipation organized a project which ran from 1989 to 1993 in which it signed positive action agreements with companies. The company undertook to set up and implement a positive action plan, while the State Secretariat made positive action expertise available to the company free of charge. Approximately 40 companies participated in this project, although the number of participants declined over the years.

In 1992 it was established by Royal Decree (Loninklijk Besluit, 7 December 1992) that companies are required to include positive action plans for women in their reorganization plans.

As in the UK, in Denmark there is an employers' association, The Danish Employers' Confederation (DEC), which actively supports positive action. In 1985 the DEC made approximately £500,000 available within the context of a 'Women for future jobs' project to furnish information to employers and women, to facilitate the exchange of information on projects and to support local initiatives targeting the recruitment of women in non-traditional professions (Simonsen, 1989 and 1991). In 1986 employers and employees signed a so-called Co-operation Agreement establishing a co-operation council in which the two parties would meet regularly to discuss issues of common interest. Since 1991 one of these issues has been the subject of equal opportunities for men and women. The DEC has also attempted to encourage its affiliates to hire more female managers, believing this to be the only way that an organization can guarantee having a management staff which represents maximum qualifications and experience. Another important issue is the problem of combining working life and family responsibilities. The measures proposed by the DEC include flexible working hours and company-based daycare facilities. Hanne Simonsen

(1991, p. 106), the department head of the DEC, has described the attitude of her organization thus: 'Creating equal opportunity at work is in the employer's best interests . . . Change is on its way, but accepting men and women as equal partners is inextricably linked to information and the education of all parties concerned. This is a primary task for the employer in the Europe of tomorrow.'

EXAMPLES OF GOOD PRACTICE IN EUROPEAN BUSINESS

In the previous section we saw that national governments in the EU encourage companies in several ways to adopt positive action programmes. The question arises whether these efforts have been successful. A study commissioned by the European Commission showed that its own recommendations, the publicity campaigns set up by the member states and the strategy of encouraging employers and unions have not resulted in a massive move toward positive action in the private sector. The study, which was carried out in 1990, involved the clients of an international accounting firm with branch offices in each member state. A questionnaire was distributed among a sample of 2,700 companies, grouped according to member state, sector and company size. Of the companies which returned the questionnaire, 15% indicated that they had introduced a policy of positive action. Those which had not frequently pursued policies in areas relevant to the position of women, for example by offering the option of working part time or the possibility of interrupting one's career, or by instituting training selection committees (ER Consultants, 1990).

The very low rate of response (13%) made it difficult to obtain a reliable estimate of the percentage of European companies that had introduced positive action measures, but the conclusion that positive action has not been successful as a policy concept seems justified. Similar percentages have been obtained in studies on positive action in trade and industry carried out in a number of member states. According to a study conducted in Germany, 5% of the businesses involved had drafted positive action plans (Herrmann, 1991). We have already mentioned a Dutch study which found positive action agreements in only 4% of business (DCA/LTD, 1990).

Notwithstanding this, women in some companies have gained more satisfactory career prospects than in the past because their employers offer them a package of secondary employment terms related to specific aspects of personnel policy. Before we discuss three such companies, in the UK, the Netherlands and Germany, we will first look at a sector which has led the rest in the field of positive action: the banking industry.

Positive action in the banking industry

In 1977 a study carried out at the initiative of the London School of Economics and supported by the European Commission commented on the position of women in the banking industry. The study focused on several large banks in different countries (the UK, France, Belgium and the Netherlands). In the

British, Belgian and Dutch banks the study was a catalyst for the formulation of an emancipation policy.

The British bank involved was National Westminster, which, as a consequence of the study, introduced an employee reintegration scheme in 1981. Both male and female employees who wished to leave the bank's employ in order to care for a child were allowed to return to the bank at the same job level within a maximum period of five years. During his or her absence the employee was obliged to attend a meeting one day each year, and had to be prepared to work a maximum of two weeks each year as a replacement. Those whose work was evaluated as good were guaranteed a job upon returning. For the others, the bank promised only to explore re-entry options.

The first study on this issue in the Netherlands involved Amro Bank and led in 1982 to the bank's supervisory board drafting a declaration of intent in which it stated that the bank would undertake to appoint more women to senior positions and consider more women as career candidates (de Jong, 1983). To encourage the promotion of women, the various bank departments drafted their own plans which were to be submitted for approval to the supervisory board. Unfortunately, the objectives were rather vaguely described and the bank failed to co-ordinate and supervise the various departments in drafting their plans, so that this decentralized approach to policy implementation proved ineffectual. A number of concrete measures were undertaken at corporate level, however. Within just a few years, the policy of targeting women among university graduate candidates led to a rise from 15 to 30% in the number of women taken on as management trainees. To stimulate the appointment of women in non-traditional positions, the bank developed a video programme which was used both internally and during recruitment campaigns. Women employees were further given the option of taking up six months of unpaid maternity leave following their pregnancy leave.

Two banks in Belgium also participated in the EU study: the Générale de Banque and the Banque Bruxelles-Lambert. An equal opportunity video was made which was intended primarily for in-company management courses. Both banks also agreed that between 1979 and 1991, one-third of the trainees taken on would be women. They also introduced special management training programmes for women (Chalude, de Jong and Laufer, 1994).

Since the introduction of these measures, the policy on positive action in the banking industry in both Great Britain and the Netherlands has been intensified and extended. By late 1990 all the bigger banks in the UK had introduced positive action programmes which involved the following elements (de Jong and Povall, 1991):

1 a concrete policy, usually set out in guidelines;
2 one or more central policy staff, sometimes supported by a steering committee or working party; in the largest banks special branch staff are appointed to oversee equal opportunities policy;
3 a reintegration programme for staff who wish to leave the employ of the bank temporarily to care for children;
4 training programmes for management staff focusing on the principle of equal treatment, usually as part of a middle-management training course;

5 training programmes for women, generally focusing on how to combine a career and family responsibilities;
6 the analysis of selection procedures and criteria with the goal of eliminating discrimination and arriving at gender-free evaluation;
7 record-keeping concerning the percentage of women employed at certain job levels, participating in training programmes and management courses, and recruited from among young university graduates. In some cases targets are used to evaluate progress.

A number of banks have further expanded and improved their policy on women since then. The banking industry still leads the way in this respect. In 1992, for example, Barclays and Midland Bank were awarded the Employer of the Year Trophy by the Working Mothers Association. Barclays's policy included the following striking elements:

1 extended maternity leave – up to 52 weeks;
2 emergency carer's leave – employees can take 5 days' unpaid leave or 'borrow' paid holiday from the following year's entitlement;
3 responsibility break – staff with personal responsibility for elderly, sick or disabled relatives can take a complete break from work or work on a temporary part-time basis for up to 6 months;
4 career skills development course for women in non-managerial positions.

According to Barclays, the policy has had a definite effect: women now form 40% of staff in the senior non-managerial grades; the number of women in management has increased from 513 in 1985 to 1,325 in 1992; women constitute 20% of the new management appointments; and the maternity return rate has more than doubled in a period of 5 years, reaching almost 80% (WMA, 1994).

In 1984 the supervisory boards of the Dutch ABN and NMB Banks formally adopted an equal opportunities policy for women. The Postbank, privatized in 1986, introduced a positive action programme based on the far-reaching policy of KPN, the Dutch Post Office. The policy included specific targets for the percentage of women employed per department, child care, paid emergency leave and a grievance procedure in the event of sexual harassment.

In 1988 and 1989 NMB and ABN undertook steps to ensure that the policy on positive action, which had until then existed only on paper, was actually implemented. The approach chosen by ABN is based on the idea that within the office network the districts themselves take responsibility for implementing policy, with the active support of the main personnel department. After merging with Amro Bank, a project has been set up to encourage the introduction of part-time work in senior positions. A manual is being put together which indicates which positions and departments are most suitable for part-time appointments.

The 1990 collective bargaining agreement for the banking industry was the first to include an emancipation protocol setting out guidelines which target equal opportunities for women and men. The protocol mentions the following: recruitment and promotion, part-time work, reintegration into employment, pregnancy and maternity leave, child care, educational and training facilities and measures to prevent sexual harassment. The agreements in principle are very promising. Although in most cases the employer is obliged to make facilities available only if the organization or budget permits, it may be assumed that the protocol will serve as an important stimulus within the sector, and certainly for the bigger banks.

As in the UK, the large banks in the Netherlands continue to play a prominent role in the field of positive action. Nevertheless, the results after 10 years of emancipation policy are not all that impressive. The percentage of women in senior positions is still well below 5%. The various banks differ very little in this respect. On the other hand, the percentage of women in middle management and specialist positions has risen over the past 10 years. Here the differences between banks appear to be related to the degree to which each has pursued an active emancipation policy. At the beginning of 1989 the Postbank, which has the most progressive emancipation policy, also had the largest share of women at this level (15%), while the Rabobank, which was less interested in positive action compared with other banks, had the lowest (7%).

Examples of positive action measures in 3 European companies

It is true that the larger banks are well ahead of other sectors of industry when it comes to implementing positive action plans, but that does not mean that other sectors have failed to take steps in this direction as well. Like the banks, companies in other industries have drafted plans to improve the position of women within businesses. Such plans are generally not full-scale positive action programmes; they usually involve a number of more or less independent measures which contribute to improving the position of women in the company in various specific ways. These may include, for example, measures concerning child care, flexible working hours, special recruitment campaigns, and so on. In what follows we will describe three examples of such measures undertaken in companies in the UK, the Netherlands and Germany.

THE UK   The nationwide chemists' chain, Boots, has long had a 'women-friendly' policy. The Working Mothers Association calls Boots 'a pioneer in their field . . . with a well-established reputation in the equal opportunities field' (WMA, 1994, p. 8). Boots also participates in the Opportunity 2000 campaign. Boots's policy includes the following important elements:

1 various forms of flexible work, i.e. flexitime, part-time, job-sharing and term-time working;
2 specific courses for women re-entering employment;
3 equal opportunity awareness training for all staff and store managers;
4 specific measures to promote women's careers, for example by ensuring equal access to management training courses;
5 specific recruitment of women for non-traditional positions;
6 an annual evaluation of women's status within the company based on the percentage of women in the various positions and their participation in management training courses.

The Boots branch in Nottingham also provides a relatively broad package of child-care facilities. There is, for example, a child-minding network which passes on the names of three child-minders to 'Boots' mothers' at their request. The branch also reserves a limited number of places in various Nottingham-based nurseries. There is also a holiday playscheme, a kind of summer camp where Boots employees can send their children (between the ages of 5 and 14) during the summer holidays to take part in recreational activities.

Boots's efforts have met with success (Opportunity 2000, 1993), as the following examples demonstrate: from 1990–91 to 1992–93, the percentage of women returning to work after maternity leave rose from 29% to 49%; in 1992/93 women formed 20% of the lorry drivers working in warehousing and distributing.

THE NETHERLANDS In the Netherlands the PGGM (Pension Fund for Health, Mental and Social Interests) has set a good example of how organizations can set up an emancipatory personnel policy (PGGM, 1993). As far back as 1988 PGGM began to consult on the introduction of a policy plan to improve the position of women within the company. In 1989 it introduced the first measures, which were subject to an evaluation in 1990. During the 1991 collective bargaining round, new agreements were made on positive action. These led in 1992 to a study on the position of women, which in turn resulted in a new policy plan that same year.

The new plan views emancipatory personnel policy specifically as an element of human resource management (HRM). Within the context of HRM, personnel duties and responsibilities are entrusted to line management, while emancipation policy is largely the concern of the various different departments. A project team has been appointed for a period of 2 years on behalf of the management to advise, support and encourage the different departments in developing and implementing a department-specific emancipation policy; this group will also assess progress on an annual basis.

Each department also has the task of developing its own policy, although they are obliged to establish set targets per job cluster in their plan and take steps to encourage the recruitment and promotion of women and to discourage their leaving the company.

The following steps have been taken at the central level:

1 a checklist is being developed which can be used to establish important part-time positions at the senior and/or management level;
2 the company has made enough child-care places available to accommodate the demand for such places among personnel; after-school facilities are being arranged and the opening hours of the creche are being extended;
3 in 1993 two management positions were reserved for women;
4 there will be more training facilities for women; women who intend to train for a future position are also eligible for full reimbursement of the associated fees;
5 a study is being carried out on the most suitable forms of flexible working hours during school holidays and when children become ill;
6 the company offers support and facilities in setting up a women's network.

It has also been agreed that the central and local policy results will be evaluated on an annual basis. The departments are expected to provide statistical material for this purpose on turnover among female employees, on the number of women per job cluster, and on the implementation of the intended measures. Based on the evaluation, the project team will investigate to what extent policy should and must be adjusted.

PGGM's policy plan has only recently been drawn up, and the company is still in the process of developing each department's specific policy. Consequently no information is available yet on the results.

GERMANY   The German car manufacturer BMW is a good example of a company which has introduced a variety of measures to improve the position of women within the organization. BMW took the first steps in this direction in 1990 in the form of an integrated plan entitled *Personalentwicklung für Frauen im Zeichen von Individualität und Mobilität* (Herrmann, 1991, p. 120). The plan included the following measures:

1 Measures intended to encourage individual career paths: annual discussions between employers and employees to evaluate job or career. The discussions covered future career prospects and were intended to result in decisions on such issues as job rotation, refresher seminars, foreign apprenticeships or participation in interdisciplinary project teams.
2 Measures intended to individualize working structures and working hours and make them more flexible:
  (a) in addition to the legal requirements to provide 6 months' parental leave, since 1 January 1992 employees have been entitled to 1 or 2 years' of unpaid leave (*Familienpause*) per birth without jeopardizing their appointment.
  (b) various forms of flexible work were introduced, for example part-time work, home-work contracts, job-sharing, seasonal working hours and the possibility of saving up unused holiday and overtime to take 6 months' leave at once. Other experiments were conducted into different forms of part-time work in managerial positions.
3 Measures to qualify employees, whether male or female:
  (a) to encourage the reintegration of employees re-entering the company's employ (for example, after a period of parental leave), monthly information days were organized to publicize BMW's training programmes and individual reintegration programmes were set up intended to make the transition to working life smoother.
  (b) during the *Familienpause* a specific group of employees had the option of participating in a model project entitled 'Distance learning for women with families' which offered various vocational courses and training programmes. Some fees were reimbursed by BMW.
4 Measures targeting the recruitment of new employees: BMW attempted to recruit more women and interest them in a career path within the company, for example by co-operating with other companies in organizing public information days for girls and by undertaking public information activities targeting schools and universities. In addition, the company made more apprenticeship places available to female students.

The company plan described above was set up in conjunction with the works council in order to draw attention to the issue of women's emancipation. Opinions have changed over the years, however. The plan is still in effect, but it no longer targets women alone. Emancipation policy is no longer the most pressing issue – the emphasis now is on a *Familienpolitik* aimed at both mothers and fathers. BMW wants to offer better opportunities to combine working life and family responsibilities by setting up schemes for reintegration and part-time work. The measures described above regarding unpaid parental leave have now become general law. In addition, the company offers additional support in cases of re-entry, for example by providing training either during or after the period of leave and by offering employees on leave the possibility of working for short periods of time as a replacement.

Other schemes have made it possible for employees to save up for a half-year 'sabbatical leave'. With respect to child care, BMW makes arrangements through the Kinderburo, an independent private agency which the company hires to advise parents on various child-care options and to arrange child-care facilities for them. The office was initially set up and financed by BMW, but it now operates independently and also works for other large companies.

BMW's experiences and its 'family policy' have been positive: an increasing number of men are also availing themselves of the opportunities for parental leave, and employees have shown themselves more than willing to maintain their ties with the company by filling in temporarily for other employees during their absence or by working at home during leave. Very few parents on leave have participated in the training programmes offered, however.

CONCLUSION AND DISCUSSION

Summing up we conclude that it is in the public sector in particular that the EU member states have attempted to improve the position of women in employment by means of positive action. Positive action has not really caught on in the private sector, where resistance to measures such as preferential treatment and targets has been particularly strong. Neither have trade and industry been convinced by arguments focusing on the principle of social justice, which in the early 1980s gave the emancipation movement a large measure of legitimacy.

Views on emancipation and the best way to promote the participation of women in employment have changed since the first positive action measures were introduced in Europe. Down through the years the social justice argument has gradually been replaced by the idea that offering women a better chance in the job market is an economic necessity. There were predictions of employee shortages in sectors where women had previously been under-represented. Women were seen as an important reserve work-force. By now, this argument too has lost a great deal of its force. There is no evidence of a shortage of personnel in the majority of member states. Indeed, the trend seems to be toward rising unemployment in almost every sector of the labour market.

This situation has given rise to new demands which support the concept of an emancipation policy, such as the need for greater flexibility in the way employees are utilized and in what they can do. To achieve flexibility, companies need more flexible work structures and working hours, and they have come to recognize how important it is to concentrate on staff qualifications. Human resources management (HRM) has once again stepped into the limelight in this connection – a personnel policy such as those described above must make it possible to do justice to the individual qualities of the employee, to develop these qualities and to utilize them in a flexible way as the needs of the company change.

Emancipation policy as seen within the context of HRM is based on the *individual approach*; no distinction is made between female and male employees and both individual women and individual men are offered the same chances to grow within the company. The responsibility for ensuring career success lies with the individual. He or she must have enough ambition and be sufficiently motivated to make the most of the (equal) opportunities that are offered.

In theory, an unadulterated HRM policy is not compatible with the introduction of specific schemes aimed at women or arrangements in which targets are set to encourage their recruitment and promotion. For these reasons, HRM cannot be equated with emancipation policy. In everyday practice, after all, women are generally not afforded the same opportunities as men to achieve their career goals. The difference between the sexes lies in the responsibility of caring for a home and family. If work–family issues become more integrated into HRM than they are now, however, HRM may still have an emancipatory effect.

As long as the responsibility of care is not shared equally by the sexes, there can be no possibility of equal opportunities for men and women, even in the event that HRM is the principle upon which a personnel policy is based. Any personnel policy intending to offer equal opportunities must take account of the fact that some employees – men, but in particular women – have responsibilities above and beyond the work which they are paid to do. There should be more opportunities to hold part-time senior and managerial positions. Another important point is to arrive at better agreements concerning the period during which employees, both male and female, are raising children, with particular attention to sustaining suitable career prospects despite the need to combine work and family. All of this leads us to raise the question whether 'classic' positive action isn't after all the most suitable approach in a number of instances. Sometimes emancipation measures can serve as a catalyst, for example when a conscious decision is taken to appoint a few women to high-profile positions. In the end, emancipation policy is not just about good intentions. What really counts are the results, and to get results it may sometimes be necessary to replace the principle of equality by the principle of inequality – meaning the temporary preferential treatment of women, of course.

REFERENCES

AMSTEL, R. VAN, BERG, T. and VERSCHUREN, R. (1994) *Positieve actie: er moet gewerkt worden*, VUGA, Den Haag.
BMW PERSONALENTWICKLUNG (1993) *Das BMW Modell für Beruf und Familie*, BMW AG, München.

BUNDESMINISTERIUM FÜR FRAUEN UND JUGEND (1992) *Frauen in der Bundesrepublik Deutschland*, Bonn.
BUNDESMINISTERIUM FÜR FRAUEN UND JUGEND (1994a) *Die Chance – Frauen kehren in den Beruf zurück*, Bonn.
BUNDESMINISTERIUM FÜR FRAUEN UND JUGEND (1994b) *Bundestag beschleßt Gleichberechtigungsgesetz*, Pressemitteilung no. 21, Bonn.
CHALUDE, M., DE JONG, A. and LAUFER, J. (1994) Implementing equal opportunity and affirmative action programmes in Belgium, France and the Netherlands, in M. J. Davidson and R. J. Burke (eds.), *Women in Management: Current Research Issues*, Paul Chapman, London.
COMMISSION OF THE EUROPEAN COMMUNITIES (1986) *Equal Opportunities 2nd Action Programme: 1986–1990*, Women of Europe Supplement, 23, Brussels.
COMMISSION OF THE EUROPEAN COMMUNITIES (1987) *Women and Men of Europe in 1987*, Brussels.
COMMISSION OF THE EUROPEAN COMMUNITIES (1988) *Report on the Implementation of the Promotion of Positive Action for Women, 13 December 1984*, (Com. 88–370), Brussels.
COMMISSION OF THE EUROPEAN COMMUNITIES (1991) *Equal Opportunities for Women and Men, 3rd Action Programmes*, 1991–1995, Brussels.
COUNCIL RECOMMENDATIONS OF 13 DECEMBER 1984: regarding the encouragement of positive action for women (84/635/EEG).
DCA/LTD (DIENST COLLECTIEVE ARBEIDSVOORWAARDEN EN DE LOONTECHNISCHE DIENST) (1991) *Emancipatie in arbeidsorganisaties*, deel 1; een gezamenlijk onderzoek naar emancipatie-aspecten in CAO's en arbeidsorganisaties, Ministerie van Sociale Zaken en Werkgelegenheid, Den Haag.
EMANCIPATIERAAD (1987) *Positieve actie internationaal*, een studie naar positieve actie in Canada, Australië, Noorwegen en Frankrijk, Den Haag.
ER CONSULTANTS (1990) *An Evaluation Study of Positive Action in Favour of Women*, Commission of the European Communities, Brussels.
GALLAGHER, M. (1984) *Employment and Positive Action for Women in the Television Organizations of the EEC Member States*, Commission of the European Communities, Brussels.
HERRMANN, H. (1991) *Betriebliche Maßnahmen zur Vereinbarkeit von Familie und Beruf sowie zur Förderung der Berufsrückkehr nach Zeiten ausschließlicher Familientätigkeit*, Materialien zue Frauenpolitik 15/91, Bundesministerium für Frauen und Jugend, Bonn.
JONG, A. DE (1983) *Gelijke behandeling en het personeelsbeleid*, Kluwer, Deventer.
JONG, A. DE (1984) Antidiscriminatiewetgeving en positieve actie in de VS, *Sociaal Maandblad Arbeid*, Vol. 39, no. 2, pp. 90–100.
JONG, A. DE and POVALL, M. (1991) Positieve actie in de banksector; een terugblik op tien jaar emancipatiebeleid, *Bank en Effectenbedrijf*, Vol. 40, November, pp. 45–50.
Koninklijk Besluit houdende maatregelen tot bevordering van gelijke kansen voor mannen en vrouwen in de overheidsdiensten, 27 februari 1990.
KREBSBACH-GNATH, C. and SCHMID-JÖRG, I. (1985) *Wissenschaftliche Begleituntersuchung zu Frauenförderungsmaßnahmen*, Verlag W. Kohlhammer, Stuttgart.
LAUFER, J. (1982) *Equal Opportunities in Banking in the Countries of the EEC*, Commission of the European Communities, Brussels.
LEGGE 10 April 1991, no. 125, Azzione positive per la realizzazione della parità uomo-donna nel lavoro.
MINISTERIE VAN BINNENLANDSE ZAKEN (1993) *Servicepuntinfo* no. 22, November.
MINISTERIUM FÜR DIE GLEICHSTELLUNG VON FRAU UND MANN DES LANDES NORDRHEIN-WESTFALEN (1994) *Das Frauenförderungsgesetz des Landes Nordrhein-Westfalen*, Sachstand und Argumente, Düsseldorf.
OOSTERHUIS-GEERS, J. A. (1994) Doorstroom van vrouwen naar hogere, leidinggevende posities in het bedrijfsleven, *M&O*, no.4, pp .405–23.
OPPORTUNITY 2000 (1993) *Towards a Balanced Workforce*, second year report, London.
PGGM (PENSIOENFONDS VOOR DE GEZONDHEID, GEESTELIJKE EN MAATSCHAPPELIJKE BELANGEN) (1993) *Emancipatoir Personeelsbeleid bij het Pensioenfonds PGGM*, Zeist.
SHAEFFER, R. G. (1980 *Nondiscrimination in Employment – and Beyond*, The Conference Board, New York.
SIMONSEN, H. (1989) *Positive Actions and Social Partners*, Panel 1-2, Evaluacion de politica comunitaria en materia de igualdad de opportunidades, Toledo.
SIMONSEN, H. (1991) The employer's role in the Europe of the future, in the Commission of

the European Communities, Directorate-General for Employment, Industrial Relations and Social Affairs, Social Europe, *Equal Opportunities for Women and Men*, no. 3, pp. 104–6.

SOCIAAL ECONOMISCHE RAAD (1993) *Vrouwen in hogere functies, lessen uit de praktijk*, Den Haag.

VOGEL-POLSKY, E. (1989) *Positive Action and the Constitutional and Legislative Hindrances to Its Implementation in the Member States of the Council of Europe*, Council of Europe, Strasbourg.

WMA (WORKING MOTHERS ASSOCIATION) (1994) *UK Employers Initiatives, Working Examples of Family Friendly and Equal Opportunities Policies*, WMA, London.

CHAPTER 12

The Comparable Worth Strategy

ANNEKE VAN DOORNE-HUISKES

INTRODUCTION

The preceding chapters have dealt with various aspects of policy to improve the position of women in the European labour market. Chapter 8, for example, looked at the general framework of the European Union's equal opportunity policy, while Chapter 9 considered the existing legislation in this area. Chapter 11 dealt with the strategy of affirmative action: a systematic approach at company or organization level aimed at ensuring equal representation of women in all jobs and at all levels.

The present chapter focuses on a different policy strategy, namely that of so-called comparable worth. This strategy concerns itself with the existing inequality in pay between men and women. The core of the comparable worth concept is the thesis that work done by women is of equal value to work done by men if that work requires equal or comparable qualifications. The strategy of comparable worth assumes that when attempts are made to create a system of equal pay for men and women, what is involved is not primarily attempts to eliminate distinctions between male and female jobs. It is, rather, a question of whether male and female jobs have distinctions in pay which cannot reasonably be traced to differences in qualifications and efforts required by these jobs. If it turns out that female jobs are paid less intrinsically, in other words purely because of the fact that the work is done by women, then the comparable worth strategy attempts to change this situation.

DIFFERENCES IN PAY BETWEEN MEN AND WOMEN

In Chapter 3 it was pointed out that the average hourly pay for women in all countries of the European Union is lower than for men. This is true of both manual and non-manual workers. Seen as a percentage of men's pay, the hourly wage for female workers in 1991 varied between 67% in the UK and 85% in Denmark. Although the figures indicate that there has been some improvement in the situation over the past decade and that pay for men and women is gradually being evened out, a substantial difference remains.

Chapter 7 presented various theoretical explanations for this stubborn phenomenon of unequal pay for men and women. According to the human capital theory, differences in hourly wage between men and women are primarily due to the differences between them in qualifications and investment. Discrimination theories provide additional explanations. Such discrimination may be direct, with employers preferring to reserve interesting and demanding – and therefore well-paid jobs – for men rather than for women. Such behaviour may be the result of prejudices against women: they are supposedly too emotional, too indecisive and insufficiently rational to cope with a demanding job. An employer's choice of employee may also be based on mechanisms of statistical discrimination. In other words, individual women who apply for a position are evaluated by employers on the basis of statistical regularities in the behaviour of women as a group. These regularities show that women interrupt their careers more frequently than men or that they take (or wish to take) part-time work more frequently than men. For many employers, these facts consequently make women less attractive as employees.

Discrimination against women may also come about in other ways. The differences in hourly wages are supposed to be due partly to lower pay in so-called female jobs, even when these jobs require the same qualifications as so-called male jobs (Wittig and Lowe, 1989). Bergmann (1986) also points to the relationship between female jobs and lower pay. Employers tend to exclude women from better jobs so that, according to Bergmann, women are crowded into female jobs. This crowding creates downward pressures on pay. England (1992) points out that women's jobs typically provide less on-the-job training, indicating that women's jobs may consequently become less skilled relative to men's jobs. Female jobs are also attached to shorter mobility ladders than male jobs, thus reducing women's chances for promotion (Bielby and Baron, 1986; DiPrete and Soule, 1988). In addition, very few female jobs involve supervision of other workers (England, 1992).

It is clear that there is a connection between occupational segregation by sex and the lower pay earned by women. There are various suggestions as to how this fact can be reflected in policy measures. These suggestions depend on whether or not one primarily targets the individuals or the jobs involved. Programmes of affirmative action generally do the former. Apart from other measures (see Chapter 11), they often include plans to eliminate occupational segregation by sex, in other words to allow more women to break into traditional male jobs. If more women are given access to well-paid male jobs, their average hourly pay will increase. This is also true when more women move up into senior positions, which are occupied largely by men. Such a strategy helps individual women, but structural discrimination with respect to women's jobs continues to exist. The comparable worth strategy is aimed at the pay differences between the jobs; in other words, it is not individuals but the jobs which are the object of policy intervention. The principle of equal pay for work of equal value regardless of such characteristics as sex, race or ethnic origin is therefore the starting point.

This principle is a recent one. History shows that differences in pay for men and women have for centuries been accepted, even when the actual work involved was precisely the same, European Union legislation (cf. Chapter 9) has, in principle, put an end to this situation. Nevertheless, it is worth taking a short look at the past. It is, after all, very likely that what was taken for granted historically still influences the value placed on men's and women's work. These values then become institutionalized in systems of job evaluation (see below). We will first take a look at the past.

THE VALUE OF MEN'S AND WOMEN'S WORK: A HISTORY

The surprisingly well-documented work of the German historian and economist Lily Braun (1902) on the 'women's question' (*De vrouwen Kwestie*, 1901) devotes a great deal of space to the developments during the 19th century in women's participation in the labour market. This growth had to do with the fact that at the end of the century more and more occupations were slowly being opened up to women. Nevertheless, the number of professions which women could choose continued to be restricted, with the result that large numbers of women applied for a single job. The crowding effect, mentioned in the previous section in relation to the low wage levels in many female jobs, was very noticeable. For example, a French study of 1890 (Braun, 1902, p. 170) states that in the Seine *département* alone more than 8,000 women applied for 193 vacancies in teaching. Almost 5,000 applied for 200 new jobs with the Post Office. At the Bank of France, which had an annual maximum of 25 new jobs available, more than 6,000 women applied in search of work. Given these figures, we can see that fear of competition from women, one of the most important reasons for men to oppose strongly the appearance of women in all sorts of jobs, was not entirely unfounded. This picture becomes clearer if we examine the differences in pay. In all areas women's pay, even for the same work, was less than that of men. In the USA, for examples, male civil servants at the end of the 19th century had an annual income of between $800 and $2,000. Women, on the other hand, had a minimum starting salary for the same posts of $500, rising to a maximum of only $1,200 (Grace H. Dodge, *What Women Can Earn*, New York, 1898; quoted by Braun, 1902). In England the situation was similar (*Women in Professions*, London Congress; quoted by Braun, 1902). Female librarians had an income of only £40 to £80 a year, half that of their male colleagues. Nursing – at the end of the 19th century entirely a women's job – received, besides board and lodging, only between £12 and £30 a year. There were also clear differences between male and female post office employees: in the higher ranks men had an income of up to £900, whereas the few women at the same level earned only £400 (Sidney and Beatrice Webb, *Problems of Modern Industry*, London 1898; quoted in Braun, 1902). At the French Post Office the picture was just the same.

It was not only in the so-called 'bourgeois' occupations that there was unequal pay for men and women; it was also the norm in industry, where throughout Europe the situation of the workers was generally dreadful. In around 1880 male workers in spinning mills located in Haut-Rhin, Alsace (Braun, 1902, p. 266) earned between 1.8 and 4 marks a day, while women earned between 1.7 and 2 marks. These differences were already present among child workers: boys generally received 30% higher pay than girls.

The differences between men's and women's pay in industry were partly the result of the fact that women did not do the same work as men. That situation still exists. Different work generally means work which is classified as inferior. Both in the past and still today, it was the least skilled work which was reserved for women. But it was not always a matter of men and women doing unequal work. Braun (1902, p. 267) reports on office-ledger manufacturers in Berlin at the end of the 19th century. Both men and women performed the job of embossing titles on the gilding press. Men received 1 mark per 100 and women 70 pfennigs.

The situation was sometimes more complicated. Women did what was basically the same work but there were still differences. Braun mentions a printing works in Glasgow, for example (Royal Commission on Labour, *Employment of Women*, London, 1894). Women typesetters earned 2 pence per 1,000 letters less than their male colleagues 'because they have not mastered all the tasks. When performing correction work they have to call upon their male colleagues to help them and they cannot be used to perform more difficult printing tasks.' Braun does not question whether the female typesetter could not have learned the more difficult tasks. It is likely that they were simply not given the opportunity.

The road to equal pay for men and women has been a long and difficult one. The following section deals with it in more detail. First, however, we would like to give an example of the discussions which took place during the process of progressing towards equal pay. The example (taken from Kim, 1989) concerns the California State Civil Service, referred to as Publica. In 1931 Publica's salary structure was systemized. Beforehand, the existing salary levels were the object of extensive classification and study. With the approval of Publica's Personnel Board, it was decided that sex should be one of the criteria determining the level of pay. A 1930 policy document states:

> Question 5   Shall any differences in pay on account of sex be made? Some of the possible methods of answering this question are as follows: (1) to pay men consistently more than women doing the same kind of work; (2) to pay men and women doing the same kind of work the same, regardless of sex; (3) when men and women do the same kind of work to make no difference, but to pay somewhat higher for those occupations filled predominantly by men than for those occupations filled predominantly by women, where, aside from sex, the qualifications are substantially the same. The compensation staff recommends the third of the methods outlined above be followed, the differentials to be limited to those kinds of occupations where in the commercial world distinctions are made in the pay for workers engaged in occupations predominantly filled by men as compared to those predominantly filled by women.

> (cited in Kim, 1989)

The procedure recommended became the policy followed. In doing so, Publica was in part following a progressive course: equal pay for men and women for precisely the same work. In part it was confirming the existing inequalities in pay between men and women: those jobs which were occupied primarily by men would be more highly paid than those taken primarily by women. This was also the case, and this is an important issue, when the qualifications required for the jobs were substantially the same. We will come across that same point again, both in the history of the relevant legislation and when the comparable worth strategy is being formulated.

LEGISLATION ON EQUAL PAY FOR WORK OF (VIRTUALLY) THE SAME WORTH

Chapter 9 has already dealt with the legislation governing equal pay. France was the first West European country to include equal pay for men and women in its legislation. This took place in 1946 and France was followed in the 1950s and 1960s by the (then) Federal Republic of Germany, Iceland, the UK, Spain, Austria, Luxembourg and Belgium. When the European Community was set up in 1957, it was again France which exerted pressure for inclusion in the founding treaty of a specific article covering equal pay for men and women. France's motives in doing so were less a matter of emancipation than one of economics. It was feared that increased unification of the European market would bring about an invasion of cheap female labour on the French labour market (Verhaaren, 1987).

Article 119 of the EU Treaty speaks of 'the principle that men and women should receive equal pay for equal work'. Directive 75/117 EEC of 10 February 1975 adds that it is not merely a matter of equal work but also of work of equal value. The directive does not elaborate on how one is to decide whether or not work has the same value. The Dutch law on equal pay lays down that 'work must be valued according to a proper system of job classification'. 'Proper' means in this connection that job classification systems are not allowed to make either direct or indirect distinctions based on sex. It is an interesting question whether the existing systems meet that requirement. We will deal with this issue below.

The basis for job comparison was also broadened in the UK via the 1983 Equal Pay Amendment Regulations, which amended the 1979 Equal Pay Act. That basis had hitherto been restricted to identical jobs or jobs previously graded as equivalent. From 1983 on, the comparison was to be based on the criterion of equal value, even in enterprises that did not have a standard job classification system (Eyraud *et al.*, 1993).

Although Directive 75/117 EEC therefore does not go into the principle of equal worth in detail, points of reference can be found in the case law of the European Court of Justice, (Boelens and Veldman, 1993; Van Stigt, 1994). The Court has determined that the principle should be applied to the economy as a whole. In *Defrenne II* (*Defrenne v Sabena II*, JUR 1975, 455) the Court makes clear that comparisons between a male and female function may be made within the whole economic sector. The 'reference person' does not, therefore, need to be employed by the same company. The Court indicates that any method of job classification may be used if it meets the criteria stated in *Rummler v Dato-Druch GmbH* (JUR 1986, 1607):

1 the criteria must correspond to the actual job requirements;
2 the system must be capable of measuring all relevant job requirements;
3 indirect distinguishing criteria must be commensurate with the effort required to perform the job;
4 if the system as a whole precluded discrimination on the grounds of sex, employers may use criteria for which one particular sex has a particular aptitude, provided that these are compensated by criteria which are to the advantage of the other sex.

Directive 75/117 and the case law of the Court of Justice would seem to offer sufficient reference points for clear measures intended to combat discrimination in job classification (Boelens, 1993). In practice, however, there are differences between the various member states of the EU. In the UK in particular, work is being done on developing a sex-neutral system of job evaluation (see, for example, London Equal Value Steering Group, 1987a and 1987b and National Joint Council for Local Authorities' Services, 1987).

In their efforts to give practical effect to this principle of equal value, many governments have tried to make the concept more operational by giving a more precise definition of the elements to be compared. Many laws establish specific criteria for comparison. In general, these are skill, responsibility, effort and conditions of work.

METHODS OF JOB EVALUATION

'Job Evaluation' is generally understood to mean a method of classifying jobs within an organization according to how demanding they are. Such a tool has been developed primarily to enable regulation of pay differences. The fact that the development of job evaluation was linked to existing differences in pay is made clear by the history of job evaluation systems in the Netherlands. The first such system in the Netherlands dates from shortly after the Second World War (see Remery and Van Doorne-Huiskes, 1992). The so-called committee of experts developed a method which was intended to determine the demands of jobs within Dutch industry. The method was tested a number of times in Dutch companies. The tests at first showed that the method's hierarchy was not the same as that which had been developed in actual business practice. The method was then tinkered with until it was brought into line with actual practice. When the criticism was levelled that this merely accommodated existing differences, the committee of experts responded as follows: that is precisely the intention; job evaluation systems are a means to express the differences as they actually exist (Scholten, 1981, pp. 20–3). The previous section has shown what the differences were like between male and female jobs.

There are various types of job evaluation systems. England (1992) distinguishes 4 methods: ranking, classification, factor comparison and the point-factor method. Ranking is the simplest of the 4 systems. Jobs are simply ordered according to their 'payworthiness'. What leads to one job being placed higher than another is not explicitly stated. The classification method does identify 'factors'. On the basis of all the factors taken together, a job is given a certain place. No points are given for each separate factor. This makes it difficult to classify jobs which score high on one factor and low on another. Since the weights of the various factors are not stated explicitly, the ranking of the jobs within this system is difficult to monitor.

The factor comparison method is a comparative method which works with 'key' jobs or 'benchmark' jobs. Because this method has neither the simplicity of a simple ranking system nor the sophistication of the point-factor system, the factor comparison method is seldom used today (England, 1992). The point-factor method is the most explicit of the 4 methods mentioned. It first describes the jobs. Rewardable factors are then chosen. This generally means such factors as skill, effort, complexity, responsibility, working conditions, contact. For each job it is determined to what extent these factors are necessary for proper performance. Each factor per job is then given a score. The score varies according to the extent to which the factor is considered a requirement within that job. The factor 'responsibility', for example, may be considered to be 'hardly' applicable to a certain job, whereas in another it may be 'highly applicable'. Point-factor methods often make use not only of separate factors but also of relative weights of the various factors. Within a certain job evaluation system, for example, the factor 'responsibility' may be considered twice as important as the factor 'contact'. The total number of points which a job is eventually given is therefore dependent on the factors which are considered relevant for the job, on the weight that is given to those factors within the system being used and on the extent to which the different factors are considered to occur within the specific job. The total number of points indicates in its turn a certain salary level.

Are job evaluation systems sex-neutral?

It was a long time before the question of whether job evaluation systems have an indirect sex-discriminatory effect was raised. When such suggestions were made, they were resolutely rejected, particularly by those involved in the actual practice of job evaluation. Their most important argument was that it is jobs which are the object of evaluation and not the people, men or women, who carry out those jobs. Jobs are described and analysed by means of certain features. Values are then assigned, on the basis of the system being used, to those features. These values, or point totals, refer in turn to the associated salary levels. Given such an objective course of events, sex discrimination factors can hardly be involved? Nevertheless, that is precisely the question which is being asked more and more frequently within the world of research into the differences in pay between men and women. At least 2 considerations are involved: first, that job evaluation systems cannot be seen separately from the social reality within which they are placed. In the sociological sense, job classification systems can be considered as institutions: rules as to what is considered just within a particular culture. Judgements as to social justice cannot be viewed separately from the history of a society. This leads to the second consideration. Women's work has, historically speaking, almost always been valued as inferior to that carried out by men. How men managed throughout history to define their work as more important than that of women is one of the core questions of women's studies. This question is, however, outside the scope of this chapter. It would involve consideration of cultural anthropology, philosophy and theology and probably of psychoanalysis. But even without such excursions into cultural history, job evaluation systems can be analysed as social constructions. They are social constructions containing notions of what the value of women's work is in comparison with that of men. This question is explicitly posed within the comparable worth strategy.

What can go wrong?

How can job evaluation systems contribute to lower pay for jobs in which it is primarily women who work, in comparison to jobs carried out primarily by men, even when the qualifications required for such jobs do not differ? The legal position 'equal pay for work of equal value' historically has a place in so-called equity theories, which relate to the question of when and on the basis of what criteria people consider particular distributions – for example income levels – to be equitable (Homans, 1961; Adams, 1965; Major, 1989). The general hypothesis is that people consider something to be equitable if there is an equilibrium between the contributions a person makes and what he or she receives for them. Contributions is a concept that needs to be interpreted broadly. Contributions include, for example, skills, efforts, training, education and experience. In deciding whether the relationship between contributions and reward is equitable, groups or individuals are compared with one another. Judgements are based on what counts in the culture and in the society as being in general equitable. In Western culture, for example, it is more or less accepted that a higher level of education gives the right to a higher level of income. One might, however, also argue that education as such functions as a reward and that it does not need to be given extra compensation in the form of pay. England (1992) refers in this connection to so-called framing effects. Framing models have been developed by some psychologists and economists in order to make the assumption of rational choice and rationality in behaviour more explicit (see Kahneman and Thaler, 1991). A frame refers to features of the situation surrounding a decision that affect what an option is compared to, and this affects how the option is valued (England, 1992). In relation to comparable worth, one can assume on the basis of framing effects that the present pay differences between male and female jobs are taken as the point of departure when evaluating what an equitable pay level is. It is not only employers who are supposed to base their decisions on the present differences but also those in male and female jobs. In addition, people do not simply compare themselves with anyone. Major (1989) states that people within privileged groups are more likely to compare themselves with one another than with people in deprived groups. That is also so in the case of people within deprived groups. This means that existing inequalities between men and women on the labour market (segregation, lower pay for female jobs, fewer chances for women) influence the way in which men and women compare their income situation and evaluate it as being equitable. Women are supposedly able to be satisfied with the pay they earn because their income is not at all bad in comparison with that of other women. The fact that it is less than what men earn may well be true, but that is not necessarily viewed as a problem, certainly not if men do work of a different type.

What we are dealing with is a vicious circle. Structural inequalities between men and women on the labour market influence judgement as to what is equitable and what is not. This is true not only for employers and for male and female workers. The designers and users of job evaluation systems, too, form part of a particular culture. If 'care' within that culture has for decades been paid less than 'planning' or 'organization', then many consider that to be normal. If existing job evaluation systems serve to express such a hierarchy, that is not surprising. They reconfirm the 'world which is taken for granted', and this world contributes in its turn to the lasting structural inequalities between men and women.

One of the things taken for granted is – it has already been pointed out – that what most women do is less economically valuable than what most men do. Such a principle influences the way people evaluate their own work. Women often do not have a very high opinion of what they do. This is seen, for example, in the study of Gender and Skill carried out in the United Kingdom in the late 1980s (Horrell, Rubery and Burchell, 1990). The study, among other things, asked 600 men and women working in the Northampton area whether they considered their own job to be skilled or unskilled. Women were more likely to call their job 'unskilled' than men. In part, this is associated with the fact that more women had part-time jobs. Part-timers in this study consider their level of skill to be lower than do full-timers, even when the qualifications required for the jobs are objectively the same. Aside from this part-time effect, however, more full-time working women than men are of the opinions that their work is unskilled.

The same picture is found at all qualification levels. Some quotations are highly indicative of the situation: 'Anyone who knows how to sew could do it'; 'Just working with old people is not a skilled job'; or 'Just a shop assistant'. The answers show that people often related the level of skill to whether or not they had undergone formal training. 'I suppose I haven't actually trained – more a caring job than a skill.'

It is highly likely that such things also find their way into official systems and that they make their own contribution to maintaining the pay differentials between men and women. In addition, there are other mechanisms at work when job evaluation systems are being applied. Within a single organization, for example, there may be several job evaluation systems in use. Because of the segregation of the internal market by gender, these differences often coincide with the difference between men's and women's work. It is therefore not possible to compare the results in evaluation with one another (see Wittig and Lowe, 1989). It may be that job descriptions are lacking or incomplete, precisely at the lower job levels at which women work (Wittig and Lowe, 1989; Veldman, 1991). Sometimes 'female' qualities such as 'tact', 'social sensitivity', 'neatness' and 'accuracy' are not formulated as requirements for the post concerned. They are in fact necessary for carrying out certain tasks effectively, but because they are often considered to be character traits rather than acquired skills they are not the subject of a separate evaluation.

Examples of non-sex-neutral job evaluation systems

Veldman (1991) investigated the job evaluation system used in the Netherlands within a company whose core activity is the design, marketing and maintenance of a high-tech product. The job evaluation system is divided into 2 independent components: Plan A for the operational functions and Plan B for independent and management functions. Plan A has 9 'factors', grouped in 3 clusters: skills; working conditions and physical effort; responsibility. The women who come under Plan A almost all work in administrative posts. The Plan A men almost all have technical jobs. When we examined the working conditions factor more closely, we see that points are assigned to this factor only when laboratory or shop-floor work is concerned. Such jobs as telephonist, receptionist or secretary do not receive points for the working conditions factor. In the case of physical effort, 'tiredness as a result of repetitive actions' is mentioned, but this relates only to the activities of (technical) production staff. It does not apply to secretaries or typists. Plan B mentions the factor 'creative/analytical ability'. This factor turns out, however, to apply only to positions in engineering, finance and planning. Personnel and other support staff positions, in which there are more women, do not receive points for this factor. The highest level of complexity is assigned only to activities requiring technical abilities. The factor 'contact' is not valued highly within Plan B. The marketing information officer provides the company's (future) clients with information. She answers questions, solves problems and is the intermediary between the client and the marketing department. This post is a prime example of a communicative post and involves the person holding it in representing the company. Nevertheless, the post of marketing information officer is assigned only one more point for the 'contact' factor than a fitter and one less than the male member of the technical service department who visits clients and is required to investigate the problems they have with the product before repairs are carried out.

In conclusion, we wish to give an example of points being assigned to jobs in the form of both scores for features of the jobs and of so-called weights. When we compare the job of fitter with that of nurse (see Table 12.1), it turns out that the relative weight of the various different job characteristics, as expressed in the weights, is to the disadvantage of the nurse (Buningh and Colenbrander, 1982).

Although the nurse scores higher than the fitter on many job characteristics, this effect is lost because of the values of the weights. The factor 'working conditions' produces striking results. In the case of fitters these would seem to be considered highly significant, but that is not so in the case of nurses. The greater weight assigned to this factor accentuates the difference in value. In this example the physical activities involved in being a nurse are

Table 12.1   **Example of discriminatory factor weighting**

FACTORS	FITTER	NURSE	WEIGHT (%)	FITTER'S SCORE	NURSE'S SCORE
Basic knowledge	6	8	7	0.42	0.56
Complexity of tasks	6	7	8	0.48	0.56
Training	5	7	7	0.35	0.49
Responsibility for people	3	8	15	0.45	1.20
Responsibility for materials	8	6	15	1.20	0.90
Mental effort	5	6	8	0.40	0.48
Visual attention	6	6	10	0.60	0.60
Physical activity	8	5	15	1.20	0.75
Working conditions	6	1	15	0.90	0.15
Total				6.00	5.66

SOURCE: Buningh and Colenbrander (1982)

underestimated in comparison with those of a fitter. One interesting question is whether the job of a fitter involves as much mental effort as that of a nurse.

On the basis of these examples, the question of whether job evaluation systems are sex-neutral can no longer be answered affirmatively. This is in any case true when we start by assuming the present distribution of men and women over the various different jobs. This distribution has in its turn been partly responsible for shaping job evaluation systems. Complex social and sociological processes are involved, and these maintain one another in the form of a vicious circle. Cultural attitudes and practices which are taken for granted are laid down in rules, and these rules then contribute to maintaining the status quo. However, it is possible to test the legitimacy of the status quo. The question is then always whether 'female jobs' are taken as seriously as 'male jobs'.

In the USA the Equal Employment Opportunity Commission (EEOC) commissioned the Committee on Occupational Classification and Analysis to investigate job classifications in the light of the comparable worth concept. In Canada there are already fully worked-out versions of job classification systems which claim to be more sex-neutral. These will be dealt with in brief in the following section.

An attempt to ensure sex-neutrality in job evaluation systems

Treiman and Hartman, (1981) members of the Committee on Occupational Classification and Analysis (see above), published their findings, which were drawn from the study commissioned by the EEOC. Their study revealed that women's jobs are less highly valued than men's jobs, even taking into account differences in complexity and difficulty and differences in the qualifications and experience of those carrying out the jobs. The American researchers recommend that job classification systems should be used more carefully. In this context 'more carefully' means that the 4 central job features – the level of skill or training, the necessary effort, the amount of responsibility required and the conditions under which the activities are carried out – are clearly defined, without the gender composition of the jobs having any influence.

Statistical procedures can help to determine whether or not the latter is the case. Using multiple-regression analysis, for example, it is possible to estimate the average earnings of the jobs within a given company. In order to arrive at an estimate of the earnings of the different jobs, such relevant features as skill, effort, responsibility and working conditions have to be included in the regression model. In addition, a factor should be included indicating the percentage of women in the job. In this way it is possible to determine whether and to what extent the latter feature - given that the other features of the job remain the same – contributes to the differences in earnings of male and female jobs. On the basis of the relative contribution of the feature 'percentage of women in the job' to the differences in earnings, a policy plan can then be developed with which to minimize this effect of gender composition of the jobs. The latter will relate primarily to regauge the 4 central features mentioned: skill, effort, responsibility and working conditions.

The so-called Hay System, used in Canada for example, is an attempt to do this. Table 12.2 gives an outline of this system.

Table 12.2 **The Hay System**

Factor 1	Factor 2	Factor 3	Factor 4
Know-how	Problem-solving	Accountability	Working conditions
The sum of total of knowledge and skills needed for acceptable performance	The amount of original, selfstarting thinking required for analysing, evaluating, creating, reasoning, arriving at conclusions	Answerability for actions and consequences	Conditions under which the job is performed
Subfactors	*Subfactors*	*Subfactors*	*Subfactors*
Substantive, managerial and human relations know-how	Degree of structure, challenge and/or difficulty of problems	Degree of discretion, magnitude measured by dollars affected, directness of impact	Physical effort, sensory attention, physical environment, mental stress

SOURCE: Hay Management Consultants (1988)

Considered from the point of view of sex-neutrality, this system has a number of interesting features. The 'human relations know-how' in the first factor is noticeable as well as the 'degree of discretion' in the third and the 'sensory attention' and 'mental stress' in the fourth. Naturally enough, such an abstract system will meet with a whole range of difficulties when the attempt is made to apply it to the entrenched actual practice of all sorts of different jobs. However, the same goes for the more conventional systems. The Hay System does in any case attempt explicitly to set out features of female jobs in order to be able to evaluate them explicitly.

CONCLUSION

This chapter has focused on the policy strategy of comparable worth: in other words, attempts to reduce the pay differentials between men and women by revaluing female jobs. Whereas desegregation projects concern themselves with the question of how to allow more women to enter male jobs, the comparable worth strategy leaves the present distribution into male and female jobs intact. It is not the employees who form the target of policy efforts but the jobs themselves. The comparable worth strategy can be characterized as a collective strategy aimed at changing systems. Research carried out by the European Network of Experts on the Situation of Women in the Labour Market (1994) within the member states of the European Union shows that collective rules and regulations have a positive effect on the level of pay equality between men and women. It was established, for example, that in countries with general minimum wage systems the pay differentials between men and women are smaller than in countries without a legal minimum wage. Centralized and integrated collective bargaining systems also seem to be a favourable precondition for closing the gender pay gap. Within companies, transparent payment systems which minimize the scope for managerial discretion contribute to reducing pay differentials between men and women. If we contrast this fact with the expected developments in the organization of work in the direction of increased flexibility and deregulation (see Chapter 14), we are faced with a dilemma. It would seem highly likely that central regulations with respect to employment terms and conditions and industrial relations will very soon lose their force. Whether (sex-neutral) job classification systems will be able successfully to resist the tendency towards deregulation and flexible working practices is a question which is difficult to answer at the moment. The same holds for the plans of the European Commission, announced in the White Paper on Social Affairs, to introduce codes of practice on equal pay for work of equal value, on training and on vertical desegregation.

REFERENCES

ADAMS, J. S. (1965) Inequality in social exchange, in L. Berkowitz (ed.), *Advances in Experimental Social Psychology*, Vol. 2, Academic Press, New York, pp. 267–99.

BERGMANN, B. R. (1986) *The Economic Emergence of Women*, Basic Books, New York.

BIELBY, W. T. and BARON, J. N. (1986) Men and women at work: sex segregation and statistical discrimination, *American Journal of Sociology*, Vol. 91, no. 4, pp. 759–99.

BOELENS, L. (1993) *Vrouwenwerk: naar waarde betalen*, Instituut Vrouw en Arbeid, The Hague.

BOELENS, L. and VELDMAN, A. (1993) *Gelijkwaardige arbeid, gelijk gewaardeerd*, NISER, Utrecht.

BRAUN, L. (1902, original edn 1901) *De vrouwenkwestie*, Soep, Amsterdam.

BUNINGH, C. A. and COLENBRANDER, P. B. (1982) *Functie en beloningsverhoudingen*, Samson, Alphen aan den Rijn.

DIPRETE, TH. and SOULE, W. (1988) Gender and promotion in segmented job ladder systems, *American Sociological Review*, Vol. 1, pp. 26–40.

ENGLAND, P. (1992) *Comparable Worth. Theories and Evidence*, Aldine de Gruyter, New York.

EUROPEAN NETWORK OF EXPERTS ON THE SITUATION OF WOMEN IN THE LABOUR MARKET (1994) *Bulletin on Women and Employment in the EU*, Brussels, October.

EYRAUD, F. *et al.* (1993) *Equal Pay Protection in Industrialised Market Economies*, International Labour Office, Geneva.

HAY MANAGEMENT CONSULTANTS (1988) Employment equity for women, *A University Handbook, the Committee on the Status of Women*, Council of Ontario Universities, Toronto.

HOMANS, G. C. (1961) *The Human Group*, Harcourt Brace, New York.

HORRELL, S., RUBERY, J. and BURCHELL, B. (1990) Gender and skills, *Work, Employment and Society*, Vol. 4(2), June, pp. 189–216.

KAHNEMAN, D. and THALER, R. (1991) Economic analysis and the psychology of utility: application to compensation policy, *American Economic Review*, Vol. 2, pp. 341–6.

KIM, M. (1989) Gender bias in compensation structures: a case study of its historical basis and persistence, *Journal of Social Issues*, Vol. 45, no. 4, pp. 39–50.

LONDON EQUAL VALUE STEERING GROUP (1987a) *A Question of Earnings: A Study of the Earnings of Blue Collar Employees in London Local Authorities*, LEVEL, London.

lONDON EQUAL VALUE STEERING GROUP (1987b) *Job Evaluation and Equal Value: A Study of White Collar Job Evaluation in London Local Authorities*, LEVEL, London.

MAJOR, B. (1989) Gender differences in comparison and entitlement: implications for comparable worth, *Journal of Social Issues*, Vol. 45, no. 4, pp. 99–115.

NATIONAL JOINT COUNCIL FOR LOCAL AUTHORITIES' SERVICES (1987) *Review of Grading Structure Assimilation and Assessment*, National Joint Council for Local Authorities' Services, London.

REMERY, C. and VAN DOORNE-HUISKES, J. (1992) Functiewaarderingsystemen: discriminerend voor vrouwen?, *Tijdschrift voor Arbeidsvraagstukken*, Vol. 1, pp. 6–18.

SCHOLTEN, G. (1981) *Passen en meten met functiewaardering*, Samsom, Alphen aan den Rijn.

STIGT, J. VAN (1994) *Implementatie van comparable worth in functiewaarderingssystemen*, Emancipatie-Raad, Den Haag.

TREIMAN, D. J. and HARTMAN, H. I. (eds.) (1981) *Women, Work and Wages*, National Academy Press, Washington D.C.

VELDMAN, A. G. (1991) Functiewaardering, vrouwenarbeid en het recht, *Tijdschrift voor Arbeidsvraagstukken*, Vol. 7, no. 2, pp. 32–43.

VERHAAREN, N. (1987) Gelijke beloning in West-Europa, *Nemesis*, Vol. 3, pp. 251–7.

WITTIG, M. A. and LOWE, R. H. (1989) Comparable worth theory and policy, *Journal of Social Issues*, Vol. 45, no. 4, pp. 1–21.

CHAPTER 13

Women, Trade Unions and European Policy

NOOR GOEDHARD AND JACQUES VAN HOOF

INTRODUCTION

By and large, and in many different respects, women have still not attained a position equal to that of men in the labour markets of the various countries which comprise the European Union. In the first part of this book we presented material in support of this observation and attempted to find explanations for this state of affairs. In the second part we looked at policy measures undertaken to reduce the differences between men and women in the labour market, and at the various obstacles which stand in the way of doing so. In recent years the official EU documents show evidence of a growing awareness that the equal treatment of men and women can be achieved only if women become more closely involved in policy-making in the social field, both within the member states and at the European level. The 1993 Green Paper on European Social Policy cited the lack of participation by women in decision-making as one of 3 major problems which should be given top priority (the other two were the difficulty in combining family life and occupational responsibilities and the segregation of the labour market).

One important means of involving women more closely in decision-making is through the trade unions. The labour movement has traditionally focused on improving the position of employees and it has tried, both directly and indirectly, to influence government social policy. In the course of time, the trade unions have also turned more of their attention to the position of female employees. The trade unions have joined forces at the European level in the European Trade Union Confederation (ETUC) and are attempting in this fashion to influence the policy pursued by the European Union. The ETUC has, furthermore, clarified its own position on the EU's equal opportunities policy, stimulated in this task by its highly active Women's Committee.

In this chapter we explore to what extent women can use the channel of the trade unions to gain more influence on policy-making in the social field. The chapter is divided into 3 sections. In the first we look at the position of women within the trade unions in the member states, focusing not only on the degree to which women join trade unions but also on the extent to which they hold prominent positions within these unions. The second section focuses on the trade union movement at the European level and the role which the Women's

Committee plays with respect to the affiliated union federations and the ETUC's policy on the position of women. The third section, finally, looks at the ways in which trade union women might influence European policy. In this connection we explore the relationship between the union federations and employers' associations at the European level and the European institutions.

WOMEN AND TRADE UNIONS IN EUROPE

In this section we compare the participation of women in unions to that of men in the various member states. We explore participation by looking at female union density rates (the percentage of female employees who are members of trade unions) and at the role which women play within the trade unions. At the same time we also discuss various explanations for the differences between men and women with respect to these two forms of participation.

Union density rates

The statistics on union membership in the European Union suffer from various flaws and imperfections. That becomes most obvious when we attempt to separate the figures for male and female membership, and find that we can do so for only a few of the EU member states. In addition, the period of time during which the data were collected varies considerably from country to country. Table 13.1 is therefore incomplete. What we have done is to add data from the 3 countries which recently joined the Union: Austria, Finland and Sweden. For the sake of completeness, we should report that the union density rates have been calculated without taking into account the unemployed, old-age pensioners or benefits recipients. The figures therefore only represent the percentage of men/women of the active male/female labour force who have union membership.

When looking at these figures, we should first be aware that in almost all the countries of Western Europe, with the exception of Sweden, Finland and Norway, overall union density dropped after 1980, (Visser, 1994). As a result, union density among women also fell in most of the countries included in Table 13.1. Looking at the differences between men and women, we see that women in the countries which made up the European Union before 1995 are less likely to be a member of a trade union than men. This is particularly true of the Netherlands and Germany. The gap between the density rates of men and women has, however, narrowed over time. The 2 Scandinavian countries, Finland and Sweden, display an entirely different pattern. Not only is union density among both men and women higher than in the other countries, but in both countries women are (even) more likely to be union members than are men. Both countries therefore have a labour movement with a strong basis of support among the working population and in which women (at least numerically) have a solid position. Their admission to the EU will probably increase support for the EU's equal opportunities policy.

Tabel 13.1   **Union density rates (%) in some European counties**

	1970		1980		1989	
	FEMALES	MALES	FEMALES	MALES	FEMALES	MALES
Germany	15.3	42.4	20.3	47.0	21.6	46.7
France			15.0	29.0	7.0	13.0
Ireland	43.4	56.1	47.3	59.9		
Netherlands	13.9	43.7	18.0	44.2	13.0	35.2
United Kingdom	29.1	54.2	36.8	60.6	33.3	44.0
Austria	44.6	72.8	40.1	63.0		
Finland					74.9	68.6
Sweden	53.7	77.4	78.9	80.9	88.3	82.4

SOURCE: Based on *OECD Employment Outlook*, 1991, Table 4.8, p. 116

Explanations for the lower union density rate among women

A number of studies have been carried out in various EU member states and in such countries as Canada and the USA exploring the differences in male and female union density rates. Visser *et al.* (1991) have distinguished 2 explanations arrived at in such international studies. The first focuses on differences between individuals in their willingness to join a union and in how they evaluate unions. The other focuses on labour market differences.

Little support was found in international research for the first hypothesis: women do not have a more negative attitude towards trade unions than do men, nor is their evaluation of the labour movement more negative. Their was more evidence in support of the second hypothesis. In some studies male–female differences even fade into the background if the features of the employment situation remain constant. Bain and Elsheikh (1979) conclude from their research in Britain that the differences between sectors in male and female union density rates cannot be attributed to the gender difference but, rather, to the fact that women tend to work in less organized sectors. In 2 American studies, 65% and 80% respectively of the differences in union density between men and women could be attributed to the difference in sectoral union density rates (Anton, Chandler and Mellow, 1980; Freeman and Medoff, 1984).

The features of the employment situation include the characteristics of the particular company and/or industry, but also whether the person concerned works part time or full time. Part-timers are less likely than full-timers to join a union. The low rate of union density among women in the Netherlands is closely related to the large number of women who work part-time. Among part-timers as such, female part-timers in 3 of the Dutch trade unions are equally or even more likely to be unionized than their male counterparts (van den Putte and Sips, 1992). Based on their own study of the Dutch situation, Visser *et al.* (1991) point out that differences in the features of the employment situation also imply differences in the likelihood of an employee being recruited by a trade union representative. Women are more likely to work in an environment in which there is only a small chance that they will be recruited.

Tabel 13.2 **Participation of women within trade unions, 1993**

COUNTRY/UNION	MEMBERSHIP	WOMEN (%)	WOMEN CONGRESS DELEGATES (%)	WOMEN ON EXECUTIVE COMMITTEE (%)
Austria OGB (Österreichischer Gewerkschaftsbund)	1,633,480	31	14	8*
Belgium FGTB (Fédération Générale du Travail de Belgique)	1,093,623	40	n/k	7
Denmark AC (Akademikers Centralorganisation)	122,442	29	29*	18
Denmark LO (Landes Organisation)	1,296,000	49	30	14
Finland SAK (Suomen Ammattilittojen Keskusjaresto)	1,000,000	45	49*	23
Finland ACAVA (Confederation of Unions of Academic Professionals)	215,400	48	35*	10*
France CFDT (Confédération Française Démocratique du Travail)	586,000	35	21	25*
France FO (Force Ouvrière)	1,015,000	48	35	8
Germany DAG (Deutsche Angestellten Gewerkschaft)	565,726	53*	36*	35*
Germany DGB (Deutscher Gewerkschaftsbund)	9,100,000	32	22	13
Greece GSEE (Greek General Confederation of Labour)	300,000	n/k	4	11
Ireland ICTU (Irish Congress of Trade Unions)	600,000	38	29*	17*
Italy CISL (Confederazione Italiana Sindicati Lavoratori)	3,000,000	40	18*	7
Italy CGIL (Confederazione Generale Italiane del Lavoro)	1,300,000	41	7*	12
Luxembourg CGT (Confédération Générale du Travail)	43,885	25	11	15
Netherlands FNV (Federatie Nederlandse Vakbeweging)	1,107,832	22	20	19
Netherlands CNV (Christelijk Nationaal Vakverbond)	326,135	20	2	14
Portugal UGDT (Uniao General Dos Travalhadores)	251,000	41	n\k	13
Spain CSCO (Confederation Sindical de Commissiones Obreras)	600,000	42	15*	20*
Spain UGT (Union General Trabajadores de España)	600,000	29	n\k	13
Sweden LO (Landes Organisation)	1,972,255	45	26	13*
Sweden TCO (Tjanstemannens Centralorganisation)	1,157,705	59	43	18
United Kingdom TUC (Trades Union Congress)	7,600,000	36	22*	31*

n\k = not known   * Special measures to increase the number of women, e.g. a quota system or a number of reserved places.

SOURCE: Membership details from the relevant organization to the ETUC (30 June 1993); data on percentage of women members for Belgium and France from ICFTU (1991); other details concerning 1993 from Braithwaite and Byrne (1994)

In explaining the relatively low level of female participation in the decision-making process within the trade unions, we will emphasize the obstacles which women encounter within a movement still dominated largely by men. This factor seems to have been neglected in the studies mentioned above, which focused on membership statistics. Nevertheless, it may be of importance. Daalder (1994) conducted research in the Netherlands on the enormous difference between the number of men and women who turn in their union membership. Career and occupational differences could play a role, but it is unclear whether this explains the sharp contrasts between the different unions. Daalder found that the 4 unions in which men and women differed most with respect to relinquishing union membership also had the smallest percentage of female members. This may indicate that women find it less attractive to retain membership in a union which has relatively few other female members.

Male–female differences within the labour movement

The ETUC's and the ICFTU's (International Confederation of Free Trade Unions) women's conferences give union women an opportunity to collect data, but one of the striking things about their doing so is that they give so little attention to female union density as such. The data they collect often relate to the relative position of women within trade unions, with regard both to membership and to female representation in union leaderships. They demonstrate the relatively disadvantaged position of women in order to stimulate measures for improvement. Braithwaite and Byrne (1994) were commissioned by the ETUC Women's Committee to study women and the decision-making process within ETUC union affiliates. Table 13.2, based on their results, summarizes the position of women compared with that of men, preceded by membership data pertaining to the relevant union federation. The table indicates the percentage of women in total membership, conference delegations and appointments to national executive committees. For the final 2 categories an indication is also given as to whether a policy exists to encourage the participation of women. Table 13.2 covers only European Union member states, including the countries which joined in 1995.

The nature of the national union federations included in the table can vary. In some countries the various federations are organized according to different ideological orientations. For example, in the Netherlands there is one large, general federation (FNV) and a small Christian federation (CNV). In other countries the dividing lines are formed by the occupational categories of the members who make up the union federation. In Denmark, for example, there is a tradition of blue-collar (the LO) and white collar (the AC) trade unions. It is important to keep these different organizational principles in mind when assessing the differences in membership. The German DAG and Swedish TCO, in which women constitute the majority of the membership, are both federations focusing on specific occupational groups (civil servants, middle and senior management staff). Unions of public servants in other countries also have a relatively large number of female members.

Strikingly enough, the Danish LO, which organizes blue-collar workers, still has the largest number of female members after the federations mentioned above. This is because the LO has one unique affiliate, a union which has exclusively female members and which focuses explicitly on the collective and individual interests of women: Kvindeligt Arbejderforbund. It had over 100,000 female members in 1990 working, for example, in the cleaning sector and in industry. Other countries do not have separate unions for women, but they do have women's committees, often supported by an 'office of women's affairs'. The FNV in the Netherlands has a separate women's union, but it is not involved in direct negotiations over terms and conditions of employment.

In general it appears that the share of women on national executive committees is much smaller than the share of women who make up the membership. A large percentage of female members does not automatically mean a correspondingly large percentage of female conference delegates and national executive committee members. Although caution is advised, we can obtain an impression by adding up the differences in percentage points between membership and participation in conference delegations on the one hand and between membership and participation in national executive committees on the other. The Swedish union federation TCO shows up relatively badly. The Dutch FNV comes out on top, followed by the Danish AC, the Finnish SAK and the British TUC, all union federations which have introduced policy measures to promote women to positions of leadership within the unions. Such measures do not as yet guarantee a high level of participation, as the Spanish CSCO demonstrates, but the problem here may be that Table 13.2 does not show when the policy was introduced.

Explanations for the fact that women are under-represented at the decision-making level

The membership studies described above often consisted of large-scale quantitative research, whereas those discussed below on the participation of women in decision-making are largely qualitative. They place greater emphasis on the barriers which actively prevent women from participating in decision-making than they do on obstacles to membership as such. Braithwaite and Byrne summarized these barriers in the following way:

- family responsibilities: women have less free time available than men . . .
- traditional views and stereotypes: resulting in women lacking in confidence and [in their] finding it difficult to be accepted as representatives and spokespersons and in men [being] unwilling to give up their power
- job segregation; union structures which reflect the sex-segregated character of the labour market can create barriers for women's advancement
- male-dominated 'discriminatory' environment: the traditional (masculine) image of union leaders, traditional meeting procedures, union jargon, etc.

(Braithwaite and Byrne, 1994, p. 15)

The factors summarized above, all of which make it difficult for women to assume leadership positions, largely correspond with the restrictions discussed elsewhere in this book (see, for example, Chapters 7 and 11). Like other types of organization, the trade union can be viewed as an organization whose structure and culture do not invite women to take up leadership positions. For example, officials are often recruited from among groups of active trade union members. If the expectation is that a future trade union leader must first prove himself (or herself) in practice, a criterion such as this reduces the chance that women will be selected. To meet this requirement, women must not only combine working life and family responsibilities but also take an active part in trade union activities in their spare time. Seen in this light, it is not at all surprising that the first female union officials were very frequently single women.

An original contribution comes from Ledwith *et al.* (1991) in their study of female activists and union officials within the Society of Graphical and Allied Trades, a TUC affiliate. The study focused on the role of family members and partners, a subject which has been given scant attention in the literature on career development. The fathers (and to a lesser extent the mothers) of these women were themselves trade unionists and had impressed upon their offspring the importance of trade unionism from a very early age. One of the women summarized it in the following way: 'We got our father's politics rammed down our throats' (Ledwith *et al.*, 1991, p. 116). Three-quarters of the female activists had a male partner who was a member of a trade union, and half of them had partners who were themselves activists. Ledwith *et al.* also observed that women who were just starting a trade union career needed 'sponsorship' to overcome such obstacles as insufficient active support from the female rank and file or resistance among male colleagues. The majority of the women they described had had active support from above.

Below we will describe how the ETUC's Women's Committee has struggled to strengthen the position of women within the trade unions and to ensure a rise in the number of female officials. That justifies our questioning whether appointing female officials does in fact increase the consideration given to women's issues and improve attitudes towards women within the trade unions. The conclusion reached by Heere and Kelly in their study is 'yes'. They investigated whether the TUC's female full-time officials (FTOs) were more likely than their male counterparts to raise issues important to women in negotiations and to mobilize women:

> The results suggest that women FTOs are more likely to make a priority of issues such as equal pay, childcare, maternity leave and sexual harassment in collective bargaining. There is also evidence that women FTOs are more committed to the recruitment of women workers into trade unions and to developing participation in union activities among the existing female membership.
>
> (Heere and Kelly, 1988, p. 502)

In addition, they may also manage to introduce changes in the trade union's own personnel policy which make it easier for women officials to combine their job with child-care activities, as examples within Dutch trade unions have shown.

THE EUROPEAN TRADE UNION CONFEDERATION
(ETUC) AND ITS WOMEN'S COMMITTEE

The ETUC was founded in 1973 as a forum for the national union federations at the European level. In 1993 its affiliates consisted of 47 national federations from 22 European countries. Through these affiliates, 95% of all unionized employees in Western Europe are represented in the ETUC (Tegzes and Sips, 1993). This demonstrates that its affiliates are not restricted to trade unions in the EU member states. The ETUC has always advocated expanding the European Union, particularly in the direction of the Scandinavian countries, whose trade unions play an important role within its ranks.

The ETUC's general goal is to expand the social dimension of a united Europe. The European market should concentrate in the first place on social issues and should work towards creating jobs and improving the terms and conditions of employment of European employees. 'Social dumping', the process of adjusting the social policy of the member states downwards to the lowest level found within the Union, should be avoided at all costs. Regional economic differences, which at times take on striking proportions, should be reduced so as to strengthen social cohesion within the EU. The ETUC is also a warm proponent of attempts to lay down a number of basic social rights for workers in European law. Its efforts to gain recognition for such rights and to prevent unfair competition have also led the ETUC to advocate equal opportunities for men and women.

The ETUC's Women's Committee plays an important role in developing ideas and instigating campaigns on the issues mentioned above. As early as 1973, the year it was founded, the ETUC set up a Working Party on Women's Work, the forerunner of the present Women's Committee. The Committee did not achieve its influential position in decision-making and the authority to mobilize women trade unionists on its own overnight. In the course of time the Women's Committee has developed close contacts with the national union federations, and in particular with their women's committees. Both the task and the position of the Committee have been clearly laid out in a resolution adopted by the ETUC in 1992 and entitled 'A gender perspective in ETUC policy'. Known as the 'gender resolution', it describes the task of the Women's Committee as encouraging the incorporation of a gender perspective in each element of ETUC policy (ETUC, 1992, p. 4). At the same time, the Committee is to serve as the driving force behind the promotion of equal opportunities policies in the labour movement. The Committee was given the status of 'standing committee'. Prior to each ETUC conference, a separate women's conference was to be held.

We will now consider the activities of the Committee in more detail. From the very start, the Women's Committee has concentrated on analysing the position of women in the labour market and on encouraging the ETUC's national affiliates to adopt a common policy on improving this position. In 1985, for example, at the suggestion of the Women's Committee, the ETUC adopted a programme 'to obtain equal rights and opportunities for women'. The programme set out a series of recommendations regarding employment, combating (hidden) unemployment among women, education and vocational training, working and living conditions, pay, and so on. The goal was to stimulate the national federations to achieve the proposed improvements in their own countries. In 1989 the ETUC's research office, the European Trade Union Institute (ETUI), investigated the impact of these recommendations (ETUI, 1989). Some countries (Portugal, Italy) reported that the programme had galvanized them into assessing the policy of their union federations, whereas others (Britain, the Netherlands) reported that the recommendations had had little effect on the existing policy.

The Women's Committee's second area of attention, one which it has gradually come to emphasize more and more, is the attempt to increase participation by women within the trade unions themselves and to use the ETUC as a channel for promoting organizational policies within the national union federations which take more account of women's issues. The Committee has drafted several resolutions in this regard which have been adopted at ETUC conferences. The study mentioned above by Braithwaite and Byrne (1994) makes various recommendations on increasing the participation of women in the decision-making process. These recommendations were discussed at a seminar organized by the Women's Committee in March 1994 for the purpose of drafting proposals for the 1995 ETUC conference.

During its first few years of existence, it was not the Women's Committee's top priority to develop a common strategy regarding the European Union. The 1985 programme mentioned above scarcely makes mention of the European Union. It is only in the section on 'discrimination in taxation, social security and family allowances' that the programme refers to the fact that 'the EEC is planning several directives which could eliminate these discriminations' (ETUI, 1989, p. 82). This apparent lack of interest has been rectified in the past few years: the EU's policy on special women's issues is now one of the Committee's major concerns. It generally supports the use of directives to improve the position of women and has itself taken steps to initiate such directives, in keeping with the ETUC's general goal of having the basic rights of workers laid down by law. In addition to influencing the actual decision-making process within the EU, the Women's Committee also tries to encourage national efforts to implement the decisions taken at European level. For example, the Committee published a set of guidelines to accompany the third action programme on equal opportunities (ETUC, 1993).

It will be clear that the EU's general economic and social policy is also an important factor influencing the position of women, and there is evidence that the Women's Committee is growing increasingly aware of this fact. For example, in 1990 at an ETUC meeting in Paris, some 200 trade union women formulated a list of demands within the framework of an action programme entitled 'Women in a social Europe: our demands' (ETUC, 1990). In addition to articulating demands specifically related to women, its attention has also been directed towards general programmes such as Eurotechnet, Comett, Force, Delta, Petra, Lingua and Erasmus, half of whose beneficiaries or participants should in its view be women. It is also looking into the degree to which ESF programmes benefit women, advising that the committees for equal opportunities in the countries involved should offer mandatory recommendations concerning the implementation of ESF programmes for each country. The Committee also demands that the European Commission separate data on the development and projected impact of unemployment and educational measures by sex.

Like other Women's Committee's activities, those described above are entirely in line with the ETUC's own ideas. In its resolution on 'a gender perspective in ETUC policy', the ETUC described the Women's Committee's explicit task as being to examine the ETUC's position on general policy issues in terms of gender. The future will reveal how this resolution can and will affect the work of the Women's Committee and particularly the ETUC's position, and what its influence will be on general policy.

We may conclude that women have gradually achieved an important role within the ETUC. They are attempting not only to encourage the affiliated national federation to consider women's issues (including the position of women within the trade unions themselves) but also to influence European-level decision-making through the channel of the ETUC. With regard to the latter, the critical factor does not appear to be the influence that the Women's Committee exercises on the ETUC's own position but, rather, the restricted options open to the ETUC to influence policy in Brussels. That is the subject of the final section of this chapter.

TRADE UNION WOMEN, THE SOCIAL DIALOGUE AND EUROPEAN POLICY

In this section we outline the way in which the ETUC (and its major opponent on the employers' side, the UNICE) are involved in the EU's decision-making process. We first discuss the 'Social Dialogue' and look at the UNICE's position on equal opportunities policy. Using a concrete example (i.e. the history of the directive on maternity leave), we then indicate how women in the ETUC can influence European policy and the problems that they face in doing so. We finish with a brief look ahead.

The 'Social Dialogue'

Employers and employees have been meeting one another in the Economic and Social Committee (ECOSOC) since the very earliest days of the European Community. ECOSOC is a vast committee whose members are appointed by the member states. In addition to employer and employee representatives, there are members who represent other socio-economic interests. ECOSOC is an advisory committee which the European Council of Ministers and the European Commission are obliged to consult on certain specific subjects and which has the right to make unsolicited recommendations on the remaining Union affairs.

For quite some time the European Commission felt the need to involve European employer and employee representative organizations directly in preparing policy. This became particularly urgent in the mid-1980s, when the European Commission under the presidency of Jacques Delors tried to pick up the pace of the European unification process. In 1985, the same year as the publication of the famous White Paper on the Single European Market, Delors took steps to give the social dimension of the unification process more substance and to improve relations with the so-called 'social partners', i.e. labour and management. From 1985 on, they began to meet regularly, at the invitation of the European Commission. These periodic meetings came to be known as the 'Social Dialogue'. The meetings focused on a number of subjects, for example vocational training, but the participants did not achieve much more than the formulation of 'joint opinions' which had no direct bearing on policy.

Around the same time the Commission began to draft new social policy initiatives. In 1989 the Community Charter of Fundamental Social Rights of Workers (usually referred to as the 'Social Charter') was adopted, with the UK as the only member state to vote against it. That marked the start of a period of 'activism', as Hall calls it, in the field of European social policy. The hallmarks of this period were several EU directives, recommendations and action programmes (Hall, 1994). The directive on maternity leave, which we will discuss below, is an example.

While the ETUC advocated a more explicit role for the social partners and supported Delors's initiatives, the employers were less enthusiastic. They recognized that the creation of an internal market was an absolute necessity if Europe was to remain competitive at the global level. They therefore agreed with the 1985 White Paper and responded to Delors's call to intensify the Social Dialogue. According to Huntjens (1991), their support was based on an initial assumption that the EU's social policy would serve as an additional policy impetus for the internal market: in their view, the purpose of social policy was to increase flexibility and mobility in the labour market. They were, however, critical of the change in direction towards more direct intervention on the part of the Community in social affairs, as took place after 1989 with the adoption of the Social Charter. According to the UNICE, if European agreements were indeed desirable, it would be better to hammer them out in negotiations between employers' associations and trade unions. In 1991 an agreement was reached linking collective bargaining between the social partners with European policy-making in the social field. This was incorporated in the Social Protocol which was appended to the Maastricht Treaty.

The Social Protocol gives the social partners direct access to European decision-making. The European Commission must first consult the social partners about the general outline of its initiatives in the social policy field. If the Commission then wishes to lay down an initiative in law, it is obliged to consult these organizations about its proposal a second time. The social partners have the option at that point to negotiate over the material and to conclude an agreement of their own at EU level. In anticipation of the results of these negotiations, the Commission must withhold its proposal for a period of 9 months (which can be extended). In this way, a round of negotiation is incorporated into the process of creating social policy. If they so desire, the social partners have 9 months to draft their own joint proposals. It will be clear that the commitment to the Social Dialogue may be raised considerably through this process.

The ETUC and its Women's Committee therefore have more than one method of influencing European decision-making in the social policy field (see Figure 13.1).

To begin with there is ECOSOC, which is consulted when important social and economic measures are being proposed. Although this is a committee representing employers and employees from the member states, both the

Figure 13.1   European decision-making in the social policy field

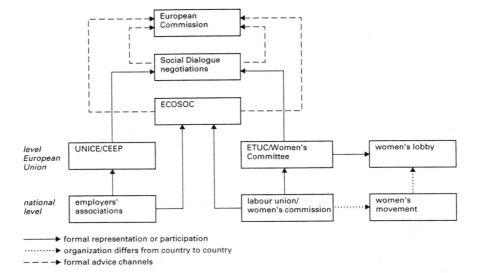

————➤ formal representation or participation

···········➤ organization differs from country to country

— — — ➤ formal advice channels

ETUC and the UNICE play an important role in co-ordinating the various points of view. In addition, the ETUC and UNICE may choose a much more active form of involvement by choosing to negotiate directly with each other over important issues and presenting the results of these negotiations to the Commission, which submits them to European Council of Ministers. Finally, for women's issues in particular the ties between the ETUC's Women's Committee and the European women's lobby are important (the role of the women's lobby was discussed in Chapter 8).

Before discussing in detail the various ways in which the ETUC and its Women's Committee can influence European social policy (and the problems associated with doing so), we will first look briefly at the position taken by the ETUC's major opponent, the UNICE, on equal opportunities.

UNICE and equal opportunities policy

UNICE (Union of Industrial Employers' Confederation of Europe) is the most important employers' association at European level. Above we described UNICE's conviction that the EU's social policy should concentrate on removing the barriers to the internal market. If we look more closely at UNICE's recent comments concerning the policy on women, we see that it has not deviated in the least from this position.

While each comment confirms that UNICE supports the principle of equal treatment and equal opportunities for men and women at work, in this respect supporting the third action programme, UNICE is also of the opinion that with regard to equal treatment, 'the directives which have been adopted till now [provide] an adequate framework. Therefore, there is no need for new legal instruments in this field' (UNICE, 1991a, p. 1). UNICE also believes that employers and employees should settle a number of matters among themselves. For example, the comment on the proposals for a Council Recommendation on Child Care says this: 'Leave arrangements for employed parents with responsibility for the care of children is a matter to be dealt with by employers and employees and/or their representatives and this is not a matter for EC intervention' (UNICE, 1991b, p. 1). Some measures are even seen as counterproductive. A case in point is the Commission's proposed remuneration policies, as described in the draft memorandum on equal pay for work of equal value (UNICE, 1993b). Paying women in traditional women's occupations higher wages, such as the Commission recommends, can only lead to women becoming mired in less profitable sectors and eventually losing their jobs as a result. The idea of obliging companies to introduce positive action measures by the fixing of quotas is also considered inefficient and even sometimes counterproductive (UNICE, 1994).

The background is UNICE's avowed conviction that greater flexibility in general would benefit both the position of employees and their situation in the labour market. That applies to women as well as to men: 'flexibility is the key to ensuring more participation by women in the labour market' (UNICE, 1991a, p. 1). In 1994 flexibility seemed to be the cure for all ills. UNICE does acknowledge the importance of the 3 action points mentioned in the Green Paper, intended to reinforce the position of women: reconciliation of employment and family responsibilities; desegregation of the labour market; and more participation by women in decision-making (Commission, 1993). But it ends its comments by stating that 'each of these points would be best addressed by more flexibility at the level of employment area' (UNICE, 1994, p. 2).

We may conclude that UNICE supports the principle of equal opportunities, but that it is suspicious of new EU initiatives in this field because they may lead to statutory measures which would have a negative effect on the flexibility of the labour market.

An example: the directive on maternity leave

The options open to the ETUC's Women's Committee to influence European policy and the problems associated with this process can be illustrated effectively by looking at the history of the directive on maternity leave (discussed briefly in Chapter 8). The lengthy battle over this directive, which lasted from 1989 to 1992, is not only an important gauge of the degree of influence women have on Union policy, it also offers us a good example of how the European Commission and a number of member states are attempting to increase the social dimension of the unification process and use the new instruments made available in the Single European Act (1986) (specifically the possibility of qualified majority voting). We will first briefly review the events which preceded the adoption of the directive by the Council of Ministers, from the very first steps undertaken by the Women's Committee, and then look at the way in which the ETUC and/or Women's Committee attempted to influence these events and assess their degree of success. Our description is based on Pedler (1994).

The European institutions had long intended to consider a measure governing paid parental leave, but a 1984 draft directive was rejected by the UK. The Framework Directive on Health and Safety at Work, adopted by the Council in 1989, appeared to the Women's Committee to offer a new opportunity: the national states had after all a tradition of incorporating protective measures for pregnant women into their policy on working conditions. By anchoring the issue of maternity leave in the health and safety field, moreover, its proponents could also benefit from the fact that it had recently become possible for the Council of Ministers to vote on the basis of qualified majority in this policy area.

The first step in the direction of a directive was naturally an attempt to place the issue on the European agenda. That became possible thanks to the excellent informal relationship between the Women's Committee and the European Commission's Equal Opportunities Unit. At the same time, the Women's Committee received the unqualified support of the ETUC, which adopted the Women's Committee's proposals for a 16-week period of paid leave. To avoid the complexity involved in working with different social security schemes in the various member states and the effect that these differences would have on the various premiums and wage-based contributions, the ETUC adopted the employee's 'take-home pay' (i.e. wages less taxes and social security contributions) as the point of departure.

The next move was the European Commission's. In 1990 it announced its draft directive, which was presented as part of the Social Action Programme and as an elaboration of the Framework Directive on Health and Safety, in accordance with the ETUC's recommendations. After consulting the social partners, however, the Commission had opted for a 'politically realistic approach' (Pedler, 1994, p. 246), to some extent prompted by the desire of the member states to keep the costs down. That meant that the directive in fact established only minimum norms which the member states were free to supplement if they so desired. In the eyes of the Commission, the minimum provision was to be 14 weeks of paid leave. No mention was made of take-home pay.

This draft directive was discussed in ECOSOC and the European Parliament. In the first, it transpired that both the trade unions and the employers' association (UNICE) were favourably inclined towards the draft directive. As commented upon by Pedler, the desire to establish minimum norms was entirely in keeping with UNICE's position on social policy in general (Pedler, 1994, p. 256). Parliament was more critical. The socialists attempted to expand the directive by extending the period of paid leave to 16 weeks and by arguing for parental rather than maternity leave. The Commission managed to thwart these improvements, however, by referring to the restricted scope of the Framework Directive (which could accommodate the protection of pregnant women but not parental leave, which could be taken up by men).

The directive which the Commission submitted to the Council was therefore largely unaltered. The Council engaged in a long, drawn-out discussion closely related to its deliberations on other proposals in the social field and to the amendments to the Treaty of Rome which were to be hammered out in Maastricht. Finally, at the end of 1991, a common position was announced. The Commission saw its proposal watered down on one important point: the criterion for an adequate allowance during the (minimum) 14-week leave was no longer full payment of wages, but the benefit received by employees in case of sickness. There was no 'unanimity' about this common position; it was adopted by qualified majority.

The European Parliament once again deliberated over the draft directive and came up with an interim proposal (based on the situation in Italy): 16 weeks of leave and a benefit based on 80% of the salary of the recipient. This proposal was once again rejected by the Council. The parties threatened to reach deadlock, a situation which might have had painful consequences (partly because of the public controversy which had broken out in various member states about the Maastricht Treaty). The directive was finally adopted on 19 October 1992 (again by qualified majority), with the length of leave and size of allowance untouched by the Ministers.

The result, then, is a directive which on a few essential points deviates considerably from what the ETUC and the Women's Committee originally intended. Was this a lost opportunity for the ETUC? There are 3 ways that it can attempt to influence European decision-making: by using its direct contacts within the European institutions and/or among representatives in these institutions; by attempting to mobilize the trade unions in the member states to put pressure on national politicians; and by exploiting its role in the European women's lobby.

With regard to the first, it is clear that the ETUC's contacts within the European Commission were in any event essential for raising the issue in the first place. These contacts could not, however, prevent the Commission from choosing a position which deviated from that adopted by the ETUC. It is, incidentally, interesting to note that ECOSOC, in particular the employers, did not raise any objections to the draft directive. Indeed, the greatest resistance came from a number of countries within the Council.

The second channel, mobilizing the national trade unions, requires sound management on the part of the ETUC. Unfortunately, it was precisely in the area of management and control over the national federations that the ETUC failed. As described above, almost every country has a women's committee which the ETUC's Women's Committee can call upon for support when attempting to mobilize the national trade unions. The ETUC did try to mobilize the national trade unions on the topic of maternity leave but, according to Pedler (1994, p. 257), 'The federal structure of ETUC was too unwieldy to transmit a clear and constant message at the key moments and in the key places around the EU.' This message was further undermined because the ETUC allowed itself to be convinced by the Commission – even before the latter had drafted its own proposal – that it was necessary to take a 'realistic' approach, i.e. to establish only minimum norms. It goes without saying that women in many countries were less than enthusiastic about such a meagre measure, making it impossible to generate a strong, unanimous position on the issue.

The third channel open to the ETUC's Women's Committee is its participation in the European women's lobby, which also includes representatives from the women's movement in the individual member states. unfortunately, even here it proved impossible to reach an undivided position. Pedler (1994, p. 257), observes that the Women's Committee failed to argue its proposal in such a way that it became a 'strong women's issue all over Europe'. The women's lobby even considered whether it would not be better quietly to remove the directive from the decision-making agenda. This debate arose after the European Parliament, having initially argued for an allowance based on the recipient's full salary, announced that it would support an allowance equal to 80% of wages. The question within the lobby was: do we stick to our guns (100% allowance) and lose the battle, or do we support Parliament's position in the final phase of decision-making (Ophuysen, 1994, p. 67)? The lobby chose to stick to its guns. Pedler (1994, p. 256) comments that 'minimum norms don't motivate people and the women in the lobby didn't understand the process of EU decision making'.

In the ETUC's eyes the result was a disappointment. Extending a minimum level of protection to women in Europe may have symbolic significance, but any actual improvement has been restricted to women in a small number of countries. It turned out to be difficult to ensure that the women's lobby and the ETUC supported the same position, and equally difficult to mobilize the affiliated national union federations to undertake co-ordinated action. The lengthy consultation process meant expending a great deal of energy lobbying the Commission and Parliament, even though the final decision was taken by the Council. The experiences described above are nevertheless viewed as part of a learning process, and the most important conclusion is that better channels must be found in the future to influence the Council (i.e. the national ministers).

We mentioned before that the activities related to the maternity leave directive are a good illustration of the way in which the European Commission is attempting to improve the EU's social policy by working with employers and employees and by taking advantage of the new decision-making rules within the Council. It is also, however, a good illustration of the limitations to these attempts. In Pedler's view, this case shows that even in the event of qualified majority voting, the member states which support a social policy aimed at upward harmonization are still very reluctant to make excessive use of this leverage. 'The case shows that there is an enormous amount of "inertia" in the Council' (Pedler, 1994, p. 257). In recent years the rise in unemployment and the national governments' concern about loss of competitiveness has certainly not inspired the Council to overcome this inertia. In the years ahead, we can expect that there will be only limited scope to pursue an active social policy aimed at improving the position of women.

DILEMMAS FOR THE FUTURE

Given the result of the debate on maternity leave, the changing climate concerning European legislation in general and, lest we forget, the increasing preoccupation with unemployment in the various member states, we must question whether we have witnessed the passing of a time when progress could be made in the field of equal treatment through the adoption of directives and recommendations (see also the final chapter). If that is indeed the case, then the ETUC and its Women's Committee will have to undergo a strategic reorientation.

One option open to them is to negotiate directly with employers, based on the agreements reached in 1991 on the eve of the Maastricht Summit. It seems likely that the employers at the European level will attempt to hammer out issues through negotiation rather than allow them to be settled through legislation. It is by no means conclusive that substantive results can be achieved in this fashion, but there is scope for creating general frameworks within which employers and employees can work out details at the national or even the industry level. Bridgeford and Stirling (1994) observe that until now there have been precious few examples of transnational bargaining arrangements, but they see signs of change. The dynamics of this process will probably be prompted by bargaining at the sector level rather than by negotiations at the most general level.

The ETUC certainly does not oppose bargaining, but it has always been a fervent advocate of laying down the basic rights of employees at the European level. Indeed, it still sees that as a way of increasing the involvement of the average citizen in the European Union. Until now, new draft directives such as the one on part-time employment were frequently blocked by countries such as the UK, Germany and the Netherlands. The relationships in this area have changed, on the one hand because the UK has removed itself from policy-making in the social field, and on the other because there are now a number of Scandinavian countries in the European Union. These are countries with strong labour movements and high union density rates among female employees, as we described earlier. Given the attitude of their female populations, it is not unimaginable that the governments of these countries will want to make clear to their citizens that entering the European Union will not undermine the position of women. The Swedish government, for example, has already announced that it intends to make an issue out of equal opportunities. If it does, the ETUC will have won support for its preference for sound legislation.

Even then, however, it will not be any easier for the ETUC to plan an effective strategy. On the one hand, various national federations and their affiliated women's committees continue to question whether the EU's policy can actually improve the position of women in their own countries. These doubts played a role in the way the various federations responded to the ETUC's efforts to take a firm stand on the maternity leave directive. On the other hand, the various affiliated federations have adopted different views on some of the issues which concern women. That means that it is not always easy to arrive at a common position. A case in point is the present discussion on part-time work.

In the Commission's most recent White Paper, which will be dealt with in the final chapter, the observation is made that the EU member states have met with varying degrees of success when it comes to increasing the number of jobs by reducing the average number of working hours or by increasing the number of part-time employees (Commission, 1993). In the Netherlands part-time work is the major reason for the increase in employment among women. The Dutch scenario is described as commendable in the White Paper, and a number of countries are certainly interested in following the example of the Netherlands. The German Labour Minister, for instance, observed that there would be jobs for 2 million more people if Germany achieved the part-time levels of the Netherlands (Labour Research, 1994). Should the trade unions therefore negotiate with employers to encourage part-time work? The ETUC has long been unanimous in its 'defensive' position: part-time employees should enjoy the same rights and privileges as full-time employees. But, as became clear at the ETUC's 'Work and Time' seminar in 1993, trade unions in many countries are still reluctant to adopt a policy that favours the conversion of full-time jobs into part-time jobs. Delegates from a number of countries worried that women would end up in second-rate jobs with second-rate employment conditions. There was no unambiguous decision in favour of an offensive position during the seminar.

This example will suffice to illustrate that the complexity of developing an adequate strategy for the future lies not only in the changes in the European balance of power, but also in the fact that the various traditions of labour participation, and the roles played by employers and employees in the various member states, influence and are reflected in the Women's Committee and the ETUC itself.

REFERENCES

ANTOS, J. R., CHANDLER, M. and MELLOW, W. (1980) Sex differences in union membership, *Industrial and Labour Relations Review*, Vol. 33, pp. 162–9.

BAIN, G. S. and ELSHEIKH, F. (1979) An inter-industry analysis of union growth in Britain, *British Journal of Industrial Relations*, Vol. 17, no. 3, pp. 137–57.

BRAITHWAITE, M. and BYRNE, C. (1994) *Women in Decision-Making in Trade Unions: A Study of the Literature and a Survey of the European Trade Union Confederation and Its Affiliated National Confederations and European Industry Committees*, ETUC, Brussels.

BRIDGFORD, J. and STIRLING, J. (1994) *Employee Relations in Europe*, Blackwell, Oxford.

COMMISSION OF THE EUROPEAN COMMUNITIES (1993) *European Social Policy; Options for the Union*, Green Paper, Brussels.

COMMISSION OF THE EUROPEAN COMMUNITIES (1993) *Growth, Competitiveness, Employment: the challenge and ways forward into the 21st century*, White Paper, Brussels.

DAALDER, A. (1994) *Vrouwen en jongeren eerst, een statistische verkenning van het ledenverloop van de FNV in 1992*, Nimmo, Amsterdam.

ETUC (1990) *Women in a Social Europe: Our Demands*, ETUC, Brussels.

ETUC (1992) *Resolution: A Gender Perspective in ETUC Policy*, adopted by the Executive Committee at its meeting in London on 3 and 4 December 1992.

ETUC (1993) *Guidelines for the ETUC Women's Committee, Review of the 3rd Action Programme of Equal Opportunities 1991–1995*, ETUC, Brussels.

ETUI (1983) *Info 6: Women's Representation in Trade Unions*, ETUI, Brussels.

ETUI (1987) *Women and Trade Unions in Western Europe*, ETUI, Brussels.

ETUI (1989) *Positive Action for Women in Western Europe*, ETUI, Brussels.

FREEMAN, R. B. and MEDOFF, J. (1984) *What Do Unions Do?*, Basic Books, New York.

HALL, M. (1994) Industrial relations and the social dimension of European integration: before and after Maastricht, in R. Hyman and A. Ferner (eds.), *New Frontiers in European Industrial Relations*, Blackwell, Oxford.

HEERE, E. and KELLY, J. (1988) Do female representatives make a difference? Women full-time officials and trade union work, *Work, Employment and Society*, Vol. 2, no. 4, pp. 487–505.

HUNTJENS, A. M. (1991) Sociaal beleid en de voltooiing van de interne markt, *Nieuw Europa*, Vol. 17, no. 4, December, pp. 17–22.

ICFTU (INTERNATIONAL CONFEDERATION OF FREE TRADE UNIONS) (1991) *Equality: the Continuing Challenge – Strategies for Success*, working paper for the 5th world women's conference in Ottawa, Canada.

LABOUR RESEARCH (1994) Europush for 'flexibility', July, pp. 11–12.

LEDWITH, S., COLGAN, F., JOYCE, P. and HAYES, M. (1991) The making of women trade union leaders, *Industrial Relations Journal*, Vol. 21, no. 2, pp. 112–25.

OPHUYSEN, T. (1994) *Vrouwen en Europa Over werk, beleid en invloed in de EG*, Stichting Burgerschapskunde/Nederlands Centrum voor Politieke Vorming, Leiden.

PEDLER, R. H. (1994) ETUC and the pregnant women, in R. H. Pedler and M. P. C. M. van

Schendelen (eds.) *Lobbying the European Union Companies, Trade Associations and Issuegroups*, Dartmouth, Aldershot, Brookfield USA, Singapore, Sydney.

PUTTE, B. VAN DEN and SIPS, C. (1992) Deeltijd en lidmaatschap, met halve kracht vooruit, *Zeggenschap*, September/October, pp. 50–4.

TEGZES, B. and SIPS, C. (1993) *De rol van de vakbeweging bij de totstandkoming van Europese wetgeving*, FNV, Amsterdam.

UNICE (1991a) *UNICE Comments on the Third Medium-Term Community Action Programme on Equal Opportunities Between Women and Men*, COM (90) 449, UNICE, Brussels.

UNICE (1991b) *UNICE Comments on the Proposal for a Council Recommendation on Childcare*, COM (91) 233 final, UNICE, Brussels.

UNICE (1993a) *Letter Sent to COREPER Members; Proposals for a Directive on the Burden of Proof in the Field of Equality of Remuneration and Equality of Treatment Between Women and Men*, UNICE, Brussels.

UNICE (1993b) *UNICE Comments on the Draft Memorandum on Equal Pay for Work of Equal Value*, UNICE, Brussels.

UNICE (1994) Green paper on European social policy – options for the Union: UNICE comments, in *UNICE Comments*, UNICE, Brussels.

VISSER, J. (1994) Trade unions: the transition years, in R. Hyman and A. Ferner (eds.), New Frontiers in *European Industrial Relations*, Blackwell, Oxford.

VISSER, J., KERSTEN, A., VAN RIJ, C. and SARIS, W. (1991) Waarom zijn zo weinig vrouwen lid van de vakbeweging?, in Carolien Bouw et al. (eds.), *Macht en onbehagen. Veranderingen in de verhoudingen tussen mannen en vrouwen*, SISWO/SUA, Amsterdam, pp. 167–81.

CHAPTER 14

Epilogue:
Emancipation at the Crossroads

JACQUES VAN HOOF AND ANNEKE VAN DOORNE-HUISKES

INTRODUCTION

The previous chapters have explored various facets of the position which women occupy in the labour market within the 12 countries which made up the European Union until 1995. We discussed a number of theories which attempt to explain that position and the behaviour of women, and placed these theories within a theoretical framework. The European Union's policy on equal opportunities was also described, as well as the degree of harmonization between this policy and that pursued by the individual member states and by organizations within those countries.

In this final chapter we review the developments discussed previously from a broader perspective by linking them to general changes in the labour market, within organizations and in industrial relations practices in the various countries of the EU. We hope in this way to shed more light on which barriers to emancipation still exist and which new challenges European and national policy will face.

A MIXED IMPRESSION

The impression that the previous chapters have given us of the situation of women in the labour market is a mixed one: women have in fact made progress on a few important fronts in the various countries of the EU, but in other respects not very much has changed since 1980. The biggest leap forward was in employment: even after factoring in all the differences between countries, there are still far more women (in particular married women) in the labour market than at any other time (see Chapter 1). This observation is echoed in Chapter 5, which covers the career patterns of women: for many women, the abrupt interruption of their careers upon marriage or the birth of their first child has given way to a temporary interruption, and a growing group of women no longer interrupt their careers at all, but attempt to continue working, although they make important adjustments in the form of part-time work and so on.

The credit side of the ledger also includes the fact that the percentage of women working in the professional and technical occupational sector has risen. In various countries, moreover, the share of women taking up management positions has also increased (see Chapter 2). The rising educational level of women has apparently allowed them to infiltrate the highest occupational categories. They have done so despite all the obstacles that they continue to face and which mean that women are still strongly under-represented at the top of the occupational hierarchy.

We have furthermore observed that European legislation on equal pay and equal treatment combined with the case law of the European Court of Justice has prompted the countries that lagged behind in this respect to update their national legislation (as described in Chapter 9). Finally, we should mention that in most countries women have become more firmly entrenched in the labour movement (see Chapter 13). The result (we may assume) is that their interests are taken into account more during collective bargaining.

There are also a number of items on the debit side, however. The growing number of women in the labour force has been accompanied by the over-representation of women in low-paid, unstable, low-skill and undemanding jobs (see Chapter 3, for example). The more that employment growth in the EU is based on these types of job, the more important this observation becomes. Although the feminization of certain categories of employment cannot simply be equated with greater flexibility (see Rubery and Fagan, 1994a), the availability of a large category of women who are prepared to accept atypical employment conditions in exchange for access to paid employment has certainly been convenient for employers in their attempts to make the deployment of personnel more flexible. As a consequence, the unemployment figures for women in all of the countries of the EU, with the exception of the UK, are higher than those for men (see Chapter 1). These differences have scarcely altered since the early 1980s. The pay gap between men and women also still exists, even when we take into account the different job and personal characteristics of men and women (see Chapter 3). We also discovered in Chapter 4 that in each of these respects women from ethnic minorities do even worse than indigenous women.

One extremely stubborn phenomenon faced by women in the labour markets of all the EU member states is occupational segregation. As Chapter 2 showed, a greater participation in employment does not necessarily lead to a reduction in segregation. In the past 15 to 20 years the supply of women has apparently been absorbed into the labour market without that having any substantial mitigating effect on the rigid distribution of occupations and jobs between men and women. Breaking through this segregation requires more than employment growth. The division of paid labour between men and women is of course inextricably bound up with the division of unpaid labour. In this are, too, the changes have been marginal at best, as the analysis of available data in Chapter 6 demonstrated.

The overall impression, then, is that progress has also been accompanied by stagnation. The question is how the relationship between these two tendencies will develop in the next few years. Until recently the prospects seemed optimistic based on forecast demographic changes. We will look at this optimistic scenario first, and then see how well it stands up to the most recent changes in the labour market, within organizations and in industrial relations practice.

THE OPTIMISTIC SCENARIO

Around 1990 most of the official EU and national policy documents on emancipation were infused with optimism: the policy promoting emancipation was right on track and very much in line with socio-cultural and technical and economic developments. The foremost task for the years ahead would be to integrate the policy of emancipation into the general socio-economic policy of the Union (still called the Community) and its member states.

As pointed out before, this optimism was based primarily on forecasts of demographic changes which, in the eyes of the policy-makers, would have far-reaching consequences for the labour market and for the policy of companies. These expectations were expressed, for example, in the European Commission's 1989 report, *Employment in Europe* (Commission of the European Communities, 1989). The birth rate was expected to continue to drop, which, combined with an increase in life expectancy, would lead to an ageing European population. Although the rate of change would differ from one country to the next, they were expected to follow the same trend: relatively fewer younger people, relatively more older ones. This demographic shift would be reflected in the composition of the labour force: in all the countries of Europe, the labour force would begin to age.

According to the optimistic scenario, this process of ageing would have an important impact on the labour market. From the perspective of the national governments, the ageing of the population would mean rising social security expenses. Governments could hope to cover these expenses only if as many people as possible of working age actually took up employment and helped to reduce the rising cost of social security by paying taxes and social security contributions. More people had to be put to work, was the conclusion. That meant not only adjusting the Europe-wide early retirement trend but also encouraging the employment of women to a greater extent than before. Employers would also be forced to make changes, the argument continued. For them, the ageing of the labour force meant in the first place that highly skilled young people would become a scarce commodity on the labour market. They could no longer afford to treat female 'human capital' in a slipshod manner and would have to find ways of increasing the commitment of women who wanted to combine a career with family responsibilities. That would mean creating an organizational environment which was more responsive to the needs of women, making it possible to break through rigid working-time and career patterns and perhaps contributing to reducing occupational and job segregation.

The demographic changes described above were to lead, therefore, not only to changes in the labour market but also (according to this scenario) to organizational changes. In that respect they were very compatible with processes of organizational innovation, prompted by market changes and forcing entrepreneurs to concentrate on more flexible, quality-conscious and customer-oriented production. On the one hand that would frequently lead to employers introducing a far-reaching redistribution of authority and tasks, but on the other it could also result in a personnel policy focusing on the most efficient possible use of the work-force's skills. If applied consistently, the principles of human resource management (HRM) would offer women better opportunities because, more than ever before, (future) personnel would be evaluated on qualities such as dedication and performance. In an achievement-oriented climate such as this one, there would be no room for sexual stereotypes.

In this scenario, then, the convergence of various demographic, socio-cultural, organizational and economic and technical changes would contribute to improving the position of women in paid employment. There was even guarded optimism concerning the division of labour within the home, because women with a good education would be more likely to make demands on their partner, and because from the perspective of household finances it would make little sense to ignore the earning capacity of such women. If the government and trade and industry created better opportunities to combine paid and unpaid work (child-care facilities, leave arrangements), family and household responsibilities would not have to stand in the way of greater and more satisfactory employment for women.

RECENT DEVELOPMENTS

This optimistic scenario, which, as mentioned, left its mark on many official policy documents around 1990, has by now lost a great deal of its lustre. Recent developments have made the one-sidedness of the scenario more obvious. Below we will look more closely at these recent changes in the labour market, within organizations and in industrial relations.

Employment and the labour market

The optimistic scenario rests on the assumption that the economy and employment will continue to grow. The rise in the number of jobs between 1985 and 1990 was projected through to the year 2000, more or less automatically. Another assumption underlying the scenario is that there would be a gradual, across-the-board upgrading of employment, the result of technological innovation and of the gradual transition within trade and industry to more diversified and quality-oriented production (Sorge and Streeck, 1988), forcing companies in turn to depend more than ever on the skills of their employees.

In the past few years, however, the dream of a rising employment level has been disturbed. The recent economic decline has brought growth to a screeching halt, and in some countries it has even led to a decline in employment. More important, perhaps, is that economic recovery seems to make the prospect of jobless growth a reality. Growth in employment is in any case not keeping pace with the present signs of economic recovery. And while the employment forecasts have been adjusted negatively, in various countries the projections concerning the labour force have been adjusted in the opposite direction. That is the result of the increasing participation of women in employment, the rising level of immigration and/or the successful attempts to reduce the number of early retirement cases. It will be a while before overall supply and demand in the labour markets of the member states reach a degree of balance. The projected general shortage in the supply of well-trained employees (male *and* female) reported in the optimistic scenario has been postponed for the time being until after the turn of the century.

Women will naturally be affected by changes in the employment figures within the sectors and occupations where they account for a larger share of employment. The traditional women's occupations in the secretarial, commercial and service sectors have done well in the past 15 to 20 years in terms of job opportunities. They are among the 'occupational winners' in the labour market, unlike the typical male occupations in the industrial sector. The recent economic collapse and the way in which large companies are responding to it have made it clear, however, that in the near future major job losses can be expected in sectors which employ a large number of women (for example banking and insurance), and that the processes of rationalization will be aimed with increasing zeal at secretarial and commercial positions (including middle management). If we also add in the cutbacks in the public sector (which are now making themselves felt in many countries of the EU) and the consequences that they will have on employment in, for example, education and health care, then it will be clear that the situation for many female occupations will become less favourable in the years ahead (particularly if the overall participation in employment continues to increase).

The expectation that there will be an across-the-board upgrading of employment seems equally over-optimistic when considered against the background of the second half of the 1980s and the early 1990s. Part of the growth in employment – the exact portion varied from country to country – took place in the segment of low-skill, poorly paid and unstable jobs, in which women, as we know, are over-represented. In respect of the immediate future, we should emphasize in this connection the new doctrine which has captured labour-market policy and which Jacques Delors's White Paper has given pride of place to: we need more jobs at the lower end of the labour market in order to combat unemployment (which is, after all, highest among unskilled and low-skilled workers) (Commission of the European Communities, 1993a). In so far as this policy is successful, it will lead to a further expansion of the secondary segment, and if part-time employment is stimulated as well to increase the overall effect on employment as much as possible, it will further encourage the feminization of the lower end of the labour market.

Changes within organizations

Commentators everywhere are convinced that companies must cast off their old identities as traditional organizations based on Taylorist principles and re-evaluate their trusted principles of personnel management. That does not mean that the new principles of organizational design and the deployment of human resources have already been put into practice on a massive scale. The strategy of diversified quality-oriented production is not the only or even the most obvious option for many companies. Many of them still expect to gain greater rewards by competing on price rather than on quality and will there-fore attach greater value to lower wages than to highly trained personnel. A mixed bag of old and new principles, the foremost example of which is 'Toyotism', seems to be more attractive to companies than a consistent policy of business process re-engineering based on socio-technical concepts. In any event, there are major differences in the degree and direction of organizational change from sector to sector and from country to country (as authors such as Sorge, Warner and Lane have demonstrated convincingly).

Against this background it must be said that organizational renewal presents women with a variety of different prospects. We cannot deny that flexible and quality-oriented organizations are more likely to meet the demands of women and do justice to their skills. But that is not the end of the story. Organizational renewal in many cases also means flattening the internal structure. In particular it means thinning out the ranks of middle management. Lindley's observation that Britain is in the midst of a far-reaching reorganization of managerial and supervisory job hierarchies also holds for other countries of the European Union (Lindley, 1994b). That naturally has a negative impact on career prospects, not only for men but also for women, whose rising educational level has made them eligible for promotion to the managerial ranks. They will in any case have to face greater competition, and that does not seem to be a good basis for eliminating sexual stereotypes, which already make promotion so difficult for them.

Even more important in our opinion is that in many organizations the patriarchal culture is able to survive the storm of organizational renewal largely intact. Organizational culture presently plays a major role in the various blueprints for flexible, slimmed down and effective organizations. Consistently the goal is to develop a strong team spirit and a tremendous concentration on performance and achievement (a combination not devoid of contradictions). Employers are in any event required to offer their loyalty and commitment to the organization. It is a culture with unmistakably macho qualities, in which 'strong men' and strong leadership occupy the central position and bellicose metaphors are very popular. In a culture such as that, women will probably have less scope to combine work and care responsibilities.

It should therefore come as no surprise that, time and again, gender differences are simply replicated during the organizational renewal process, so that there is very little change in internal occupational and job segregation. A good example is the segregation of the sexes in the computer professions, discussed in Chapter 2. Another is the evolution of typical 'women's' jobs and careers in management, as observed by Crompton (1994). According to her, women who gain access to management positions largely end up in sex-differentiated managerial jobs in sales or personnel or on the soft side of engineering, where they can manage other women rather than men.

We may conclude that the positive consequences of organizational innovation will not be as unqualified for women as the optimistic scenario predicts. The longer it takes for the shortage of well-trained young people forecast in the scenario to manifest itself, the less positive these consequences will be.

Changing industrial relations

The optimistic scenario also assumes that women will have greater access to decision-making processes at sector and company levels, and that they will therefore be able to influence the agreements and decisions that impact on their own situation. Chapter 13 looked at the position of women within the trade unions from this perspective. We wish to add a few comments here on the transformation of industrial relations within the countries of the EU in general and on the possible consequences that this transformation will have on the position of women.

Industrial relations experts agree that the 1980s saw a change of direction in industrial relations, although this change manifested itself in different ways in the various countries of Europe (see, for example, Baglioni and Crouch, 1992). One important reason for the change is that economic uncertainty, rising unemployment, declining union density rates and the changing social and political climate of the previous decade tipped the balance of power in favour of the employers. Another reason is that the governments of most countries ended a tradition of intervening in industrial relations. This break with tradition went much further in some countries than in others, and in extraordinary circumstances governments intervened temporarily anyway, but in general they gave employers' associations and trade unions a freer hand and were less inclined to interfere with national-level collective bargaining than they had been in the 1970s. At the same time there was an undeniable tendency to relax the constraints on the labour market.

All these factors combined meant that the locus of industrial relations shifted downwards: a process of decentralization took place in which individual companies were given more scope to conclude their own collective bargaining agreements or to interpret and supplement sector-level agreements in consultation with trade unions or employee representatives. European industrial relations became increasingly dominated by the struggle to achieve more flexibility and deregulation. One could even say that industrial relations is at present undergoing a process of individualization, given employers' attempts to differentiate the terms and conditions of employment on the grounds of the skills, performance and market value of the various employee categories. The introduction of HRM principles seems to reinforce this process and consequently to undermine the influence exercised by the unions on company social policy.

This entire chain of events is also important for the position of women. In general, collective organization, protective government measures and agreements that restrict the scope of individual employers are all beneficial for the weaker parties in the labour market. That was, after all, the point of departure for the collectivization of industrial relations in the 20th century. The present trend towards de-collectivization may be advantageous for certain employee categories, but it has a less favourable impact on more vulnerable employees, for example members of ethnic minorities *and* large groups of women. Seen from this perspective, deregulation and flexible working practices are precarious developments for many women. For example, any assault on minimum wage regulations and/or any absence of acceptable statutory measures governing part-time employment will effect the income and job security of many women. Deregulation increases the chance that the pay gap between men and women will grow larger. Rubery and Fagan (1994a, p. 162) have stated that 'the more centralized the system of pay determination, the narrower the differences between industries and occupations and the smaller the overall gender gap'. They conclude that where decentralization and deregulation have occurred in payment systems, vulnerable groups of employees, such as women, get the short end of the stick.

Deregulation and flexible working practices may also lead to problems within companies. Chapter 12 pointed out the tension between a further refinement of the job evaluation system based on the comparable worth principle and the employers' desire to introduce more wage flexibility. And in Chapter 11 the possibility was raised that the individualization trend enshrined in HRM may clash with attempts to use positive action to improve the position of women within organizations. These difficulties emphasize once again how important it is that women, particularly at the company level, find ways of influencing decision-making. The further the process of decentralization progresses within industrial relations, the more improvements must be hammered out precisely at that level.

Our conclusion is that the changes in industrial relations practices will not have an unconditionally positive impact on the labour-market situation of women within the EU. However much some categories of women (specifically those with a good education) can benefit from a more far-reaching differentiation of employment terms and the introduction of HRM principles, for the majority of women flexible working practices and deregulation will mean greater vulnerability in respect of income and job security. Given the weakened position of the trade unions in many European countries, a strong female presence within these organizations will neutralize these threats to a certain extent only.

THE SECOND SCENARIO

In our previous discussion the value outline of a second scenario began to emerge. According to this scenario, the persistent supply surplus on the labour market, employer rationalization strategies and government policy encouraging atypical employment at the lower end of the labour market will lead to further growth in the segment of low-paid, unstable and undemanding jobs (the so-called 'junk jobs'). These jobs are particularly prevalent in certain branches of the private services sector (hospitality industry, retail, personal services, etc.), but they will also increasingly be found in those areas of the public sector hit by government economy measures. The increasing participation of (married) women will to a large extent be absorbed by the growth of this category of job. The result will be the rise of a post-industrial proletariat (Esping-Andersen *et al.*, 1993) in which women will be over-represented.

At the same time, business strategies aimed at flexible customer- and quality-oriented production, and the associated restructuring of organizational and personnel policy, will be limited to specific sectors and types of company. In these sectors and companies productivity will indeed increase, but not so the number of jobs: jobless growth or even growth combined with job losses will be the trend here. That means that only a small portion of the female work-force (consisting largely of young, well-trained women) will enjoy the blessings of organizational renewal and HRM. They will probably also have to pay a price for these blessings: they will have to carve out a place for themselves within an achievement-oriented and patriarchal organizational culture. That will not make it any easier to combine paid employment and care responsibilities in the home.

These trends will lead to growing divisions between the separate categories of women. The dual economy, in which the sectors with high-end and those with low-end jobs will grow further and further apart, will also bring about polarization between women in the labour market. The mid-range category of women in skilled clerical, sales and service occupations will decrease proportionally in scale thanks to employers' redoubled efforts to rationalize their organizations, while the categories at the lower end and probably also at the top end of the female occupational hierarchy will increase in scale. According to Rubery and Fagan (1994, pp. 32–3) this trend has already become visible in every country of the EU.

In this scenario, movement in the direction of a flexible labour market will continue unabated, with the hardship this produces being borne by the weakest groups of workers. At the same time, the likelihood of a separate emancipation policy for women will decrease, at both the national and the company level. National governments will increasingly adopt the point of view that the policy on emancipation must be integrated into overall social and economic policy as such, and they will restrict any specific policy on the labour-market situation of women to those measures which concur with neo-liberal concepts: career information, training measures and the individualization of social security (provided that it does not cost too much). Other issues will be left to collective bargaining between employers and employees, or (if the issues involve household and care tasks) will be considered a private matter. On their part, employers, who had little enthusiasm for positive action anyway, will increasingly prefer an HRM policy that makes no formal distinction between men and women to any specific policy for women. It will become more and more difficult, then, to pursue a policy aimed at the collective improvement of the position of women.

This scenario is clearly more pessimistic than the one described at the start of this chapter. We do not wish to create the impression that we believe that developments in the near future will entirely follow the line set out in the second scenario. More probable is that we will see elements of both scenarios in the years ahead, just as we did in the second half of the 1980s, despite the official optimism described above. We should also add that the mixture of elements from the 2 scenarios will differ from one country to the next within the EU, depending on the economic circumstances, the political climate, the dominant mentality in employer circles, but also on the institutional arrangements which developed over time in such areas as education, industrial relations and social security.

Welfare state regimes

We wish to return in this connection to Esping-Andersen's 3 types of social welfare state: the social democratic, the conservative/corporatistic and the liberal welfare state, which were introduced in Chapter 7. This distinction is an important one when considering various aspects of the labour-market situation of women discussed in this book and the associated policies:

employment, the pay gap, legislation on equal treatment, child-care facilities and parental leave arrangements. In a recent publication Esping-Andersen uses this distinction to investigate the lower end of the labour market. The main question he poses is to what extent a post-industrial service proletariat is emerging in the various Western societies (Esping-Andersen, 1993). He led an investigation comparing 3 English-speaking countries with a liberal welfare state (the UK, the USA and Canada), two Scandinavian countries which serve as models for the social-democratic welfare state regime (Sweden and Norway) and one country which represents the conservative/corporatist model (the former Federal Republic of Germany).

Based on this comparison, Esping-Andersen came to the conclusion that there is as yet no strictly demarcated post-industrial proletariat. The number of low-skilled service jobs has remained within reasonable bounds (5–15% of overall employment in the countries investigated). There is, furthermore, a high degree of social fluidity among the unskilled service workers. Their jobs are frequently transitional, stop-gap jobs, especially for the young. Germany alone is an exception in this respect. At the same time, however, women are tied to this segment much more than are men. For women lacking in skills, there is clearly a closed mobility circuit between unskilled services, (low-end) sales and (low-end) clerical work (Esping-Andersen, 1993, p. 235). Men, especially young males, have more mobility options open to them.

There are also striking differences between countries, however. Germany has the smallest share of low-skilled service jobs, but it also draws the sharpest line between this segment and the rest of the labour market. That is because this line also separates those who have a vocational training diploma from those who do not. In Germany, more than in any other country, such a diploma is the passport to a job as a semi-skilled or skilled worker. The share of low-skilled service jobs is much larger in the English-speaking and the Scandinavian countries than in Germany. Still, there is a big difference between the two: in the former category, these jobs are primarily in the market sector, whereas in the latter they can be found largely in the public sector. That is a particularly relevant difference for women: they have much greater job security and more opportunities for promotion in the 2 Scandinavian countries than in the UK (and the USA and Canada). The influence of the various welfare state regimes is obvious.

In a certain sense, the various categories of country represent certain policy options. Germany, more than the other countries, is attempting to limit the number of low-skilled service jobs by introducing qualitatively advanced production and by expanding vocational training in general. At the same time, of all the countries described here, Germany has the lowest participation rate of women in employment. Employment at the high end of the labour market is apparently accompanied by a relatively far-reaching exclusion of women. The participation of women in paid employment is much higher in the Scandinavian and English-speaking countries. This level of participation has been achieved thanks to the presence of a substantial number of low-skilled service jobs. But there are apparently two ways of approaching the issue: the social-democratic welfare state uses the public sector to achieve acceptable conditions for the employees (especially women) who must resort to these jobs, whereas in the liberal model of the English-speaking countries these jobs are associated with low pay and minimal security.

What happens to these 3 'models' in the next few years is very important for the future position of women within the European Union. It is likely that the German model, in which every effort is made to prevent the creation of low-skilled jobs, will be able to survive the increasing participation of women in employment only by cutting back on working hours – a more crucial issue in Germany than in the other EU countries. The social-democratic model will live or die depending on whether and to what extent the population and companies are willing to foot the bill for the welfare state without this harming the level of consumption and the competitive position of trade and industry. If these 2 models cannot survive the economic fluctuations of the near future and/or if they succumb to the prevailing neo-liberal climate, only the third model will remain. In that event, the second, pessimistic scenario of the future labour-market situation of women would be the more realistic of the two.

POLICY IMPLICATIONS

The previous discussion leads us to conclude that the changes in the labour market, within organizations and in industrial relations practice appear to be heading us towards the second scenario and all that that implies for the position of women. That raises the rather crucial question of how we can prevent this scenario from becoming reality. Can the government and trade and industry implement a policy that will strengthen the position of women and reduce the differences between the sexes, even under these altered circumstances? Can the European Union make a contribution to this effort? These are the questions we will be dealing with in the final section of this chapter.

It will be obvious that we do not believe that women can rely on measures which aim to deregulate the labour market further and make collective bargaining agreements more flexible. Neither will it be enough to take steps aimed at the supply side of the labour market, for example by eliminating tax disincentives for employment, expanding facilities which make it easier to combine care responsibilities and paid employment, improving the educational level of women and influencing their educational and career choices. What is needed most of all is an active employment policy, in other words a policy which does not leave the creation of jobs to the market alone and which, furthermore, is not aimed only at the lower end of the labour market.

If we elaborate on our previous discussion of the various welfare state regimes, we arrive first at the public sector and the redistribution of labour. It may not seem very realistic to argue for the expansion of the public sector when the reduction of the budget deficit has been given top priority in every country of the EU. Nevertheless, in many EU member states the paradoxical situation has arisen that the public services which have been cut back reappear anyway in some other form, for example as volunteer work, workfare schemes or temporary job programmes for the unemployed. It is therefore not so much a question of the market taking over these services as it is the destructuring of employment in the public sector, i.e. the replacement of real jobs by quasi-jobs or unpaid work. In our opinion this trend, which will have a very negative impact on employment for women, must in any event be stopped.

Chapter 1 of this book has already discussed the redistribution of labour as an essential addition to a labour-market policy which intends to create more jobs at the lower end of the labour market. In the first half of the 1980s various EU countries experimented with a modest form of collective working-time reduction. This quickly turned out to be a dead end. The fact that the average number of working hours within the EU was reduced anyway (with the exception of the UK) was largely a consequence of growth in the number of part-time jobs. However, this growth has had two sides to it for women, as we have seen: part-time employment increases their chance of combining paid employment and care responsibilities, but it is also linked to low wages and little job security (a factor which varies from country to country; compare the UK and the Netherlands or Denmark, for example).

A further increase in the number of part-time jobs is a good way to give women more employment opportunities (and to give men more time to participate in domestic tasks – see Chapter 6). More than in the past, however, a policy such as this should aim at creating part-time jobs of more than 20 hours a week, the creation of part-time positions at upper and management levels and the improvement of employment terms for part-time employees at the lowest levels. The introduction of a statutory right to part-time work might provide an important impetus.

Another way of reducing the average number of working hours is to extend the existing leave arrangements. At several points in this book mention was made of pregnancy and/or parental leave, with the observation that these arrangements could stand considerable improvement in most countries of the EU (see Chapters 10 and 13). Such leave arrangements could be expanded into a general care leave scheme, which would also provide for a leave of absence to care for sick relatives (see De Bruijn, 1992). In addition, there is the question of the sabbatical or educational leave. Although there have been rudimentary attempts to introduce educational leave arrangements in various EU member states, until now these efforts have not made any significant contribution to reducing the average number of working hours. It is unnecessary to explain in detail why these meagre results are at odds with the importance which is being ascribed on all sides to 'permanent learning'. It will suffice to emphasize that women in particular can benefit from satisfactory educational leave arrangements as compensation for the discontinuities in their careers.

There are, therefore, various ways of reducing the average number of working hours. The advantages and disadvantages of specific measures aimed at women can be discussed at length, but this is not the place to do so. We do, however, wish to emphasize that, in our opinion, the employment problem which the EU countries face will not be solved without further reducing the average number of working hours, and that the future labour-market situation of women will depend to a very large extent on the success of a policy on this point.

An active general policy on employment, as argued above, will not make a specific policy on women superfluous. Both at national and company level we cannot do without specific measures to eliminate the disadvantages suffered by groups of women. Various such measures were discussed in this book. Again, women-specific policy must focus not only on the supply side of the labour market but also in in particular on the demand side. After all, women are only partly to blame for the obstacles which stand in the way of their achieving a more complete and satisfactory participation in employment.

The stubborn persistence of occupational and job segregation is a case in point. It is of course possible to encourage girls and young women to choose 'male' programmes and occupations, and the governments of various countries have introduced striking campaigns intended to influence women in their choice of vocational programme. But without a corresponding policy on the part of employers to abolish formal and material barriers to recruiting and promoting women, to mitigate the influence of sexual stereotypes during the reorganization of tasks and jobs, to provide extra incentives to women to participate in training programmes and courses, to increase women's access to decision-making processes – whether or not under the banner of 'positive action' – the ultimate impact of such campaigns will remain limited.

A role for the European Union?

We are left at the end of this final discussion with the question whether the European Union will in fact be able to contribute to a policy which can circumvent the dangers of the second scenario. This is not an easy question to answer, certainly now that the Union has recently gained 3 new member states and the consequent new balance of power is still uncertain. One positive point seems to be that at least 2 of the new member states (Finland and Sweden) are trail-blazers when it comes to women's emancipation and will no doubt cast a suspicious eye on any measure which women in their own countries might consider disadvantageous.

The second positive point is that in the White Paper mentioned earlier in this chapter, *Growth Competitiveness and Employment*, a cautious attempt is made to raise the possibility of introducing 'an adjustment in working hours' as an employment policy instrument. The document cites the example of the Netherlands to illustrate that a reduction in the average number of working hours (achieved in the Netherlands largely because of the spectacular growth in the number of part-time jobs) can have a considerable effect on employment (Commission of the European Communities, 1993a, pp. 139–40). No European policy on this point has been announced, however, and indeed it would be difficult for the EU to do so, since – in keeping with the present division of authority between the Union and its member states – the labour market is primarily the member states' concern.

As we saw in Chapter 8, the EU's policy on women is part of its social policy. In recent years the European Commission has made considerable efforts to step up the implementation of this policy based on the Social Charter adopted in 1989 by 11 of 12 member states. At first glance these efforts do not appear to be entirely without success. The Social Protocol attached to the Maastricht Treaty also appears to increase the opportunities for a social policy, since the UK can no longer play the role of spoilsport and the issues subject to qualified majority voting in the European Council of Ministers have been expanded.

We nevertheless have the impression that efforts in the field of social policy have run out of steam. One illustration is the course of events related to the draft directives on 'atypical work' (meaning part-time and temporary work). We hardly need point out (after the previous discussion) that this is a very important issue for women. At the time of writing, 2 of the 3 directives have not yet been adopted. In our opinion, the reason these expanded opportunities are not being exploited is that the employment problem is stealing the limelight away from social policy both at European level and in the individual member states. In addition, the financial scope for new policy has shrunk (see also Hall, 1994).

The effect that the Union's equal opportunities policy has had in the individual member states depended, as we saw in Chapter 9, on a combination of directives (in other words, binding legislation) and the associated case law of the European Court. This combination may gradually lose its impact, certainly in the northern member states. By appealing to the principle of subsidiarity, the EU is showing more caution over adopting directives in general. In addition, the new directives, such as the one covering maternity leave, increasingly prescribe only minimum standards and will therefore have a significant impact only in the most backward countries. The course of events related to the directive on maternity leave, which was discussed in the previous chapter, clearly illustrates the limits which the Union's social policy will run up against in the years ahead.

It is therefore questionable whether in the near future the EU's social policy will offer many new incentives to improve the position of women in the member states. The influence of the EU will probably become more indirect. That may mean that the European Commission will raise the possibility of a policy option such as the redistribution of labour in such documents as the White Paper for discussion in the member states. But these effects will be relatively marginal when compared with the impact of the agreements governing European Monetary Union (EMU), which oblige most member states to reduce their budget deficits. The economy measures that will accompany their efforts (for example, in social security or in the size of the public sector) may accelerate any tendencies in the direction of the second scenario.

REFERENCES

BAGLIONI, G. and CROUCH, C. (eds.) (1992) *European Industrial Relations: The Challenge of Flexibility*, Sage, London.
BRUIJN, J. G. M. DE (1992) Arbeidsparticipatie en informele zorg voor jong en oud, *Tijdschrift voor Arbeidsvraagstukken*, Vol. 9, no. 2, pp. 122–3.
CROMPTON, R. (1994) Occupational trends and women's employment patterns, in Lindley (1994a).
COMMISSION OF THE EUROPEAN COMMUNITIES (1989) *Employment in Europe*, Brussels.
COMMISSION OF THE EUROPEAN COMMUNITIES (1993a) *Growth, Competitiveness and Employment*, White Paper, Brussels.
COMMISSION OF THE EUROPEAN COMMUNITIES (1993b) *European Social Policy; Options for the Union*, Green Paper, Brussels.
ESPING-ANDERSEN, G. et al. (1993) *Changing Classes: Stratification and Mobility in Post-industrial Societies*, Sage, London.
HALL, M. (1994) Industrial relations and the social dimension of European integration: before and after Maastricht, in Hyman and Ferner (1994).
HOOF, J. J. VAN (1993) Organiseren in een veranderend arbeidsbestel, in W. J. van Noort, J.

P. Laurier and M. C. Dozy (eds.), *Organiseren op een breukvlak*, Siswo, Amsterdam.

HYMAN, R. and FERNER. A. (1994) *New Frontiers in European Industrial Relations*, Blackwell, Oxford.

LINDLEY, R. (1994a) *Labour Market Structures and Prospects for Women*, Equal Opportunities Commission, Manchester.

LINDLEY, R. (1994b) Economic and social dimensions, in Lindley (1994a).

RUBERY, J. and FAGAN, C. (1994a) Does feminization mean a flexible labour force?, in Hyman and Ferner (1994).

RUBERY, J. and FAGAN, C. (1994b) Occupational change: plus ça change . . . ?, in Lindley (1994a).

SORGE, A. and STREECK, W. (1988) New technology: the case for an extended perspective, in R. Hyman and W. Streeck (eds), *New Technology and Industrial Relations*, Blackwell, Oxford.

Index